AF848152

EBI Studies in Banking and Capital Markets Law

Series Editors
Danny Busch, Financial Law Centre (FLC), Radboud University Nijmegen, Nijmegen, The Netherlands
Christos V. Gortsos, National and Kapodistrian University of Athens, Athens, Greece
Antonella Sciarrone Alibrandi, Università Cattolica del Sacro Cuore, Milan, Italy

General Series Editors
(all members of the EBI Academic Board)
Danny Busch, Financial Law Centre (FLC), Radboud University Nijmegen, Nijmegen, The Netherlands
Christos V. Gortsos, National and Kapodistrian University of Athens, Athens, Greece
Antonella Sciarrone Alibrandi, Università Cattolica del Sacro Cuore, Milan, Italy

The European Banking Institute
The European Banking Institute based in Frankfurt is an international centre for banking studies resulting from the joint venture of Europe's preeminent academic institutions which have decided to share and coordinate their commitments and structure their research activities in order to provide the highest quality legal, economic and accounting studies in the field of banking regulation, banking supervision and banking resolution in Europe. The European Banking Institute is structured to promote the dialogue between scholars, regulators, supervisors, industry representatives and advisors in relation to issues concerning the regulation and supervision of financial institutions and financial markets from a legal, economic and any other related viewpoint.

As of May 2021, the Academic Members of the European Banking Institute are the following: Universiteit van Amsterdam, University of Antwerp, University of Piraeus, Alma Mater Studiorum–Università di Bologna, Universität Bonn, Academia de Studii Economice din Bucureşti (ASE), Trinity College Dublin, University of Edinburgh, Goethe-Universität, Universiteit Gent, University of Helsinki, Universiteit Leiden, KU Leuven University, Universidade Católica Portuguesa, Universidade de Lisboa, University of Ljubljana, Queen Mary University of London, Université du Luxembourg, Universidad Autónoma Madrid, Universidad Carlos III de Madrid, Universidad Complutense, Madrid, Johannes Gutenberg University Mainz, University of Malta, Università Cattolica del Sacro Cuore, University of Cyprus, Radboud Universiteit, BI Norwegian Business School, Université Panthéon—Sorbonne (Paris 1), Université Panthéon-Assas (Paris 2), University of Stockholm, University of Tartu, University of Vienna, University of Wrocław, Universität Zürich.

Supervisory Board of the European Banking Institute:
Thomas Gstaedtner, President of the Supervisory Board of the European Banking Institute
Enrico Leone, Chancellor of the European Banking Institute
European Banking Institute e.V.
TechQuartier (POLLUX), Platz der Einheit 2
60327 Frankfurt am Main, Germany
Website: https://www.ebi-europa.eu

Editorial Board
(All members of the EBI Academic Board)
Dariusz Adamski, University of Wroclaw
Filippo Annunziata, Bocconi University
Jens-Hinrich Binder, University of Tübingen
William Blair, Queen Mary University of London
Concetta Brescia Morra, University of Roma Tre
Blanaid Clarke, Trinity College Dublin, Law School
Veerle Colaert, KU Leuven University
Guido Ferrarini, University of Genoa
Seraina Grünewald, Radboud University Nijmegen
Christos Hadjiemmanuil, University of Piraeus
Bart Joosen, Free University Amsterdam
Marco Lamandini, University of Bologna
Rosa Lastra, Queen Mary University of London
Edgar Löw, Frankfurt School of Finance & Management
Luís Morais, University of Lisbon, Law School
Peter O. Mülbert, University of Mainz
David Ramos Muñoz, University Carlos III of Madrid
Andre Prüm, University of Luxembourg
Juana Pulgar Ezquerra, Complutense University of Madrid
Georg Ringe, University of Hamburg
Rolf Sethe, University of Zürich
Michele Siri, University of Genoa
Eddy Wymeersch, University of Ghent

Filippo Annunziata ·
Christos Hadjiemmanuil · Bart Joosen
Editors

Central Bank Digital Currency

The Birth of the Digital Euro

palgrave
macmillan

Editors
Filippo Annunziata
Bocconi University
Milan, Italy

Christos Hadjiemmanuil
University of Piraeus
Piraeus, Greece

Bart Joosen
Faculty of Law
Leiden University
Leiden, The Netherlands

ISSN 2730-9088 ISSN 2730-9096 (electronic)
EBI Studies in Banking and Capital Markets Law
ISBN 978-3-031-80956-9 ISBN 978-3-031-80957-6 (eBook)
https://doi.org/10.1007/978-3-031-80957-6

© The Editor(s) (if applicable) and The Author(s), under exclusive license to Springer Nature Switzerland AG 2025

This work is subject to copyright. All rights are solely and exclusively licensed by the Publisher, whether the whole or part of the material is concerned, specifically the rights of translation, reprinting, reuse of illustrations, recitation, broadcasting, reproduction on microfilms or in any other physical way, and transmission or information storage and retrieval, electronic adaptation, computer software, or by similar or dissimilar methodology now known or hereafter developed.
The use of general descriptive names, registered names, trademarks, service marks, etc. in this publication does not imply, even in the absence of a specific statement, that such names are exempt from the relevant protective laws and regulations and therefore free for general use.
The publisher, the authors and the editors are safe to assume that the advice and information in this book are believed to be true and accurate at the date of publication. Neither the publisher nor the authors or the editors give a warranty, expressed or implied, with respect to the material contained herein or for any errors or omissions that may have been made. The publisher remains neutral with regard to jurisdictional claims in published maps and institutional affiliations.

Cover illustration: Teekid/gettyimages

This Palgrave Macmillan imprint is published by the registered company Springer Nature Switzerland AG
The registered company address is: Gewerbestrasse 11, 6330 Cham, Switzerland

If disposing of this product, please recycle the paper.

Series Editor's Preface

This collective volume perfectly fits with EBI's mission of promoting high-quality research in the field of banking studies. It provides a comprehensive analysis of a reform project touching upon one the most intimate chords of our European financial system: the single currency. More than twenty years after the fulfilment of the European monetary sovereignty, the fast pace of digitalisation patterns of financial markets, matched with the prospect of tokenisation being the "next generation for markets" as recently pictured by Larry Fink, solicits the opportunity to give "new (digital) clothes" to our central bank money.

The Council of the European Union has stressed the need of a restyling exercise of central bank money so as to safeguard the European Union's "open strategic autonomy, promoting financial sector innovation and delivering benefits for citizens, businesses, and member states, while preserving the role of central bank money as an anchor for the monetary system".

This study contributes to this demanding exercise, with an insightful assessment of the legal status of a central bank digital currency, engaging in the theoretical effort of testing the legal implications of the birth of a digital complement to cash. The fruits of this academic effort, as merged in this book, are extremely timely given that after the issuing of the relevant legislative proposals by the Commission, in October 2023 the Governing Council of the ECB announced the start of the preparation and experimentation phase of the digital euro, which is expected to last about three years.

Stimulated by this tight policy agenda, the volume explores the legal anatomy of the central bank digital euro, meeting the scientific standards of rigour and originality needed to inform the ongoing reflections at European political level.

Indeed, the well-reasoned theoretical analysis is alert to the highly complex and varied practical pitfalls of such an ambitious project, to be differently declined within the prism of financial regulation's and banking supervision's established normative schemes. From this standpoint, traditional principles driving financial and banking regulation, such as technological neutrality, market neutrality, price stability and financial integrity, are first of all confronted, bottom up, with a new ecosystem evolving around the digital euro construction site, necessarily involving new categories of "external" subjects to which central banks have to turn to, namely IT providers and technology regulators. Once more, the frontiers of the banking system are called into question by technological, well before legal, formants.

The diverse legal interests—of both public and private nature, with purely economic as well as social and personal bearing—impacted by the introduction of a digital euro could not have been better detected than by a young cohort of excellent financial law scholars, who have participated in this book project and have again confirmed the active and cutting-edge work of the Advanced Researchers Group (ARG) of the European Banking Institute. Their critical thinking and intellectual curiosity have been key for approaching such a novel topic, under the general logical frame that has been wisely set out by the editors, Filippo Annunziata, Christos Hadjiemmanuil and Bart Joosen.

With the chosen topic, the authors take up a pioneering task, given the initial (perhaps is it too early to say intermediate?) standpoint of the ongoing debates, which requires a good balance between a forward-looking approach and the concrete factual perspectives that can be seized today. Against this backdrop, the research questions addressed by the study are to be traced back to the (i) general mapping of the opportunities and risks arising from the CBDC; (ii) public governance and supervisory aspects; and, ultimately, (iii) the implications on the payment system and, more in general, on the banking sector.

In accordance with these general lines of reasoning, the first section with Chapter 2 by Eugenia Macchiavello outlines the main rationales and downsides underlying the creation of a CBDC, also highlighting—amongst others—the difficulties of achieving an effective financial inclusion, an aspect that is further investigated in Chapter 6 by Federico Riganti and Anne-Marie Weber. The constitutional foundations of the CBDC from the perspective of the EU treaties are explored in the second section with Chapter 3 by Christy Anne Petit. The third section unveils the digital euro's role in the payment system; Chapter 4 by María Cecilia del Barrio Arleo contextualises the CBDC in the general payment system, whereas Chapter 5 by Panagiotis N. Politsidis tackles the concrete demands of a digital euro on the side of the beneficiaries of the retail payment system. The fourth and last section zooms in from the theory to the envisaged practice of the digital euro, considering the "mechanics" of the CBDC, in relation to its issuance and governance. From this last perspective, Chapter 7 by Ioannis E. Linaritis foreshadows the possibility of a co-participated governance of the CBDC, and Chapter 8 by Nikos Maragopoulos looks into the impact scenarios of the advent of the digital euro with respect to the banking system. Finally, Chapter 9 by Andrea Minto evaluates the delicate interface between the CBDC system and another recently reformed area of financial regulation: AML.

A brief outline of the vast array of topics addressed by this scientifically dense enquiry immediately reassures the readers that they will find many answers regarding the controversial integration of a central bank digital euro into our financial and banking system or they may hopefully come up with even more new questions.

A final note: the foundations for this volume were laid at an ARG workshop held in Athens on 29 September 2022. The EBI is grateful to the Bank of Greece, in particular Governor Yannis Stournaras and Deputy Governor Christina Papakonstantinou, for hosting the workshop, and to the Department of International and European Studies of the University of Piraeus for its financial support. It is also grateful to Ms. Maria Katsigianni and Ms. Michelle Snippenburg for their invaluable assistance to the editors.

It is important to note that the manuscript for this volume was closed in the autumn of 2023. Consequently, subsequent developments, particularly those relating to the digital euro, are not discussed in an elaborate manner within these pages.

Rome, Italy Antonella Sciarrone Alibrandi

Author's Note

All the authors are member of the Associate Researcher Group (ARG) of the European Banking Institute (EBI) at Frankfurt a/M, Germany. The ARG consists of senior academics having obtained their Ph.D. degree and being positioned within the organisations that employ them as advanced researcher. The ARG has been established by the EBI to stimulate the continued researching efforts of its members and to stimulate the participation in joint research under the auspices of the EBI.

Contents

Part I General Discussion

1 **Introduction** 3
Filippo Annunziata, Christos Hadjiemmanuil, and Bart Joosen

2 **Objectives, Rationale, Opportunities Versus Main Risks of a CBDC: Principles for a Coherent European Financial Regulation** 23
Eugenia Macchiavello

Part II Constitutional Issues/EU Treaties

3 **Central Bank Digital Currency and the Treaty Mandate of the European Central Bank** 71
Christy Ann Petit

Part III Role in EU Payment System/Demand—Missing Market

4 **The Digital Euro and the EU Framework for Payments** 105
María Cecilia del Barrio Arleo

5 **The Demand for CBDC in the Perspective of Existing (Retail) Payment Systems** 129
Panagiotis N. Politsidis

6 Digital Euro and Financial Inclusion Considerations on Trust, the Digital Divide and Financial Literacy 161
Federico Riganti and Anne-Marie Weber

Part IV Mechanics: Governance, Form of Issuance, Impact on Banking System

7 Governance Issues Concerning the Issuer of CBDC, Who Supervises and Controls the CBDC Scheme? 183
Ioannis E. Linaritis

8 Exploring the Impact of the Digital Euro on Euro Area Banks 257
Nikos Maragopoulos

9 Anti-Money Laundering (AML) Implications of Central Bank Digital Currencies (CBDC) 287
Andrea Minto

Index 331

Notes on Contributors

Filippo Annunziata (1963) is a Professor of Financial Markets and Banking Legislation at Bocconi University, Milan, Italy. He is member of the Faculty of the Ph.D. in Legal Studies at Bocconi University. He is also Professor of Musicology at Università degli Studi di Milano, Visiting Professor at Ca' Foscari University, Venice, Italy, and Visiting Professor at Leuven University, Belgium, and Co-Chair of the Advanced Researchers Group (ARG).

María Cecilia del Barrio Arleo obtained her Ph.D. from the School of International Studies of the University of Trento, Italy. Her dissertation focused on the transformation of banking supervision and supervisory practices in the euro area since the establishment of the Single Supervisory Mechanism. Cecilia works as a banking supervisor at the ECB. Her current research focuses on financial technology topics including CBDCs and payments.

Christos Hadjiemmanuil (1964) is a member of the General Council of the Bank of Greece and a Professor of International and European Monetary and Financial Institutions at the University of Piraeus and Visiting Professor at the Law School of the London School of Economics. He is a member of the Athens Bar Association and Co-Chair of the ARG.

Bart Joosen (1963) is a Professor of Financial Law at the Faculty of Law of Leiden University, Hazelhoff Centre for Financial Law. He is a part-time Professor at the Florence School of Banking and Finance, of the Robert Schumann Institute for Advanced Studies of the European University Institute. He is a Fellow of the European Banking Institute in Frankfurt a/M, Germany and Co-Chair of the ARG.

Ioannis E. Linaritis is Assistant Professor at the Faculty of Law of Democritus University of Thrace. He is also active as attorney-at-law in National Bank of Greece S.A. and private practice, specialising in banking law, company law, capital markets and information technology law.

Eugenia Macchiavello is Assistant Professor in Economic Law at the University of Genoa and Academic Fellow of the Jean Monnet Centre of Excellence in Sustainable Finance (EuSFIL). Formerly a Visiting Fellow at the NYU Center of Financial Institution, certified attorney-at-law in Italy and participant to the Italian Capital Markets Authority (Consob) Working Group on FinTech, she is an internationally renowned expert in alternative finance and fintech regulation.

Nikos Maragopoulos is Head of Resolution Planning & Banking Regulation at Eurobank and Associate Researcher at European Banking Institute with a Doctor of Philosophy (Ph.D.) focused on European Banking Law.

Andrea Minto is the Jean Monnet Professor in Law and Regulation of Financial Markets at Ca' Foscari University, Venice, Italy, and he holds the Chair in Digitalisation in EU Financial Studies (EUDIFIN), financed by the European Commission. He is Professor of Law at the University of Stavanger—Business School (Universitetet i Stavanger—UiS), Norway.

Christy Ann Petit is Assistant Professor, Dublin City University (DCU), and Deputy Director of DCU Brexit Institute. Christy Ann Petit holds Ph.D. in Law (European University Institute), LL.M. (EUI and College of Europe), and agrégée in economics & management (Ecole Normale Supérieure).

Panagiotis N. Politsidis is Associate Professor, Finance Department, Audencia Business School, France.

Federico Riganti is an Assistant Professor of Economic Law and Financial Market Regulation in the Department of Management, University of Turin. He earned his Ph.D. summa cum laude at the University of Bologna. Federico Riganti specialises in financial market regulation and company law. He is a member of the Associated Researchers Group of the

European Banking Institute and an academic member of the European Corporate Governance Institute.

Anne-Marie Weber is an Assistant Professor in the Department of Commercial Law, Faculty of Law and Administration, University of Warsaw. She is a graduate of the Master of Laws (LL.M.) programme at Berkeley Law School. Anne-Marie Weber specialises in financial market regulation and company law. She is a Fellow of the European Law Institute and an academic member of the European Corporate Governance Institute.

Abbreviations

AIFMD	Alternative Investment Fund Managers Directive
AIS	Account Information Service
AML	Anti-Money Laundering
AML/CFT	Anti-Money Laundering and Countering the Financing of Terrorism
AMLA	Anti-Money Laundering Authority
AML-CT	Anti-Money Laundering and Combating Terrorism
AMLD	Anti-Money Laundering Directive
ARG	Advanced Researchers Group
ATM	Automated Teller Machine
BIS	Bank for International Settlements
BoE	Bank of England
BRRD	Bank Recovery and Resolution Directive
CBDC	Central Bank Digital Currency
CDD	Customer Due Diligence
CJEU	Court of Justice of the European Union
CPMI	Committee on Payments and Market Infrastructures
CPSS	Committee on Payment and Settlement Systems
CRD IV	Capital Requirements Directive, 2013/36/EU
CRR	Capital Requirements Regulation, Regulation (EU) No 575/2013
DFR	Deposit Facility Rate
DGS	Deposit Guarantee Schemes
DLT	Distributed Ledger Technology
DORA	Regulation of the European Parliament and of the Council on Digital Operational Resilience for the Financial Sector

DSA/DMA	Digital Services Act/Digital Markets Act
EBA	European Banking Authority
EBF	European Banking Federation
EBI	European Banking Institute
EC	European Commission
ECB	European Central Bank
ECHR	European Convention on Human Rights
ECJ	European Court of Justice
e-CNY	Electronic Chinese Yuan
EDPB	European Data Protection Board
EDPS	European Data Protection Supervisor
EEA	European Economic Area
EIOPA	European Insurance and Occupational Pensions Authority
ELTEG	Euro Legal Tender Expert Group
EMU	Economic and Monetary Union
EP	European Parliament
EPC	European Payments Council
ERPB	Euro Retail Payments Board
ESA	European Supervisory Authority
ESCB	European System of Central Banks
ESFS	European System of Financial Supervision
ESMA	European Securities and Markets Authority
ESRB	European Systemic Risk Board
EU	European Union
EUR	Euro
FATF	Financial Action Task Force
FCA	Financial Conduct Authority
FDIC	Federal Deposit Insurance Corporation
FED	Board of Governors of the Federal Reserve System of the United States of America
FIAT CURRENCY	Government-Issued Currency
FIU	Financial Intelligence Unit
FMI	Financial Market Infrastructure
FSB	Financial Stability Board
FSC	ECB's Financial Stability Committee
GBIC	German Banking Industry Committee
GDP	Gross Domestic Product
HQLAs	High-Quality Liquid Assets (HQLAs)
ID	Identification
IMF	International Monetary Fund
IOSCO	International Organization of Securities Commissions
IT	Information Technology
KYC	Know Your Customer

LCR	Liquidity Coverage Ratio
MEP	Member of the European Parliament
MiCAR	Regulation (EU) 2023/1114 of the European Parliament and of the Council of 31 May 2023 on markets in crypto-assets, and amending Regulations (EU) No 1093/2010 and (EU) No 1095/2010 and Directives 2013/36/EU and (EU) 2019/1937
MiFID	Markets in Financial Instruments Directive, 2004/ 39/ EC
MiFID II	Markets in Financial Instruments Directive II, 2014/ 65/ EU
NCA	National Competent Authorities
NCB	National Central Bank
NSFR	Net Stable Funding Ratio
OECD	Organisation for Economic Co-operation and Development
P2P	Person-to-Person
PAN	Primary Account Number
PBOC	People's Bank of China
PIS	Payment Initiation Services
PISA	Payment Instruments, Schemes and Arrangements
POS	Physical Point of Sale
PoS	Proof of Stake. A consensus mechanism in which an individual or "validator" validates transactions or blocks
PoW	Proof of Work. A consensus mechanism in which each block is 'mined' by a group of individuals or nodes on the network
PSD	Payment Services Directive, 2007/ 64/ EC
PSD2	Payments Services Directive II, (EU) 2015/ 2366
PSPs	Payment Service Providers
RMC	Risk Management Committee
RSA	Rivest, Shamir, Adleman
RTGS	Real-Time Gross Settlement
SEPA	Single Euro Payment Area
SFD	Settlement Finality Directive
SIPS	Systemically Important Payment Systems
SPACE	Study on the Payment Attitudes of Consumers in the Euro Area
SSM	Single Supervisory Mechanism
STABLECOIN	Any cryptocurrency pegged to a stable asset, like fiat currency or gold
SWIFT	Society for Worldwide Interbank Financial Telecommunication

TEU	Treaty on the European Union
TFEU	Treaty on the Functioning of the European Union
TOKEN	A token represents an asset built on an existing blockchain
TPP	Third Party Providers
UN	United Nations
US	United States
VASP	Virtual Asset Service Provider
WALLET	A designated storage location for digital assets (cryptocurrency) that has an address for sending and receiving funds. The wallet can be online, offline or on a physical device
WHO	World Health Organization
WSBI	World Savings and Banking Institute

List of Figures

Chapter 4

Fig. 1 Chart-author's elaboration (*Source* own elaboration) 115

Fig. 2 Proposed roles of intermediaries and Eurosystem (*Source* Adapted from ECB, "Progress on the investigation phase of a digital euro—second report" [December 2022], 6) 120

Chapter 5

Fig. 1 Share of payment instruments used at the POS and P2P (in terms of the number and value of transactions). Data are for the euro area (all 19 countries). The category "Cards" includes credit and debit cards. The category "Others" refers to payments with mobile phones, bank cheques, credit transfers, direct debits and other (unidentified) payment instruments, and includes the answer "Don't know". Due to their low frequency of use, these instruments have been grouped into a single category. (*Source* European Central Bank's SPACE survey) 131

Fig. 2 Means of payments that euro area companies prefer to be paid with distribution of preferences across means of payment for the four sectors of interest: Retail trade, hotels, restaurants and cafes, and arts, entertainment and recreations. DK stands for "Don't know", while NA stands for "No answer". (*Source* European Central Bank [2022]) 134

Fig. 3 Volume of worldwide non-cash transactions for years 2021–2026 (in USD billions). (*Source* Capegemini research institute for financial services, 2022; ECB statistical data warehouse, BIS statistical explorer, countries' central bank annual reports). (*Note* 2021 non-cash transaction data is sourced from central banks. Forecasted figures were used when data was unavailable. Figures are forecasted for 2022 and beyond) 136
Fig. 4 Number of card payments per inhabitant (2014–2017). The chart shows card payments with cards issued by EU-resident payment service providers, except cards with an e-money function only. (*Source* European Central Bank [2019]) 142
Fig. 5 Preference for some digital euro features based on top five rankings. The figure shows the number of respondents to a multiple-choice question about ranking in order of importance a list of specific features that a digital euro should offer (followed by a field to add comments). (*Source* European Central Bank [2021]) 145
Fig. 6 Size of shadow economy in European countries in 2016 (percent of GDP). (*Data source* kelmanson, Kirabaeva, Medina, Mircheva and Weiss [2019]) 149

List of Tables

Chapter 3

Table 1	Overview of the available legal bases and corresponding types of CBDC for the digital euro - Author's own elaboration	78

Chapter 8

Table 1	Impact on the Eurosystem's balance sheet (mild scenario)	263
Table 2	Impact on banks' balance sheets (mild scenario)	264
Table 3	Impact on banks' balance sheets (adverse scenario)	265
Table 4	Impact on Eurosystem's balance sheet (adverse scenario)	267

PART I

General Discussion

CHAPTER 1

Introduction

Filippo Annunziata, Christos Hadjiemmanuil, and Bart Joosen

1 The Discussion of the Birth of the Digital Euro

This volume, part of the EBI Studies in Banking and Capital Markets Law, analyses the new phenomenon of Central Bank Digital Currencies (CBDC) with a focus on the launch of the Digital Euro in the European Union. The book is the result of the research carried out by members of the EBI's Associated Researchers Group (ARG). This group was formed during the COVID-19 pandemic and its members had hardly seen each

F. Annunziata (✉)
Bocconi University, Milan, Italy
e-mail: f.annunziata@aclaw.eu

C. Hadjiemmanuil
University of Piraeus, Piraeus, Greece
e-mail: c.hadjiemmanuil@lse.ac.uk

B. Joosen
Leiden University, Leiden, Netherlands
e-mail: e.p.m.joosen@law.leidenuniv.nl

© The Author(s), under exclusive license to Springer Nature Switzerland AG 2025

F. Annunziata et al. (eds.), *Central Bank Digital Currency*, EBI Studies in Banking and Capital Markets Law,
https://doi.org/10.1007/978-3-031-80957-6_1

other in their roles within the ARG until 2022. The in-person meeting happened for the first time during a mini-conference organised in preparation for the establishment of this book in Athens, where the ARG was a guest of the Bank of Greece.

The book analyses the subject of CBDC from various perspectives, with each of the authors formulating viewpoints regarding this new phenomenon, focusing particularly on the Digital Euro. The contributions were all written at a time when there was still much uncertainty about how the European Central Bank (ECB) would follow up on the CBDC project, for which it would be responsible, *and the manuscripts for all the Chapters have been closed by the authors in August 2023.* At the time of the conclusion of this book, there is greater clarity available on the Digital Euro, not only because of the publication of the framework by the ECB in October 2023 on the Digital Euro, but especially because of the regulatory basis that will potentially be created, based on the European Commission's proposals of 28 June 2023 for the Single Currency Package.

In this introductory chapter, we present a brief overview of the main topics of interest in this area, while also linking to the comprehensive analyses reviewed in detail by the various authors of Chapters 2, 3, 4, 5, 6, 7, 8, and 9.

2 The ECB's Project on the Digital Euro

The Eurosystem published its 'Report on a Digital Euro'[1] on 2 October 2020. The report provided the basis for gathering broader views on the benefits and challenges of issuing a Digital Euro, as well as on its possible design. The report was followed by the 'Public consultation on a digital euro,' which started on 12 October 2020 and ran until 12 January 2021.

In the Report on a Digital Euro, the launch of an investigation on the need and desirability of the introduction of a digital version of cash tender, for which the Eurosystem bears exclusively the responsibility within the Eurozone, was mainly motivated by emphasising the mission of the Eurosystem "to provide citizens with riskless money for their payments".[2]

[1] www.ecb.europa.eu/pub/pdf/other/Report_on_a_digital_euro.

[2] Introduction of the ECB President and the ECB Executive Board Member and Chair of the Eurosystem HighLevel Task Force on Central Bank Digital Currency, Foreword on page 2 of the Report on the digital euro.

Although it was noted by the ECB that cash payments still accounted for the vast majority of payments in the Eurozone (an unstated claim that had to be put into some perspective afterwards), the time was deemed ripe to explore an alternative to those cash payments.

The 2020 report was silent when it came to the final design of the Digital Euro, partly so as not to pre-empt the discussion with society and all stakeholders that needed to be involved. However, at the time, the ECB did indicate that a Digital Euro should meet a number of key requirements and features, namely "accessibility, robustness, safety, efficiency and privacy—while complying with relevant legislation".[3]

This discussion with society and stakeholders had to take place without prior biases; however, obviously, some preconditions were formulated in advance. Now, most of these preconditions cannot be considered highly controversial: the efficiency, reliability and robustness of a possible issuance of the Digital Euro being self-evident in this respect. Other preconditions put forward by the ECB may have made the debate more subjective.

One can, of course, consider the aspect of privacy, which was indeed put forward in the public consultation as a highly important, if not the most important, feature established therein, in which, nonetheless, the consequences of a system leading to optimal safeguards of privacy entail conflicting interests, for instance when it comes to the monitoring of possession of fiat currency and transactions committed from the perspective of anti-fraud measures and/or other illegal activities.

In April 2021, the ECB reported on the outcome of the consultation in a comprehensive document entitled 'Eurosystem report on the public consultation on a digital euro'[4] ('Consultation Report'). This Consultation Report shed interesting perspectives on the views shared with the ECB on the need and desirability of a Digital Euro and the prerequisites the Digital Euro should meet according to the stakeholders consulted. For this reason, we devote some attention to the main outcomes of the consultation held.

Over 8000 responses to the 18 questions raised by the ECB had been submitted in the course of the consultation. The ECB noted that these

[3] Foreword on page 2 of the Report on the digital euro.

[4] www.ecb.europa.eu/pub/pdf/other/Eurosystem_report_on_the_public_consultation_on_a_digital_euro.

contributions would form an important basis for the decision-making processes to be organised within the ECB as to the launch of the Digital Euro, especially considering the decision of whether a further investigation of this novel means of payment means would be required. From all the participants in the consultation, 95% identified themselves as citizens and the remainder as professionals.[5] What is clear is that the possible launch of a Digital Euro has created quite a stir among the people of the Eurozone.

A very striking statistic concerns the representation of participants from different parts of the Eurozone. The absolute majority of participants are from Germany, followed by participants from France and Italy. Remarkably, only about six other Member States gave input of any significance (with a participation between 1 and 5%); from the remaining Member States, the participation is low and represents less than 1% per Member State. It is thus certain that the possible launch of a Digital Euro (at least not in 2020/2021) cannot count with very broad support in all Member States of the Eurozone.[6]

Notable is the division between respondents from the private sector and professionals participating in the consultation, including a large contingent of FinTechs. Private individuals prefer that the features for the Digital Euro should mainly be built around an offline solution, while the professional private individuals prefer a hybrid solution, in which the Digital Euro should be made available offline as well as online, and from that perspective should also facilitate online payment transactions. From the various answers, the following preferences can be thus distilled: most important for a Digital Euro is privacy (43%), then security (18%), usability across the euro area (11%), the absence of additional costs (9%) and offline use (8%).[7] The ECB puts this ranking in further perspective as follows:

[5] Page 2 of the Consultation Report.

[6] Page 2 of the Consultation Report. The ECB itself observes: "When reading this report, it should be taken into account that these biased demographic characteristics do not represent the euro area population. The replies from both citizens and professionals do, however, provide valuable input to the Eurosystem's reflections on a digital euro." Notwithstanding these doubts about broad support, the ECB has not questioned the viability of the Digital Euro project ever since. To the contrary, the current narrative as conveyed in the establishment of further preparations rather suggests that broad support of the launch of the Digital Euro is to be expected.

[7] Page 11 Consultation Report.

> Privacy emerges as the key feature that a digital euro should offer, according to respondents to the public consultation. This is confirmed both indirectly – by the presence of comments on the importance of privacy in the responses to most questions – and directly – by the choice of two in five citizen respondents to rank privacy first among the nine features proposed in this question.[8]

This emphasis on privacy may also be one of the explanations for which further studies by the ECB considering the functionality of the Digital Euro through the application of innovative solutions (such as embedding in SmartContracts, where spending targets or spending limits can be determined by the technological environment) have found that it was better not to move further with such initiatives at this point in time.

In addition, the consultation also revealed that in the distribution of the Digital Euro, there is also an understanding among private respondents of the need to come up with adequate solutions in terms of monitoring the system, to prevent it from being abused for illegal purposes, such as money laundering. For this reason, many expressed a preference that the design for how to distribute the Digital Euro should reserve a role for existing intermediaries, such as banks and payment institutions, or the central bank itself, which should continue to be able to use information on the users and holders of the Digital Euro for monitoring and preventing its illicit use.[9]

It can therefore be concluded that a majority of respondents choose to tailor the use of the Digital Euro into the existing payment infrastructure in order to enable its smooth introduction. In doing so, there is also a preference for maintaining the cross-border functionality, and in addition, an overwhelming preference for maintaining cross-currency payments, all at (the same) low cost for current transactions, which is a result of the steps taken over the past decades in the European Union.[10]

Ease of use is of primary importance, and, in this sense, the ECB observes that:

> Simplicity of use is especially important to ensure that all segments of the population can use a retail payment solution such as the digital euro,

[8] Page 11 Consultation Report.

[9] Page 18 Consultation Report.

[10] See further in more detail: Page 29 Consultation Report.

> with the aim of fostering the participation of all citizens and businesses in the increasingly digital economy. The Eurosystem finds this aspect of the design of a digital euro to be especially important, and participants in the public consultation were therefore asked to provide their input on this.[11]

This aspect touches on the knowledge gained in scholarly research and public authority studies on citizens' accessibility of financial services. At a time when personal attention to customers of financial institutions in local bank branches is increasingly being replaced by online services and remote approaches to service provision, there is a fear that large groups of citizens are being excluded from using financial services, even when it comes to simple products, such as payments for consumer spending or even for fulfilling obligations to public institutions (remittances of taxes and the like more). The ECB raises this problem of older generations as a possible bottleneck to be solved with the Digital Euro. Perhaps this is one of the main drivers for the ECB to come up with the introduction of the Digital Euro.

In short, the public consultation provided no reason for the ECB to halt or delay the initiative to move towards the introduction of the Digital Euro; on the contrary, the Eurosystem sees in its introduction an important and (almost inevitable) step in the further development of the (retail) payment system in the Eurozone (and possibly beyond). In any case, shortly after the conclusion of the public consultation, the ECB took a number of important follow-up steps. These amounted to a decision by the Governing Council on 14 July 2021 to further develop the various aspects of the introduction of the Digital Euro, in the form of large-scale trials of sub-projects that should further highlight and test all aspects of the Digital Euro.

In the context of the finalisation of that first phase, the ECB announced in July 2021 that it would commence a further investigation phase that would take 24 months. In this further investigation, key issues concerning the functional design of the Digital Euro would be explored, to ensure that the Digital Euro would meet users' needs. A further project included is the investigation as to the required changes to the legislative framework needed in order to introduce the Digital Euro, whose proposals will be discussed and decided upon by the European

[11] Page 16 Consultation Report.

co-legislators. The investigation would furthermore consider the potential market impacts of the Digital Euro, identifying "the design options to ensure privacy and avoid risks for euro area citizens, intermediaries and the overall economy."

The investigations were supposed to build further on the experimentation work undertaken by the ECB and national central banks in the preceding period. Accordingly, such experimentation concerned: (a) the Digital Euro ledger; (b) privacy and anti-money laundering; (c) limits on Digital Euro in circulation; and (d) end-user access while not connected to the internet and facilitating inclusiveness with appropriate devices.[12]

In the fourth progress report issued on 13 July 2023,[13] the ECB provided further information on the results achieved in the various investigations on topics as highlighted above. The ECB again stressed the importance of the joint collaboration of the work on the establishment and design of the Digital Euro, particularly also by involving the Euro Retail Payments Board (ERPB[14]) in the work undertaken by the Eurosystem.

The fourth progress report provided further depth on the issue of the compensation model. That model should, according to the ECB, assume a basic service by the relevant intermediaries at a cost fee equal to the fees currently charged for 'regular' retail payment services. The Eurosystem will bear its own costs, as is currently the case for cash tender (coins and banknotes). In this way, access to the Digital Euro should continue to be ensured for retail consumers without entailing any additional costs, compared to the use of regular retail payment services.

Further work by the ECB in the context of the fourth report concerned the so-called porting of balances held at a 'wallet' managed by one intermediary to a wallet system of another intermediary. In addition, the report comprised research on methods for ensuring financial inclusion and on fraud detection and prevention. At the time,

[12] ECB, press release 'Eurosystem launches digital euro project', 20 July 2021, https://www.ecb.europa.eu/press/pr/date/2021/html/ecb.pr210714.

[13] Approachable via: www.ecb.europa.eu/paym/digital_euro/investigation/governance/shared/files.

[14] The Euro Retail Payments Board (ERPB) is a high-level strategic body tasked with fostering the integration, innovation and competitiveness of euro retail payments in the European Union. It was launched on 19 December 2013 by the ECB and replaced the SEPA Council.

the ECB concluded that the work was so advanced in the summer of 2023 that all steps had been taken for further decision-making by the ECB's Governance Council in autumn 2023.

Importantly, the ECB also provided insight into further technical work on the design of the Digital Euro. The policy reports indicated that the Digital Euro should be available in both an online variant and an offline variant, with the understanding that the technology to be applied will differ for both variants. Further work was being undertaken to develop the Rulebook for the Digital Euro scheme, to ensure (i) attractiveness of the use of the Digital Euro, (ii) compatibility with exiting (retail payment) schemes and (iii) customer identification and authentication. Additional developments on the infrastructural aspects of the Digital Euro were also undertaken by the Rulebook Development Group.

The fourth progress report confirmed the readiness of the investigations towards the establishment of the Digital Euro and the ability for the Governing Council to take further decisions on the next phase in autumn of 2023. The relevant decisions and final design features of the Digital Euro will be further discussed.

3 Single Currency Package

As discussed, in the context of the introduction of the Digital Euro, European Institutions adopted the stance that the legislative framework should be designed in a way that would allow for, inter alia, the incorporation of some aspects of the operation of the Digital Euro in the existing payment system, the confirmation of the Digital Euro as other means of payment and the incorporation of this new payment instrument into existing rules.

The legislative package ultimately introduced by the Commission on 28 June 2023 consists of two important regulations: the regulation on the establishment of the Digital Euro[15] (DigEuro-Reg) and the regulation on the legal tender of euro banknotes and coins[16] (Legal Tender-Reg). The background to both legislative proposals is briefly discussed below.

[15] Proposal of the European Commission of 28 June 2023 for a Regulation of the European Parliament and of the Council on the establishment of the digital euro, COM (2023) 369 final.

[16] Proposal of the European Commission of 28 June 2023 for a Regulation of the European Parliament and of the Council on the legal tender of euro banknotes and coins, COM (2023) 364 final.

Each of the legislative instruments has different objectives. The DigEuro-Reg will provide the frameworks for the issuance and circulation of the Digital Euro, while the Legal Tender-Reg aims to ensure that the use of cash in the Eurozone is facilitated in the most optimal way. The legislative proposals provide insight into the tension that underpins the introduction of the Digital Euro: whether it would lead to even greater downward acceptance of cash (coins and banknotes) as a means of payment in the context of consumer spending. This touches upon the insight that the use of cash in the European Union, but also especially in the Eurozone, where more research is being carried out on the matter, is under strong pressure. In some Member States, for example, it is reported that retail outlets refuse to accept cash altogether, and only allow card payments.

Regarding the desirability or undesirability of this phenomenon, while highly an ad-hoc study on the subject is highly encouraged for future research, it falls out of the scope of the present volume on CBDC and the Digital Euro. Nonetheless, it should be noted that this policy objective indeed raises concerns among regulators, and this resulted in the proposals included in the Legal Tender-Reg.

For example, the European Commission notes in the introduction of the Legal Tender-Reg:

> The growth of electronic payments, a trend accelerated by COVID-19, has led to a general decline in cash payments and the reduction of automated teller machine (ATM) networks in a number of Member States means there are risks to access to cash. Thus, the issue of the scope and meaning of the legal tender status of cash has become more prominent in the EU policy agenda, as outlined in the Commission's Retail Payments Strategy and in

view of the recent ruling of the Court of Justice of the European Union[17] on the matter.

With respect to the more institutional issues on the exclusive competences of the European Institutions in the context of the issuance and circulation of 'legal tender' (the tension surrounding the provisions of the TEU and TFEU which, of course, were conceived considering the role of the ESCB in relation to the issuance of banknotes and the minting of coins and their circulation, but not the issuance of a Digital Euro), we refer to *Chapter* 3 written by *Christy Ann Petit*.

Here we briefly indicate the essence of the rules to be introduced by the Legal Tender-Reg, which, in our view, can be seen as compensating

[17] Reference is made to CJEU 26 January 2021 in Joined Cases C-422/19 and C-423/19 (Johannes Dietrich and Norbert Häring v. Hessischer Rundfunk). The following parts of that judgement are noteworthy : (46) "It should be noted in that regard that the concept of 'legal tender' of a means of payment denominated in a currency unit signifies, in its ordinary sense, that that means of payment cannot generally be refused in settlement of a debt denominated in the same currency unit, at its full face value, with the effect of discharging the debt," and (49) "Point 1 of Recommendation 2010/191 sets out, as its title indicates, the common definition of 'legal tender', stating that, where a payment obligation exists, the legal tender of euro banknotes and coins should imply, first, mandatory acceptance of those banknotes and coins; second, their acceptance at full face value; and, third, their power to discharge from payment obligations. That point therefore shows that that concept of 'legal tender' encompasses, inter alia, an obligation in principle to accept banknotes and coins denominated in euro for payment purposes" and, somewhat nuancing the absolute obligations to accept cash as a means of payment: "However, it cannot be considered necessary for the use of the euro as the single currency within the meaning of Article 133 TFEU and, more specifically, for the establishment of the status of legal tender of banknotes denominated in euro, as provided for in Article 128(1) TFEU and in the third sentence of the first paragraph of Article 16 of the Protocol on the ESCB and the ECB, to impose an absolute obligation to accept those banknotes as a means of payment. It follows from the information contained in paragraphs 46 to 49 of the present judgment that that status as legal tender calls only for acceptance in principle of banknotes denominated in euro as a means of payment, not for absolute acceptance. Nor, moreover, is it necessary for the use of the euro as the single currency and, more specifically, for the preservation of the effectiveness as legal tender of cash denominated in euro that the EU legislature lay down exhaustively and uniformly the exceptions to that fundamental obligation, provided that every debtor is guaranteed to have the possibility, as a general rule, of discharging a payment obligation in cash."

for the discussion that has started regarding the binding status of Recommendation 2010/191,[18] which was the subject of the debate in the case that led to the CJEU decision of 26 June 2021.

The essence of the provisions of the Legal Tender-Reg is set out in Articles 4 and 5. In particular, Article 5 establishes that there may be exceptions to the acceptance of cash as a means of payment, if the *ex-ante* exclusion is imposed in good faith, and is of a temporary nature or if agreed beforehand. In particular, the rules highlight the operational aspects of excluding the use of cash as a means of payment, for example because the recipient of the cash excludes payment with large denominations given the low value of the payment transaction or the absence of change money. Another important reason for refusing, for example, payment with large denominations (preventing money laundering) is not mentioned as an objective justification for such an exclusion, in our view. Article 4 contains the main rule and deserves to be quoted in full:

Article 4
Legal tender

1. The legal tender status of euro banknotes and coins shall entail their mandatory acceptance, at full face value, with the power to discharge from a payment obligation.
2. In accordance with the mandatory acceptance of cash, the payee shall not refuse euro banknotes and/or coins tendered in payment to comply with that obligation.
3. In accordance with the acceptance at full face value of cash, the monetary value of euro banknotes and/or coins tendered in settlement of a debt shall be equal to the amount in euro indicated on the banknotes and/or coins. Surcharges on the settlement of debt with euro banknotes and coins shall be prohibited.
4. In accordance with the power to discharge from a payment obligation, a payer shall be able to discharge from a payment obligation by tendering euro banknotes and coins to the paye"e.

[18] Commission Recommendation of 22 March 2010 on the scope and effects of legal tender of euro banknotes and coins (2010/191/EU), OJEU L 83 of 30 March 2020, pp. 70–83.

There are well-known rules concerning the status of legal tender and the incorporation of the euro into this legal concept. The rules also partly stem from the 2010 Recommendation cited above and should therefore be seen as a further codification of the relevant rules that were contained therein. The legal tender status of cash presupposes the obligation to accept cash as a means of payment and the discharge of the payer's payment obligation to the payee when cash is used. The payment is at the face value of the relevant cash resources, and the recipient of the cash may not charge additional fees or stipulations in this regard.

The remaining rules of the Legal Tender-Reg contain numerous procedural aspects, but also a framing of the scope of application, for example by excluding that the regulation will apply to online payments. In our view, it would be wise to also further define the concept of 'online payments,' to clarify that this includes bank transfers (credit transfers) through payment systems, which in our view should just as well be considered a payment in 'legal tender.'

The implications of this regulation are incalculable. There is a steady trend in many Member States where cash payments have been banned altogether, especially when it comes to low-value transactions (settling instant consumer spending, paying for public transport travel, *et cetera*). Many of these measures are aimed at protecting the people involved from crime (robberies with violence and the like more so); in many cases, it also relates to cost control. It is safe to say that there is a completely different picture in the European Union in this respect, some Member States are moving towards a completely cashless economy, while in other Member States the use of cash is still very important.

The compatibility of these rules with the measures taken in another area, namely the AML/CTF rules in the new AMLR framework that include rules to control the volume of cash payments and the admissibility of anonymous payments, is discussed in detail by *Andrea Minto* in *Chapter* 9.

The second important legislative proposal concerns the DigEuro-Reg, an instrument aiming to shape the legal foundation of the Digital Euro to be issued by the ECB. It is fair to say that, unlike the Legal Tender-Reg which encompasses and codifies known legal concepts, this Regulation will be a complete novelty in the regulatory environment of the European Union.

Importantly, the European Commission outlines the need and purpose of the introduction of the Digital Euro, also referring to the drivers of the initiatives that the ECB adopted on the Digital Euro. The Commission states:

> Banknotes and coins - which are the only current forms of central bank money with legal tender available to the general public (including people, public authorities and businesses) – alone cannot support the EU's economy in the digital age. Their use in payments therefore diminishes as online purchases increase and payment habits of the general public shift towards the large variety of private digital means of payment offered in the EU. This puts at stake the desirable balance between central bank money and private digital means of payment. This trend could even be reinforced in the future, with the emergence of third country central bank digital currencies (CBDC) and stablecoins issued by private firms, which could challenge the role of the euro in payments, in the EU and outside.
> The lack of a widely available and usable form of central bank money technologically adapted to the digital age could also diminish trust towards commercial bank money, and ultimately towards the euro itself. Trust towards commercial bank money relies on the possibility of depositors to convert at par their deposits into central bank money with legal tender, which currently is only available in the form of cash. Lacking a form of a central bank money that can be used in the digital economy and is convertible at par with commercial bank deposits may undermine the monetary anchor role of central bank money, weakening financial stability and monetary in the EU.[19]

What is indicated as one of the arguments is also seen as one of the important drivers for the ECB to come up with the Digital Euro, namely the developments surrounding the proposed introduction of the Libra payment product by Meta and the fears that it raised regarding interference of such a large-scale payment product in the settlement of retail payment transactions, and its possible monetary consequences. *Eugenia Macchiavello* discusses the issue in more detail in *Chapter* 2 of this book.

The Commission here notes concerns about the over-dominance of private party payment products, on the one hand, and foreign CBDC, on the other, and the consequent loss of the position of euro central bank currency in the form of bank notes and coins. From a historical perspective, the development of a payment solution by BigTechs does represent a risk in the view of European authorities. In particular, it is feared that this

[19] Paragraph 1 (Context of the Proposal), DigEuro-Reg, page 1.

would lead to a loss of sovereignty in terms of drawing the boundaries of macroeconomic policy and monetary frameworks. It is interesting to note that while the Digital Euro study and the consultations conducted revealed that future users have high demands on the issue of privacy, the European authorities, when assessing the desirability of payment solutions developed by private parties, do not pay any attention to the possible bottlenecks in this area.

In addition, the disappearance of the claim available in the form of cash to the central bank could also have implications for confidence in commercial parties' payment products, as the implicit assumption is that the holders of claims on the commercial parties should be able to convert them into a claim on the central bank (withdrawing cash). This argument mirrors the position taken by the ECB at the launch of the Digital Euro project, by stating upfront that a key mission of the ECB is "to provide citizens with riskless money for their payments".[20] On the implications for the banking industry of the introduction of a Digital Euro, see in detail *Chapter* 8 by *Nikos Maragopoulos*.

4 The Next Phase of the Digital Euro: The Preparation Phase

On 18 October 2023, the Governing Council of the ECB decided to start the Digital Euro preparation phase after the conclusion of the investigation phase. The preparation phase was planned to take another two years. In accordance with the ECB communication, the "preparation phase will lay the foundations for a potential Digital Euro, with work to include finalising rulebook and selecting providers to develop platform and infrastructure."[21] The decision follows the completion of the investigation phase that has been described in previous paragraphs.[22]

[20] Ibidem, Report on the Digital Euro, page 2.

[21] ECB, Press Release, "Eurosystem proceeds to next phase of digital euro project", to be consulted at: https://ec.europa.eu/commission/presscorner/detail/en/ip_23_3501.

[22] The results of the investigation phase and the forward looking planning for the next phase, the preparation phase, are laid out in ECB's publication 'A stocktake on the digital euro; Summary report on the investigation phase and the outlook on the next phase', 18 October 2023, www.ecb.europa.eu/euro/digital_euro/timeline/profuse/shared/pdf/ecb.dedocs231018.en.pdf.

The proposed design options for the Digital Euro, as presented by the ECB in October 2023, were based on the results of a comprehensive public consultation and an experimentation phase that involved the private sector and other central banks. The main objectives of the design were to ensure that the Digital Euro is accessible, secure, efficient and interoperable, while preserving the benefits of cash and respecting the principles of privacy and data protection. The design also aimed to prevent potential negative effects on financial stability and monetary policy transmission, as well as to foster innovation and competition in the European payment market.

One of the key features of the proposed Digital Euro design is that it would be a digital equivalent of cash, enabling users to make payments in any scenario, both online and offline, with full privacy protection and instant settlement in central bank money. No other existing digital payment method offers such a combination of benefits. The Digital Euro would thus complement cash and fill a gap in the European payment landscape.

The next stage of the Digital Euro project, the preparation phase, began on 1 November 2023 and was expected to last for two years initially. This phase would focus on finalising the rules and standards for the Digital Euro and selecting potential providers who could develop the platform and infrastructure for the Digital Euro. It would also involve testing and experimentation to ensure that the Digital Euro meets the expectations and needs of users, as well as the requirements of the Eurosystem, in terms of user experience, privacy, financial inclusion and environmental impact. The ECB continued to consult and engage with the public and relevant stakeholders throughout this phase. After the end of the two years, the Governing Council will decide whether to proceed to the next phase of preparations, which would set the stage for the possible future issuance and roll-out of the Digital Euro.

The start of the preparation phase does not imply a decision to issue the Digital Euro. Such a decision will only be considered by the Governing Council after the completion of the legislative process in the European Union, as highlighted above. The ECB will take into account any changes to the design of the Digital Euro that may result from the legislative discussions.[23]

[23] See Christos V. Gortsos, "Towards a central bank digital currency (CBDC) for the euro area," EBI Working Paper Series, 2024—no. 170, 29 (April 2024).

5 Further Outline of the Book

In creating this book, the group of ARG members first tested which topics deserved further discussion. This led to the development of the various contributions as included in this book. As mentioned, all the Chapters 2, 3, 4, 5, 6, 7, 8, and 9 have been completed in August 2023 and have not considered any developments beyond that closing date. Below is a brief reading guide to the remainder of the book.

5.1 Background and Rationale of CBDC

The history and rise of CBDC, and in particular its developments in Europe, are discussed in detail in *Chapter* 2 by *Eugenia Macchiavello*. In it, she discusses the different viewpoints on the subject and a deeper background and rationale. Her chapter discusses in detail the input of international institutions, such as the Bank for International Settlements, and academic research in this area.

How should CBDC be seen in relation to other payment methods as operated by existing industry players? What is the additional value offered by CBDC? This aspect gets extensive attention in *Chapter* 5 by *Panagiotis Politsidis*.

5.2 Role of the Central Bank and ECB in Respect of CBDC

Chapter 3 by *Christy Ann Petit* examines the European institutional and constitutional aspects of the introduction of the Digital Euro and the role of the ECB in it. How does the current treaty regime provide for supporting this new role that the ECB will play? This chapter was a prospective analysis before the publication of the Single Currency Package on 28 June 2023. *Chapter* 4, by *Maria Cecilia del Barrio Arleo*, then discusses the role of the ECB in the retail payment system and how the future issuance of the Digital Euro will need to fit into the existing system.

5.3 Financial Inclusion

As also prominently highlighted in the Commission's introduction to the DigEuro-Reg, it is a key policy objective of the European Institutions to create safeguards and incentives for the sufficient financial inclusion of citizens, and the initiatives to move towards a Digital Euro should be seen as consistent with the policy objective of:

> financial inclusion, the initiative is inspired by the approach adopted under Directive (EU) 2014/92 (Payment Accounts Directive), which aims at ensuring a universal access to payment accounts with basic features for all consumers, including financially excluded persons.[24]

Chapter 6 by *Federico Riganti* and *Anne-Marie Weber* discusses this important aspect in detail.

5.4 *Impact on Existing Banking Sector*

In *Chapter* 8, *Nikos Maragopoulos* discusses the potential impact of the introduction of the Digital Euro on the banking sector, from a micro-prudential perspective. In that chapter, he discusses the various design options of the Digital Euro presented and the potential impact on the balance sheet composition of banks.

5.5 *Governance of the Issue of the CBDC*

Needless to say, with the introduction of the Digital Euro, the ECB will take on numerous new tasks. Particularly in the operationalisation of the Digital Euro, there will be major implications. In *Chapter* 7, *Ioannis Linaritis* discusses in great detail the governance aspects of these new roles of the ECB, the extent to which the current institutional arrangements provide for such task performance and makes concrete proposals for further design and operation of the governance to be established around the Digital Euro.

5.6 *AML/CTF Aspects*

Finally, in *Chapter* 9, *Andrea Minto* discusses the AML/CTF aspects of the newly introduced Digital Euro, shedding light on the implications of the online variant, but especially the offline variant. Here, there seems

[24] Paragraph 1 (Context of the Proposal), DigEuro-Reg, page 3.

to be tension between the ECB's and the Commission's prominently stated objective of safeguarding privacy and allowing a largely anonymised payment circuit, and the fight against money laundering and terrorist financing.

6 Final Observations

It has become clear from the above that the Digital Euro will most probably happen, although the road to the final launch still seems to be a long one. The European Commission's comments on the occasion of the Single Currency Package speak of a long legislative process before it can come to the launch.[25] The ECB too is cautious in its pronouncements (e.g. the fourth progress report last July 2023) about the time frame and path ahead. But it does seem that the point of no return has been reached.

The long preparations are also indicative of the massive turnaround that can be expected from the introduction of the Digital Euro. Not only does it obviously require the creation of a completely new infrastructure both at the level of the Eurosystem and at the level of the (in all likelihood playing a major role) existing operators of the retail payment systems, both when it comes to the banks and payment institutions (as far as the online variant is concerned) and at the acceptance points (as far as the offline variant is concerned). After that has been done, the phase of actually using the Digital Euro will begin. In other words, the period during which the Digital Euro is used by consumers and businesses as a means of payment alongside existing means of payment, not only cash (banknotes or coins), but also card transactions and other electronic means of payment, such as, for instance, the rapidly evolving use of Apple Pay and Google Pay with Smartphones.

Those long preparations also include thorough research into the various aspects of this new phenomenon, as this too is entering *terra incognita*. While past experience has been gained by the private sector in introducing similar new payment methods,[26] the immense scale on

[25] European Commission, Press release, 28 June 2023, Brussels, 'Single Currency Package: new proposals to support the use of cash and to propose a framework for a digital euro', https://ec.europa.eu/commission/presscorner/detail/en/ip_23_3501

[26] For instance in the 90s, an 'offline' payment instrument had been introduced in the Netherlands, embedded on existing payment cards in the form of a programmable chip ('Chipknip' and 'Chipper'). This chip was the storage of value loaded through transactions

which the Digital Euro will be introduced as a means of payment in the Eurozone is completely new. What will be interesting to watch in the coming years is the extent to which the Digital Euro will be embraced equally within all Member States as a means of payment, or whether differences will emerge in terms of market penetration. In other words, will the Digital Euro belong to all of us as European citizens? This book elaborates on some key aspects along the lines set out above. It constitutes a contribution to the necessary scholarly debate on this important phenomenon.

carried out at ATMs. The product required the complete exchange of existing payment cards in circulation (more than 10 million cards), the introduction of new equipment facilitating the load transactions, and such operational aspects more. The introduction of this payment instrument took some years to implement all these required operational changes. The payment product was subsequently never accepted by consumers as a trustworthy means of payment, and consumers hardly used the product because, as appeared in use cases and research, consumers were concerned about the risks of loss of money when the payment card would be lost or stolen, including the embedded value. Consumers typically used the offline payment product for very small amounts and never loaded the stored value to more than approximately EUR 100. The scheme operators (the Dutch banks) decided to completely terminate the payment scheme after some years and concluded that this costly project failed, and wrote of the development costs (amounting to hundreds of millions of euro) off in a amortisation scheme agreed upon between the Dutch regulator and the industry to avoid sudden drops in profitability of the banks.

CHAPTER 2

Objectives, Rationale, Opportunities Versus Main Risks of a CBDC: Principles for a Coherent European Financial Regulation

Eugenia Macchiavello

1 Introduction: Structure and Aim of the Chapter

Control over money remains one of the most strategic and strong powers. Projects and experimentations for the creation of CBDCs are flourishing around the world also to allow central banks and their states not to lose such control: in 2022, 80% of central banks are considering launching a CBDC or have already done so, despite the required substantial amount

E. Macchiavello (✉)
Department of Law, University of Genoa, Genoa, Italy
e-mail: eugenia.macchiavello@unige.it

© The Author(s), under exclusive license to Springer Nature Switzerland AG 2025

F. Annunziata et al. (eds.), *Central Bank Digital Currency*, EBI Studies in Banking and Capital Markets Law,
https://doi.org/10.1007/978-3-031-80957-6_2

of economic, human and technical resources needed to study and implement this type of projects.[1] This chapter will, first of all, identify the immediate causes of this sudden and widespread blooming. Secondly, it will critically discuss the main arguments used to support the introduction of CBDCs in terms of the opportunities and the attainment of public goals against the corresponding risks and downsides. Finally, the present chapter will conclude by assessing the ability of the digital euro project in balancing different public goals and its coherence with the overall framework of European Union (EU) Financial Regulation, deriving, where possible, suggestions for its design.

The discussion will take into account the variety of alternatives at disposal in the design of CBDCs and its infrastructure, as well as the current stage of the digital euro project.

In fact, the design options and related implications from a regulatory point of view are multiple.[2] For instance, the use of blockchain to develop the infrastructure for CBDCs should not be taken for granted, as other more traditional systems have been considered (e.g., in the case of the Jamaican Jam-Dex). However, Distributed ledger technology (DLT)-based systems seem to be at the centre of the discussion.[3] Moreover, while wholesale CBDCs have received attention and considered for implementation, retail CBDCs (with retail accounts at the central bank) are the ones with greater revolutionary potential and most widespread.[4] Account-based CBDCs (with bank-like accounts and system) would replicate existing structures (with KYC identification procedures), ensuring

[1] PricewaterhouseCoopers, *Global CBDC index and stablecoins overview* (PwC, 2022), 5, https://www.pwc.com/gx/en/new-ventures/cryptocurrency-assets/pwc-global-cbdc-index-stablecoin-overview-2022.pdf. The cut-off date for all sources is 15th September 2023 (last possible update of the chapter/book).

[2] About CBDCs in general, see Chapter 1, by Annunziata, Hadjiemmanuil and Joosen.

[3] Raphael Auer et al., "Rise of the central bank digital currencies: drivers, approaches and technologies," Working Paper no. 880 (Bank for International Settlements, 2020), 5, https://www.bis.org/publ/work880.pdf.

[4] On the prevalence of retail CBDCs, see: European union blockchain observatory and forum, *CBDCs trend report* (EUBOF, 2022), 2, https://www.eublockchainforum.eu/sites/default/files/reports/CBDC_Trend_Report%20September2022_0.pdf. The most important projects for retail CBDCs in 2022 were: Nigeria, Bahamas, China, Jamaica, Eastern Caribbean, Ukraine, Uruguay, Thailand, Sweden, Korea; for wholesale CBDCs: Thailand, Hong Kong, Singapore, Canada, France, South Africa, United Arab Emirates, Japan, Saudi Arabia, Switzerland: PwC, *Global CBDC Index*, 10, 12; Auer et al., "Rise", 4ff.

interoperability with current payment systems and easy regulatory adaptation. Token-based CBDCs (based on the transfer of a token and the verification of its validity) and (semi-) decentralized structures (based on the consensus among different multiple nodes about the recording of ownership), instead, would mimic Bitcoin's anonymity and democratic model, but also its potential inefficiency, operational risks and the need for regulatory adaptations.[5] Finally, indirect systems, where the central bank (CB) simply issues the digital money and the financial intermediaries, such as banks, manage the rest and have a lower level of innovation and therefore advantages; on the other hand, direct models, with the CB managing all the process from the CBDC issuance to the interface with the client, would transform the role of CBs in the financial sector (see below 5.1). Therefore, hybrid models are most likely, where the CB issues the CBDC, becomes the client's counter-party and manages the infrastructure, while banks and other financial intermediaries create retail accounts and manage the user interface (e.g., CBDC projects in China, Sweden and the EU).[6] In particular, the ECB has expressed a preference

[5] Alexander Bechtel et al., "The future of payments in a DLT-Based european economy: A roadmap," in *The future of financial systems in the digital age: Perspectives in law, business and innovation*, ed. Markus Heckel and Franz Waldenberger (Springer: Singapore, 2022), 94. See also: Spitzer Kai Gereon and Loi Giacomo, "Digital Euro. Reviewing the progress to date and some open questions," *EGOV Briefing PE 741.498*, European Parliament, March, 2023. https://www.europarl.europa.eu/RegData/etudes/BRIE/2023/741498/IPOL_BRI(2023)741498_EN.pdf.

[6] About the design options, see: Bank for international settlements, *Central Bank Digital Currencies* (BIS, 2018), https://www.bis.org/cpmi/publ/d174.pdf; Gina Pieters, "Digital currencies and central banks," *The Palgrave Handbook of Technological Finance* (2021); Raphael Auer et al., "Central bank digital currencies: motives, economic implications and the research frontier," Working Papers no. 976 (BIS, 2021), 4, https://www.bis.org/publ/work976.pdf; Bechtel et al., "The future of payments"; Bank for International Settlements, *CBDCs: an opportunity for the monetary system*, Annual Economic Report, 2021, https://www.bis.org/publ/arpdf/ar2021e3.pdf; European Union Blockchain Observatory and Forum, *Central Bank Digital Currencies and a Euro for the Future* (EUBOF, 2021), 22ff, https://www.eublockchainforum.eu/sites/default/files/reports/CBDC%20Report%20Final.pdf; Francesca Mattassoglio, *Moneta e tecnologia* (Torino: Giappichelli, 2022), 115. About the current stage of the digital euro project and design options: European Central Bank, *Progress on the investigation phase of a digital euro*, Third Report (ECB, 2023), https://www.ecb.europa.eu/paym/digital_euro/investigation/governance/shared/files/ecb.degov230424_progress.en.pdf; European Central Bank, *Progress on the investigation phase of a digital euro*, Second Report (ECB, 2022), https://www.ecb.europa.eu/paym/digital_euro/investigation/governance/shared/files/ecb.degov220929.en.pdf. About China and Sweden: Auer et al., "Rise",

for a hybrid system where the digital euro represents a direct liability of the ECB and ownerships are recorded on a central ledger operated by the ECB, through an account-based model, but with financial intermediaries creating and operating users' individual accounts, performing clients' on boarding (the same as under Payments Services Directive II, (EU) 2015/2366 - PSD2) and know-your-customer (KYC) checks.[7]

The present chapter will briefly anticipate some relevant topics discussed further in detail in the rest of the book, with the aim of providing a first overview of the main regulatory issues, as well as the bigger picture, to contribute to the better understanding of the details and the deepening of more specific aspects.

2 Why a CBDC? Immediate Causes and Triggers

Many different types of sciences distinguish between immediate or proximate causes of an event and underlying or remote causes of it. The first are easier to identify, but the second might be more important, especially from a regulatory perspective, since they tend to be rooted in long-lasting factors and can also serve as legal basis and rationale for a legal reform.

Starting with the immediate triggers of CBDC projects, the development of crypto-currencies, such as Bitcoin since 2008, has been sometimes indicated as an incentive for the public power to consider the adoption of a CBDC and, in this way, provide an attractive alternative for users and fight against the prominence of private money. Nonetheless, crypto-currencies like Bitcoin have never represented a true threat for public money, despite the widespread narrative of substituting fiat money with crypto one. In fact, such crypto-currencies have never been able to work as units of account or a mean of exchange at a global scale, because

22ff. On the predominance of hybrid models: Ibid., 4; Michael Lloyd, "The Future of Money: Central Bank Digital Currencies", *Atlantic Economic Journal*, 50 (2022): 85–98, 96–97 (forecasting for the near future the prevalence of retail non-DLT account-based CBDCs); Tao Zhang and Zhigang Huang, "Blockchain and central bank digital currency", *ICT Express* 8, no. 2 (2022), 264–270 (regarding non-DLT based CBDCs or anyway permissioned CBDCs as most likely).

[7] Spitzer and Loi, "Digital Euro", 3; European Central Bank, *Digital euro—Prototype summary and lessons learned* (ECB, 2023), https://www.ecb.europa.eu/pub/pdf/other/ecb.prototype_summary20230526~71d0b26d55.en.pdf; ECB, *Progress*, third report, 5.

of their high volatility and technical limits (slow, costly, non-scalable and energy consuming/polluting system).[8]

Nonetheless, and as a response to these highlighted limits, the market has developed a more effective alternative: stablecoins.[9] These are crypto-currencies characterized by (a variety of) stabilization mechanisms (linked to a single fiat money or a basket of fiats) which aims at ensuring a stable value to the token. This, together with other comparable advantages (rapid settlement, rich transaction data, potential global reach), has made such private money more likely to serve as store of value and a mean of exchange and therefore attribute to the notion of money.

Stablecoins represent, thus, the immediate trigger for moving forward CBDCs projects and a faster pace. Facebook (now Meta) announced in 2019 its Libra (now Diem) project,[10] a global stablecoin anchored to a basket of fiats: shortly after, the United States (US) and the EU rushed to announce the future adoption of the digital dollar and digital euro, respectively.[11] CBs have been in fact reacting not only to defend their 'territory', but also because they concerned for the related risks and threats for the monetary and financial system, in terms, for instance, of CB's loss of control over money and impossibility to realize monetary policy,

[8] See, among others, Bank for International Settlements, *Cryptocurrencies: looking beyond the hype*, Annual Economic Report, 2018, https://www.bis.org/publ/arpdf/ar2018e5.pdf.

[9] For an overview of different types of stablecoins and stabilization mechanisms: Elliott Davis, "Stablecoins: Fiat-backed vs Crypto Collateralized vs Algorithmic," August 16, 2022, https://www.elliottdavis.com/stablecoins-fiat-backed-vs-crypto-collateralized-vs-algorithmic/; BIS, *CBDCs*, 77ff; Financial Stability Board, *Regulation, Supervision and Oversight of "Global Stablecoin" Arrangements*, Final Report and High-Level Recommendations (FSB, 2020), https://www.fsb.org/wp-content/uploads/P131020-3.pdf; PwC, *Global CBDC Index*, 46.

[10] Libra Association, "An Introduction to Libra", White Paper (2019), https://www.docdroid.net/kudDQUQ/librawhitepaper-en-us-pdf.

[11] See Mattassoglio, Moneta e tecnologia, 97; Anton Didenko and Ross Buckley, "Central bank digital currencies: A Potential Response to the Financial Inclusion Challenges of the Pacific," *UNSW Law Research Paper* (2021) https://www.adb.org/sites/default/files/publication/720016/central-bank-digital-currencies-pacific.pdf; Auer et al., *Central bank digital currencies*, 3; Codruta Boar et al., "Impending arrival: a sequel to the survey on central bank digital currency," (BIS Paper) no. 107 (Bank for International Settlements, 2005), https://www.bis.org/publ/bppdf/bispap107.pdf; Auer at al., "Rise", 3; Wilko Bolt et al., "Getting the balance right: Crypto, stablecoin and CBDC," DNB Working Paper no. 736 (DeNederlandscheBank, 2022), 9, https://www.dnb.nl/media/jo3h1dlu/working_paper_no-_736.pdf .

decline of banks' role and its ability to finance the real economy and the risks for consumers (data governance, losses, etc.). Such threat becomes even more serious when the stablecoin is realized at a global scale by a Big tech: such companies, with their enormous (economic and technical) resources and global consumer base, present the risk of dominating the entire economic system and create market concentration in a systemically important area.[12]

US and EU plans for CBDCs have been accelerated, not only through a public–private money competition, but also by a public-public money race: the announcement of the Digital Yuan has made more vivid the scenarios where a national currency replaces the others as the internationally-accepted one for cross-border payments and even domestic transactions in more instable and economically-weak countries, putting pressure on the other economically powerful areas not to lose their positions.[13]

The plans for CBDCs adoption have been spurred also by the COVID-19 emergency: pandemic-related restrictions, government recommendations to avoid cash not to spread the virus and better availability of

[12] European Central Bank, *Report on a digital euro* (ECB, 2020), 11–12, https://www.ecb.europa.eu/pub/pdf/other/Report_on_a_digital_euro~4d7268b458.en.pdf; BIS, *CBDCs*, 68; Ehrentraud et al., "Big tech regulation: in search of a new framework", FSI Occasional Paper 20 (Band for International Settlements, 2022), 4, 8–10, https://www.bis.org/fsi/fsipapers20.pdf; Christine Legarde and Panetta Fabio "Key objectives of the digital euro", *ECB blog*, July 13, 2022, https://www.ecb.europa.eu/press/blog/date/2022/html/ecb.blog220713~34e21c3240.en.html#:~:text=It%20would%20protect%20the%20strategic,innovation%20in%20the%20private%20sector.

[13] Buckley et al., "Sovereign Digital Currencies: Reshaping the Design of Money and Payments Systems", *Journal of Payments Strategy and Systems* 15(1), no. 7 (2021), 21-61. See also the explicit statement by the US administration in The White House, "Executive order on Ensuring Responsible Development of Digital Assets," March 9, 2022, section 4.a.iii, https://www.whitehouse.gov/briefing-room/presidential-actions/2022/03/09/executive-order-on-ensuring-responsible-development-of-digital-assets/: "A United States CBDC that is interoperable with CBDCs issued by other monetary authorities could facilitate faster and lower-cost cross-border payments and potentially boost economic growth, *support the continued centrality of the United States within the international financial system, and help to protect the unique role that the dollar plays in global finance.*" Instead, denying a "first-mover advantage" in a CBDCs context: Ken Isaacson et al., "An Examination of First-Mover Advantage for a CBDC", FEDS Notes (Washington: Board of Governors of the Federal Reserve System, November 25, 2022), https://doi.org/10.17016/2380-7172.3230.

convenient card and mobile payments have increased the use of digital payments among several societal groups.[14]

3 The Main Rationales to Create a CBDC: Opportunities

Introducing a CBDC and setting up its infrastructure, however, cannot be based on a temporary threat, but it needs more rooted arguments and reasoning. The basic argument used to justify such revolutionary reform is to deal with the inevitable decline in cash and therefore build on the advantages offered by crypto, while offering to users a convenient and more reliable alternative to private digital payments and crypto-currencies, overcoming the above-mentioned negative consequences and risks.[15]

[14] In Europe, 31% of consumers use less cash than before the pandemic: European Central Bank, *Study on the payment attitudes of consumers in the euro area (SPACE)* (ECB, 2022), https://www.ecb.europa.eu/stats/ecb_surveys/space/html/ecb.spacereport202212~783ffdf46e.en.html. See also Buckley et al., "Sovereign digital currencies" *Journal of Payments Strategy & Systems* 15, no. 1 (2021); ECB, *Report on a digital euro,* 10; Raphael Auer et al., "Covid-19, cash, and the future of payments," BIS Bulletin no. 3 (Bank for International Settlements, 2020), https://www.bis.org/publ/bisbull03.pdf; Auer et al., "Central bank digital currencies," 3; European Central Bank, *Progress on the investigation phase of a digital euro,* First Report, 2022, 3, https://www.ecb.europa.eu/paym/digital_euro/investigation/governance/shared/files/ecb.degov220929.en.pdf; Didenko and Buckley, "Central bank digital currencies", 39–40.

[15] See also Jess Cheng et al., "Preconditions for a general-purpose central bank digital currency", FEDS Notes (Washington: Board of Governors of the Federal Reserve System, 2021), https://doi.org/10.17016/2380-7172.2839. About CBDCs' rationale, among others: BIS, *CBDCs*; BIS, *Central Bank Digital Currencies*, 7; Bank for International Settlements, *Central bank digital currencies: executive summary* (BIS, 2021), https://www.bis.org/publ/othp42.pdf; ECB, *Progress,* first report; BIS, *Central Bank Digital Currencies*; Didenko and Buckley, "Central bank digital currencies", 36; Walter Engert and Fung Ben Siu Cheong, "Central bank Digital Currency: Motivations and Implications," Staff Discussion Paper no. 2017-16 (Bank of Canada, 2017), 7–8, https://www.bankofcanada.ca/wp-content/uploads/2017/11/sdp2017-16.pdf; G7 United Kingdom 2021. *Public Policy Principles for Retail Central Bank Digital Currencies (CBDCs)*, UK Presidency, 2021, 3, https://assets.publishing.service.gov.uk/government/uploads/system/uploads/attachment_data/file/1025235/G7_Public_Policy_Principles_for_Retail_CBDC_FINAL.pdf; Bank of England and HM Treasury, *The digital pound: a new form of money for households and businesses?*, Consultation Paper, February (BoE, 2023), https://www.bankofengland.co.uk/-/media/boe/files/paper/2023/the-digital-pound-consultation-working-paper.pdf.

The discussions about the opportunity for CBDCs have been articulated and complex. The most relevant arguments will be identified below for supporting the introduction of CBDCs, grouping them into clusters characterized by similar rationales. Carefully analysing such rationales is extremely important since picking one over another has an impact on CBDCs legal bases, design, chances for success, supervision and financial system's coherence.

3.1 Preservation

A recurring objective emerges from CBDCs' policy papers and official documents: preserving the role of public money and monetary sovereignty in the digital economy to maintain stability, customer protection (from data abuse, discontinuity and frauds) and other public goals.[16]

The plan is to design a CBDC able to replace crypto-currencies and Big tech's solutions, presenting similar advantages, while offering solutions to the former's limits and therefore, appearing more trustworthy, resilient, efficient (e.g., in terms of speed 24/24 operativity), environmentally sustainable, more protective of customer's data and not endangering competition and stability as Big techs' money.

In countries like Sweden, with an extremely low level of cash use due to a high degree of digitalization in the society and banking sector (see the early introduction of the digital ID), the issuance of a CBDC can be seen in line with the CB's objective of ensuring everyone's access to trustworthy and safe money. Economic and psychology literature, in fact, shows that even when private money is available to the public in substitution of cash, public money—and convertibility of private money into the former especially in time of crisis—might still be needed to reassure people fearing banks' credit risk (despite bank resolution measures and deposit insurance) and to maintain the CB's control over inflation (despite

[16] ECB, *Progress*, second report; ECB, *Progress*, first report, 3; Brooks 2021; Bank for International Settlements, *Central Bank Digital Currencies: Foundational Principles and Core Features*, Report no. 1, 2020, https://www.bis.org/publ/othp33.pdf; International Monetary Fund, "Digital money across borders: macro-financial implications," Policy Paper no. 50 (IMF, 2020), https://www.imf.org/en/Publications/Policy-Papers/Issues/2020/10/17/Digital-Money-Across-Borders-Macro-Financial-Implications-49823.

bank capital requirements and other measures to avoid over-lending).[17] Where the decline in cash makes a scenario of stablecoins diffusion more likely, CBDCs are able to ensure the widespread availability of official money issued and/or backed by the government.[18] The CB might also want to preserve its 'seigniorage' (revenue stream based on the value of outstanding banknotes), in order not to rely on government's funding.[19]

Moreover, CBDCs are also able to ensure customer data protection, while Big techs' model—and therefore their money—relies on a massive use and resale of customer data. Furthermore, single private digital payment solutions might reach such a level of adoption and market size to endanger competition, resilience and stability (e.g., in case of discontinuity of private payment services in a naturally concentrated market). For instance, Sweden developed the e-krona project to address the concerns about stablecoins, but also in order to counteract the high diffusion of the Swish—a popular mobile payment system developed by six dominant banks—and its likely prominence over cash in the near future.[20]

[17] Hanna Armelius et al., "Is central bank currency fundamental to the monetary system?," Economic Review (Sveriges Riksbank, 2020), 19–32, https://www.riksbank.se/globalassets/media/rapporter/pov/artiklar/engelska/2020/200618/2020_2-is-central-bank-currency-fundamental-to-the-monetary-system.pdf. About the UK: BoE & HM Treasury, *The digital pound*, 10, 28.

[18] This would overcome the remaining instability of stablecoins, which, despite the narratives, remain untrustworthy as demonstrated by the Terra-Luna crash, which has brought down also Tether: see Steven Kelly, "Stablecoins do not make for a stable financial system: Applying the logistics of financial stability to the cryptoverse," *Financial Times*, August 11, 2022, https://www.ft.com/content/0f979c98-ea78-4848-8282-52c2b68a9d19b.

[19] Engert and Fung, "Central bank digital currency", 2-3, 13; Elina Sidorenko et al., "Legal and Economic Implications of Central Bank Digital Currencies (CBDC)," in *Economic Systems in the New Era: Stable Systems in an Unstable World* (Springer International Publishing, 2021); Svetlana Igorevna Ashmarina et al., *Economic systems in the new era: Stable systems in an unstable world*. Lecture Notes in Networks and Systems 160 (Springer International Publishing, 2021), 498.

[20] Florian Misch, *The Pros and Cons of Central Bank Digital Currency: Insights From The Riksbank's E-Krona Project*, Sweden selected issues, Country Report no. 21/62, International Monetary Fund, 2021, https://www.elibrary.imf.org/view/journals/002/2021/062/002.2021.issue-062-en.xml; Hanna Armelius et al., "The Rationale for Issuing E-krona in the Digital Era", *Economic Review* no. 2 (Sveriges Riksbank, 2020), 6–18, https://www.riksbank.se/globalassets/media/rapporter/pov/artiklar/engelska/2020/200618/2020_2-the-rationale-for-issuing-e-krona-in-the-digital-era.pdf.

Another preservation objective targets international threats: countries want to avoid losing their economic and political importance over a foreign CBDC, developed before and at a faster pace, able to occupy the whole market on a 'first come – first served' basis and endanger even national cohesion.[21] The ECB has expressly stated that the digital euro would 'contribute to Europe's strategic autonomy and economic efficiency'.[22] Some developing countries have experimented CBDCs to maintain monetary sovereign against widespread and strong foreign currencies (e.g., Bahamas and Jamaica).

An extreme argument looks at CBDCs as an instrument to eliminate/reduce the systemic risk, associated with commercial banks—which justify public support and consequent sovereign crises (despite in the EU, the BRRD reform and its, in principle, prohibition of bail-out)—simply by completely bypassing banks themselves through retail and direct CBDCs.[23] This would eliminate/reduce the need of deposit insurance and therefore banks' moral hazard.[24] As discussed further below in this chapter, as well in other parts of the book, cutting banks out of the financial system would have, per se, very serious negative consequences; moreover, CBDCs, especially certain designs (decentralized models), might increase systemic risk (e.g., in terms of operational risks). However, as already anticipated above, the ECB is considering adopting a hybrid system, with a relevant role played by banks, also to prevent the risk of disintermediation and its disruptive effects (e.g., deposit run, high capital cost for banks and banks' inability to finance families and businesses, etc.).

[21] Monetary policy autonomy tends to be reduced in countries which do not have a CBDC: Massimo Ferari Minesso et al.,"Central Bank Digital Currency in an Open Economy," Working Paper Series no. 2488 (ECB, 2020), https://www.ecb.europa.eu/pub/pdf/scpwps/ecb.wp2488~fede33ca65.en.pdf. See also: Skylar Brooks, "Revisiting the Monetary Sovereignty Rationale for CBDCs," Staff Discussion Paper (Bank of Canada, 2021) https://www.bankofcanada.ca/wp-content/uploads/2021/12/sdp2021-17.pdf.

[22] ECB, *Progress*, first report, 4.

[23] Buckley et al., "The future of payments," 15.

[24] Paolo Fegatelli, "Central Bank Digital Currencies: The Case of Universal Access to Central Bank Reserves." Cahier D'Études Working Paper no. 130 (Central Bank of Luxembourg, 2019), 6–9, https://www.bcl.lu/en/publications/Working-papers/130/BCLWP130.pdf; Annelieke Mooij, "A digital euro for everyone: Can the European System of Central Banks introduce general purpose CBDC as part of its economic mandate?," *Journal of Banking Regulation* no. 24 (2021), 89–104.

Operational risk might come, in any case, from the complexity of the hybrid mode and infrastructure (see below).

3.2 Modernization

An important objective of CBDCs projects is to contribute to the digitalization of the economy and spur innovation.[25] One of the first new frontiers envisaged is that of a programmable money/token, through which parties can limit the permissible uses of the money, for instance, excluding certain goods, like tobacco or alcohol, or automatically save a small percentage of money for every purchase or limiting the use of credit to certain agreed goals.[26] Going further, having programmable digital money would empower the CBs to more effectively realize monetary policy and innovative 'helicopter money drops' (i.e., direct transfer of CB's funds to individuals and firms) and distribute economic support to socially/financially-excluded people. Other public authorities might use programmable money to limit the possibility to spend subsidies on certain services and products.[27] Ukraine has announced to be interested in developing a programmable retail CBDC that might also be linked to targeted welfare payments.[28]

[25] ECB, *Report on a digital euro*, 10; European Commission, "Targeted Consultation on a Digital Euro," Consultation Document, 2022, https://finance.ec.europa.eu/system/files/2022-06/2022-digital-euro-consultation-document_en.pdf. About the digital euro where no other solutions are available: European Banking Federation, *EBF response to the European Commission's Targeted Consultation on a digital euro* (EBF, 2022), 2, https://www.ebf.eu/wp-content/uploads/2022/06/FINAL-EBF-Response-to-EC-Consultation-on-a-Digital-Euro.pdf; BoE and HM Treasury, *The digital pound*, 5, 29.

[26] See also Ibid., 32; EUBOF,*CBDCs Trend Report*, 53ff (reporting the technical possibility to implement programmability within CBDCs even when not DLT-based at 61); Cyril Monnet, *Digital Euro: An assessment of the first two ECB progress reports*, (EGOV, 2023), 17, https://www.europarl.europa.eu/RegData/etudes/IDAN/2023/741508/IPOL_IDA(2023)741508_EN.pdf.

[27] Hossein Nabilou, "Testing the waters of the Rubicon: the European Central Bank and central bank digital currencies," *Journal of Banking Regulation*, 21 (2020), 305; Engert and Fung, "Central bank digital currency," 10; Mattassoglio, *Moneta e tecnologia*, 126ff. On helicopter drops: Ben Dyson and Graham Hodgson, "Digital Cash: Why Central Banks Should Start Issuing Electronic Money," *Positive Money* (2016), https://positivemoney.org/wp-content/uploads/2016/01/Digital_Cash_WebPrintReady_20160113.pdf.

[28] PwC, *Global CBDC Index*, 22.

At present, public money and the most private payment means are not compatible with interesting innovations, such as digital ID, payments integrated in DLT-based platforms and programmable (or conditional/ automatic) and stream payments.[29] Although this does not seem to represent the priority for worldwide CBs, CBDCs can even create a bridge between mainstream economy and crypto-economy (especially in case of token-based CBDCs), facilitating the integration of these two worlds, as long as this could be accepted by both public powers and crypto-anarchists.[30]

Another interesting area of future payment innovation is the Metaverse. Although there is no unique or official definition of the Metaverse, this can be broadly described as a digital environment conceived to be shared within a large network and allow parallel lives in a virtual augmented reality, including virtual friends, cars and purchases.[31] At present, the only payment solutions considered compatible with the Metaverse from a technical point of view are crypto-based. CBs might be interested in developing public money compatible with and therefore spendable also in this new world, again not to lose control over a (potentially) relevant part of the economy. Nonetheless, even if it was possible to develop a CBDC compatible with both current payment systems and the Metaverse, considering the current opacity and uncertainty surrounding the Metaverse project and therefore about the ability to oversee the activities and transactions conducted, there might be also reasons for the public money to stay away from it, at least until more clarity is reached.

As anticipated above (§3.1), CBDC would allow public money to better align with innovative payment solutions and respond to people's preference, especially after COVID-19, for digital payments over cash,

[29] Programmable or automatic payments allow parties to execute payments only where and when certain conditions are met (*e.g.*, delivery of the good). Stream payments consist in the consecutive execution of micro-payments to pay for on-demand and low-value services and products (*e.g.*, video, music, electricity recharging): see European Commission, "Targeted Consultation."; BoE and HM Treasury, *The digital pound*, 32; EUBOF, *CBDCs Trend Report,* 54ff; G7 United Kingdom 2021, *Public Policy Principles*, principle 9.

[30] Iris Chiu, *Regulating the Crypto Economy* (Oxford: Hart, 2021), 246ff; Iris Chiu, "Building out the Crypto Economy in Europe: a Proposal for Central Bank Digital Euros," *European Law Review*, 4 (2021); Bechtel et al., "The future of payments".

[31] On the metaverse and law, see Richard Pate, "Legal issues inside the unnatural world of Metaverse", *Business Law Review*, 43, no. 5 (2022), 188–193.

providing a cheap, easily accessible, cash-like experience.[32] To replicate a cash-like experience and support the digital euro legal tender status, the ECB is considering allowing person-to-person (P2P) and off-line transactions through varied forms of technological devices (still to be developed) meeting customers' demand.[33] As regards the design of CBDCs is also important to ensure interoperability with other private payment instruments.

3.3 *Response to Needs and Crises*

As happens with crypto-currencies and fintech in general, CBDCs are presented as instruments to improve the access of individuals and (smaller) businesses to the financial system (financial inclusion; see the eNaira in Nigeria and the Sand dollar in the Bahamas). In particular, the decline in the use of cash creates a need for convenient and cheap payment solutions (compared, for instance, to certain credit card fees), accessible also to low-income people.[34] Moreover, some believe that CBDCs might be able to broaden access for people with disabilities, reducing physical barriers.[35]

[32] BIS, *CBDCs*; ECB, *Progress*, second report.

[33] Eurogroup, "Eurogroup statement on the digital euro project," Statement, January 16, 2023, https://www.consilium.europa.eu/en/press/press-releases/2023/01/16/eurogroup-statement-on-the-digital-euro-project-16-january-2023/. See also the following ECB market study, which identifies p2p payments, off-line transactions and conditional payments as the most desired ones: European Central Bank, *Study on Digital Wallet Features*, Report, March (Kantar Public: 2023), https://www.ecb.europa.eu/press/pr/date/2023/html/ecb.pr230424_1_annex~93abdb80da.en.pdf. On the need to protect such devices from manipulation and therefore likely adoption later than the online tools for the low level of readiness of existing technologies: Spitzer and Loi, "Digital Euro," 4; ECB, *Digital euro—Prototype*, 12–13.

[34] BIS, *CBDCs*, 68; ECB, *Report on a digital euro*. About CBDC and social/financial inclusion, see in the present Book Chapter 4 by Riganti and Weber. Studies attest a preference of unbanked people for payment methods also for small amounts, off-line, low or no fees, and even with the possibility to borrow small amounts during difficult months: ECB, *Study on New Digital Payment Methods*, Report, March (Kantar Public: 2022), 12, https://www.ecb.europa.eu/paym/digital_euro/investigation/profuse/shared/files/dedocs/ecb.dedocs220330_report.en.pdf.

[35] European Commission, "Targeted Consultation."; See, however, again in the present Book, Riganti and Weber's chapter 6.

Furthermore, CBDCs are deemed to respond to significant shortcomings in the current cross-border payment system. While the EU has solved most problems of payments among Member States (e.g., through SEPA, TARGET instant payments settlement, etc.), this segment of the international financial system, in fact, suffers from slowness, technical barriers, lack of interoperability when one looks at payment flows with non-EU countries. CBDCs, instead, are expected to increase the level of compatibility, interconnection and potential integration of national infrastructures into a single system, facilitating remittances and international trade.[36]

The current supply of micro and peer-to-peer payments is also inadequate and CBDCs have the potential to attract customers, when responding to such customers' needs.[37] The aim to create a global and interoperable Financial Market Infrastructure (FMI) has also motivated the Fnality Global Payment Project, an initiative of a consortium of international banks for wholesale payments and settlement.[38] This will consist of separate national, distributed, DLT and token-based interoperable FMIs (regulated as payment systems). Settlements will be based on pre-funded settlement balances fully 'backed' by CB money—in the form of reserve accounts at the CB—to eliminate banks' credit risk (basically, synthetic CBDCs: see below §6.1).[39] The introduction of an official/public CBDC, instead, will allow CB to retain control over the retail payment systems.

[36] ECB, *Progress*, third report, 12; Bank for International Settlements, *Central bank digital currencies for cross-border payments*, Report to the G20 (BIS, 2021), https://www.bis.org/publ/othp38.pdf; BIS, *CBDCs*, 85ff; IMF, "Digital."; Didenko and Buckley, "Central bank digital currencies," 14; Boar et al., "Impending arrival," 5 (improving cross-border payments is regarded by economically developed countries as one of the main motivations for wholesale CBDCs); G7 United Kingdom 2021, *Public Policy Principles*, principle 12.

[37] Bank for International Settlements, *Central bank digital currencies: user needs and adoption*, Report no. 3, 2021, https://www.bis.org/publ/othp42_user_needs.pdf.

[38] The shareholders are Banco Santander, BNY Mellon, Barclays, CIBC, Commerzbank, Credit Suisse, ING, KBC Group, Lloyds Banking Group, Mizuho Financial Group, MUFG Bank, Nasdaq, Sumitomo Mitsui Banking Corporation, State Street Corporation and UBS. The fiat currencies that will be initially covered are CAD, EUR, GBP, JPY & USD. See Fnality Team. 2021. Fnality Global Payments—The Fnality Narrative, 4, https://f.hubspotusercontent10.net/hubfs/5546019/Fnality%20International%20Narrative%20Q3%202020.pdf; see also Fnality Frequently Asked Questions at https://www.fnality.org/what-we-do.

[39] Ibid.

A CBDC might also have a relevant role in terms of geopolitical difficulties. As evidenced by the Ukraine war, digital payments can be more accessible than cash or bank money in time of war. Depending on the specific district, a CBDC might respond to additional shortcomings and deficiencies of that country, such an inefficient payment system or a weak bank infrastructure.[40] As an example, the Sand dollar has been conceived also to improve the payment system and its resilience especially in the aftermath of natural disasters.[41]

At the same time, private digital payment entities are often located outside the EU: the digital euro would avoid the danger of leaving such transactions and other relative data in the hands of foreign entities and their countries or being affected by political frictions.[42]

Finally, CBDCs would improve the instant settlement, continuous operability of the payment system, and allow a better overview of the system, also at the benefit of the tax system and frauds prevention.[43]

4 Careful About What You Desire: Relevance for CBDC's Legal Basis, Design and Potential for Success

The rationales listed above are generally used jointly to support the launch of CBDCs. Nonetheless, each of them might be linked to a different legal basis for the CBDC and influence differently the CBDC design. For instance, as will be discussed in length in another part of this book,[44] the use of the digital euro to preserve and enact ECB's monetary policy would be grounded in Articles 128(1) Treaty on the Functioning of the

[40] Boar et al., "Impending arrival," 4. Such argument has been apparently used also in the UK, where anyway the House of Lords has manifested scepticism about CBDCs and used the efficiency of the British payment system to challenge the validity of a digital Pound: House of Lords, *Central bank digital currency: a solution in search of a problem*, 3rd Report of Session 2021–22, January 13, 2022, https://publications.parliament.uk/pa/ld5802/ldselect/ldeconaf/131/131.pdf.

[41] Misch, *The Pros and Cons*, 5.

[42] ECB, *Progress*, second report; Legarde and Panetta, "Key objectives of the digital euro."

[43] Sofie Blakstad and Robert Allen, "Central Bank Digital Currencies and Cryptocurrencies," in *FinTech Revolution* (Cham: Palgrave Macmillan, 2018), 91.

[44] See Chapter 3 in the present Book by Petit.

EU (TFEU) and 20 European System of Central Banks (ESCB) (e.g., issuance of banknotes). Such Treaty provisions are not likely to represent the legal basis for CBDCs in case of programmable money, considering the diversity of function between cash and the latter,[45] and would clash with the proposed holding caps and remuneration features.[46] At the same time, if the main justification for the digital euro is financial inclusion, the legal bases would be Article 127(1) TFEU, support of price stability and economic policies in line with Article 3 Treaty on the EU (TEU); instead, if the main rationale is efficiency through the creation of accounts opened directly with the CB, the legal bases would be Articles 127(2) TFEU and 17 ESCB (i.e., ECB's competence to promote the smooth, efficient and safe functioning of the payment system, including the power to open accounts for financial institutions and market participants). Moreover, modernization of payment systems and replication of cash-like experience rationales would find their grounds in Articles 128 TFEU and 16 ESCB (about ECB's power to issue banknotes). Finally, if the main goal aims at improving cross-border payments, Articles 127(2) TFEU and 22 ESCB would instead represent the potential legal reference.[47]

Considering such complexity, from a regulatory point of view and design of CBDCs projects, some authors have advanced the possibility, in principle, to separately issue different types of 'tailored' CBCDs, with the objective to maximize the benefits of each solution and thus, to reduce the corresponding risks.[48] On the other hand, such solution seems to be quite complex in practical terms, as well as costly, leading therefore to the development of a universal and unique type of digital money.

[45] Nabilou, "Testing the waters of the Rubicon," *Journal of Banking Regulation*, 308.

[46] See also Seraina Grünewald, *A legal framework for the digital euro: An assessment of the ECB's first three progress reports*, Economic Governance and EMU Scrutiny Unit at the request of the ECON Committee, May (European Parliament, 2023), 18, https://www.europarl.europa.eu/RegData/etudes/IDAN/2023/741518/IPOL_IDA(2023)714518_EN.pdf.

[47] See also ECB, *Report on a digital euro*; Hubert de Vauplane, "Cryptocurrencies and central banks," in *Fintech Law and Regulation*, ed. J. Madir, (Cheltenham: Edward Elgar, 2021), 141ff; Nabilou, "Testing the waters of the Rubicon," *Journal of Banking Regulation*, 307–308; Bengamin Geva et al., "The e-Banknote as a 'Banknote': A Monetary Law Interpreted," *Oxford Journal of Legal Studies*, 41, no. 4 (2021), 1119; Mooij, "A digital euro for everyone," 4ff.

[48] Tod Keister and Daniel Sanches, "Should Central Banks Issue Digital Currency?" *The Review of Economic Studies*, 90, no. 1 (2023).

At the same time, pitfalls and potential for failure are intrinsic to these same rationales. For instance, the introduction of CBDC, to last and be successful, should not be simply a reaction to crypto-currencies (immediate cause), but be based on solid, reasonable and realistic grounds. If the main and real reason to launch a CBDC is competing with private crypto-currencies, the efforts are likely mis-directed and the potential for success scarce. In fact, based on recent data,[49] crypto-currencies are used on average in the EU only by 4% of the population, with peak of 8% in Slovenia and Luxembourg. Moreover, among this part of the population, the majority holds crypto-currencies for investment purpose only, or for both investment and payment (with the payment function prevalent exclusively in Slovenia). In addition, although based on anecdotic evidence, the motivations of many crypto-currency users reside in factors not applicable to future CBDCs (except for curiosity for technology and low fees), such as the hope of becoming rich, the pleasure of betting or illegal use,[50] the need of keeping their anonymity, or the aversion towards banks and user empowerment.[51]

Similarly, CBDCs might not represent the most effective instrument for financial access, considering that a recent study underlines low-income people's preference for cash or anonymous solutions, while a minimum level of KYC on boarding is inevitable, with CBDC to preserve other financial regulation's objectives, such as anti-money laundering and combating terrorism (AML-CT).[52] Moreover, low-income population

[49] ECB, *Study on the payment attitudes.*

[50] Omar Alqaryouti et al., "Users' Knowledge and Motivation on Using Cryptocurrency," in *European, Mediterranean, and Middle Eastern Conference on Information Systems* (Cham: Springer International Publishing, 2019).

[51] Lena Cavusoglu and Idil Goksel, "Exploring Motivations of Cryptocurrency Enthusiasts," *International Journal of Business and Management Invention* 8, no. 10 (2019), https://www.ijbmi.org/papers/Vol(8)10/Series-1/F0810014553.pdf; Irni Eliana Khairuddin et al., "Exploring Motivations among Bitcoin Users," Lancaster University, 2016, https://eprints.lancs.ac.uk/id/eprint/78254/1/Exploring_Motivations_among_Bitcoin_Users_Final_Submission.pdf. See also Sarah Meiklejohn et al., "A fistful of bitcoins: characterizing payments among men with no names," in *Proceedings of the 2013 conference on Internet measurement conference* (2016), https://dl.acm.org/doi/10.1145/2896384; Aaron Yelowitz and Matthew Wilson, "Characteristics of Bitcoin users: an analysis of Google Search data," *Applied Economics Letters*, 22, no. 13 (2015); Lui, S. "The demographics of Bitcoin (Part 1 Updated)." *Simulacrum. April* 3 (2013), http://simulacrum.cc/2013/03/04/the-demographics-of-bitcoin-part-1-updated/.

[52] See in this Book Chapter 9 by Minto.

generally need better infrastructures and more custom-centred solutions, rather than a CBDC.[53] More generally, financial inclusion seems not to be the most important drivers, at least in economically developed jurisdictions (particularly in the Eurozone), and other instruments might be more effective in meeting such goal.[54]

Another example of CBDCs' utility is related to the goal to fix cross-border payments' problems: considering the variety of technical options considered by different CBs around the world and ID systems, ensuring interoperability among CBDCs would require enormous cooperation efforts among countries, which at present seems at least as difficult as fixing existing cross-border payments channels.[55] Token-based CBDCs would probably better serve cross-border payments' needs and such corresponding rationale but, as mentioned above, do not correspond to the most widespread model. Anyhow, the presence of the global, market-led, token-based Fnality initiative for wholesale settlements put pressure on the CBs of the involved jurisdictions to make efforts in ensuring interoperability of the future public, (likely) centralized retail system with the former private decentralized one.

Certain rationales might also conflict with each other: the choice about which one should prevail will impact the design and be decisive for the success of the project. For instance, the true competitors of CBDCs are bank money and private electronic payments.[56] In this regard, CBDCs can really respond to customers' demand for convenient

[53] Greta Bull et al., "Is Financial Inclusion a Reason to Push Central Bank Digital Currencies?," *CGAP*, May 13, 2021, https://www.cgap.org/blog/is-financial-inclusion-reason-to-push-central-bank-digital-currencies.

[54] Engert and Fung, "Central bank digital currency," 7–8; Boar et al., "Impending arrival," 4 (in surveys, financial inclusion is listed as very important motivation only by emerging market economies). However, the digital euro might facilitate cross-border remittances by workers living in the EU to their families in non-EU countries: Ignazio Angeloni, *Digital Euro: When in doubt, abstain (but be prepared)*, European Parliament, 2023, 19, https://www.europarl.europa.eu/RegData/etudes/IDAN/2023/741507/IPOL_IDA(2023)741507_EN.pdf.

[55] See also: House of Lords, *Central bank digital currency*; BIS, *CBDCs*, 87; BIS, *Central bank digital currencies*; Bank for International Settlements, *Options for access to and interoperability of CBDCs for cross-border payments*, Report to the G20, 2022, https://www.bis.org/publ/othp52.pdf.

[56] Fabio Panetta, "A digital euro that serves the needs of the public: Striking the right balance," Report, March 30, European Central Bank, 2022, https://www.ecb.europa.eu/press/key/date/2022/html/ecb.sp220330_1~f9fa9a6137.en.html.

and cheap digital payment, through a flexible design, lower costs and solutions to existing gaps (e.g., peer-to-peer, conditional or cross-border payments).[57] Nonetheless, technical obstacles and the required involvement of traditional intermediaries, such as banks and the persistence, as already mentioned, of mandatory on boarding and KYC under the current digital euro project and therefore costs might clash with this goal.[58] In addition, certain potential features announced by some studies might make a CBDC unattractive for customers, hindering the attainment of a sufficiently wide network: traceability, same KYC procedure as traditional channels, programmable limits to spending or holding would dissuade customers to use the CBDC and therefore limit the achievement of the objective to reinforce ECB's monetary power.[59]

Although certain narratives describe CBDC as the anonymous digital version of cash, digital public money cannot ensure complete anonymity to limit frauds, money laundering and financing terrorism. Even if anonymity might correspond to an actual preference of customers, this cannot be satisfied when it corresponds to the need to conduct or support an illicit activity or avoid payment of taxes or disguise the property of the user of the digital currency.[60]

In this regard, the ECB, also in order to find a balance between customers' privacy and money laundering prevention, for instance, has been considering a hybrid and tiered system (see above §1): the ECB would issue the digital euro and operate the settlement infrastructure, but private intermediaries (e.g., banks) would manage individual accounts and deal with customers' onboarding. As a result, customers' identities and personal data would not be available to the CB, preserving their

[57] Fearing the absence of a market demand for a digital euro and consequent failure with a reputational damage for the ECB: Angeloni, *Digital Euro*.

[58] For instance, about the need to make the digital euro attractive for merchants (to overcome existing merchants' resistance to allow customers' payments with cards): Monnet, *Digital Euro*.

[59] Against holding caps as limiting the monetary anchor goal of the digital euro and its resemblance to cash: Grünewald, *A legal framework for the digital euro*.

[60] On the balance between privacy and prevention of money-laundering and other public goals, see Chapters 5 by Politsidis and 9 by Minto.

privacy towards public authorities and bodies (similarly to the Swedish e-krone).[61] Moreover, 'selective privacy' and a risk-based approach would allow more privacy/anonymity in case of low value transactions, while stricter rules would apply to larger amount and offline transactions up to a certain amount,[62] in line with EDPB's recommendations.[63] Also token-based CBDCs might allow tiered solutions, mid-way between cash and account-based money.[64] The UK is considering a CBDC based on wallets, which, if implemented, would allow only the third-party providers (TPP) to see the personal data, while the Bank of England (BoE) and other national banks would be left with the possibility to see the anonymous transaction recorded.[65]

5 The 'Other Side of the (Digital) Coin': Adding CBCDs' Risks to the Picture

The above discussion, so far, has focused on the reasons and opportunities to launch a CBDC. Nonetheless, any reform and innovative policy obviously needs to be assessed also against the risks it would add to

[61] Payments data would anyway be transferred in a pseudonymized/aggregated form to the ECB for settlement, supervisory and statistical purposes. Since such data include personal data (*e.g.*, spending habits, mean of transport used, etc.) and are not completely anonymized, some authors still see relevant privacy issues: Mooij, "A digital euro for everyone", 19ff.

[62] ECB, *Progress*, 78; Eurogroup, Eurogroup *statement on the digital euro project*. See also Auer et al., "Rise", 25; ECB, *Digital euro—Prototype*, 10.

[63] European Data Protection Board, *EDPB letter to the European institutions on the privacy and data protection aspects of a possible digital euro*, June 18 (EDPB, 2021), 4-5, https://edpb.europa.eu/system/files/2021-07/edpb_letter_out_2021_0111-digitaleuro-toecb_en_1.pdf; European Data Protection Board, *Response of the EDPB to the European Commission's targeted consultation on a digital euro*, June 14 (EDPB, 2021), https://edpb.europa.eu/system/files/2022-06/edpb_responseconsultation_20220614_digitaleuro_en.pdf. Banks' representatives seem to favour instead the adherence to the same standards used for banks' money, likely to ensure competition: see EBF, *EBF response*, 3. About privacy and CBDC, see also G7 United Kingdom 2021, *Public Policy Principles*, principle 3.

[64] Raphael Auer and Rainer Boehme, The technology of retail central bank digital currency, *BIS Quarterly Review*, March (Banks for International Settlements, 2020), 88, https://www.bis.org/publ/qtrpdf/r_qt2003j.pdf. The EDPB supports a cash-like digital euro: EDPB, *EDPB letter*, 4–5.

[65] BoE and HM Treasury, *The digital pound*, 11–12.

the system and other regulatory concerns,[66] especially in the view of an impact and cost–benefit analysis under a better-regulation perspective. Risks might not represent impediments to CBDC's adoption, but need to be addressed and contained through CBDC design choices and other regulatory measures.

The present section has the aim of providing a first overview of the 'other side of the coin' to supply a first complete picture of CBCDs from a regulatory point of view. However, for their importance, such issues deserve a deeper analysis in the subsequent and insightful chapters of this book.

5.1 The Risk of Crowding Out Banks

One of the most debated risks of CBDCs, as anticipated above, is the reduced role of banks. Should CBDC turned out to be successful in attracting customers through cheap retail accounts held directly at CBs', depositors might be induced to transform their commercial bank deposits into central bank liabilities, with a higher risk of bank run in times of crisis.[67] Consequently, banks would lose a relevant part of their customers' base and their cheapest source of funding, having to recur to wholesale funding at higher costs and/or riskier forms of lending. Banks would also further lose their residual information advantage over clients' transaction data based on a relation banking model: this has been already impaired by the PSD2 open banking model, requiring banks to share customers' data with TPP and other fintechs. Such phenomenon

[66] Addressing specifically also CBDCs' risks: BIS, *Cryptocurrencies*; Buckley et al., "Sovereign digital currencies."

[67] See also Chapter 8 by Maragopoulos. For a more optimistic view: Iris HY Chiu and Christian Hofmann, "Unlimited Central Bank Digital Currency: The Case for a Public Good in the Euro Area and its Regulatory (and Deregulatory) Implications for Modern Finance," *North Carolina Journal of International Law* 48, no. 1 (2023) (looking at this bank run as an opportunity for banks' supervisors to redirect their attention from depositors' protection to stability); Christian Hofmann, *Digital Euro: An assessment of the first two progress reports - The case for unlimited holdings of digital euros*, Economic Governance and EMU Scrutiny Unit at the request of the ECON Committee, April (European Parliament, 2023), 19ff, https://www.europarl.europa.eu/RegData/etudes/IDAN/2023/741511/IPOL_IDA(2023)741511_EN.pdf (the digital euro would allow safer and quicker reconversions after bank runs or negative interest rate periods); Monnet, *Digital Euro*, 13 (no caps on digital euro holdings would bring healthy competition in the market for deposits).

has been later aggravated by Big tech's dominance over customers' data from their platform-based ecosystem.[68] All this would inevitably lead to higher interest rates on bank loans and lower banks' ability to finance the real economy, as well as to more instability for the entire financial system.[69] Moreover, leaving CBs to manage millions of retail accounts and related transactions, customer on boarding and other typical activities performed by financial intermediaries would completely change the role of CBs, transforming them from independent and technical authorities to market actors in (unfair) competition with financial intermediaries, subject to potentially suboptimal choices and political risk, without considering the substantial investments needed to realize such transition.[70]

To address the above risks, the ECB has proposed several design solutions and additional policy measures. As regards the former, as already mentioned, a model based on direct claims with the ECB where the distribution takes place through retail accounts at banks has been advanced (see above §1 and §4, last paragraph). Moreover, to eliminate the substitution between deposits and CBDCs and make the latter unattractive as an instrument of store of value, no interest or negative interest rates above certain amount (while remunerating small holdings, to be used for payment purposes) and caps on holdings (e.g., 3,000–4,000 per capita)[71]

[68] See also BIS, *CBDCs*, 67–68. On the impact of open banking and Big techs' entrance in the financial services industry on banks' role, please also refer to Eugenia Macchiavello, "Digital Platforms, Capital Raising and EU Capital Markets Law: Different Shades of Decentralisation." *European Business Law Review*, 33, no. 7 (2022), 1057.

[69] BIS, *CBDCs*; ECB, *Report on a digital euro*, 16; EBF, *EBF response*, 21; see also (on the cost of funding): Ulrich Bindseil, "Central Bank Digital Currencies in a World with Negative Nominal Interest Rates," in *The Future of Financial Systems in the Digital Age. Perspectives in Law, Business and Innovation*, ed. Heckel, M., Waldenberger, F. (Singapore: Springer Springer Singapore, 2022); Keister and Sanches, "Should central banks"; Jay Cullen, "Economically inefficient and legally untenable: constitutional limitations on the introduction of central bank digital currencies in the EU." *Journal of Banking Regulation*, 23, no. 1 (2022), 31–41, 31, 35; Nabilou, "Testing the waters," 308–09.

[70] Harry Leinonen, "Electronic central bank cash: To be or not to be?," *Journal of Payments Strategy & Systems*, 13, no. 1 (2019), 20–31; BIS, *Central bank digital currencies*, 14ff; Nabilou, "Testing the waters," 306; Chiu, *Regulating the crypto economy*, 244–45; Mooij, "A digital euro for everyone," 11-16; Angeloni, *Digital Euro*.

[71] See Fabio Panetta, "The digital euro and the evolution of the financial system," *Introductory statement at the Committee on Economic and Monetary Affairs of the European Parliament*, European Central Bank, 2022, https://www.ecb.europa.eu/press/key/date/2022/html/ecb.sp220615~0b859eb8bc.en.html.

have been presented as additional corrective measures (although raising new issues).[72]

The open finance strategy[73] and other EU initiatives in the area of data and platform economy should address the remaining highlighted problems.

5.2 *An Ambitious Project, Filled with Complexity: The Difficult Balance Between Technical, Private and Public Powers*

Creating a big infrastructure to operate CBDCs will require, as already mentioned, substantial resources and extremely high technical skills.[74] Governments are notoriously lacking knowledge on the latest technologies or capacity to attract high-skilled professionals, making unavoidable private sector's involvement in CBDCs' projects.[75]

CBs have been in fact running experiments with the private sector (e.g., banks, e-money providers), as well as technological companies. The ECB announced in September 2022 the collaboration with five companies (including Amazon and Nexi) to develop user interfaces for the

[72] ECB, *Progress*, second report; Ulrich Bindseil, "Tiered CBDC and the financial system," Working paper (European Central Bank, 2020), https://www.ecb.europa.eu/pub/pdf/scpwps/ecb.wp2351~c8c18bbd60.en.pdf; Markus Brunnermeier and Jean-Pierre Landau, "The digital euro: policy implications and perspectives," European Parliament, 2021, https://www.europarl.europa.eu/RegData/etudes/STUD/2022/703337/IPOL_STU(2022)703337_EN.pdf; EBF, *EBF response*, 3 (favouring hard caps over soft rate disincentives); BoE and HM Treasury, *The digital pound*, 14 (on caps on the holding of the digital pound at least in the initial phase); EUBOF, *CBDCs Trend Report*, 68. Against instead such caps (saved for an initial phase) to better protect depositors, enhance CBs' control over banks' liquidity provision, and support competent authorities' resolution efforts: Hofmann, *Digital Euro*; in favour of only high caps and no remuneration to ensure wide acceptance of the digital euro while preserving stability: Grünewald, *A legal framework*. About negative remuneration as in violation of the EU charter of fundamental rights: Annelieke Mooij, "Digital euro's legal framework—The legal framework concerning legal tender, privacy and inclusion," European Parliament, 2023, 14, https://www.europarl.europa.eu/RegData/etudes/IDAN/2023/747840/IPOL_IDA(2023)747840_EN.pdf.

[73] European Commission, *Open finance framework—enabling data sharing and third party access in the financial sector*, Published initiatives on the Web site, https://ec.europa.eu/info/law/better-regulation/have-your-say/initiatives/13241-Open-finance-framework-enabling-data-sharing-and-third-party-access-in-the-financial-sector_en.

[74] BoE and HM Treasury, *The digital pound*, 17–18.

[75] Bechtel et al., "The future of payments," 108 (in favour of a privately-issued digital euro).

digital euro.[76] In its second progress report, the ECB has recognized that 'the close involvement of the private sector is seen as a key factor for successful implementation of a digital euro. A digital euro will need to draw on the experience and best practices used in the market'.[77] If the final infrastructure had to be created and even managed in cooperation with powerful technological companies, this would make the public power and a systemically relevant infrastructure dependent on one/some of such companies.[78] Again, competition, stability, resilience and consumer protection objectives must be taken under consideration.[79] Managing, also from a legal point of view, the responsibility within the system among the CB/public power and private actors would require new regulatory models.

In any case, the implementation of a new system, especially if based on a new technology as the DLT, would increase operational risk for a relevant infrastructure and therefore, a relevant concentrated point of failure.[80]

5.3 *Social Risks and Additional Sustainability Concerns*

Although fascinating, solutions entailing programmable money might clash with the competence of CBs generally limited to monetary policy and overview of payment systems. In fact, if CBs could issue public money embedded with use restrictions and other similar features, their competence would be questionably extended to re-distribution policies

[76] ECB, *ECB selects external companies for joint prototyping of user interfaces for a digital euro*, MIP News, September 16, 2022, https://www.ecb.europa.eu/paym/intro/news/html/ecb.mipnews220916.en.html. See also ECB, *Digital euro—Prototype*.

[77] ECB, *Progress*, second report, 4.

[78] Although referred to financial institutions' over-reliance on Big -techs (instead of CBs): "Excessive dependence by financial institutions on third-party providers generates operational risks. When those services are of a technological nature, the vulnerabilities become more pronounced due to possible cyber incidents affecting the continuity of services and data protection. Moreover, the concentration of some of those services within a relatively small set of (big tech) providers results in the consequences of operational risks being particularly pronounced and potentially systemic" (Ehrentraud et al., "Big tech regulation," 4).

[79] G7 United Kingdom 2021, *Public Policy Principles*, principles 1, 2, 4 and 5.

[80] Leinonen, "Electronic central bank cash," 22. About the governance of CBDC infrastructure and operational risk, see Chapter 7 in the present Volume by Linaritis.

and intervention in the economy. Even in case of a CBDC programmable by public authorities with extended competence, there would be the risk of excessive intrusion of the state in people's choices, especially in less democratic jurisdictions. For instance, fears have been advanced on China's ability to collect, through the digital Yuan, additional data on citizens and increase controls, limits to spending and monitoring. Based on similar considerations, the Eurogroup has expressed concern over a programmable digital euro and advise against it.[81] The ECB has clarified that, while the digital euro will not be programmable money, it will allow programmable (or conditional) payments, meaning that people will be able to pre-authorize an automatic payment where pre-defined conditions are met, through value-added services provided, on a voluntary basis, by supervised financial intermediaries, participating to the new digital euro system.[82]

Negative consequences, from a socially-sustainable perspective, might occur in an international economy perspective: the adoption of a strong digital currency, like the digital dollar or euro or Yuan, might cause currency substitution in third countries, further undermining the sovereignty of certain countries.[83]

A wide diffusion of CBDCs might have the effect of excluding a part of population, such as the elderly and other categories not digitally savvy.[84] Moreover, the wide adoption of digital ID—often considered in combination with CBDCs—has increased the opportunity for frauds and identity theft, especially in the elderly and other non-sophisticated customers.[85]

[81] Eurogroup, *Eurogroup statement*. About the risks of programmable money, see also Pieters, "Digital currencies," 149.

[82] Fabio Panetta, "The digital euro: our money wherever, whenever we need it," European Central Bank, 2023, https://www.ecb.europa.eu/press/key/date/2023/html/ecb.sp230123~2f8271ed76.en.html; Spitzer and Loi, "Digital Euro," 4–5; ECB, *Progress*, third report, 2, 11.

[83] See G7 United Kingdom 2021, *Public Policy Principles*, principle 7 (spillovers).

[84] The FCA estimated that, in February 2020, 4.7 million adults were digitally excluded, representing almost 10% of the population: Financial Conduct Authority, *Financial Lives 2020 survey: the impact of coronavirus Key findings from the FCA's Financial Lives 2020 survey and October 2020 Covid-19 panel survey,* The Financial Lives survey, February 11 (FCA, 2021) https://www.fca.org.uk/publication/research/financial-lives-survey-2020.pdf; see also BoE and HM Treasury, *The digital pound*, 88.

[85] About the rise in frauds with digital payments and digital IDs in Sweden and other Nordic countries, see, Marte Eidsand Kjørven, "who pays when things go wrong? Online

Market studies attest the importance, for certain categories of the population and for the general acceptance of CBDCs, to maintain cash, but also allow multiple devices to use CBDC, including currently widespread ones, such as cards, Proof of Stake (PoS) and smartphones.[86]

Finally, in a world becoming more and more aware of climate change and the importance of sustainable solutions, it is important to ensure that CBDCs are not less environmentally sustainable than existing or alternative systems (e.g., Real-Time Gross Settlement—RTGS—or TIPS).[87] In particular, as already mentioned, the majority of current CBDCs projects rely on DLT, which results in high computational cost, with negative effects on energy consumption. The number and location of the nodes, the need for additional physical security measures and back up servers can have an impact on the energy costs.[88] RTGS technology, therefore, should be preferred in case energy consumption is a priority since it seems to be less energy consuming than the current credit card system.[89] Anyway, existing CBDCs projects do not recur to public block chains and Proof of Work (PoW) consensus method (the Bitcoin one), but to PoS and permissioned systems, which allow to save more than a thousand times energy compared to PoW.[90] Such costs should be offset, in any case, by the savings in terms of environmental impact coming from the reduction in cash production, use and storage and they might be limited

financial fraud and consumer protection in scandinavia and europe," *European Business Law Review*, 31, no. 1 (2020), 77–110.

[86] EDPB, *Response of the EDPB*, 8; Sidorenko et al., "Legal and economic implications," 499. See also BIS, *Central bank digital currencies*, 3.

[87] See also G7 United Kingdom 2021, *Public Policy Principles*, principle 8.

[88] Soohyang Lee and Jinhee Park, *Environmental Implications of a Central Bank Digital Currency (CBDC)*, Korea Office Innovation and Technology Note Series 8 (World Bank Group, 2022), https://documents1.worldbank.org/curated/en/099143507042228192/pdf/IDU0110707310d28b041b70bb560cc1f4b1f41d4.pdf; Itai Agur et al., "Digital currencies and energy consumption," FinTech Notes no. 006 (International Monetary Fund, 2022), 2, 13ff, https://www.imf.org/en/Publications/fintech-notes/Issues/2022/06/07/Digital-Currencies-and-Energy-Consumption-517866.

[89] Lee and Park, *Environmental Implications*, 9–11 (reporting a lower energy use by card network compared to cash and blockchain assets); Agur et al., *Digital currencies and energy consumption*, 13.

[90] See, in a crypto-currency context: Carlo Gola and Johannes Sedlmeir, "Addressing The Sustainability of Distributed Ledger Technology," Occasional Paper no. 670 (Bank of Italy, 2022), 10.

through the recourse to renewable energy as source. Finally, the higher the number of access means to the system (cards, hardware-based wallets, etc.) and of the intermediaries involved, the higher the energy costs.[91] These means add complexity to the choice about the design and structure of the CBDC's system, which might be managed, again, balancing different goals (e.g., universal access and financial inclusion, stability and banks involvement, environmental sustainability).

6 Conclusions: CBDCs and the Coherence and Consistency of EU Financial Regulation

The digital euro project has been developed by the ECB, without a significant involvement of the European legislators, within its monetary mandate. At the same time, the considerable amount of EU strategies, action plans and relative legislative proposals and texts dedicated to digital finance,[92] Capital Markets Union, retail payments[93] and consumers,[94] at most, just mention CBDCs without really deal with their issues and position within the overall plan. Only recently, the Eurogroup and the European Parliament have stated the importance of other institutions' involvement in the digital euro project, going beyond simple updates from the ECB and the Commission.[95] The introduction of a CBDCs can

[91] Agur et al., *Digital currencies and energy consumption*, 13ff.

[92] European Commission, *Digital finance strategy for the EU*, COM (2020) 591 final, 2020 (which only briefly mentions generally CBDCs, page 10), https://eur-lex.europa.eu/legal-content/EN/TXT/PDF/?uri=CELEX:52020DC0591&from=EN.

[93] European Commission, *Retail payments strategy for the EU*, COM (2020) 592 final, 2020 (where, at 14, CBDCs are mentioned in a short paragraph and as a work which 'complements the Commission's proposed regulatory framework on asset-referenced tokens used for payment purposes'), https://eur-lex.europa.eu/legal-content/EN/TXT/PDF/?uri=CELEX:52020DC0592.

[94] European Commission, *New Consumer Agenda: Strengthening consumer resilience for sustainable recovery*, COM (2020) 696 final, 2020 (no reference to, generally, CBDCs or, specifically, digital euro), https://eur-lex.europa.eu/legal-content/EN/TXT/PDF/?uri=CELEX:52020DC0696.

[95] Eurogroup, *Eurogroup statement on the digital euro project*: "*The Eurogroup considers that the introduction of a digital euro as well as its main features and design choices requires political decisions that should be discussed and taken at the political level*". More recently, the ECB has announced that it will present a Proposal for on the digital euro based on an ordinary legislative procedure (and Article 133 TFEU) to address the role of financial intermediaries in the distribution of the digital euro (including obligations to distribute),

have a significant impact on the whole (national and EU) legal framework, also requiring adaptations of the same, starting with its legal classifications, legal acceptance, as well as other relevant issues pertaining to tax law, accounting/company law (capital contributions through CBDCs), etc.

Considering the potential significant impact on the European financial sector (e.g., on banks and payments, as mentioned above) and the inevitable interactions with it, the European regulator should ensure coherency within the overall legal framework and with the financial regulation objectives.

The digital euro project appears in line with other digital finance strategy ones: for instance, both the digital euro and MiCAR[96] aim at contrasting stablecoins and other unregulated private 'money'. Again, the digital euro, the Digital Services Act / Digital Markets Act (DSA/DMA), the oversight framework for critical ICT third-party service providers under DORA[97] and current discussions/proposals about Big tech treatment within financial regulation (e.g., revision of the notion of banking

eligibility of users, protection from counterfeiting fees and compensation, privacy issues, etc.: European Commission, "Targeted Consultation."

[96] European Commission, *Proposal for a Regulation of the European Parliament and of the Council on Markets in Crypto-assets, and Amending Directive,* COM (2020) 593 final, 2020/0265 (COD), 2020, https://eur-lex.europa.eu/resource.html?uri=cellar:f69f89bb-fe54-11ea-b44f-01aa75ed71a1.0001.02/DOC_1&format=PDF. The text that eventually adopted on 20 April 2023 is available at https://www.europarl.europa.eu/doceo/document/TA-9-2023-0117_EN.pdf. About MiCAR see: Christos Gortsos, "The Commission's 2020 Proposal for a Markets in Crypto-Assets Regulation ('MiCAR'): A Brief Introductory Overview," *available at SSRN 3842824 (2021)*: https://ssrn.com/abstract=3842824; Dirk Zetzsche et al., "The Markets in Crypto-Assets regulation (MiCA) and the EU digital finance strategy," *Capital Markets Law Journal*, 16, no. 2 (2021); Paolo Giudici and Guido Ferrarini, "Digital Offerings and Mandatory Disclosure: A Market-Based Critique of MiCA," in *Digital Finance in Europe: Law, Regulation, and Governance,* no. 5 (De Gruyter, 2021).

[97] Regulation (EU) 2022/2554 of 14 December 2022 on digital operational resilience for the financial sector and amending Regulations (EC) No 1060/2009, (EU) No 648/2012, (EU) No 600/2014, (EU) No 909/2014 and (EU) 2016/1011 (available at: https://eur-lex.europa.eu/legal-content/EN/TXT/PDF/?uri=CELEX:32022R2554), Official Journal [2022] L 333/1 (available at: https://eur-lex.europa.eu/legal-content/EN/TXT/PDF/?uri=OJ:L:2022:333:FULL). About DORA: Stavros Kourmpetis, "Management of ICT Third Party Risk Under the Digital Operational Resilience Act," in *Digitalisation, Sustainability, and the Banking and Capital Markets Union*, EBI Studies in Banking and Capital Markets Law, ed. L. Böffel and J. Schürger, (Cham: Palgrave Macmillan, 2023); Dirk Clausmeier. "Regulation of the European Parliament and the

group/financial conglomerate to account for Big tech's non-financial core activities; open finance and extension of covered services and obliged entities beyond banks) aim at reducing Big tech's lack of accountability towards users of their technology and therefore, the inability of financial sector participants to be accountable to the supervisory authorities themselves in the financial industry. The EU action to introduce an EU Digital ID, moreover, would perfectly support all these projects, facilitating distant on boarding and therefore digital services and products.

Nonetheless, despite this general continuity and alignment in principles, we need to further assess the coherence of the overall legal framework, looking closer at the specific regulatory tools used. Such assessment is complicated by the above-mentioned complex nature of CBDCs: different rationales and, therefore, goals are present and need to be balanced: not only monetary policy objectives, but also financial sector stability, client protection, competition, efficiency of the payment system, etc. The assessment, nevertheless, can also provide useful indications for the future design, supervision of CBDCs.

The remaining of the chapter will try to recap the discussion mentioned above in this perspective and focusing on the relationship among goals and the consequent implications in terms of CBDC design.

6.1 Conflicts Among Different Goals: Preservation of Monetary Function Versus Financial Stability of the Banking System

As discussed, the introduction of the digital euro and, therefore, the pursue of ECB's primary goal of price stability (Article 127(1) TFEU; Article 2 ECB Statute) can impair banks' functions and consequently, stability. Nonetheless, the ECB shall also support other EU policies and contribute to the achievement of other goals set out in Article 3 TEU, including the internal market and competition (again, Article 2 ECB Statute and Article 119(1)-(2) TFEU), as well as financial stability (as pursued by Member States or by itself within the Single Supervisory Mechanism (SSM): Article 127 TFEU).[98] A direct and 'solo' involvement of the ECB in the provision of the digital euro-related

Council on digital operational resilience for the financial sector (DORA)," *International Cybersecurity Law Review*, 4, no. 1 (2023).

[98] See also G7 United Kingdom 2021, *Public Policy Principles*, principle 1.

services would violate the principle of market neutrality and its task of promoting the smooth operation of payment systems (Article 127(2) TFEU) and contribute to competition, stifling the development of alternative payment instruments and infrastructures.[99]

In this case, all these goals (monetary, competition and stability) might be achieved through a careful design of the digital euro, implementing the variety of tools already mentioned (e.g., direct CB's liability, but hybrid model, initial holding caps, etc.). Anyway, this makes evident the necessity to avoid the direct competition of the ECB, as provider of financial services, with other providers, as well as the preference for hybrid models, with involvement of private operators for the provision of financial services related to CBDCs.

At the same time, hybrid models are complex and the cooperation between the ECB and private actors (other financial intermediaries and technological companies) cannot leave the system and the ECB in the hands of these private actors, to reduce a different type of operational risk: therefore, it is advanced that the ECB would retain the ownership and operation of the blockchain and settlement system. Nonetheless, the exact details of the functioning of such system as well as its regulatory framework remain uncertain (see below § 6.3).

6.2 *Internal Conflicts: Financial Inclusion Versus Financial Inclusion*

Several layers of complexity are present in CBDCs projects, in conflict within the same regulatory goal: for instance, the digital euro is supported, as mentioned, as a tool to improve the financial inclusion of un-banked. However, the same might lead to the exclusion of other non-digitally expert categories, such as the elderly. Again, a balance might be achieved with a careful impact assessment and design of the overall system: digital euro also for off-line and P2P payments, variety of devices to use it, maintenance of cash and other payment instruments as well as traditional IDs, financial and digital education, etc.

[99] See above §5.1; Cullen, "Economically inefficient and legally untenable", 31; De Nederlandsche Bank, "Central Bank Digital Currency: Objectives, preconditions and design choices," Occasional Studies Volume 20-01 (DNB, 2020), https://www.dnb.nl/media/espadbvb/central-bank-digital-currency.pdf.

Similarly, the involvement of banks and other intermediaries is required to maintain stability and competition preserving their functions but, on the other hand, where too many functions and responsibilities are left to private actors, systemic risk increases in the form of operational risk (risk of interruption, disruption of payments, etc.).

6.3 Regulation of Financial Intermediaries and Financial Regulation Internal Coherence: Level-Playing Field and 'Same Risk-Same Rules' Principles

CBCDs cannot be confused with or put on the same level as private money (crypto-currencies, bank money) and private payment instruments. However, a partial fungibility, from a customer's perspective, among the two classes and therefore, competition among providers, is undeniable. Thus, such providers should be subject to similar principles and rules to respect the level-playing field. As anticipated, the relationship between the digital euro project and other legislative packages in the financial sector, in particular in the digital finance area, is not discussed, nor explicitly addressed.

The recently adopted DORA, aiming at introducing harmonized and cross-sectoral rules for containing digital operational risks and a new oversight regime for critical ICT third-party service providers, contains no reference to the digital euro: however, it states that '[…] in light of the evolving payment services market becoming increasingly dependent on complex technical solutions, and in view of emerging types of payment services and payment-related solutions, participants in the payment services ecosystem, providing payment-processing activities, or operating payment infrastructures, should also be considered to be ICT third-party service providers under this Regulation, with the exception of central banks when operating payment or securities settlement systems, and public authorities when providing ICT related services in the context of fulfilling State functions' (recital 67). Payment systems and entities involved in payment-processing activities remain outside this framework at the moment, but it is expected that the Commission, also within the review of the PSD2, will evaluate the future inclusion of these entities within the DORA framework and the application to the same of an appropriate oversight (Article 58(2) DORA). Consequently, it can be derived that DORA would not apply in any case to the ECB, when issuing the digital euro and operating the infrastructure and settlement system; the intermediaries involved in the system would be covered, instead, when corresponding to the obliged entities under Article 2(1) DORA (e.g., credit institutions, investment firms, payment institutions, account information services provider, crypto-asset service providers, etc.) and offering payment or other financial services, while they might become subject to DORA and an oversight regime, when co-operating the system only in the future.

While the original MiCAR Proposal did not contain a textual reference to CBDCs,[100] the most recent compromise text approved by the Council in October 2022[101] and the one adopted by the European Parliament and Council on 20 April 2023 explicitly exclude the ECB, its CBDCs and related serviced offered by the ECB from such framework.[102] This makes completely sense since, as mentioned, MiCAR has been imagined to cover crypto-assets, otherwise not subject to any already existing financial regulation regime and to set a minimum level of customer protection and stability and level-playing field in the financial sector. CBDCs, instead, are public money, issued and backed by the CB, per se safer than private money.[103] Moreover, the exclusion of national, international and public authorities when acting in their official public capacity from the scope of financial regulation is typical of many EU legal acts.[104]

What could be covered by MiCAR are instead stablecoins issued by private intermediaries and referenced to the euro (e-money tokens under

[100] Anyway, 'it excluded Crypto-assets issued by central banks acting in their monetary authority capacity or by other public authorities' from its scope (recital 7 MiCAR proposal) and the ECB from the obliged entities (Article 2(3)(a) MiCAR Proposal).

[101] Council of the European Union, *Proposal for a Regulation of the European Parliament and of the Council on Markets in Crypto-assets, and amending Directive (EU) 2019/1937 (MiCA)*. Letter to the Chair of the European Parliament Committee on Economic and Monetary Affairs, October 5, 2022, https://data.consilium.europa.eu/doc/document/ST-13198-2022-INIT/en/pdf.

[102] Recital 13 MiCAR (text adopted on 20 April 2023): 'Digital assets issued by central banks acting in their monetary authority capacity, including central bank money in digital form, or crypto-assets issued by other public authorities, including central, regional and local administrations, should not be subject to the Union framework for markets in crypto-assets. Nor should related services provided by such central banks when acting in their monetary authority capacity or other public authorities be subject to that Union framework'. See also Article 2(2), letter c) MiCAR (April 2023 adopted text).

[103] See Hofmann, *Digital Euro*, 12–13.

[104] See, for instance, CRD (Article 2(5)(2)), PSD2 (Article 1(1)(e)), EMD (Article 1(1)(d)), AIFMD (Article 2(3)(c)).

MiCAR) or synthetic CBDCs, i.e., token issued by banks (private money) and therefore a bank's liability (not a central bank's) although fully backed by the central bank money (e.g., through mandatory reserves).[105] The latter, therefore, is not a 'pure' CBDCs but neither a crypto-currency like Bitcoin: it presents a certain counter-party/credit risk, but it is backed by CB's money, therefore safer and more 'mainstream' than other types of e-money tokens.

Anyway, MiCAR only excludes from its scope the ECB, the CBDC issued by the same and the related services provided by the ECB in its monetary capacity, while it does not explicitly exclude the private financial intermediaries involved in the process and providing CBDCs-based services. However, CBDCs considered 'funds, as defined in Article 4 (25) of Directive 2015/2366/EU', would not be anyhow subject to MiCAR (Article 2(4)(c) April 2023 adopted text) and therefore, neither the intermediaries offering CBDCs-related services. Only in case the CBDC could be instead classified as crypto-asset[106] under MiCAR, the private financial intermediaries offering related services might be subject to the same; nonetheless, such classification of CBDCs as crypto-asset seems to be excluded by recital 13 which excludes from MiCAR all crypto-assets issued by CBs or public authorities.[107]

The issue on how to regulate CBDCs' intermediaries, however, is of extreme relevance from the perspective of assessing the coherence of financial regulation and compliance with the level-playing field principle.[108]

[105] About synthetic CBDCs see: Simon Hess, "Regulating Central Bank Digital Currencies: Towards a Conceptual Framework," *available at SSRN 3582501* (2020), 13–14, https://papers.ssrn.com/sol3/papers.cfm?abstract_id=3582501; Leinonen, "Electronic central bank cash," 22–23. See also European Central Bank, *Digital euro glossary* (ECB, 2023) https://www.ecb.europa.eu/paym/digital_euro/investigation/profuse/shared/files/dedocs/ecb.dedocs220420.en.pdf?b268d673898445396fb1a59efbcf01f3.

[106] Article 3(1), No. 5 MiCAR adopted version: "'crypto-asset' means a digital representation of a value or a right that is able to be transferred and stored electronically, using distributed ledger technology or similar technology".

[107] Zetzsche et al., "The Markets in Crypto-Assets regulation", 223–24 (although not discussing this particular classificatory issue in this context, recommend excluding CBDCs intermediaries from MiCAR scope).

[108] On CBDCs and payment services framework, see also in this Book, Chapter 8 by Del Barrio Arleo.

One alternative is to regulate such intermediaries through a new special regulation to better calibrate the rules to the particular and unusual infrastructure and architecture for CBDC's issuance and related service. Although it depends on the particular model adopted (token/account-based, direct/indirect/hybrid, etc.), assuming a hybrid model, the rules for CBDC-intermediaries cannot be similar to MiCAR's since in case of the digital euro system, the intermediaries potentially involved are already regulated ones (e.g., banks, e-money institutions and payment service institutions) and the assets are direct liabilities of the CB. Nonetheless, it would be possible to imagine additional requirements for the intermediaries authorized to provide CBDC-related services, tailored to the role played and the risks faced, in consideration of the system relevance and the risk also of natural monopoly of intermediaries[109]: for instance, additional capital requirements for operational risk and additional measures for cyber risk, interoperability, etc. Moreover, some authors have highlighted a new conflict of interests, unaddressed by existing laws or ECB projects, in a context where it is still unclear how the costs for distributing the digital euro will be split among participants (e.g., ECB and national central banks, intermediaries, merchants, users, etc.): banks would have low incentives to contribute to the digital euro success and to invest in adapting their structure since a wide CBDC adoption would erode their profits derived from deposits and bank money payments.[110]

The second alternative, at the opposite side of the spectrum, is to leave such intermediaries only regulated under their main regime (e.g., banks, payment institutions, etc.) to avoid excessive regulation and incentivize intermediaries' participation to the system and therefore, network effects. Moreover, additional requirements, where only justified by the use of CBDC technology and its risks, might be regarded as a violation of the technology-neutrality principle: if CBDCs are equivalent to cash, similar rules should apply.[111]

In any case, special rules would be required to regulate the relationships between the ECB and other actors in managing and operating the

[109] On this latter risk see: Sidorenko et al., "Legal and economic implications", 499.

[110] Angeloni, *Digital Euro*; Monnet, *Digital Euro*, 15ff; Spitzer and Loi, "Digital Euro", 6; Grünewald. *A legal framework*, 16.

[111] See Misch, *The Pros and Cons*, 8: "Entities offering transfer, storage, or custody of e-krona should be held to equivalent regulatory and prudential standards as firms offering similar services for cash or existing digital money"; BIS, *Central Bank Digital Currencies*.

system. On the one side, the system might appear partially similar to the bank-TPPs relationship under the PSD2; on the other side, it presents similarities also to payment systems or financial markets infrastructure. Also, in consideration of its peculiar character, a calibrated mix between the two regimes can serve as starting model.

Nonetheless, so far, no proposal addressing these issued has been presented, but the ECB has stated that '*A digital euro scheme would establish a set of common rules, standards and procedures that supervised intermediaries would need to adhere to in order to distribute the digital euro*'.[112] Such initial descriptions seem to refer to the need to ensure a harmonized end-user experience, not to prudential concerns or other types of requirements on intermediaries. Anyway, in its third progress report, the ECB seems to consider existing regulations in the area (PSD2, PAD, AML/CT, Settlement Finality Directive, etc.) as the main legal framework and references, disregarding the fact that so far only banks had access to ECB's accounts.[113]

The UK has taken since the beginning a stronger position about the design of the digital pound and the regulation of intermediaries: not only a hybrid system with the BoE issuing the digital pound and operating the infrastructure and banks managing the interface with the client, but also a wallet-based system. The digital pound would be recorded and transferred through wallets, provided by third-party wallet providers, in order to ensure privacy and prevent the BoE or banks from having access to the details of the transactions. Such firms providing wallets would be regulated to ensure payments using digital pounds are resilient, reliable and compatible with other payments.[114]

In conclusion, countries and their CBs will be required, in the very next years to evaluate the opportunity to issue a CBDC and carefully design its features and infrastructure. In this context, the rationales indicated as in support for CBDCs adoption are extremely important to correctly fund CBDCs' legal basis and to direct their specific design

[112] European Central Bank, *ECB seeks scheme rulebook manager for the digital euro*, MIP News (ECB, 2022), https://www.ecb.europa.eu/paym/intro/news/html/ecb.mipnews221010.en.html; see also ECB, *Progress*, second report, 10.

[113] ECB, *Progress, third report*, 6, 7. Suggesting the need to adjust some of these regimes, in particular, the Settlement Finality Regime: Spitzer and Loi, "Digital Euro"; Grünewald, *A legal framework*, 15, 22.

[114] BoE and HM Treasury, *The digital pound*, 12, 53ff.

features. Each design option, in fact, should be evaluated through the lenses of the main rationales and pondered based on the priority of goals in that particular jurisdiction (including common currency areas such as the euro). In the EU, at present, the focus seems to be placed on the need to maintain the euro internally and internationally competitive, while not compromising stability through the crowding out of the banks. Only time, instead, will tell whether the EU will ultimately succeed also in serving users' needs (in terms of service quality and cost, innovation, privacy, broad access, etc.) and sustainability concerns. In any case, consistency and coherence within the financial sector and therefore with legislative framework will be also fundamental.

References

Agur, Mr Itai, Jose Deodoro, Xavier Lavayssière, Soledad Martinez Peria, Mr Damiano Sandri, Hervé Tourpe, and Mr German Villegas Bauer. "Digital currencies and energy consumption." FinTech Notes no. 2022/006, International Monetary Fund, 2022. https://www.imf.org/en/Publications/fintech-notes/Issues/2022/06/07/Digital-Currencies-and-Energy-Consumption-517866.

Alqaryouti, Omar, Nur Siyam, Zainab Alkashri, and Khaled Shaalan. "Users' knowledge and motivation on using cryptocurrency." In *European, mediterranean, and middle eastern conference on information systems*, pp. 113–122. Cham: Springer International Publishing, 2019.

Angeloni, Ignazio. *Digital Euro: When in doubt, abstain (but be prepared)*. European Parliament, 2023. https://www.europarl.europa.eu/RegData/etudes/IDAN/2023/741507/IPOL_IDA(2023)741507_EN.pdf.

Armelius, Hanna, Carl Andreas Claussen, and Scott Hendry. *Is central bank currency fundamental to the monetary system?*. Economic Review no. 2020–2. Sveriges Riksbank, 2020, 19–32. https://www.riksbank.se/globalassets/media/rapporter/pov/artiklar/engelska/2020/200618/2020_2-is-central-bank-currency-fundamental-to-the-monetary-system.pdf.

Armelius, Hanna, Gabriela Guibourg, A. Levin, and Gabriel Söderberg. "The rationale for issuing e-krona in the digital era." *Sveriges Riksbank Economic Review* 2, no. 2020 (2020): 6–18. https://www.riksbank.se/globalassets/media/rapporter/pov/artiklar/engelska/2020/200618/2020_2-the-rationale-for-issuing-e-krona-in-the-digital-era.pdf.

Ashmarina, Svetlana Igorevna, Jakub Horák, Jaromír Vrbka, and Petr Šuleř. *Economic systems in the new era: stable systems in an unstable world*. Lecture Notes in Networks and Systems 160. Springer International Publishing, 2021.

Auer, Raphael, and Rainer Böhme. "The technology of retail central bank digital currency." Quarterly Review, March. Bank for International Settlements, 2020. https://www.bis.org/publ/qtrpdf/r_qt2003j.pdf.

Auer, Raphael, Giulio Cornelli, and Jon Frost. "Covid-19, cash, and the future of payments". BIS no. 3, Bank for International Settlements, 2020.

Auer, Raphael, Giulio Cornelli, and Jon Frost. "Rise of the central bank digital currencies: drivers, approaches and technologies." Working Paper no. 880, Bank for International Settlements, 2020. https://www.bis.org/publ/work880.pdf.

Auer, Raphael, Jon Frost, Leonardo Gambacorta, Cyril Monnet, Tara Rice, and Hyun Song Shin. "Central bank digital currencies: motives, economic implications, and the research frontier." Working Paper no. 976, Bank for International Settlements, 2021. https://www.bis.org/publ/work976.pdf.

Bank for International Settlements. *Central Bank Digital Currencies*. Committee on Payments and Market Infrastructures, March. Basel: BIS, 2018. https://www.bis.org/cpmi/publ/d174.pdf.

Bank for International Settlements. *Cryptocurrencies: looking beyond the hype*. Annual Economic Report, 2018. https://www.bis.org/publ/arpdf/ar2018e5.pdf.

Bank for International Settlements. *Central bank digital currencies: Foundational Principles and Core Features*. Report no. 1 in a series of collaborations from a group of central banks, 2020. https://www.bis.org/publ/othp33.pdf.

Bank for International Settlements. *CBDCs: an opportunity for the monetary system*. Annual Economic Report, 2021. https://www.bis.org/publ/arpdf/ar2021e3.pdf.

Bank for International Settlements. *Central bank digital currencies*. Executive summary, 2021. https://www.bis.org/publ/othp42.pdf.

Bank for International Settlements. *Central bank digital currencies: user needs and adoption*. Report no. 3 in a series of collaborations from a group of central banks, 2021. https://www.bis.org/publ/othp42_user_needs.pdf.

Bank for International Settlements. *Options for access to and interoperability of CBDCs for cross-border payments*. Report to the G20, 2022. https://www.bis.org/publ/othp52.pdf.

Bank of England (BoE) and HM Treasury. *The digital pound: a new form of money for households and businesses?*. Consultation Paper, 2023. https://www.bankofengland.co.uk/-/media/boe/files/paper/2023/the-digital-pound-consultation-working-paper.pdf.

Bechtel, Alexander, Agata Ferreira, Jonas Gross, and Philipp Sandner. "The future of payments in a DLT-based European economy: a roadmap." In *The future of financial systems in the digital age: perspectives from Europe and Japan*, edited by Markus Heckel and Franz Waldenberger, 89–116. Singapore: Springer Singapore, 2022.

Bindseil, Ulrich. "Central bank digital currencies in a world with negative nominal interest rates." In *The future of financial systems in the digital age: perspectives from Europe and Japan*, pp. 75–88. Singapore: Springer Singapore, 2022.
Bindseil, Ulrich. "Tiered CBDC and the financial system." Working Paper Series no. 2351, European Central Bank, 2020. https://www.ecb.europa.eu/pub/pdf/scpwps/ecb.wp2351~c8c18bbd60.en.pdf.
Blakstad, Sofie, and Allen, Robert. "Central bank digital currencies and cryptocurrencies." In: *FinTech Revolution*, 87–112. Cham: Palgrave Macmillan, 2018.
Boar, Codruta, Henry Holden, and Amber Wadsworth. "Impending arrival—A sequel to the survey on central bank digital currency." BIS paper no. 107, Bank for International Settlements, 2020. https://www.bis.org/publ/bppdf/bispap107.pdf.
Bolt, Wilko, Vera Lubbersen, and Peter Wierts. "Getting the balance right: Crypto, stablecoin and CBDC." DNB Working Paper no. 736, De Nederlandsche Bank, 2022. https://www.dnb.nl/media/jo3h1dlu/working_paper_no-_736.pdf.
Brooks, Skylar. "Revisiting the monetary sovereignty rationale for CBDCs." Staff Discussion Paper, Bank of Canada, 2021. https://www.bankofcanada.ca/wp-content/uploads/2021/12/sdp2021-17.pdf.
Brunnermeier, Markus K., and Jean-Pierre Landau. "The digital euro: policy implications and perspectives." Publication for the committee on Economic and Monetary Affairs, Policy Department for Economic, Scientific and Quality of Life Policies. European Parliament, 2022. https://www.europarl.europa.eu/RegData/etudes/STUD/2022/703337/IPOL_STU(2022)703337_EN.pdf.
Buckley, Ross P., Douglas W. Arner, Dirk A. Zetzsche, Anton N. Didenko, and Lucien J. Van Romburg. "Sovereign digital currencies: reshaping the design of money and payments systems." *Journal of Payments Strategy & Systems* 15, no. 1 (2021): 7–22.
Bull, Greta, William Cook, Mehmet Kerse, and Stefan Staschen. "Is financial inclusion a reason to push central bank digital currencies?." *CGAP*, May 13, 2021. https://www.cgap.org/blog/is-financial-inclusion-reason-to-push-central-bank-digital-currencies.
Cavusoglu, Lena, and Idil Goksel. "Exploring motivations of cryptocurrency enthusiasts." *International Journal of Business and Management Invention* 8, no. 10 (2019): 45–53. https://www.ijbmi.org/papers/Vol(8)10/Series-1/F0810014553.pdf.
Cheng, Jess, Angela N. Lawson, and Paul Wong. "Preconditions for a general-purpose central bank digital currency." FEDS Notes. Washington: Board of

Governors of the Federal Reserve System, February 24, 2021. https://doi.org/10.17016/2380-7172.2839.

Chiu, Iris HY. "Building out the crypto economy in europe: a proposal for central bank digital euros." *European Law Review* 4 (2021).

Chiu, Iris HY. *Regulating the crypto economy: business transformations and financialisation.* Oxford: Hart, 2021.

Chiu, Iris HY, and Christian Hofmann. "Unlimited central bank digital currency: the case for a public good in the euro area and its regulatory (and deregulatory) implications for modern finance." *North Carolina Journal of International Law* 48, no. 1 (2023): 1–77.

Clausmeier, Dirk. "Regulation of the European Parliament and the council on digital operational resilience for the financial sector (DORA)." *International Cybersecurity Law Review* 4, no. 1 (2023): 79–90.

Council of the European Union. *Proposal for a Regulation of the European Parliament and of the Council on Markets in Crypto-assets, and amending Directive (EU) 2019/1937 (MiCA).* Letter to the Chair of the European Parliament Committee on Economic and Monetary Affairs, October 5. Council of the EU, 2022. https://data.consilium.europa.eu/doc/document/ST-13198-2022-INIT/en/pdf.

Cullen, Jay. "Economically inefficient and legally untenable: constitutional limitations on the introduction of central bank digital currencies in the EU." *Journal of Banking Regulation* 23, no. 1 (2022): 31–41.

Davis, Elliott. "Stablecoins: Fiat-backed vs Crypto Collateralized vs Algorithmic," August 16, 2022, https://www.elliottdavis.com/stablecoins-fiat-backed-vs-crypto-collateralized-vs-algorithmic/.

De Nederlandsche Bank. *Central Bank Digital Currency: Objectives, preconditions and design choices.* DNB Occasional Studies Volume 20–01, April. DNB, 2020. https://www.dnb.nl/media/espadbvb/central-bank-digital-currency.pdf.

de Vauplane, Hubert. "Cryptocurrencies and Central Banks." In *Fintech. Law and Regulation*, edited by J. Madir. Cheltenham: Edward Elgar, 2021.

Didenko, Anton N., and Ross P. Buckley. "Central bank digital currencies: A potential response to the financial inclusion challenges of the Pacific." *UNSW Law Research Paper* (2021): 21–63.

Dyson, Ben, and Graham Hodgson. "Digital cash: Why Central Banks should start issuing electronic money." Positive Money (2016), https://positivemoney.org/wp-content/uploads/2016/01/Digital_Cash_WebPrintReady_20160113.pdf.

Ehrentraud, Johannes, Jamie Lloyd Evans, Amélie Monteil, and Fernando Restoy. "Big tech regulation: In search of a new framework." Financial Stability Institute, Bank for International Settlements, 2022. https://www.bis.org/fsi/fsipapers20.pdf.

Engert, Walter, and Ben Siu-Cheong Fung. "Central bank digital currency: Motivations and implications." Discussion Paper no. 2017–16, Bank of Canada, 2017. https://www.bankofcanada.ca/wp-content/uploads/2017/11/sdp2017-16.pdf.

Eurogroup. "Eurogroup statement on the digital euro project." Statement, January 16, 2023. https://www.consilium.europa.eu/en/press/press-releases/2023/01/16/eurogroup-statement-on-the-digital-euro-project-16-january-2023/.

European Banking Federation. *EBF response to the European Commission's Targeted Consultation on a digital euro*. EBF: June 16, 2022. https://www.ebf.eu/wp-content/uploads/2022/06/FINAL-EBF-Response-to-EC-Consultation-on-a-Digital-Euro.pdf.

European Central Bank. *Report on a digital euro*. ECB, 2020. https://www.ecb.europa.eu/pub/pdf/other/Report_on_a_digital_euro~4d7268b458.en.pdf.

European Central Bank. *ECB seeks scheme rulebook manager for the digital eu*ro. MIP News, October 10. ECB, 2022. https://www.ecb.europa.eu/paym/intro/news/html/ecb.mipnews221010.en.html.

European Central Bank. *ECB selects external companies for joint prototyping of user interfaces for a digital euro*. MIP News, September 16. ECB, 2022. https://www.ecb.europa.eu/paym/intro/news/html/ecb.mipnews220916.en.html.

European Central Bank. *Progress on the investigation phase of a digital euro*. First Report, 2022. https://www.ecb.europa.eu/paym/digital_euro/investigation/governance/shared/files/ecb.degov220929.en.pdf.

European Central Bank. *Progress on the investigation phase of a digital euro*. Second Report, 2022. https://www.ecb.europa.eu/paym/digital_euro/investigation/governance/shared/files/ecb.degov221221_Progress.en.pdf.

European Central Bank. *Study on new digital payment methods*. March. Kantar Public, 2022. https://www.ecb.europa.eu/paym/digital_euro/investigation/profuse/shared/files/dedocs/ecb.dedocs220330_report.en.pdf.

European Central Bank. *Study on the payment attitudes of consumers in the euro area (SPACE)*. ECB: December, 2022. https://www.ecb.europa.eu/stats/ecb_surveys/space/html/ecb.spacereport202212~783ffdf46e.en.html.

European Central Bank. *Digital euro glossary*. ECB: January 7, 2023. https://www.ecb.europa.eu/paym/digital_euro/investigation/profuse/shared/files/dedocs/ecb.dedocs220420.en.pdf?b268d673898445396fb1a59efbcf01f3.

European Central Bank. *Digital euro—Prototype summary and lessons learned*. ECB, 2023. https://www.ecb.europa.eu/pub/pdf/other/ecb.prototype_summary20230526~71d0b26d55.en.pdf.

European Central Bank. *Progress on the investigation phase of a digital euro*. Third Report, 2023. https://www.ecb.europa.eu/paym/digital_euro/investigation/governance/shared/files/ecb.degov230424_progress.en.pdf.

European Central Bank. *Study on digital wallet features*. Kantar Public, March 2023. https://www.ecb.europa.eu/press/pr/date/2023/html/ecb.pr230424_1_annex~93abdb80da.en.pdf.

European Commission. *Digital finance strategy for the EU*. COM (2020) 591 final, September 24. European Commission, 2020. https://eur-lex.europa.eu/legal-content/EN/TXT/PDF/?uri=CELEX:52020DC0591&from=EN.

European Commission. *New Consumer Agenda: Strengthening consumer resilience for sustainable recovery*. COM (2020) 696 final, November 13. European Commission, 2020. https://eur-lex.europa.eu/legal-content/EN/TXT/PDF/?uri=CELEX:52020DC0696.

European Commission. *Proposal for a Regulation of the European Parliament and of the Council on Markets in Crypto-assets, and Amending Directive*. COM (2020) 593 final, 2020/0265 (COD), September 24. European Commission, 2020. https://eur-lex.europa.eu/resource.html?uri=cellar:f69f89bb-fe54-11ea-b44f-01aa75ed71a1.0001.02/DOC_1&format=PDF.

European Commission. *Retail payments strategy for the EU*. COM (2020) 592 final, September 24, 2020. https://eur-lex.europa.eu/legal-content/EN/TXT/PDF/?uri=CELEX:52020DC0592.

European Commission. "Targeted Consultation on a Digital Euro." Consultation Document, 2022. https://finance.ec.europa.eu/system/files/2022-06/2022-digital-euro-consultation-document_en.pdf.

European Data Protection Board. *EDPB letter to the European institutions on the privacy and data protection aspects of a possible digital euro*. June 18. EDPB, 2021. https://edpb.europa.eu/system/files/2021-07/edpb_letter_out_2021_0111-digitaleuro-toecb_en_1.pdf.

European Data Protection Board. *Response of the EDPB to the European Commission's targeted consultation on a digital euro*. June 14. EDPB, 2021. https://edpb.europa.eu/system/files/2022-06/edpb_responseconsultation_20220614_digitaleuro_en.pdf.

European Union Blockchain Observatory and Forum. *Central bank digital currencies and a euro for the future*. EUBOF, 2021. https://www.eublockchainforum.eu/sites/default/files/reports/CBDC%20Report%20Final.pdf.

European Union Blockchain Observatory and Forum. *CBDCs Trend Report*. EUBOF, 2022. https://www.eublockchainforum.eu/sites/default/files/reports/CBDC_Trend_Report%20September2022_0.pdf.

Fegatelli, Paolo. "Central bank digital currencies: The case of universal central bank reserves." Cahier D'Études working paper no. 130, Central Bank of Luxembourg, 2019. https://www.bcl.lu/en/publications/Working-papers/130/BCLWP130.pdf.

Financial Conduct Authority. *Financial Lives 2020 survey: The impact of coronavirus Key findings from the FCA's Financial Lives 2020 survey and October 2020 Covid-19 panel survey*. The Financial Lives survey, February 11.

FCA, 2021. https://www.fca.org.uk/publication/research/financial-lives-survey-2020.pdf.
Financial Stability Board. *Regulation, supervision and oversight of "global stablecoin" arrangements*. Final Report and High-Level Recommendations. FSB, 2020. https://www.fsb.org/wp-content/uploads/P131020-3.pdf.
Geva, Benjamin, Seraina Neva Grünewald, and Corinne Zellweger-Gutknecht. "The e-Banknote as a 'Banknote': A monetary law interpreted." *Oxford Journal of Legal Studies* 41, no. 4 (2021): 1119–1148.
Giudici, Paolo, and Guido Ferrarini. "Digital offerings and mandatory disclosure: A market-based critique of MiCA." In *Digital finance in Europe: law, regulation, and governance*, edited by De Gruyter, no. 5, pp. 87–107, 2021.
Gola, Carlo, and Johannes Sedlmeir. "Addressing the sustainability of distributed ledger technology." Occasional Paper no. 670, Bank of Italy, 2022.
Gortsos, Christos. "The commission's 2020 proposal for a markets in crypto-assets regulation ('MiCAR'): A Brief Introductory Overview." *Available at SSRN 3842824 (2021)*. https://ssrn.com/abstract=3842824.
Grünewald, Seraina. *A legal framework for the digital euro: An assessment of the ECB's first three progress reports*. Economic Governance and EMU Scrutiny Unit at the request of the ECONCommittee, May. European Parliament, 2023. https://www.europarl.europa.eu/RegData/etudes/IDAN/2023/741518/IPOL_IDA(2023)714518_EN.pdf.
G7 United Kingdom 2021. *Public Policy Principles for Retail Central Bank Digital Currencies (CBDCs)*. United Kingdom Presidency, 2021. https://assets.publishing.service.gov.uk/government/uploads/system/uploads/attachment_data/file/1025235/G7_Public_Policy_Principles_for_Retail_CBDC_FINAL.pdf.
Hess, Simon. "Regulating central bank digital currencies: Towards a conceptual framework." *Available at SSRN 3582501* (2020). https://papers.ssrn.com/sol3/papers.cfm?abstract_id=3582501.
Hofmann, Christian. *Digital euro: An assessment of the first two progress reports. The case for unlimited holdings of digital euros*. Economic Governance and EMU Scrutiny Unit at the request of the ECONCommittee, April. European Parliament, 2023.
House of Lords. *Central bank digital currency: a solution in search of a problem?*. 3rd Report of Session 2021–22, January 13, 2022. https://publications.parliament.uk/pa/ld5802/ldselect/ldeconaf/131/131.pdf.
Isaacson, Ken, Jesse Leigh Maniff, and Paul Wong. "An examination of first-mover advantage for a CBDC." FEDS Notes. Washington: Board of Governors of the Federal Reserve System, November 25, 2022. https://doi.org/10.17016/2380-7172.3230.

International Monetary Fund. *Digital money across borders: macro-financial implications*. Policy Paper. IMF, 2020. https://www.imf.org/en/Publications/Policy-Papers/Issues/2020/10/17/Digital-Money-Across-Borders-Macro-Financial-Implications-49823.

Keister, Todd, and Daniel, Sanches. "Should central banks issue digital currency?." *The Review of Economic Studies* 90, no. 1 (2023): 404–431.

Kelly, Steven. "Stablecoins do not make for a stable financial system: Applying the logistics of financial stability to the cryptoverse." *Financial Times*, August 11, 2022. https://www.ft.com/content/0f979c98-ea78-4848-8282-52c2b68a9d19b.

Khairuddin, Irni Eliana, Corina Sas, Sarah Clinch, and Nigel Davies. "Exploring motivations among bitcoin users." Lancaster University, 2016. https://eprints.lancs.ac.uk/id/eprint/78254/1/Exploring_Motivations_among_Bitcoin_Users_Final_Submission.pdf.

Kjørven, Marte Eidsand. "Who pays when things go wrong? Online financial fraud and consumer protection in Scandinavia and Europe." *European Business Law Review* 31, no. 1 (2020).

Kourmpetis, Stavros. "Management of ICT third party risk under the digital operational resilience act." In *Digitalisation, sustainability, and the banking and capital markets union*. EBI Studies in Banking and Capital Markets Law, edited by L. Böffel and J. Schürger. Cham: Palgrave Macmillan, 2023.

Lagarde, Christine, and Fabio Panetta. "Key objectives of the digital euro." *The ECB blog*, July 13, 2022. https://www.ecb.europa.eu/press/blog/date/2022/html/ecb.blog220713~34e21c3240.en.html#:~:text=It%20would%20protect%20the%20strategic,innovation%20in%20the%20private%20sector.

Lee, Soohyang, and Jinhee Park. "Environmental implications of a central bank digital currency (CBDC)." Korea Office Innovation and Technology Note Series 8, World Bank Group, 2022. https://documents1.worldbank.org/curated/en/099143507042228192/pdf/IDU0110707310d28b041b70bb560cc1f4b1f41d4.pdf.

Leinonen, Harry. "Electronic central bank cash: To be or not to be?." *Journal of Payments Strategy & Systems* 13, no. 1 (2019): 20–31.

Libra Association. "An introduction to Libra." White Paper, 2019. https://www.docdroid.net/kudDQUQ/librawhitepaper-en-us-pdf.

Lloyd, Michael. "The future of money: Central bank digital currencies." *Atlantic Economic Journal* 50, no. 3–4 (2022): 85–98.

Lui, S. "The demographics of Bitcoin (Part 1 Updated)." *Simulacrum. April*, 3 (2013). http://simulacrum.cc/2013/03/04/the-demographics-of-bitcoin-part-1-updated/.

Macchiavello, Eugenia. "Digital platforms, capital raising and EU capital markets law: Different shades of decentralisation." *European Business Law Review* 33, no. 7 (2022).

Mattassoglio, Francesca. *Moneta e tecnologia*. Torino: Giappichelli, 2022.

Meiklejohn, Sarah, Marjori Pomarole, Grant Jordan, Kirill Levchenko, Damon McCoy, Geoffrey M. Voelker, and Stefan Savage. "A fistful of bitcoins: characterizing payments among men with no names." In *Proceedings of the 2013 conference on Internet measurement conference*, pp. 127–140. 2016. https://dl.acm.org/doi/https://doi.org/10.1145/2896384.

Misch, Florian. *The pros and cons of central bank digital currency: Insights from the Riksbank's e-krona project*. Sweden selected issues, IMF Country Report 21/62, International Monetary Fund, 2021. https://www.elibrary.imf.org/view/journals/002/2021/062/002.2021.issue-062-en.xml.

Minesso, Massimo Ferrari, Arnaud Mehl, and Livio Stracca. "Central bank digital currency in an open economy." Working Paper Series no. 2488, European Central Bank, 2020. https://www.ecb.europa.eu/pub/pdf/scpwps/ecb.wp2488~fede33ca65.en.pdf.

Monnet, Cyril. *Digital euro: An assessment of the first two ECB progress reports*. Economic Governance and EMU Scrutiny Unit (EGOV), 2023 https://www.europarl.europa.eu/RegData/etudes/IDAN/2023/741508/IPOL_IDA(2023)741508_EN.pdf.

Mooij, Annelieke. "A digital euro for everyone: Can the European System of Central Banks introduce general purpose CBDC as part of its economic mandate?." *Journal of Banking Regulation* 24, no. 1 (2023): 89–104.

Mooij, Annelieke. "Digital euro's legal framework-The legal framework concerning legal tender, privacy and inclusion." European Parliament, 2023. https://www.europarl.europa.eu/RegData/etudes/IDAN/2023/747840/IPOL_IDA(2023)747840_EN.pdf.

Nabilou, Hossein. "Testing the waters of the Rubicon: the European Central Bank and central bank digital currencies." *Journal of Banking Regulation* 21 (2020): 299–314.

Panetta, Fabio. "A digital euro that serves the needs of the public: striking the right balance." European Central Bank, 2022. https://www.ecb.europa.eu/press/key/date/2022/html/ecb.sp220330_1~f9fa9a6137.en.html.

Panetta, Fabio. "The digital euro and the evolution of the financial system." *Introductory statement at the committee on economic and monetary affairs of the European Parliament*, June 15. European Central Bank, 2022. https://www.ecb.europa.eu/press/key/date/2022/html/ecb.sp220615~0b859eb8bc.en.html.

Panetta, Fabio. "The digital euro: Our money wherever, whenever we need it." European Central Bank, 2023. https://www.ecb.europa.eu/press/key/date/2023/html/ecb.sp230123~2f8271ed76.en.html.

Pate, Richard L. "Legal issues inside the unnatural world of Metaverse." *Business Law Review* 43, no. 5 (2022).

Pieters, Gina. "Digital currencies and central banks." *The Palgrave Handbook of Technological Finance* (2021): 139–160.

Price waterhouse Coopers (PwC). *Global CBDC Index and Stablecoins overview*, April 4. PwC, 2022. https://www.pwc.com/gx/en/new-ventures/cryptocurrency-assets/pwc-global-cbdc-index-stablecoin-overview-2022.pdf.

Sidorenko, Elina, Svetlana Sheveleva, and Alexandr Lykov. "Legal and economic implications of central bank digital currencies (CBDC)." In *Economic systems in the new era: Stable systems in an unstable world*, pp. 496–502. Springer International Publishing, 2021.

Spitzer, Kai Gereon and Loi Giacomo, "Digital euro. Reviewing the progress to date and some open questions." EGOV Briefing PE 741.498, European Parliament, March, 2023. https://www.europarl.europa.eu/RegData/etudes/BRIE/2023/741498/IPOL_BRI(2023)741498_EN.pdf.

The White House, "Executive order on ensuring responsible development of digital assets," March 9, 2022, https://www.whitehouse.gov/briefing-room/presidential-actions/2022/03/09/executive-order-on-ensuring-responsible-development-of-digital-assets/.

Yelowitz, Aaron, and Matthew Wilson. "Characteristics of bitcoin users: an analysis of google search data." *Applied Economics Letters* 22, no. 13 (2015): 1030–1036.

Zetzsche, Dirk A., Filippo Annunziata, Douglas W. Arner, and Ross P. Buckley. "The markets in crypto-assets regulation (MiCA) and the EU digital finance strategy." *Capital Markets Law Journal* 16, no. 2 (2021): 203–225.

Zhang, Tao, and Zhigang Huang. "Blockchain and central bank digital currency." *ICT Express* 8, no. 2 (2022): 264–270.

PART II

Constitutional Issues/EU Treaties

CHAPTER 3

Central Bank Digital Currency and the Treaty Mandate of the European Central Bank

Christy Ann Petit

Legal foundations of a universal and inclusive digital euro

1 Introduction

In March 2023, Eurogroup's President, Paschal Donohoe, stressed that 'at the heart of the digital euro project is the objective to maintain the link between citizens and central bank money'.[1] The issuance of public

[1] Paschal Donohoe, "The possibility of the digital euro," *POLITICO* (blog), March 14, 2023, https://www.politico.eu/article/finance-banking-the-digital-euro-cryptocurrency-central-banks-currency/. This Chapter presents a prospective analysis conducted before the publication of the Single Currency Package by the European Commission on 28th June 2023.

C. A. Petit (✉)
School of Law and Government, Dublin City University, Dublin, Ireland
e-mail: Christy.Petit@dcu.ie

© The Author(s), under exclusive license to Springer Nature Switzerland AG 2025

F. Annunziata et al. (eds.), *Central Bank Digital Currency*, EBI Studies in Banking and Capital Markets Law,
https://doi.org/10.1007/978-3-031-80957-6_3

money in the euro area has been the realm of the ECB for more than 25 years[2] and will face significant transformation with the digitalisation of the economy. The consumers' preferences in payments are moving away from the use of cash in retail payments,[3] while the private sector innovates in digital payment solutions and diverse crypto assets at a high pace. Several projects for developing CBDCs are at different phases worldwide[4] and, in the euro area, different forums have started reflecting on its best design and format.[5] This chapter focuses on the legal mandate of the ECB at primary level, namely following the EU Treaties, for issuing a CBDC.

The question that will be primarily addressed in this chapter is not whether the ECB is empowered to issue a digital euro (already extensively discussed in literature and by policymakers),[6] but rather how it can do so in the near future. It will therefore only briefly discuss the question whether a digital currency can be a lawful means for the settlement of euro-denominated debts in the euro area.[7] The present chapter will then focus on answering the question to what extent the EU constitutional

[2] Thomas Beukers et al., *The new European Central Bank: Taking stock and looking ahead* (Oxford, New York: Oxford University Press, 2022).

[3] European Central Bank, *Study on the payment attitudes of consumers in the euro area (SPACE)* (ECB, 2022), https://www.ecb.europa.eu/stats/ecb_surveys/space/html/ecb.spacereport202212~783ffdf46e.en.html.

[4] Bank for International Settlements, *BIS innovation hub work on Central Bank Digital Currency (CBDC)* (BIS, 2021), https://www.bis.org/about/bisih/topics/cbdc.htm.

[5] From the High-Level Task Force set by the ECB's Governing Council to the more recent consultations held by the ECB and the European Commission. The cut-off date of this chapter is 8 June 2023, before the publication of the Single Currency Package had been published. Regarding the later, see the Introduction of this volume.

[6] See excellent prior contributions on the legal framework, Seraina Grünewald et al., "Digital euro and ECB powers," *Common Market Law Review,* 58, no. 4 (2021), https://kluwerlawonline.com/journalarticle/Common+Market+Law+Review/58.3/COLA2021066; Corinne Zellweger-Gutknecht et al., "Digital euro, monetary objects, and price stability: A legal analysis," *Journal of Financial Regulation,* 7, no. 2 (2021), https://doi.org/10.1093/jfr/fjab009; and other authors stressing the inadequate current constitutional framework: Hossein Nabilou, "Testing the waters of the Rubicon: The European Central Bank and Central Bank Digital currencies," *Journal of Banking Regulation,* 21, no. 4 (2020), 310, https://doi.org/10.1057/s41261-019-00112-1; Jay Cullen, "'Economically inefficient and legally untenable': Constitutional limitations on the introduction of Central Bank Digital currencies in the EU," *Journal of Banking Regulation,* 23, no. 1 (2021), 32, https://doi.org/10.1057/s41261-021-00162-4.

[7] Note here the focus on the EU Legal Order and not its external dimensions. The latter will raise; however, several important issues as regards cross-border payments with

framework is proof for the issuance of euro banknotes, coins and digital euro alike. Here, a *digital* euro, as a type of CBDC, can be defined as a liability of the Eurosystem recorded in digital form and a complement to cash and wholesale central bank deposits.[8] Moreover, when a CBDC is used by individuals/end users to pay businesses, shops or each other, it is called a *retail* CBDC, while it is called a *wholesale* CBDC when financial institutions settle trades in financial markets.

The approach of the chapter is in public law, central banking law and EU monetary law.[9] Here is a succinct background of the sources and framework examined: the power to issue a currency is part of the monetary sovereignty held at EU level for the twenty euro area Member States and should be shielded from competing private initiatives.[10] The EU constitutional and institutional framework for the Monetary Union and the sources that created the *tangible* euro are the reference points, following its inception with the Maastricht Treaty.[11] The European System of Central Banks (ESCB)/Eurosystem would be the natural issuer of a digital currency for euro area Member States. A consensus is progressively emerging in favour of a tier model, in which 'supervised intermediaries' would comprise commercial banks and payment services providers to ensure its distribution.[12] Hence, this tier model does not imply a direct relationship between the ECB and the EU citizens via an account held at the central bank.

third countries, interoperability and in general the role of the euro as an international currency.

[8] European Central Bank, "*Report on a digital euro*" (ECB, 2020), 6, https://www.ecb.europa.eu/pub/pdf/other/Report_on_a_digital_euro~4d7268b458.en.pdf.

[9] Even if it is very difficult to disentangle this analysis from the policy and technical questions underpinning the choice of a CBDC.

[10] See: Edoardo D. Martino, "Monetary sovereignty in the digital era. The law & macroeconomics of digital private money," *Computer Law & Security Review*, 52 (27 October 2023), 105909. https://doi.org/10.1016/j.clsr.2023.105909.

[11] Emmanuel Mourlon-Druol, "History of an incomplete EMU," in *The EU law of economic and monetary union*, ed. Fabian Amtenbrink, Christoph Herrmann, and René Repasi (Oxford University Press, 2020), https://doi.org/10.1093/oso/9780198793748.003.0003.

[12] European Central Bank, "Progress on the investigation phase of a digital euro, Third report (ECB, 2023), 6, https://www.ecb.europa.eu/paym/digital_euro/investigation/governance/shared/files/ecb.degov230424_progress.en.pdf.

The policy developments, preceding the legislative initiative, sustain the issuance of digital euro under the current EU constitutional framework. Firstly, during the investigation phase, until October 2023, preparatory work among EU institutions[13] (ECB, European Parliament and Eurogroup) elaborated on a set of CBDC design options for the digital euro. The ECB Governing Council endorsed some of the designs and distribution options at the end of 2022 and stressed the objective to ensure an openly accessible, electronic means of payment, for retail,[14] which is coined by the author of this chapter as 'universal and inclusive' CBDC. This means not only to ensure the wide availability and use of the digital euro, but also to consider the complementary phases within the digital euro 'scheme',[15] namely its issuance, distribution and settlement. Secondly, in January 2023, the Eurogroup stated that the appropriate legal basis from the EU constitutional framework would require 'involving the European Parliament and the Council of the European Union based on a legislative proposal by the European Commission' and reiterated the political nature of such decision.[16] At the time of writing, a legislative initiative from the European Commission was expected in the first half of 2023,[17] for which the main legal basis was announced, namely Article 133 of the Treaty on the Functioning of the EU (TFEU). Notwithstanding this clarification, the author of this chapter fully concurs with the approach of the 'cumulation of legal bases'[18] which

[13] European Commission, *Communication from the commission—The European economic and financial system: Fostering openness, strength and resilience*, Pub. L. No. COM (2021) 32 final, 2021, 10–12, https://eur-lex.europa.eu/legal-content/EN/TXT/?uri=CELEX:52021DC0032.

[14] ECB, *Progress, third report,* 2.

[15] Fabio Panetta, "Building on our strengths: The role of the public and private sectors in the digital euro ecosystem," Introductory statement, committee on economic and monetary affairs of the European parliament, European Central Bank, 2022, https://www.ecb.europa.eu/press/key/date/2022/html/ecb.sp220929~91a3775a2a.en.html.

[16] Eurogroup, *Eurogroup statement on the digital euro project* (Eurogroup, 2023), https://www.consilium.europa.eu/en/press/press-releases/2023/01/16/eurogroup-statement-on-the-digital-euro-project-16-january-2023/.

[17] Donohoe, "The Possibility of the Digital Euro."

[18] Seraina Grünewald, *A legal framework for the digital euro: An assessment of the ECB's first three progress reports*, Economic governance and EMU scrutiny unit at the request of the ECONCommittee, European Parliament, 2023, 20–21, https://www.europarl.europa.eu/RegData/etudes/IDAN/2023/741518/IPOL_IDA(2023)714518_EN.pdf.

will enable, legally and constitutionally, the entire digital euro scheme in the euro area. The chapter is structured as follows: Sect. 2 lays down the EU constitutional and primary law analysis, by focusing on the Treaty mandate of the ECB for issuing a CBDC. Section 3 discusses the importance of legal tender for both the euro coins/banknotes and the future CBDC—despite the limits of this concept across the euro area Member States. Section 4 engages with some broader constitutional challenges in issuing CBDCs and discusses some other legal issues that can significantly influence the digital euro scheme, including at its operational level. Section 5 concludes the chapter.

2 Constitutional Law Analysis for a CBDC Issuance by the ECB

This section firstly examines the Treaty mandate of the ECB with an overview of such mandate in primary law and the issuance of euro banknotes and coins. It continues then with a detailed account of the available legal bases, before justifying the choice of combined legal bases for the issuance of digital euro as a universal and inclusive CBDC. The legal bases are also discussed for the distribution and settlement of digital euro.

2.1 EU Primary Law and Treaty Mandate of the ECB

The mandate is a construct and is not provided expressly in the Treaties with a dedicated article or chapter entitled 'mandate'. The ECB has a hierarchical mandate, with a primary price stability objective in monetary policy,[19] which ultimately maintains the value of money and falls under the exclusive competence of the Union. Despite a clear primary objective, the ECB has secondary objectives and other contributory objectives. These additional objectives are all the more important, with recent advocates calling for embracing the objective of financial stability (reinforced since the Great Financial Crisis from both a primary and secondary law

[19] Article 127(1) TFEU, Article 3(3) TEU, as well as Articles 119(2) and 282(2) TFEU and Article 2 of the ESCB and ECB Statute.

perspective) and the objectives of climate change and sustainability,[20] echoing the EU priorities in the post-pandemic era.

As argued elsewhere, the Treaty mandate of the ECB must be understood through its objectives, but also tasks and powers, as part of the ESCB/Eurosystem, which calls for a purposive and functional analysis.[21] The price stability mandate should not be impaired by the introduction of a digital euro,[22] which requires examining in detail the consequences of the design that is chosen and corresponding operations/distribution. And the reverse is also true. The non-adoption or delay in the adoption of a digital currency should not undermine the ECB/Eurosystem tasks and powers. The author of this chapter concurs with other authors,[23] who stress that the ability of the central bank to deliver its mandate might be compromised by the decline of cash use and the parallel development of (non-euro-denominated) private digital currencies. Inaction could hamper euro area monetary sovereignty. Hence, the basic ECB/Eurosystem task of promoting the smooth operation of the payment system[24] is relevant in the analysis of the ECB Treaty mandate for the issuance of the digital euro. The effects of a CBDC issuance will have impact on all the other ECB tasks, i.e., for monetary policy, the stability of the financial system and the operation of the payment system. Other concerns are outside the central banks' remit *stricto* sensu, such as the fundamental rights to conduct business and privacy, but are still important to preserve, in accordance with other primary legal sources (see Sect. 4).

[20] Agnieszka Smoleńska and Thomas Beukers, "The ECB and financial stability," in *The new European Central Bank: Taking stock and looking ahead*, ed. Thomas Beukers, Diane Fromage, and Giorgio Monti (Oxford, New York: Oxford University Press, 2022), 105–35; Rosa Maria Lastra and Kern Alexander, "The ECB mandate: Perspectives on sustainability and solidarity," Study for the committee on economic and monetary affairs (Luxembourg: European Parliament, 2020); Gianni Lo Schiavo, *The role of financial stability in EU law and policy* (Wolters Kluwer, 2017).

[21] Christy Ann Petit, "The ECB mandate—A comparative constitutional perspective," in *The new European Central Bank: Taking stock and looking ahead*, ed. Thomas Beukers, Diane Fromage, and Giorgio Monti (Oxford, New York: Oxford University Press, 2022), 365–68; For some authors functions relate to the "what" while powers to the "how", see Wouter Bossu et al., "Legal aspects of Central Bank Digital Currency: Central Bank and monetary law considerations," IMF Working Paper no. 254 (International Monetary Fund, 2020), 14, https://doi.org/10.5089/9781513561622.001.

[22] Eurogroup, *Eurogroup Statement*.

[23] Grünewald et al., "Digital euro and ECB powers," 1031.

[24] Article 127(2) TFEU and Article 3.1 of the Statute.

2.2 Monetary Policy: Primary Sources for the Issuance of Banknotes and Coins in the Eurosystem

The ECB, as an EU institution, has been conferred exclusive competence in the area of monetary policy for the euro area Member States (as per Article 3(1)(c) TFEU, combined with Article 5(2) TEU on the principle of conferral).[25] The ECB has the exclusive right to authorise the issuance of euro banknotes under Article 128(1) TFEU. The ECB, together with the national central banks (NCBs)' part of the Eurosystem, can issue these banknotes, which are the only notes that benefit from the status of legal tender. Euro area Member States can issue euro coins, subject to the ECB approval of the volume of their issue, as per Article 128(2) TFEU.

2.3 Available Legal Bases for Issuing a CBDC

This section examines the available legal bases and outlines the diverse options, before elaborating on the legal basis retained by the European Commission for its forthcoming legislative initiative and discussing its features as a universal and inclusive CBDC. Several Treaty provisions have been considered for their use as legal foundations for the ECB to issue a digital currency, with consideration for the corresponding overall design to ensure the entire digital euro scheme (without describing the technical details that depend on the development of pilots and implementation projects). Beyond the CBDC design, other variables are important, i.e., the access of the issued digital currency. Regardless of the final choice of the combined legal bases, the complementarity of the digital euro with cash is taken for granted in law and in policy (see Sect. 4).

Legal bases described hereinafter combine Articles from the TFEU and the Statute and depending on a given combination of such provisions, the CBDC may have legal tender. All options are summarised in Table 1 below. We explain hereinafter the main features of the CBDC associated with the legal bases in the following order, namely, a CBDC: as a monetary policy instrument or wholesale CBDC; as a retail account-based CBDC; as a medium of settlement; and as an instrument equivalent

[25] Court of Justice of the EU, *C-370/12 Thomas Pringle v Government of Ireland and Others, No. ECLI:EU:C:2012:756*. Judgement of the Court (CJEU, 2012), https://eur-lex.europa.eu/legal-content/EN/TXT/PDF/?uri=CELEX:62012CJ0370&qid=1706422663831.

to banknotes. This section only signals the presence of legal tender, when the legal basis allows it for the considered CBDC, while Sect. 3 will discuss the concept of legal tender as regards its effectiveness and legal interpretation. The features of the different CBDCs examined with their corresponding legal bases should not be taken in strict isolation. On the contrary, they might be used in combination to enable the issuance, distribution and settlement of the digital euro, as it will be argued in the following section.

Firstly, a CBDC could be an instrument of monetary policy. In such a case, it would be akin to central bank reserves and only accessible to central bank counterparties. The legal bases would be Article 127(2) TFEU, in conjunction with Article 20 (sentence 1) Statute ESCB and ECB. This is a wholesale CBDC with a restrictive access in essence. Secondly, a CBDC could be made available to households and other private entities through accounts held with the Eurosystem. The legal bases would be Article 127(2) TFEU, in conjunction with Article 17,

Table 1 Overview of the available legal bases and corresponding types of CBDC for the digital euro - Author's own elaboration

Legal bases underpinning a digital euro		*Type of CBDC envisaged for the digital euro*	*Addressees / beneficiaries of digital euro*
Article 127(2) TFEU	Article 20 Statute 'Other instruments of monetary control'	Wholesale CBDC Monetary policy instrument	Central Bank Counterparties ⇨ Digital euro 'to business'
	Article 17 Statute* 'Accounts with the ECB and the NCBs'	Retail account-based CBDC	Households and private entities ⇨ Digital euro 'to consumers' (and businesses)
	Article 22 Statute* 'Clearing and payment systems'	Settlement CBDC	Clearing and payment systems
Article 127(2) TFEU, Article 128 (1) TFEU and Article 133 TFEU	Article 16 Statute 'Banknotes'	Instrument equivalent to banknotes	Universal and inclusive ⇨ Digital euro to EU citizens and businesses

* The asterisk signals the possibility to amend the Statute provision, as per Article 129(3) TFEU

Statute of the ESCB and ECB. Here, this corresponds to a retail account-based model, in which the access is open to households and private entities with pseudonymised accounts at the central bank. In a simple definition, account-based can refer to a system where the payment requires to update the balances from both the payer and the payee (in contrast to token-based defined below).[26] However, such a CBDC feature would require an amendment of Article 17 of the Statute, in accordance with an ordinary legislative procedure (as per Article 129(3) TFEU), to add households as individual users and business users among the digital euro users holding accounts.[27] Thirdly, a CBDC could be issued as a medium of settlement for specific types of payment, processed by a dedicated payment infrastructure and only accessible to eligible participants. The legal bases would be Article 127(2) TFEU, in conjunction with Article 22 Statute of the ESCB and ECB.[28] In such a case, this is a settlement digital currency, with again a restrictive access, considering the eligibility criteria, i.e., clearing and payment systems are under its scope. Lastly, a CBDC could be issued as an instrument equivalent to a banknote. The legal bases would be Article 128 TFEU in conjunction with Article 16 Statute ESCB and ECB (first sentence), in addition to Article 127(2) TFEU that lists the basic tasks of monetary policy. This corresponds to a digital *equivalent* euro with an open access, also called a token-based digital euro.[29] In this regard, token-based differs from account-based insofar as the system has a record in place that updates who holds a given CBDC (regardless of its characteristics as anonymous, pseudonymous or identifiable).[30] Moreover, this type of digital currency would benefit from legal tender.

Now that the legal bases have been detailed and placed within the EU constitutional framework follows the analysis of these options: Cases 1

[26] Bank for International Settlements, *Central Bank Digital Currencies: System design and interoperability* (BIS, 2021), 4, https://www.bis.org/publ/othp42_system_design.pdf.

[27] Currently, accounts may be opened for credit institutions, public entities and other market participants, see the analysis in Grünewald, *A Legal Framework for the Digital Euro*, 20.

[28] Nabilou, "Testing the waters of the Rubicon," 307.

[29] Anne-Sophie Gógl et al., *Ahead of the digital euro—Public digital euro working group recommendations*, Digital euro association public, August (Digital euro working group, 2022), 10.

[30] BIS, *Central Bank Digital Currencies: System*, 4.

to 3—a wholesale CBDC, a retail account-based CBDC, a medium of settlement CBDC—are not without limits due to their limited access and the absence of a legal tender status for the CBDC.[31] They all rely on Article 127(2) TFEU, but in combination with a different Article in the Statute (Articles 17, 20 or 22), which underpins the different nature and access to the envisaged CBDC. As the third column of Table 1 shows, these cases correspond to an issuance of CBDC for limited uses (restrictive access for beneficiaries) or would lead to a centralised allocation of credit at the central bank[32] in the case of the account-based model.

Some scholars argued that Article 128(1) TFEU is a sound legal basis that at the same time creates some limits to the competence of the ECB.[33] The limits are related to the tied relationship of the envisaged *digital* banknotes with *tangible* banknotes, as foreseen in EU primary law provisions (see Sect. 4 on the complementarity). In particular, the digital equivalent euro could be a means of payment and a store of value (unit of account), but not a monetary policy instrument.[34] This would lead to exclude the first option. The writer concurs with this, but on different grounds, related to the beneficiaries of the digital euro, as explained in the following subsection.

If we opt for a functional and systematic approach to ensure the effectiveness of the ECB mandate (see the tasks and objectives mentioned above), the fourth option can be considered the most appropriate one. In plain wording, the currency is a vehicle for public money, whose format can change to deliver appropriately the tasks and functions of the central bank. Legally, we can consider using a reasoning by analogy that elaborates on this legal basis option. If we consider the digital euro equivalent

[31] See other limits discussed under a model that considered direct access to NCBs in the Eurosystem in Annelieke Mooij, "A digital euro for everyone: Can the European system of Central Banks introduce general purpose CBDC as part of its economic mandate?," *Journal of Banking Regulation* 24, no. 1 (2023).

[32] In breach of Article 127 TFEU and the principle of open market economy with free competition according to Nabilou, "Testing the waters of the Rubicon," 307.

[33] Grünewald et al., "Digital euro," 1033: see the mere reference to Article 128(1) TFEU also by José Carlos Laguna de Paz, "Some implications of the new global digital economy for financial regulation and supervision," *Journal of Banking Regulation* (2022), https://doi.org/10.1057/s41261-022-00189-1.

[34] Grünewald et al., "Digital euro," 1036; see other limits, though with a questionable reading of primary law and policy-makers' statements: Jay Cullen, "Economically inefficient and legally untenable,' *Journal of Banking Regulation*, 32.

to a banknote and it is treated similarly, the ECB/Eurosystem has exclusive competence to 'authorise the issue of [digital] euro [...] within the Union' (as per Article 128(1) TFEU). The addition in squared brackets reflects the adaptation of the wording of this Treaty provision to the digital reality. In other words, in lieu of euro banknotes, we read the enabling of the issuance of a digital euro within the Union and in such case, with the status of legal tender. This reasoning by analogy can be justified by the absence of any explicit exclusion (of other forms of the single currency beyond the notes) in EU primary sources.[35]

Therefore, the right to issue euro banknotes can encompass the right to determine the format or medium of 'euro banknotes', which is, in that case, transposing to the digital reality of the economy. The ECB has already considered the fourth option of Article 128(1) TFEU—a digital euro as an instrument equivalent to banknotes—the best legal basis for ensuring the issuance of digital equivalent euro (to cash) with legal tender.[36] Moreover, the adoption of secondary law, on the basis of Article 133 TFEU, will specify the conditions for issuing a digital euro with legal tender.[37] However, this will happen in combination with 127(2) TFEU and other provisions from the Statute, to ensure the entire digital euro 'scheme' is legally grounded before becoming operational.

[35] For a more restrictive reading of coins and banknotes see Bossu et al., "Legal aspects of Central Bank Digital Currency," 21.

[36] Kai Gereon Spitzer and Giacomo Loi, "Digital euro: Reviewing the progress to date and some open questions," EGOV briefing PE 741.498, European Parliament, 2023, 10, https://www.europarl.europa.eu/RegData/etudes/BRIE/2023/741498/IPOL_BRI(2023)741498_EN.pdf.

[37] Already recognised as a possibility in ECB, *Report on a Digital Euro*.

2.4 *The Legal Basis for the Digital Euro: A Universal and Inclusive CBDC*

At the time of writing, Article 133 TFEU[38] had been indicated by the European Commission for its forthcoming legislative proposal as a suitable primary law foundation.[39] This Article would give the legal basis for '***an electronic means of payment for retail payments***, *issued by the central bank and accessible to everyone in the euro area*', as indicated in the second ECB progress report.[40] This would lead to a tiered model that relies on supervised intermediaries (like payment services providers) at the centre.[41] This model gives users an ***intermediated*** access to digital euros.

In legal engineering, this legal basis implies EU law secondary acts proposed by the European Commission, e.g., an EU Regulation examined under the ordinary legislative procedure with the European Parliament and the Council, after the consultation of the ECB. This legislative action falls within monetary law, an area of exclusive competence at EU level (Article 3(1)(c) TFEU). The EU Regulation would regulate the essential aspects of the digital euro, including the rights and obligations of users and providers.[42]

The case-law of the Court of Justice of the EU supports this stance. In the preliminary ruling Joined Cases C-422/19 and C-423/19 Johannes Dietrich and Norbert Häring v Hessischer Rundfunk (hereinafter Joined Cases *Hessischer Rundfunk*), the Court clarified that the competence laid down in Article 133 TFEU empowers the EU legislature alone to specify the legal rules governing the status of legal tender, accorded to banknotes

[38] Policy objective n. 25: European Commission, *Annexes to the communication commission work programme 2023—A union standing firm and united (Com(2022) 548 Final)* (European Commission, 2022), 3, https://commission.europa.eu/system/files/2022-10/com_2022_548_1_annexe_en.pdf; Euro Legal Tender Expert Group, *Final Report of the Euro Legal Tender Expert Group* (ELTEG, 2022), 9.

[39] See already in early 2022, Eurogroup, *Eurogroup statement on the digital euro project* (Eurogroup, 2022), https://www.consilium.europa.eu/en/press/press-releases/2022/02/25/eurogroup-statement-on-the-digital-euro-project/; European Commission, *Consultation document—Targeted consultation on a digital euro* (European Commission, 2022), 3.

[40] ECB, *Progress*, third report, 2.

[41] Ibid., 7.

[42] Spitzer and Loi, "Digital Euro," 9.

and coins, in so far as it is necessary for the use of the euro as the single currency.[43] If the digital form of the euro were to be treated as equivalent to banknotes (following the above reasoning by analogy), the competence of determining its legal tender status is automatically the EU legislature's responsibility following this judgement.[44]Moreover, it would be necessary for the use of the *digital* euro, as the single currency, to paraphrase the judgement and translate it to the digital euro reality.

Finally, next to the issuance within the digital euro scheme, additional legal bases could be used in combination within the EU constitutional framework sources (see Sect. 2.3) to support the digital euro infrastructure in its distribution and settlement (Articles 17 and 22, Statute ESCB and ECB, together with Article 127(2) TFEU, see Table 1). In this regard, the approach of the 'cumulation of legal bases' is the correct one to enable, legally and constitutionally, the entire digital euro scheme.[45]

The ECB also has a role in deciding on the technical features[46] of the digital euro relying on its regulatory powers in monetary policy. Nevertheless, this raises the fundamental question of the dividing line and coherence between the co-legislators' role and the ECB's responsibility in adopting and implementing parts of the digital euro framework.

[43] Court of Justice of the EU, *Joined Cases C-422/19 and C-423/19: Hessischer Rundfunk—Judgment of the Court (Grand Chamber) of 26 January 2021, No. ECLI:EU:C:2021:63*, Judgement of the Court (CJEU, 2021), para 51.

[44] To be sure, the EU exclusive competence precludes any competence on the part of the Member States in the matter, unless they are acting on the basis that the European Union has empowered them to do so or for the implementation of EU acts, see ibid., para 52.

[45] Grünewald, *A Legal Framework*, 20–21.

[46] See the legal basis and subsidiarity check in European Commission, *Call for evidence for an impact assessment—A digital euro for the EU*, Pub. L. No. Ref. Ares (2022) 2567612, 2022, https://ec.europa.eu/info/law/better-regulation/have-your-say/initiatives/13392-A-digital-euro-for-the-EU_en.

3 CBDC and Legal Tender

Is legal tender a mandatory requirement for the issuance of a CBDC in the euro area? The author argues that it is for several reasons[47]: the preservation of the singleness of monetary policy, the credibility of the issuer—the ECB—as well as its independence. However, this concept is not without limitations as it suffers already a number of exceptions (and misapplications), related to national legal frameworks that may ultimately impinge on the effectiveness of legal tender of banknotes and coins as discussed in this section. This analysis allows for a positive and normative approach to the status of legal tender for digital euros, which would take the shape of a universal CBDC.

Furthermore, the European Commission's work programme foresaw a legislative initiative based on Article 133 TFEU, to address the scope and effects of legal tender of euro banknotes and coins.[48] This will cover the 'essential characteristic'[49] of legal tender for the digital euro. Should the legal tender of euro coins and banknotes be reviewed simultaneously,[50] this may change the nature of the act, underpinning legal tender to a binding legal act, in replacement of the 2010 Commission's recommendation currently in force.[51] This legislative review can be the opportunity to fix some of the shortcomings observed in some EU Member States that apply legal tender more loosely—apart from the exceptions that can be justified on public interest grounds (e.g., cash payments).

[47] For a different view see Grünewald et al., "Digital euro," 1053; Christian Hofmann, "The changing concept of money: A threat to the monetary system or an opportunity for the financial sector?," *European Business Organization Law Review*, 21, no. 1 (2020), 42, https://doi.org/10.1007/s40804-020-00182-z.

[48] Policy objective n. 25 European Commission, *Annexes*, 3

[49] European Commission, *Call for Evidence*, 2.

[50] ELTEG, *Final Report of the Euro*, 10.

[51] Even if a recommendation is not completely without legal effect towards national courts, see Court of Justice of the EU, *Joined Cases C-422/19 and C-423/19. Johannes Dietrich (C-422/19) and Norbert Häring (C-423/19) v Hessischer Rundfunk*. No. ECLI:EU:C:2020:756. Opinion of Advocate General Pitruzzella delivered on 29 September 2020 (CJEU, 2020), para 48, 103, https://eur-lex.europa.eu/legal-content/EN/TXT/HTML/?uri=CELEX:62019CC0422&qid=1706422172122.

3.1 Legal Tender for Euro Banknotes and Coins

Legal tender is better understood by looking at both EU primary law and secondary law. The Treaties refer to legal tender in Article 128(1) TFEU (third sentence) and Article 16 of the Statute for *banknotes*, without defining its exact scope and legal effects.[52] EU secondary law also provides for the legal tender of banknotes: in an EU Recommendation from the European Commission, while other EU secondary acts merely repeat the letter of EU primary law.[53] Euro *coins* have the status of legal tender as per Article 11 of Regulation no. 974/98. As examined above, coins may be issued by the Member States subject to the volume approved by the ECB (as per Article 128(2) TFEU). Overall, legal tender is not fully determined in EU constitutional sources.

The interpretation of the concept is found in a non-binding Recommendation of the European Commission from 2010 itself based on the prior work of the Euro Legal Tender Expert Group (ELTEG).[54] Legal tender encompasses three main elements: it guarantees mandatory acceptance; acceptance at full face value; and the power to discharge from payment obligations. These three features contribute to the confidence of the consumers and businesses and ultimately public trust. Hence, the functions of legal tender, from the perspectives of the users and of the businesses, demonstrate how important this concept is for single monetary policy in the euro area. Firstly, for the end users, legal tender can influence their expectations and their acceptance of the money. Secondly, for businesses, legal tender can ensure legal certainty and at an operational level, make them use equipment that processes public money.[55]

[52] ECB, *Report on a Digital Euro*, 25.

[53] Second sentence of Article 10, Council of the EU, *Council Regulation (EC) No 974/98 of 3 May 1998 on the Introduction of the euro*, 139 OJ L 11/05/1998 P. 0001–0005, 1998, http://data.europa.eu/eli/reg/1998/974/oj/eng; see also paras 99 and seq. CJEU, *Opinion of AG Pitruzzella in Joined Cases C-422/19 and C-423/19.*

[54] European Commission, *Recommendation on the scope and effects of legal tender of euro banknotes and coins, Official Journal of the European Union L*, 083 (2010), http://data.europa.eu/eli/reco/2010/191/oj/eng; Euro Legal Tender Expert Group, *Report of the Euro Legal Tender Expert Group (ELTEG) on the Definition, scope and effects of legal tender of euro banknotes and coins* (Brussels: ELTEG, 2009), https://ec.europa.eu/economy_finance/articles/euro/documents/elteg_en.pdf.

[55] Markus Brunnermeier and Jean-Pierre Landau, *The digital euro: Policy implications and perspectives,* Study for the committee on economic and monetary affairs, policy department for economic, scientific and quality of life policies, PE 703.337, European

The Court of Justice of the EU clarified that the concept of 'legal tender' as a means of euro-denominated payment signifies that it cannot generally be refused in settlement of a debt in euros, at its full face value, with the effect of discharging the debt.[56] While citing again the three main elements contained in the 2010 EU Recommendation, the Court considered that there is an obligation in principle to accept banknotes and coins denominated in euro for payment purposes.[57]

There is, however, a degree of uncertainty and controversy in the concept of legal tender applied across euro area countries,[58] considering a broad and somehow legally loose circumscription. This creates an uneven playing field of legal tender due to limitations to cash acceptance (as well as cash payments thresholds) among other issues, further examined in the following section.

3.2 Limitations to Legal Tender Status

The limitations are examined through the lenses of two distinct situations. On the one hand, some exceptions to the legal tender status can be considered proportionate in the public interest. On the other hand, the effectiveness of legal tender across the euro area is uneven with some (accepted or infringing) derogations.

Firstly, under the definition of legal tender, acceptance is not an absolute acceptance. The Court of Justice stressed a distinction between mandatory acceptance in principle as opposed to absolute acceptance in the Joined Cases C-422/19 and C-423/19 *Hessischer Rundfunk*.[59] The Member States may regulate the procedures for settling pecuniary obligations (under private or public law provisions). There might be specific

Parliament, 2022, 37, https://www.europarl.europa.eu/RegData/etudes/STUD/2022/703337/IPOL_STU(2022)703337_EN.pdf.

[56] CJEU, *Joined Cases C-422/19 and C-423/19*, para 46.

[57] Ibid., para 49.

[58] Robert Freitag, "Euro as legal tender (and Banknotes)," in *The EU law of economic and monetary union*, ed. Fabian Amtenbrink and Christoph Herrmann (Oxford University Press, 2020), 596–97, 610, http://oxford.universitypressscholarship.com/view/10.1093/oso/9780198793748.001.0001/isbn-9780198793748-book-part-26.

[59] CJEU, *Joined Cases C-422/19 and C-423/19*, para 55.

circumstances in the functioning of Member States' tax or public administrations that justify, on public interest grounds, a derogation from the obligation to discharge payment obligations in cash.[60] However, such restrictions must be proportionate to the public interest objectives and apply the proportionality test.[61] However, one may wonder whether this finding could be extrapolated to private parties.

Furthermore, legal tender of the euro is not effective in a similar way across the EU, in particular for cash acceptance that might be impinged by contractually agreed terms for electronic payments among parties. Already in 2009, the ELTEG reported some divergence among Member States regarding the general acceptance of cash, as some Member States argue that contractual freedom can prevail.[62] The 2021 ELTEG Report discussed the delicate balance between legal tender and contractual freedom, reporting the differences among national legal frameworks, businesses and public authorities' practices on cash acceptance.[63]

In addition, some national frameworks may suffer from legal gaps or insufficient legal certainty in complying with the Joined Cases *Hessischer Rundfunk*, requiring action at EU level, as underlined by the ELTEG.[64] The scope of action at EU level remains undetermined potentially, while awaiting the upcoming legislative proposals. Moreover, some Member States recognised having other means of payment that may be considered with a 'quasi' legal tender status.[65] For instance, Greece has made some electronic payments mandatory for some professionals/sectors by ministerial decisions, the Dutch Civil Code provides a possibility for excluding the payment through the banking system and Italy has a payment ceiling above which the means of payment must be traceable. Such a departure from legal tender questions its effectiveness across the EU.

Finally, effective enforcement of legal tender might be at odds with regulatory provisions that prioritise public policy objectives on the ground

[60] Ibid., para 56.

[61] Ibid., paras 68–70 and 78.

[62] Ireland, Germany, Finland and the Netherlands, ELTEG, *Final Report of the Euro*, 6.

[63] Ibid., 2-4.

[64] As to the existence of legal gaps or a lack of legal certainty that would need to be addressed by action at EU level as a result of the CJEU's judgment, five Member States (ES, IE, LT, SI, PT) indeed point to this risk, ibid., 3.

[65] ELTEG, *Final Report of the Euro*, 2.

of public interest. Such limitation could stem from the Anti-Money Laundering (AML) framework implementation[66] and some Member States' lower limits in cash payments in euros, as defined under national laws. This is a sensitive issue in finding the balance between money circulation and the fight against financial crime.[67] Moreover, national laws may prioritise other public policy objectives, limiting legal tender, but with the obligation to be proportionate. For instance, a recent law in Slovakia removed the option to pay contributions for social security in cash and allowed such payment via other means of payments, like bank transfer or postal money.[68] Another example is Spain, which lowered cash payments' limit in transactions with parties acting in a professional/business capacity to one thousand euros.[69] The ECB considered these regulatory changes as disproportionate and with 'an adverse and undesired impact on the legal tender status of euro banknotes',[70] but this has not been followed up by any amendments in Spanish law to date.

3.3 Legal Tender for Digital Euro as a Universal CBDC

In a similar way as tangible euros, the non-tangible form of euro can and should benefit from the status of legal tender. This claim is supported by a reasoning inferred from the silence of the legal sources and a reasoning *a*

[66] Christy Ann Petit, "Chapter 16. Anti-money laundering," in *Research handbook on EU law enforcement*, ed. Miroslava Scholten (Edward Elgar Publishing, 2023), 16.

[67] See para 4 analysing the limits to cash payments in the ongoing legislative review of the AML rulebook: European Central Bank, *Opinion of the ECB of 16 February 2022 on a Proposal for a Directive and a Regulation on the Prevention of the Use of the Financial System for the Purposes of Money Laundering or Terrorist Financing (CON/2022/5) 2022/C 210/06*" (CJEU, 2022), https://eur-lex.europa.eu/legal-content/EN/TXT/PDF/?uri=CELEX:52022AB0005&qid=1706421729701.

[68] The ECB acknowledged in its opinion that there are reasons of public interest for this limitation to cash payments, but Slovak authorities have not demonstrated its appropriateness and if it does not go beyond what is necessary to achieve the public interest objectives. See European Central Bank, *Opinion of the ECB of 7 March 2023 on the Limitation of Cash Payments for Public Social Insurance Contributions (CON/2023/7)* (ECB, 2023), paras 3.2–3.7, https://eur-lex.europa.eu/legal-content/EN/TXT/?uri=CELEX%3A52023AB0007&qid=1680615286943&home=ecb.

[69] European Central Bank, *Opinion of the ECB of 15 March 2022 on Limitations to Cash Payments (CON/2022/9)* (ECB, 2022), https://eur-lex.europa.eu/legal-content/EN/TXT/?uri=CELEX%3A52022AB0009&qid=1680615286943&home=ecb.

[70] Ibid., para 3,5.

fortiori. The argument here is in line with Advocate General Pitruzzella's position.[71] His Opinion in the Joined Cases *Hessischer Rundfunk* referred to a non-physical form of the euro and articulated a convincing reasoning to support the attributes of legal tender for the future digital currency. This section emphasises the arguments that support legal tender for a digital euro that is a universal CBDC.

The first line of argument follows a reasoning on the silence of the provision and drawing on an analogy (as examined with Article 128(1) for digital euro issuance). Advocate General Pitruzzella anticipated the fact that the sovereign power conferred exclusively on the Union by the euro area Member States encompasses the definition of 'which good or instrument (*tangible or non-tangible*) has the status of legal tender in the euro area'.[72] In particular, the AG considered that Article 128(1) TFEU and other EU sources do not exclude the possibility for the EU to assign the status of legal tender to 'other forms of currency that are not necessarily physical', alongside the euro banknotes and coins.[73] Therefore, the EU sovereign power to define legal tender can include the power to determine the instruments with legal tender status in the euro area.[74]

Another argument is made *a fortiori*. The Treaty's wording for the legal tender of euro banknotes in Article 128 TFEU makes it clear that the legal tender is restricted only to these notes. As AG Pitruzzella argued, this does not exclude legal tender for other instruments, as for coins[75]; it can be added here that the same applies to the future digital currency in the euro area, regardless of the future design options and features.

Should there be a discrepancy between the different forms of euro, the co-existence of digital-tangible euro may shift citizens' preferences with an arbitrage for the currency form, with legal tender over the other, that remains without legal tender. In such a scenario, the effects of having tangible euro with legal tender and simultaneously, digital euro without any legal tender (even in a transition period) might raise practical and

[71] For a different view, considering a Treaty amendment to Article 128(1) TFEU, see Nabilou, "Testing the waters of the Rubicon," 307.

[72] CJEU, *Opinion of AG Pitruzzella in Joined Cases C-422/19 and C-423/19*, para 93.

[73] Ibid., para 96.

[74] Ibid.

[75] Ibid., para 96 and the corresponding footnote 52.

policy difficulties.[76] It might be an issue for the legal certainty represented by the digital currency, its credibility and ability to fulfil its function under single monetary policy. Therefore, both the euro banknotes and the digital euro should benefit from effective legal tender status, ensuring legal certainty and a level playing field.

However, in the same way as for banknotes and coins, the legal tender of digital euro might suffer some exemptions.[77] They may result from Member States' legal framework in contractual arrangements and some provisions shaping the citizens' use of the digital euro (see the cash payments' limits set at different levels across Member States, as previously discussed). Exemptions may also stem from other concerns to ensure financial inclusion and the (yet to be determined) relationship of the digital single currency with other CBDCs (see Chapter6).

Furthermore, the partial acceptance of digital euro by merchants (physical and online stores) and businesses could be an impediment to effective legal tender. The industry raised some concerns as to the costs incurred by the systems required by the future implementation of the digital euro scheme. The offset of costs by benefits or potential ways to compensate remains underdetermined.[78] The industry highlighted the high investments a digital euro would entail for retailers and financial intermediaries and called for potential government funding to meet the investment costs, including the option of remuneration for commercial transactions.[79] The replacement of incentives on merchants/businesses by legal obligations has been put on the table with a binding obligation to offer digital euro services,[80] but the effectiveness of such obligation depends on the system of enforcement, once again.

[76] See Panagiotis Papapaschalis, "Retail Central Bank Digital Currency: A (legal) novelty?," in *ESCB Legal Conference 2020 (11 September–2 November 2020) proceedings*, European Central Bank, 2021, 205, https://www.ecb.europa.eu/pub/pdf/other/ecb.escblegalconferenceproceedings2020~4c11842967.en.pdf.

[77] Spitzer and Loi, "Digital Euro," 9.

[78] Ibid., 4.

[79] European Banking Federation, *EBF Response to the European commission's targeted consultation on a digital euro* (Brussels: EBF, 2022), 31, https://www.ebf.eu/wp-content/uploads/2022/06/FINAL-EBF-Response-to-EC-Consultation-on-a-Digital-Euro.pdf

[80] They compare this obligation with the current obligation to open basic bank accounts, see Spitzer and Loi, "Digital Euro," 4.

Therefore, if the issuance of digital euro without legal tender were theoretically possible, in law and in practice, this route faces several limitations, including negative repercussions for single monetary policy. However, the concept of legal tender itself is not without any limitations. The review of the legislative framework for legal tender could improve its effectiveness, while accommodating—in a proportionate manner—exceptions in the public interest. It remains to be seen if diverse approaches to legal tender could reflect the two mediums of the single currency coexisting, as tangible and digital euros have different characteristics (see the acceptance at full face value discussed above).

4 ECB's Mandate in Action for a Universal CBDC

The digital euro will involve several stakeholders in the distribution and settlement phases, after its issuance. In this regard, the digital euro scheme necessitates looking at other constitutional and operational challenges, in issuing and operating a digital euro in the euro area. The scheme encompasses not only the legal framework for the inception of a digital euro, but also the practices and standards that will be included in a dedicated 'rulebook'. There are still some elements to clarify on the private sector involvement, i.e., supervised intermediaries responsible for the distribution, or the businesses and merchants' investment in supporting infrastructures.

4.1 EU Constitutional Challenges

This section briefly discusses the constitutional challenges raised by the opportunity to keep existing tangible euro, alongside digital euro, as well as the importance of fundamental rights, with a particular focus on privacy.

Firstly, the issuance of a digital euro raises the question of the long-term life expectancy of tangible euro, i.e., cash. The EU Treaties are clear and guarantee 'the very existence of euro banknotes at a constitutional level'.[81] Therefore, a complete abolition of tangible euro is

[81] CJEU, *Opinion of AG Pitruzzella in Joined Cases C-422/19 and C-423/19*, para 95.

contrary to EU primary law. However, this legal analysis does not contradict a medium- to long-term evolution that paves the way for a further digitalisation—as embraced by citizens and businesses.

Secondly, the EU constitutional sources include legal safeguards that can protect some beneficiaries of the digital euro in their fundamental rights. As examined at length in scholarly publications, these rights range from the fundamental right to conduct a business enshrined in the EU Charter of Fundamental Rights to the fundamental right of privacy recognised in the European Convention on Human Rights (ECHR), including personal data protection under the Charter.[82] Once again, there is a balance to strike with the public interest.[83]

In particular, the fundamental right to privacy granted to end users will be weighed against public policy concerns embedded under the public interest, namely AML and countering the financing of terrorism (AML/CFT) policies, the prevention and sanctioning of tax evasion and the effective enforcement of sanctions.[84] We may anticipate that such public interest will be loosely defined and subject to interpretation with its application at both Member States and EU level. ECB Executive Board Member, Fabio Panetta, stressed the co-legislators' duty in examining and framing this delicate balance while he assured the Members of the European Parliament (MEPs) that the solutions for the digital euro would 'preserve privacy by default and by design'.[85] Privacy is a more pregnant concern in the digital reality, as citizens' views expressed during the consultations. Therefore, the upcoming legislative proposal might consider it with a risk-based approach and could consider a proportionality test. In the case of low-value and lower-risk digital euro payments, such test would allow a tilt towards higher levels of privacy and on

[82] Grünewald et al., "Digital euro and ECB powers," *Common Market Law Review*, 58, no. 4 (2021), 1045; Zellweger-Gutknecht et al., "Digital euro, monetary objects, and price stability," 305.

[83] See Ulrich Bindseil, "Issuing a digital euro", *ESCB legal conference 2020 (11 September–2 November 2020) Proceedings*, European Central Bank, 2020, 174, https://www.ecb.europa.eu/pub/pdf/other/ecb.escblegalconferenceproceedings2020~4c11842967.en.pdf.

[84] Eurogroup, *Eurogroup Statement on the Digital Euro Project.*

[85] Fabio Panetta, "The digital euro: Our money wherever, whenever we need it," *Introductory statement, committee on economic and monetary affairs of the European Parliament*, European Central Bank, 2023, https://www.ecb.europa.eu/press/key/date/2023/html/ecb.sp230123~2f8271ed76.en.html.

the other end, a simplified due diligence under the AML requirements framework.[86] This 'selective privacy'[87] corresponds to a more cash-like experience.[88] The strive to safeguard some privacy features supports the wide use and hence preserves the universal character of the digital euro.

4.2 Operational Challenges

Operational challenges in issuing a CBDC include the consequences of the design chosen—here discussed, as regards the challenge of mandatory acceptance—and the subsequent review of EU secondary legislation.

The three features of legal tender—mandatory acceptance, acceptance at full face value and the power to discharge from payment obligations—can 'significantly influence CBDC design choices'.[89] Universality, as a broad concept that underpins an effective mandatory acceptance, would require a digital euro accessible online and offline. The ministers sitting in the Eurogroup supported such offline functionality for the sake of financial inclusion.[90] Moreover, the acceptance at full face value raises challenges, as to the potential interest bearing or (controversial) remuneration,[91] in holding digital euros (considered in the interest of supervised intermediaries' business models). Policymakers seem inclined to adopt some holding limits that will ensure digital euro holders maintain their commercial bank accounts at the same time.[92]

Moreover, a significant part of EU secondary law would need to be amended or even replaced, to regulate a new era, in which single monetary policy also relies on the issuance of digital euro, in co-existence with euro banknotes and coins.

[86] Fabio Panetta, "The digital euro and the evolution of the financial system," *Introductory statement, committee on economic and monetary affairs of the European Parliament*, European Central Bank, 2022, https://www.ecb.europa.eu/press/key/date/2022/html/ecb.sp220615~0b859eb8bc.en.html.

[87] ECB, *Progress*, 8.

[88] Grünewald, *A Legal Framework for the Digital Euro,* 14.

[89] See Papapaschalis. "Retail Central Bank Digital Currency," 205.

[90] Eurogroup, *Eurogroup Statement on the Digital Euro Project.*

[91] Grünewald, *A Legal Framework for the Digital Euro*, 12, 13 and 18.

[92] For a comparison of the potential digital euros' holding limits and the Bank of England's proposal, ibid., 11–12.

Firstly, as it is argued above, both the digital euro and cash should have legal tender status to ensure a level playing field and legal certainty. As far as a new EU secondary legislation will regulate the legal tender of a digital euro, a parallel review of the definition the legal tender of euro coins and banknotes is necessary. The EU Recommendation could be repealed and replaced by an EU Regulation based on Article 133 TFEU, as well. These evolutions are not only necessary for the coherence of the legal framework applicable to cash and the digital euro,[93] but also for an equal treatment of the different forms of public money provided under single monetary policy.

Secondly, the legislative framework will need to reflect the new ecosystem represented by the issuance, distribution and settlement of digital euro. Other EU financial services legislation will be amended to ensure regulatory alignments and keep coherence and consistency in relevant EU law[94] (among others: Payment Service Directive, Payment Account Directive, e-Money Directive, AML legislation and Settlement Finality Directive). Worldwide, the Bank for International Settlements (BIS) suggested the adoption of a rulebook to formalise the roles and responsibilities of different stakeholders: operators, participants and service providers.[95] New rules will need to clarify intermediaries' responsibility and liability—beyond the issuance itself. In this respect, the elements pertaining to harmonisation of private law that may result from the adoption of the digital euro would need a different legal basis than the ones considered under Sect. 2.[96]

5 Conclusion

The answer to the initial question is positive: a digital currency can be a lawful means for the settlement of euro-denominated debts. To answer the second question—to what extent the EU constitutional framework is

[93] ELTEG, *Final Report of the Euro*, 10.

[94] Ibid., 14.

[95] Bank for International Settlements, *Central Bank Digital Currencies: Foundational Principles and Core Features*, Report no. 1 in a series of collaborations from a group of central banks, 2020, 13, https://www.bis.org/publ/othp33.pdf.

[96] See the argument of Germany to use Article 114 TFEU for this purpose: ELTEG, *Final Report of the Euro*, 9.

proof for the issuance of euro banknotes, coins and digital euro alike—this chapter examined the various legal bases for issuing a digital currency in the euro area. It concluded that, in addition to Article 127(2) TFEU, the combination of Article 128(1) TFEU with Article 16 of the Statute is the best route, while Article 133 TFEU will be the foundation of the Commission's legislative initiative for proposing measures regulating the use of the digital euro as a single currency. In narrowing down the type of digital euro that can be issued legally under the EU Treaties. The author of this chapter has argued for a universal and inclusive CBDC, which stresses the beneficiaries (see Table 1) and should preserve the inclusion of all, natural and legal persons, from an end user's perspective.

Furthermore, the effectiveness of the ECB constitutional mandate requires a legal tender status, in principle, for euro banknotes, coins and the non-tangible form of the euro alike. The issuance of a digital euro by the ECB will have significant repercussions on the daily life of citizens, the operations of the businesses within the euro area and in the international role of the euro at global level. Wide acceptance (one of the three features to ensure legal tender) requires public confidence and trust by users. In this regard, the BIS stressed the necessity for central banks to have 'clear authority', underpinning the CBDCs issuance.[97] This authority will emerge also through the implementation of one of the key principles for CBDCs for 'transparency and accountability frameworks, for both public and private sector participants'.[98] This calls for improving and keeping high standards of accountability and legitimacy in the upcoming digital euro scheme—in its issuance, distribution and settlement. This socio-economic shift also calls for a sociological analysis of the transformation of money in our society and democracy.

The year 2023 was pivotal with the decision of the ECB's Governing Council in autumn to launch the 'realisation phase' of the digital euro. However, the digital euro package was not finalised under the 9th European Parliament term that ended in mid-2024. It may take up to half a decade, or more, to clarify how the digital euro will be issued and distributed to EU citizens.[99] The CBDC will change the traditional

[97] BIS, *Central Bank Digital Currencies: Foundational*, 11.

[98] G7 United Kingdom 2021, *Public Policy Principles,* Principle 2.

[99] An EPRS briefing indicates a tentative date of 2026 for an ECB decision on possible issuance of a digital euro, see Spitzer and Loi, "Digital Euro," 11.

banking system. The likely significant increase of cross-border financial flows and payments once CBDCs are adopted and interoperable worldwide raises several challenges in macro-financial policy[100]—a concern that reaches beyond central banking strictly.[101] The question should not be (anymore) on the existence of a digital currency, but on the conditions for its creation in the twenty-first century with full awareness of its implications for the EU's social market economy.

References

Bank for International Settlements. *BIS innovation hub work on Central Bank Digital Currency (CBDC)*. BIS, 2021. https://www.bis.org/about/bisih/topics/cbdc.htm.

Bank for International Settlements. *Central Bank Digital Currencies: Foundational principles and core features*. Report no. 1 in a series of collaborations from a group of Central Banks, 2020. https://www.bis.org/publ/othp33.pdf.

Bank for International Settlements. *Central Bank Digital Currencies: System design and interoperability*. Report no. 2 in a series of collaborations from a group of Central Banks, September, 2021. https://www.bis.org/publ/othp42_system_design.pdf.

Beck, Thorsten, Stephen G. Cecchetti, Magdalena Grothe, Malcolm Kemp, Loriana Pelizzon, and Antonio Sánchez Serrano. *Three scenarios for the financial system in 2030—Will video kill the radio star? Digitalisation and the future of banking*. Reports of the advisory scientific committee no. 12, 2022. https://doi.org/10.2139/ssrn.4012413.

Beukers, Thomas, Diane Fromage, and Giorgio Monti. *The new European Central Bank: Taking stock and looking ahead*. Oxford, New York: Oxford University Press, 2022.

Bindseil Ulrich. "Issuing a digital euro." *ESCB legal conference 2020 (11 September–2 November 2020) proceedings*. European Central Bank, 2021. https://www.ecb.europa.eu/pub/pdf/other/ecb.escblegalconferenceproceedings2020~4c11842967.en.pdf.

Bossu, Wouter, Masaru Itatani, Catalina Margulis, Arthur D. P. Rossi, Hans Weenink, and Akihiro Yoshinaga. "Legal aspects of Central Bank Digital

[100] Thorsten Beck et al., *Three Scenarios for the Financial System in 2030—Will video kill the radio star? Digitalisation and the future of banking*, Reports of the advisory scientific committee no. 12, 2022, 42–43, https://doi.org/10.2139/ssrn.4012413.

[101] The ECB (ESRB) together with the Member States, as this area is still subject to coordination.

Currency: Central Bank and monetary law considerations." working papers 20, no. 254, International Monetary Fund, 2020. https://doi.org/10.5089/9781513561622.001.

Brunnermeier, Markus K, and Jean-Pierre Landau. *The digital euro: Policy implications and perspectives.* Study for the committee on economic and monetary affairs, policy department for economic, scientific and quality of life policies, PE 703.337, January. European Parliament, 2022.

Council of the EU. "Council regulation (EC) No 974/98 of 3 May 1998 on the introduction of the euro." *Official Journal L 139, 11/05/1998 P. 0001–0005.* Council of the EU, 1998. http://data.europa.eu/eli/reg/1998/974/oj/eng.

Court of Justice of the EU. *C-370/12 Thomas Pringle v government of Ireland and others.* No. ECLI:EU:C:2012:756. Judgement of the court, November 27. CJEU, 2012. https://eur-lex.europa.eu/legal-content/EN/TXT/PDF/?uri=CELEX:62012CJ0370&qid=1706422663831. Court of Justice of the EU. *Joined cases C-422/19 and C-423/19. Johannes Dietrich (C-422/19) and Norbert Häring (C-423/19) v Hessischer Rundfunk.* No. ECLI:EU:C:2020:756. Opinion of advocate general Pitruzzella delivered on 29 September 2020. CJEU, 2020. https://eur-lex.europa.eu/legal-content/EN/TXT/HTML/?uri=CELEX:62019CC0422&qid=1706422172122.

Court of Justice of the EU. *Joined cases C-422/19 and C-423/19: Hessischer Rundfunk—Judgment of the court (Grand Chamber) of 26 January 2021.* No. ECLI:EU:C:2021:63. Judgement of the court, January 26. CJEU, 2021. https://eur-lex.europa.eu/legal-content/EN/TXT/PDF/?uri=CELEX:62019CJ0422&qid=1706422985323.

European Central Bank. *Opinion of the ECB of 16 February 2022 on a proposal for a directive and a regulation on the prevention of the use of the financial system for the purposes of money laundering or terrorist financing (CON/2022/5) (2022/C 210/06).* CJEU, 2022. https://eur-lex.europa.eu/legal-content/EN/TXT/PDF/?uri=CELEX:52022AB0005&qid=1706421729701.

Cullen, Jay. "'Economically inefficient and legally untenable': Constitutional limitations on the introduction of Central Bank Digital Currencies in the EU." *Journal of Banking Regulation* 23, no. 1 (2021): 31–41. https://doi.org/10.1057/s41261-021-00162-4.

Donohoe, Paschal. "The possibility of the digital Euro." *POLITICO* (blog), March 14, 2023. https://www.politico.eu/article/finance-banking-the-digital-euro-cryptocurrency-central-banks-currency/.

Euro Legal Tender Expert Group. *Final report of the Euro Legal Tender Expert Group.* July, 2022.

Euro Legal Tender Expert Group. *Report of the Euro Legal Tender Expert Group (ELTEG) on the definition, scope and effects of legal tender of euro banknotes and coins*. January 21, 2009. https://ec.europa.eu/economy_finance/articles/euro/documents/elteg_en.pdf.

Eurogroup. *Eurogroup statement on the digital euro project*. Press release, February 25, 2022. https://www.consilium.europa.eu/en/press/press-releases/2022/02/25/eurogroup-statement-on-the-digital-euro-project/.

Eurogroup. *Eurogroup statement on the digital euro project*. Statement, January 16, 2023. https://www.consilium.europa.eu/en/press/press-releases/2023/01/16/eurogroup-statement-on-the-digital-euro-project-16-january-2023/.

European Banking Federation. *EBF response to the European commission's targeted consultation on a digital euro*. Consultation Paper, June 16, 2022. https://www.ebf.eu/wp-content/uploads/2022/06/FINAL-EBF-Response-to-EC-Consultation-on-a-Digital-Euro.pdf.

European Central Bank. ESCB legal conference 2020 (11 September–2 November 2020) proceedings. Conference proceedings, February. ECB, 2021. https://www.ecb.europa.eu/pub/pdf/other/ecb.escblegalconferenceproceedings2020~4c11842967.en.pdf.

European Central Bank. *Opinion of the ECB of 15 March 2022 on limitations to cash payments (CON/2022/9)*. ECB, 2022. https://eur-lex.europa.eu/legal-content/EN/TXT/?uri=CELEX%3A52022AB0009&qid=1680615286943&home=ecb.

European Central Bank. *Opinion of the ECB of 7 March 2023 on the limitation of cash payments for public social insurance contributions* (CON/2023/7). ECB, 2023. https://eur-lex.europa.eu/legal-content/EN/TXT/?uri=CELEX%3A52023AB0007&qid=1680615286943&home=ecb.

European Central Bank. *Progress on the investigation phase of a digital euro*. Third report, 2023. https://www.ecb.europa.eu/paym/digital_euro/investigation/governance/shared/files/ecb.degov230424_progress.en.pdf.

European Central Bank. *Report on a digital euro*. ECB, 2020. https://www.ecb.europa.eu/pub/pdf/other/Report_on_a_digital_euro~4d7268b458.en.pdf.

European Central Bank. *Study on the payment attitudes of consumers in the euro area (SPACE)*. ECB, December 2022. https://www.ecb.europa.eu/stats/ecb_surveys/space/html/ecb.spacereport202212~783ffdf46e.en.html.

European Commission. "Recommendation on the scope and effects of legal tender of euro banknotes and coins." *Official Journal of the European Union L. 083* (March 22, 2010). http://data.europa.eu/eli/reco/2010/191/oj/eng.

European Commission. *Annexes to the communication commission work programme 2023—A union standing firm and united (Com(2022) 548 Final)*. October 18, 2022. https://commission.europa.eu/system/files/2022-10/com_2022_548_1_annexe_en.pdf.

European Commission. *Call for evidence for an impact assessment—A digital euro for the EU*. Pub. L. No. Ref. Ares (2022) 2567612. European commission,

2022. https://ec.europa.eu/info/law/better-regulation/have-your-say/initiatives/13392-A-digital-euro-for-the-EU_en.

European Commission. *Targeted consultation on a digital euro.* Consultation document, April, 2022. https://finance.ec.europa.eu/system/files/2022-06/2022-digital-euro-consultation-document_en.pdf.

Freitag, Robert. "Euro as legal tender (and Banknotes)." In *The EU law of economic and monetary union*, edited by Fabian Amtenbrink and Christoph Herrmann. Oxford University Press, 2020. http://oxford.universitypressscholarship.com/view/10.1093/oso/9780198793748.001.0001/isbn-9780198793748-book-part-26.

G7 United Kingdom 2021. *Public policy principles for retail Central Bank Digital Currencies (CBDCs).* United Kingdom presidency, 2021. https://assets.publishing.service.gov.uk/government/uploads/system/uploads/attachment_data/file/1025235/G7_Public_Policy_Principles_for_Retail_CBDC_FINAL.pdf.

Grünewald, Seraina Neva, Corinne Zellweger-Gutknecht, and Benjamin Geva. "Digital euro and ECB powers." *Common Market Law Review* 58, no. 4 (2021), 1029–1055. https://papers.ssrn.com/sol3/papers.cfm?abstract_id=3807855.

Grünewald, Seraina. *A legal framework for the digital euro: An assessment of the ECB's first three progress reports.* Economic Governance and EMU Scrutiny Unit at the request of the ECONCommittee, May. European Parliament, 2023. https://www.europarl.europa.eu/RegData/etudes/IDAN/2023/741518/IPOL_IDA(2023)714518_EN.pdf.

Gógl, Anne-Sophie, Filippo Zatti, Erik Ahlborn, Cizar Bachir Brahim, Suleiman Barada, Lucia Suarez Barcia, Rosa Giovanna Barresi, et al. "Ahead of the digital euro—Public digital euro working Group recommendations." Digital euro working group, 2022. https://7869715.fs1.hubspotusercontent-na1.net/hubfs/7869715/New%20-%20Public%20DEA%20Working%20Group%20Paper.pdf.

Hofmann, Christian. "The changing concept of money: A threat to the monetary system or an opportunity for the financial sector?." *European Business Organization Law Review 21*, no. 1 (March 1, 2020): 37–68. https://doi.org/10.1007/s40804-020-00182-z.

Laguna de Paz, José Carlos. "Some implications of the new global digital economy for financial regulation and supervision." *Journal of Banking Regulation* (2022). https://doi.org/10.1057/s41261-022-00189-1.

Lastra, Rosa Maria, and Kern Alexander. "The ECB mandate: Perspectives on sustainability and solidarity." Study for the committee on economic and monetary affairs. European Parliament, June 2020.

Lo Schiavo, Gianni. *The role of financial stability in EU law and policy.* Wolters Kluwer, 2017.

Mooij, Annelieke. "A digital euro for everyone: Can the European system of Central Banks introduce general purpose CBDC as part of its economic mandate?," *Journal of Banking Regulation* 24, no. 1 (2023): 89–104.

Mourlon-Druol, Emmanuel. "History of an incomplete EMU." In *The EU law of economic and monetary union*, edited by Fabian Amtenbrink, Christoph Herrmann, and René Repasi. Oxford University Press, 2020. https://doi.org/10.1093/oso/9780198793748.003.0003.

Nabilou, Hossein. "Testing the waters of the Rubicon: The European Central Bank and Central Bank Digital Currencies." *Journal of Banking Regulation* 21, no. 4 (2020): 299–314. https://doi.org/10.1057/s41261-019-00112-1.

Panetta, Fabio. "Building on our strengths: The role of the public and private sectors in the digital euro ecosystem." *Introductory statement at the committee on economic and monetary affairs of the European parliament*, September 29. European Central Bank, 2022. https://www.ecb.europa.eu/press/key/date/2022/html/ecb.sp220929~91a3775a2a.en.html.

Panetta, Fabio. "The digital euro and the evolution of the financial system." *Introductory statement at the committee on economic and monetary affairs of the European parliament*, June 15. European Central Bank, 2022. https://www.ecb.europa.eu/press/key/date/2022/html/ecb.sp220615~0b859eb8bc.en.html.

Panetta, Fabio. "The digital euro: Our money wherever, whenever we need it." Introductory statement at the committee on economic and monetary affairs of the European parliament, January 23. European Central Bank, 2023. https://www.ecb.europa.eu/press/key/date/2023/html/ecb.sp230123~2f8271ed76.en.html.

Papapaschalis Panagiotis. "Retail Central Bank Digital Currency: A (legal) novelty?." In *ESCB Legal conference 2020 (11 September–2 November 2020) proceedings*. European Central Bank, 2021. https://www.ecb.europa.eu/pub/pdf/other/ecb.escblegalconferenceproceedings2020~4c11842967.en.pdf.

Petit, Christy Ann. "Chapter 16. Anti-Money laundering." In *Research handbook on EU law enforcement*, edited by Miroslava Scholten and Leander Stahler. Edward Elgar Publishing, 2023.

Petit, Christy Ann. "The ECB mandate—A comparative constitutional perspective." In *The New European Central Bank: Taking stock and looking ahead*, edited by Thomas Beukers, Diane Fromage, and Giorgio Monti. Oxford, New York: Oxford University Press, 2022.

Smoleńska, Agnieszka, and Thomas Beukers. "The ECB and financial stability." In *The New European Central Bank: Taking stock and looking ahead*, edited by Thomas Beukers, Diane Fromage, and Giorgio Monti, 105–35. Oxford, New York: Oxford University Press, 2022.

Spitzer, Kai Gereon and Loi Giacomo, "Digital euro. Reviewing the progress to date and some open questions." EGOV briefing PE 741.498. European Parliament, March 2023. https://www.europarl.europa.eu/RegData/etudes/BRIE/2023/741498/IPOL_BRI(2023)741498_EN.pdf.

Zellweger-Gutknecht, Corinne Benjamin Geva, and Seraina Neva Grünewald. "Digital euro, monetary objects, and price stability: A legal analysis." *Journal of Financial Regulation* 7, no. 2 (2021), 284–2318. https://doi.org/10.1093/jfr/fjab009.

PART III

Role in EU Payment System/ Demand—Missing Market

CHAPTER 4

The Digital Euro and the EU Framework for Payments

María Cecilia del Barrio Arleo

1 Introduction

June 2019 was a tipping point in the brief history of CBDCs: the announcement of (back then) Libra (subsequently Diem) triggered central banks' attention and concern towards the development of a digital version of fiat currency. What came next was an avalanche of academic and policy literature exploring features and design options that said CBDCs could take and a massive set-up of public initiatives across the world in order to accelerate a possible issuance of a digital currency.[1]

[1] According to the 2021 BIS survey on central bank digital currencies, out of a sample of 81 central banks across the globe, 90% is engaged in some form of CBDC work, see: Bank for International Settlements, "Gaining momentum—Results of the 2021 BIS survey on central bank digital currencies," BIS paper no. 125 (BIS, 2022), https://www.bis.org/publ/bppdf/bispap125.pdf.

M. C. del Barrio Arleo (✉)
European Banking Institute, Frankfurt, Germany
e-mail: cecilia.delbarrioarleo@ebi-europa.eu

© The Author(s), under exclusive license to Springer Nature Switzerland AG 2025

F. Annunziata et al. (eds.), *Central Bank Digital Currency*, EBI Studies in Banking and Capital Markets Law,
https://doi.org/10.1007/978-3-031-80957-6_4

However, the need for CBDC issuance was not automatically embraced in all jurisdictions. In fact, there was a short-lived "CBDC winter", characterised by criticisms towards the arguments in favour of digital fiat currencies, especially by some developed economies—both the United Kingdom and the US first reacted in a less than enthusiastic way by referring to CBDCs as being *a solution in search of a problem*.[2] However, the scepticism has not prevailed and both countries have moved on with their respective exploratory projects, regarding the possible issuance of a CBDC.[3]

Amidst the current uncertainties and speculation on possible CBDC timelines, design choices and integration with private sector initiatives, this chapter offers some points of attention and reflections to conceptualise the relationship between the digital euro and the European framework for payments. Contrary to other financial activities, such as banking which are (at least for the time being) better insulated from a technological blitzkrieg thanks to regulatory prerogatives, the field of payments is slightly different. New actors tend to use the provision of payment services as an entrance door to later on offering a broader set of financial services and eventually products.[4]

[2] For instance, the 2021 speech by Christopher Waller, Member of the Board of Governors of the Federal Reserve System, entitled "CBDC—A Solution in Search of a Problem?" (Christopher Waller, "CBDC—A solution in search of a problem?" *Speech at Washington DC, August 5*, Bank for International Settlements, 2021, https://www.bis.org/review/r210806a.htm) and the January 2022 report from the House of Lords Economic Affairs Committee with the same title (House of Lords—Economic Affairs Committee. *Central bank digital currencies: A solution in search of a problem?* 3rd Report of Session 2021–22, 2022. https://committees.parliament.uk/publications/8443/documents/85604/default).

[3] The Bank of England has published a digital pound consultation paper in February 2023, while the US also started to actively explore the technical possibilities for a US CBDC. See for instance the seminal paper by the Board of Governors of the Federal Reserve System, *Money and Payments: The U.S. Dollar in the Age of Digital Transformation* (Federal Reserve System, 2022), www.federalreserve.gov/publications/files/money-and-payments-20220120.pdf; Bank of England, "The digital pound: A new form of money for households and business?," Consultation paper (BoE, 2023), www.bankofengland.co.uk/-/media/boe/files/paper/2023/the-digital-pound-consultation-working-paper.pdf.

[4] The so-called BigTechs have penetrated the financial services domain via offering digital payments first. See for instance European Securities and Markets Authority, *Financial stability and investor protection: BigTech—implications for the financial sector*, Report on Trends, Risks and Vulnerabilities no. 1, 2020, https://www.esma.europa.eu/sites/default/files/trv_2020_1-bigtech_implications_for_the_financial_sector.pdf.

In response to the market dynamics recalled above, European regulators and policymakers started to advocate for the preservation of the role of central bank money in the new financial ecosystem. For instance, ECB Executive Board member, Panetta, claimed that the "*digitalisation of payments cannot be ignored by central banks [...]. Central banks cannot escape these transformations, nor should they underestimate the potential for far-reaching shifts that may occur*".[5] Such a response from public authorities is needed, in order to keep up with the pace of the ongoing developments; in fact, this is not about creating new roles or responsibilities, but instead, adapting institutions' mandates (i.e., in the case of the central bank the provision of fiat money) to the current circumstances, characterised by not just the provision of efficient payments instruments, but also new forms of money aside of commercial and central bank ones (euro stablecoins).

In order to provide some reflections on the digital euro and the European framework for payments, the chapter is structured as follows. Section 2 helps conceptualising the role of central banks and central banks' money in the payment system. Once the need for central bank action in the field of payments is identified, Sect. 3 turns to the complex legal ecosystem that is being developed around it and how the digital euro would need to organically fit in it to minimise unwanted consequences resulting from the overlap of initiatives. Sections 4 and 5 further focus on the specific features of the digital euro that concern the payment system based on the project decisions available at the time of writing the chapter, while Sect. 6 concludes.

2 A Primer on Central Banks' Role in the Payment System

Amongst the reasons that are brought forward to justify the issuance of a digital euro, the role of central banks in the payment system is of the outmost importance. However, in the light of the recent evolution of the payment system and the panoply of payment methods propelled by technological innovations, a healthy dose of scepticism seems inevitable: μήπως το παρακάτω italics.

[5] Fabio Panetta, "Central bank digital currencies: Defining the problems, designing the solutions", *Speech at US Monetary Policy Forum*, European Central Bank, 2022, https://www.ecb.europa.eu/press/key/date/2022/html/ecb.sp220218_1~938e881b13.en.html.

> If we could use the ECB's digital euro for payments, what is the benefit over and above today's existing means of payment? What is the benefit over credit cards? What is the benefit over Apple Pay or Google Pay solutions? Actually, it remains unclear.[6]

These doubts that emerge when comparing a still unclear central bank-backed digital euro with ever-convenient privately-fuelled means of payment are also statistically backed. In fact, the latest *Study on the payment attitudes of consumers in the euro area* (SPACE)[7] conducted by the ECB revealed that "cash [...] was used in 59% of transactions, down from 79% in 2016 and 72% in 2019 [and] in terms of value of payments, cards (46%) accounted for a higher share of transactions than cash payments (42%). This contrasts with 2016 and 2019, when the share of cash transactions was higher than the share of card transactions". The SPACE also shows the increase in the share of mobile apps payments and contactless card payments at the point of sale (in the latter, from 41% of all card payments in 2019 to 62% in 2022).

Such a state of affairs—a blossoming digital payment landscape, as opposed to a gradually gloomy outlook for cash—can make one wonder which is the role of central banks as public authorities in a field dominated by private initiatives. In order to address this issue and clarify why the issuance of a digital euro would eventually matter, it is useful to go back in time and review some basic concepts embedded in the functioning of the payment system. As Padoa-Schioppa observed, italics below??

> Long before central banks became responsible for monetary policy, they were the banks designated to issue banknotes: the means of payment protected by legal tender status. The origin of central banking lies precisely in this revolution in payment technology: from metal to paper, from commodity money with intrinsic value to fiduciary money.[8]

[6] Philipp Sandner and Jonas Gross, "The digital euro of the ECB: Do we need it?" *Digital euro association blog*, March 8, 2023, https://blog.digital-euro-association.de/the-digital-euro-of-the-ecb-do-we-need-it-article.

[7] European Central Bank, *Study on the payment attitudes of consumers in the euro area (SPACE)* (ECB, 2022), https://www.ecb.europa.eu/stats/ecb_surveys/space/html/index.en.html.

[8] Tommaso Padoa-Schioppa, "Shaping the payment system: A central bank's role," *Speech at bank of Korea's conference on payment systems in Seoul*, European Central Bank, 2004: 1, https://www.ecb.europa.eu/press/key/date/2004/html/sp040513_1.en.html.

It was precisely this need for a superior form of trust that is not circumscribed to the perimeter of the payer-payee relationship that paved the way for central banks' action.

2.1 *Retail and Large Value Payments: A Cursory Overview*

When it comes to the distinction between retail and wholesale payments, the difference lies in *who* are the parties to a specific transaction: the former refers to payments amongst individuals and firms, while the latter refers to "large value" payments made within the banking system. The aim of this section is to briefly explain central banks' approach to both retail and wholesale payments and how past reflections on the topic can shed light on the current discussion on the digital euro. It is interesting to note that casting doubts on central bank money and its utility in the context of emerging means of payments and the advent of a cashless society is not a new phenomenon:

> *What reasons exist for persevering with the use of the banknotes infrastructure despite the emergence of more "modern" means of payment? A good answer to this question was given to me by a colleague from the printing press of the Banca d'Italia, to whom I was talking about the advent of a cashless society. In his words, "despite all the advances in means of transport throughout the 20th century . . . the best way to move from one room of your house to another will always be to walk".*[9]

The analogy drawn between payment and transport systems introduced by former ECB Executive Board member—by which banknotes represent the ultimate walking trails that everyone needs to move from one room to the other—could not fully anticipate central banks' necessity to provide a non-physical version of said walking trails, thus partially replacing banknotes with a digital form of central bank money. In drawing lessons from the recent history of retail payments, a key aspect related to the design and distribution of a digital euro is the need for *intermediaries*. In fact, "the emergence of non-cash means of settlement is associated with that of payment intermediaries. [...]. Most non-cash payments will require the participation of [...] multiple payment intermediaries".[10] As

[9] Ibid., 2.

[10] Ibid., 3.

Sect. 4 and Sect. 5 below further elaborate, the role of intermediaries is a fundamental aspect that speaks, on the one hand, to the governance of the digital euro and the distribution of responsibilities between public and private sectors and on the other, to the incentives that the central bank provides to these actors in order to enter the CBDC game.

Central banks can be in fact the necessary *catalyst* to "foster this combination of technology and confidence, in particular, in reform processes" in which both current habits and cooperation between the parties are changing,[11] as it is the case nowadays with the issuance of CBDCs and emergence of stablecoins. What perhaps could not be anticipated back in the early 2000s was the fact that central banks were not necessarily sitting in the driver's seat, but have instead reacted due to technological developments that could potentially hamper monetary sovereignty, amidst the rise of private digital moneys. Padoa-Schioppa's reflection, however, was visionary enough to anticipate that "as the economy develops, the precise combination of cooperation, public action and competition will also evolve", thus highlighting the need to dynamically interpret the role and powers of the central bank as economic, societal and technological conditions change.

Different objectives in the retail and wholesale payment landscapes imply different roles and tasks allocation between central banks and intermediaries, respectively; the issuance of a digital euro should also mirror these different degrees of central banking intermediation. Retail payments are characterised by the need for strong competition in order to increase efficiency and provide consumers with a broader range of instruments. When it comes to wholesale payments (i.e., interbank payments settled in central bank money, being the central bank the only fully trusted third party between two banks), the role of central banks is different. In fact, the past decades have been characterised by an ever-increasing number and value of financial transactions with the accompanying technological innovation, which have triggered the need for more sophisticated tools to contain the systemic risk created by the payment system:

> *As a result of these developments, central banks undertook two paths of action. First, they upgraded their own systems to provide immediate finality; real-time gross settlement (RTGS) systems were created. Second, they defined standards to contain the risks inherent to net settlement systems. These two settlement*

[11] Ibid., 4.

> *modalities, netting and RTGS, have co-existed in many countries, thereby providing two parallel circuits for banks to settle their payments.*[12]

These settlement modalities, in turn, are based upon two different approaches to reduce systemic risk: (i) the adoption of rules requiring individual exposures to be capped; (ii) the creation of incentives for participants to actively manage their exposures. Fast-forward to our days, RTGS has become predominant and the reduction of "value and duration of payment exposures through the combined use of collateral and real-time settlement"[13] has been at the heart of central banks' systemic risk management tools in this field.

2.2 Role of Central Bank Money in the Payment System and Oversight

In order to further conceptualise the relationship between the digital euro and the EU framework for payments, it is worth considering the equilibrium maintained between the role of central bank and commercial bank money in the payment system. Leaving aside the retail and wholesale distinction made above, it is important to bear in mind two aspects pertaining to currencies. The first one relates to the central banks' role to preserve its *singleness* in the public interest, thus ensuring a unique value for commercial banks' liabilities. The second one is the simultaneous *substitutability* and *complementarity* between central and commercial bank money in the payment system: the former due to the interchangeable nature of the currency (epitomised by the nowadays less frequent *do you wish to pay by cash or card?*) and the latter due to the combined use and interactions between commercial and central bank monies along the payment cycle. The words below provide some high-level guidance regarding the digital euro design options and distribution models further elaborated in Sect. 4 and how these relate to the payment system:

> *There are three key policy decisions through which central banks preserve the composite of central and commercial bank money. It is largely up to central banks to decide, first, who may settle in central bank money, second, how to*

[12] Ibid., 5.

[13] Ibid., 7.

> *make it appealing to settle in central bank money, third, who should settle in central bank money.*[14]

One of the fundamental questions that the digital euro would need to address is precisely *who* or which entities can be involved in the distribution and settlement of the digital currency—and admittedly, with the emergence of stablecoins and in particular euro-denominated stablecoins, the panorama is slightly more complex than the one good old Padoa-Schioppa had back in 2004.

A last aspect to be considered when analysing central bank's involvement in the payment system is the *oversight* role. It is worth noting that, while the word "oversight" is currently popular and extended in the ECB parlance,[15] this was not the case in the early 2000s:

> *30 years ago most systems were owned and operated by the central bank. Central banks did not need oversight to affect their own system. Then, with increased liberalisation, many payment and settlement systems started to be provided by the private sector. The notion of oversight arises as central banks have the need to "keep an eye on" and affect the safety and efficiency of these new systems that it does not operate itself.*[16]

These words are more relevant than ever, if we consider that nowadays technology has enabled not just ubiquitous payment instruments, but the multiplication of "monies" as well. The responsibility "to promote the smooth operation of payment systems" is enshrined in Article 127(2) of the Treaty on the Functioning of the EU (TFEU) and Article 3.1 of the Statute of the ESCB and of the ECB. The levers that the central bank has to ensure the safety and efficiency of the payment system need to adapt and evolve to face the current challenges and the design choices embedded in the digital euro should go in tandem with the oversight objective (see Sect. 4 below). After having highlighted some fundamental

[14] Ibid., 8.

[15] If we consider the oversight mandate in the realm of payment systems and in the micro-prudential set-up as per the competences exercised by ECB banking supervision with regard to less significant institutions (LSIs), established in the Single Supervisory Mechanism Regulation.

[16] Padoa-Schioppa, "Shaping the payment system," 10.

aspect concerning the role of central banks role in the payment system—drawing on the recent euro area history—the next session zooms out in order to provide a broad-brush view of the current legal landscape, in which the digital euro would have to be introduced.

3 A Potentially Complex Legal Ecosystem

Before delving into specific features of the digital euro project, this section provides a broader perspective on the payment system and the ongoing initiatives, to complement the central banking view explained before. The aim is not to provide a detail account of each of the legal sources and initiatives, but simply to highlight relationships and possible overlaps between them. The digital euro, if/when adopted, would have to smoothly fit within this broader regulatory ecosystem, in order not to backfire and allow for an industry-wide participation, which in its turn would guarantee its adoption by the public.

The chart below depicts the current legal ecosystem in the field of payments—including adopted, under review and proposed legislation—but it does not consider foundational texts (i.e., treaties and relevant protocols) establishing competences in the field of payments.[17] For the sake of simplicity, national frameworks (mostly private law) have been considered as a single source. However, it has to be recalled that the issuance of a retail digital euro needs to consider, not only the legal relationship between the central bank and the intermediaries (further explored in Sect. 4 below), but also end users' rights and the ways in which Member States' legal frameworks regulate transfers.[18] To illustrate the point, it is worth considering that PSD2 "does not provide for

[17] Therefore, it considers neither the legal basis for the issuance of the digital euro nor the legal basis to grant legal tender, which have been considered in the European Commission's legislative proposal on the establishment of the digital euro (COM(2023) 369 final). Might be eventually clarified in the European Commission's upcoming legislative proposal setting out the principles for a digital euro.

[18] Aurelia Philine Birne et al., "Principles for the transfer of retail CBDC," *Recht digital*, December 15, 2022: 13, https://papers.ssrn.com/sol3/papers.cfm?abstract_id=4303955. The authors conclude their national law-focused analysis by explaining that "in order to be able to issue a digital currency functionally close to existing cash, [retail] CBDC units have to be value-based. As in the case of cash, the entitlement to a specific unit is not a prerequisite to a successful transfer. The identity of the payer is irrelevant to the validity of the transfer transaction. Instead, as with cash, the verification process should focus on the authenticity of the monetary unit itself."

a comprehensive and self-contained regulation of retail payments in the EU, but regulates 'only' the services for the handling of funds [...]. PSD2 is applied in parallel to other EU and national laws" amongst which (i) civil law provisions on monetary obligations; (ii) consumer rights' provisions on the application of fees and charges for payment services; and (iii) national implementation of the Payment Account Directive (Fig. 1).[19]

The aim of the chart is not to visually overwhelm the reader—although it probably does—but, instead, raise awareness of the increasing complexity of the current and upcoming legal framework. While it is true that the speed of technological developments applied to the financial sector has prompted a much-needed regulatory response, the legislator has not necessarily adopted a holistic approach in the development of future-proof payments regulation. Instead, the chosen legislative approach has been that of (i) drafting regulation *ex nihilo* (as it has been the case with MiCAR, DLT and DORA) or (ii) addressing deficiencies of the existing regulation on a more ad hoc basis, as it is currently the case of PSD2. While the reasons for not having brought together different initiatives in a holistic manner can be understood—as it would imply a demanding intellectual work to develop less conventional, but future-proof regulatory tools—the current approach can reveal itself as costly in the near future.

As a matter of fact, industry participants had the chance to convey some of their concerns in the recent public consultations carried out by the European Commission in the field of payments (i.e., targeted consultation on a digital euro, PSD2 review and instant payments). For instance, the European Banking federation, when providing its feedback on the digital euro consultation, expressed that the industry needed "clarity on the different policy initiatives and priorities set by the authorities, while it is not clear how the initiatives on instant payments and digital euro would go together and not overlap".[20]

[19] Costanza Iacomini and Simone Mezzacapo, "The transposition of the PSD2 in Italy: Policies and rules," in *The Payment Services Directive II: A commentary*, ed. Gabriella Gimigliano and Marta Božina Beroš (Cheltenham, Northampton: Edward Elgar Publishing Limited, 2021), 389.

[20] European Banking Federation, *EBF response to the European commission's targeted consultation on a digital euro* (EBF, 2022), 15, www.ebf.eu/wp-content/uploads/2022/06/FINAL-EBF-Response-to-EC-Consultation-on-a-Digital-Euro.pdf.

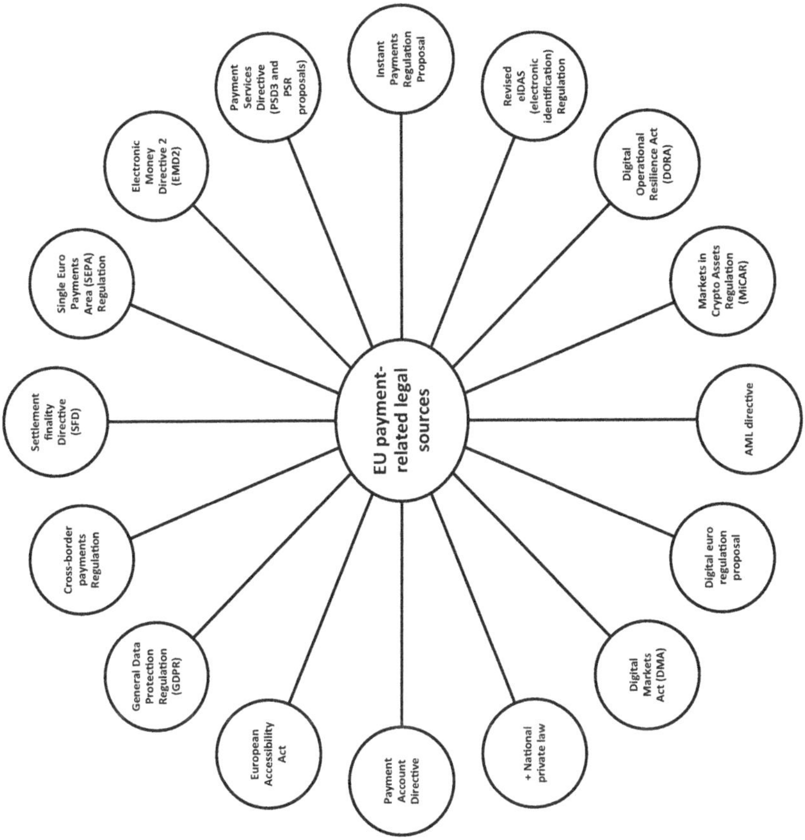

Fig. 1 Chart-author's elaboration (*Source* own elaboration)

Other market participants have more vehemently highlighted costs and undesirable consequences, when providing comments, with regard to the instant payments' proposal:

> *Legally mandating the almost exclusive use of instant credit transfers is a deep intervention into the dynamics of the market and would lead to greater costs for both banks and customers, with no certainty of providing any benefits whatsoever by doing so.*[21]

Aside of industry's complaints, it is apparent that the multiple legislative initiatives can raise not only project-specific, but also regulatory uncertainty. As a matter of fact, digital euro-related literature discusses in detail primary sources of EU law, as far as its issuance is concerned; however, the interaction between the digital euro framework and secondary EU law sources needs to be considered as well. Such normative dispersion and inflation could be attributed to the lack of an encompassing strategy, with regard to the legislative treatment of digitalisation at the EU level. Digitalisation and its transversal impact on the financial sector pose in fact a series of difficult questions at both the regulatory and supervisory levels.

To conclude, it is worth recalling that the legal harmonisation process that has so far characterised the European framework for payments could be compromised if the issues highlighted above are not properly coordinated. The interaction between different initiatives (i.e., digital euro, instant payments and adjustments to the payment services framework), as well as the legislative tools, need to be organically streamlined in order to support the development of a pan-European payment solution. The next section delves into the fundamental digital euro design options and how they could be deployed vis-à-vis the European framework for payments.

[21] German Banking Industry Committee, *Comments on the European Commission's proposal for a regulation on instant credit transfers COM (2022) 546 final* (GBIC, 2022), https://die-dk.de/en/topics/article/comments-on-the-european-commissions-proposal-for-a-regulation-on-instant-credit-transfers-com2022-546-final/.

4 Digital Euro Features and Their Relationship with the Payment System

The chapter has so far provided a framework to conceptualise the digital euro with regard to (i) central banks' role in the payment system and (ii) other payment-related initiatives at the EU level. This section analyses the fundamental digital euro design choices[22] and how they could be possibly incorporated in the framework for payments. It is important to clarify that this section does not cover the entire digital euro features agreed upon so far as a matter of fact some of these foundational design options are discussed elsewhere in this volume (e.g., privacy). At the time of writing this chapter, the public information available is high level when it comes to the actual implementation of the digital euro given that the Eurosystem is still at an early prototype phase; however, some foundational principles can be drawn from the first to fourth report on the "Progress on the investigation phase of a digital euro", published in September and December 2022, April 2023 and July 2023, respectively.[23] It should be also noted that on 18 October 2023, the ECB issued a new report entitled "A stocktake on the digital euro", right after the completion of the investigation phase.[24]

The so-called design of the digital euro comprises both (i) the selection of legal basis (and eventually the identification of legislative amendments

[22] These considerations are based on the publicly available information released until June 15, 2023.

[23] European Central Bank, *Progress on the investigation phase of a digital euro,* First report (ECB, 2022), https://www.ecb.europa.eu/paym/digital_euro/investigation/governance/shared/files/ecb.degov220929.en.pdf; European Central Bank, *Progress on the investigation phase of a digital euro,* Second report (ECB, 2022), https://www.ecb.europa.eu/paym/digital_euro/investigation/governance/shared/files/ecb.degov221221_Progress.en.pdf; European Central Bank, *Progress on the investigation phase of a digital euro,* Third report (ECB, 2023), www.ecb.europa.eu/paym/digital_euro/investigation/governance/shared/files/ecb.degov230424_progress.en.pdf.

[24] European Central Bank: "A stocktake on the digital euro—summary report on the investigation phase and outlook on the next phase" (October 2023) www.ecb.europa.eu/paym/digital_euro/investigation/governance/shared/files/dedocs/ecb.dedocs.231018.en.pdf; European Central Bank, "Progress on the investigation phase of a digital euro—fourth report," (July 2023), www.ecb.europa.eu/paym/digital_euro/investigation/governance/shared/files/ecb.degov230713-fourth-progress-report-digital-euro-investigation-phase.en.pdf?704b0eee4c20eee4dbe4970f5091a96a.

that might be needed in order to advance in the project) and (ii) the delineation of a business model for the different subjects that are part of the digital euro ecosystem. The first report identified a set of *foundational design options*, including a transfer mechanism to validate transaction, privacy (full anonymity explicitly excluded) and tools to control the amount of digital euro in circulation (to tackle potential financial stability concerns). Regarding the degree to which the digital euro could replicate cash-like features, the design choices already taken provide a flavour of what to expect. In fact, the digital euro is meant to complement, but *not* substitute cash—as a matter of fact, the former could never substitute the latter, given the intrinsically different business models and design embedded in the physical and digital central bank currencies, respectively.

The second report distinguished between *design options* and *distribution model*. This second round of design options is the key to better understanding how cooperation between the public and private sectors would unfold within a dynamic payments landscape. These more specific design options concern: (i) the role of intermediaries (see summarising table below)[25]; (ii) the settlement model, i.e., the "completion of a payment transaction with the aim of irrevocably discharging all payment obligations between a payer and payee through the transfer of funds[26]"; and (iii) funding and defunding (respectively, the possibility to convert private/commercial money into digital euro and vice versa, the conversion of digital euro into cash or private money—operations which epitomise the complementarity or interchangeable nature of currency as referred to in Sect. 2). The second and third reports further elaborate on the distribution model, which is expected to be based on a digital euro scheme.[27] The

[25] The foundational digital euro report contains some relevant guidance: "*contrary to the elements of the design and issuance of a digital euro (features such as remuneration, anonymity, infrastructure, issuance model, etc.), which cannot be outsourced, practical arrangements with no impact on the central bank's balance sheet (for example storage of units, handling of payments on behalf of the public, etc.) could, in principle, be outsourced, subject to strict Eurosystem supervision*" (European Central Bank, *Report on a digital euro* (ECB, 2020), 25).

[26] ECB, *Progress*, second report, 6.

[27] The ECB second report provides additional details on alternative distribution models, weighting pros and cons (Ibid., 9): "*a model based on a digital euro scheme is seen as the most appropriate for the initial roll-out of the digital euro. For instance, with an issuance model, the Eurosystem would only be responsible for issuing the digital money, without providing the settlement infrastructure or intervening in distribution. Alternatively, in an*

aim of said scheme is "to establish a set of common rules, standards and procedures that supervised intermediaries would need to adhere in order to distribute the digital euro"[28] to guarantee a desirable balance between the roles and responsibilities of the Eurosystem and supervised intermediaries as illustrated in the table below. According to the third report,[29] the different types of payment service providers (PSPs), as per the criteria set in PSD2, should be authorised to provide digital euro services in accordance with the services they are currently licensed to provide under PSD2 (Fig. 2).

The second report pinpoints two crucial and interrelated aspects that pertain to the framework for payments: the role of supervised intermediaries and the delimitation of roles and responsibilities between private and public actors, as well as the development of a digital euro scheme. As a matter of fact, the Settlement Finality Directive (SFD) foresees that direct participation in a designated payment system is only allowed for credit institutions, investment firms and other financial market infrastructures listed in the SFD. On the contrary, e-money institutions and payment institutions (as defined in Article 4(4) PDS2) are not allowed as direct participants in a designated SFD system.[30] In this regard, one of the aspects that the digital euro scheme would need to consider is whether the settlement of digital euro requires an SFD-designated system, given that currently e-money and payment institutions are only connected to designated payment systems in an indirect manner (e.g., via a credit institution).

If the settlement of digital euro were to also encompass other actors beyond SFD participants, the oversight perimeter with regard to the payment system could possibly broaden. It should be reminded that the

open access model, the Eurosystem would only provide the settlement infrastructure and set access rules; every entity that fulfilled these rules could then use the infrastructure in their own way. [. . .] An alternative distribution model could be imagined in which the Eurosystem would provide the full payment product in an end-to-end solution. While this model would ensure a homogenous end user experience and widespread distribution, it would reduce the role of intermediaries and could pose challenges in terms of meeting end user demands and keeping up with innovation."

[28] Ibid., 10.

[29] ECB, *Progress*, third report.

[30] Pereira Pinto Lara Sofia, "Digital Euro Project," Presentation, ESCB Legal Counsels Seminar (Frankfurt am Main: November 21, 2022).

	Intermediaries	Eurosystem
User management	Management of digital euro accounts/wallets' Provision and management of payment instruments	Management of supervised intermediaries
Transaction management	Transaction initiation Authentication Validation Post-settlement	Settlement Post-settlement
Liquidity management	Funding and defunding	Issuance and redemption

Fig. 2 Proposed roles of intermediaries and Eurosystem (*Source* Adapted from ECB, "Progress on the investigation phase of a digital euro—second report" [December 2022], 6)

Eurosystem payment oversight function covers both (i) *payment systems*—which comprise, in turn, systemically important payment systems (SIPS) and non-systemically important payment systems (non-SIPS)—and (ii) *payment instruments*, *schemes* and *arrangements*. In fact, the former encompasses the latter, as per the definition included in Article 2(1) of the SIPS Regulation[31]:

> *'payment system' means a formal arrangement between three or more participants [...] with common rules and standardised arrangements for the execution of transfer orders between the participants.*

In this sense, one of the most important developments in the payments oversight arena relates to the Eurosystem's framework for electronic payment instruments, schemes and arrangements (so-called PISA), approved by the ECB's Governing Council in November 2021. As the name indicates, it covers all three elements of the payment system: (i) electronic *payment instruments*, "which allow the transfer of value or the discharge of payment obligations between end users [...]; (ii) *schemes* defining standardised procedures for such electronic payment instruments and (iii) *arrangements* providing functionalities supporting the use of electronic payment instruments, as well as the services of payment service providers".[32]

Technological developments have triggered the need to review prior oversight provisions to include *all* electronic payment instruments that serve as value transfers between end users. Such transfers comprise not just euro funds as per the definition provided in PSD2,[33] but also 'representations of value backed by claims or assets denominated in euro or

[31] European Central Bank, "Regulation of the European Central Bank (EU) No 795/2014 of 3 July 2014 on oversight requirements for systemically important payment systems (ECB/2014/28)," *Official Journal of the EU: L 217, 23.7.2014* (ECB, 2014): 16.

[32] European Central Bank, *Eurosystem oversight framework for electronic payment instruments, schemes and arrangements* (ECB, 2021), 2, https://www.ecb.europa.eu/paym/pdf/consultations/ecb.PISApublicconsultation202111_1.en.pdf. It should be noted that the European Commission's proposal COM(2023)366 final, popularly referred to as "PSD3", has included an amended definition of "funds" in its article 2(23), according to which "funds" mean central bank money issued for retail use, scriptural money and electronic money.

[33] According to Article 4(25) PSD2, funds mean banknotes and coins, scriptural money or electronic money as defined in point (2) of Article 2 of EMD2.

redeemable in euro; or other digital assets that are accepted under the rules of a scheme for payment purposes'. This framework complements the activities covered by PSD2 by capturing those actors or entities who might not qualify as payment service providers but whose activities nevertheless fall within the remit of the Eurosystem oversight of payment systems or schemes.

The PISA framework is an attempt to take into account the increasing complexity of the payment ecosystem in the light of the proliferation of privately issued payment instruments, such as stablecoins; it can be furthermore prove relevant vis-à-vis the potential development of a digital euro scheme. As highlighted by the foundational report on the digital euro, "although central bank liabilities are not subject to regulation and oversight, in issuing the digital euro, the Eurosystem should still aim at complying with regulatory standards, including in the area of payments.[34]" Depending on the task allocation between digital euro issuance by the Eurosystem and its distribution by supervised intermediaries, novel schemes and business models can emerge. Therefore, with a view to maintain future-proof oversight standards, it would be desirable to deploy, in the course of the remainder of the investigation phase, a regulatory-sandbox approach in order to provide intermediaries safe spaces to fail.

5 Further Considerations on the Digital Euro and PSD2

As anticipated, one point of contact between a digital euro scheme and the PSD2 is represented by the distribution tasks performed by intermediaries who might fall within the Eurosystem's oversight perimeter, most importantly payment service providers (PSPs). The scope of PSD2 is represented electronic payments other than cash.[35] As a result, the digital euro is left in a possible limbo—being a digital, but cash-like means of payment. Furthermore, the fact that PSD2—as its acronym indicates—is a directive has left some areas in which Member States' implementation

[34] ECB, *Report on a digital euro*, 20.

[35] "*The Directive applies to payment services in the European Union. The Directive focuses on electronic payments, which are more cost-efficient than cash and which also stimulate consumption and economic growth*", see European Commission, Web site, https://ec.europa.eu/commission/presscorner/detail/fr/MEMO_15_5793.

varies. For instance, contractual remedies, in case PSPs do not fulfil information requirements, the legal status of monetary obligations[36] and the cross-border alternative dispute resolution methods, all differ across jurisdictions. These differences in PSD2 implementation at the national level could be problematic if the digital euro project is not accompanied by comparable legal tools amongst euro area Member States. It is precisely in this context that the European Commission has issued, on the occasion of the digital euro regulation proposal, a proposal for a directive on payment services and electronic money services in the internal market amending the Settlement Finality Directive, and repealing PSD2 and the Electronic Money Directive (Add footnote: COM (2023) 366 final, also referred to as "PSD3". The European Commission simultaneously issued a proposal for a regulation on payment services in the internal market, COM (2023) 367 final, also referred to as "PSR"). While this chapter does not focus on said directive proposal—also because it does not directly concern digital euro issues—it is worth noting that some of the key aims of the initiative were to overcome differences in PSD2 implementation across Member States and reinforce the level playing field between banks and non-banks' PSPs. It is to be seen how PSD3's harmonisation efforts could, in its turn, bring about innovation and further competition amongst PSPs in order to provide a more efficient digital euro distribution. Furthermore, one of the main changes introduced by PDS2 has been the qualification of Payment Initiation Services (PISs) and Account Information Services (AISs), as new regulated payment services; it is to be seen if/how these actors can be considered within the digital euro scheme.

When it comes to PSPs' role and their interaction with the digital euro scheme, Chapter IV of the digital euro regulation proposal on "Distribution" cannot be overlooked. This chapter consists of 2 articles only—13 and 14—but contains key aspects related to (i) the recipients of the digital euro payment services and (ii) the activities that shall be enabled by PSPs with regard to digital euro access. As the October 2023 stocktake on the digital euro report also makes clear, the distribution via PSPs is as fundamental and vital to the digital euro life as its very issuance. Section 3 of said report contains a detailed description of the roles and activities allocated to PSPs, and delineates the supporting services which shall be provided by the Eurosystem—reinforcing once again, the idea that

[36] As also explained in Aurelia Philine Birne et al., "Principles for the transfer of retail CBDC."

a successful digital euro is mutually dependent on the fluid and fruitful collaboration between the public and private sectors.

To sum up, this section has zoomed in on specific features of the design and emerging business model for the participants in the digital euro ecosystem. The development of a flexible digital euro scheme could provide a way forward to ensure, on the one hand, the necessary dose of freedom to market participants and on the other, provide a regulatory anchor in order to contribute to the integration of payments across the euro area and the legal harmonisation.

6 Conclusions and Way Forward

As stated in the introduction, June 2019 marked the before and after in the life of CBDCs and the public debate around them. It is interesting to note that a monthly report issued by Deutsche Bundesbank precisely in June 2019 entitled *Payment services in transition: instant payments, PSD2 and new competitors*, contained no intellectual trace whatsoever of the possibility to issue a central bank digital currency:

> *A new European payment procedure could mean real European alternatives for payers and payees. Such a procedure would integrate existing national payment solutions and be based, perhaps initially, on an existing infrastructure before migrating to a thoroughly modernised real—time infrastructure. The procedure would also cater for all possible payment scenarios: online, offline, P2P and mobile payments [. . .].*
> *To ensure that an efficient, secure and competitive European payments market can continue to develop, it is essential to clarify when firms that have so far thought of themselves as technical service providers need to be subject to greater oversight and brought into the scope of supervision.*

The report alludes to the challenges faced by European PSPs to create an "effective pan-European payment solution", in order to compete with global actors, but contains no hints on the development of a digital currency. What came next is history.

As this chapter highlighted, one of the key aspects to consider when analysing the digital euro vis-à-vis the payment system relates to the dynamics between the public and private sectors. The role (and relevance) of intermediaries in the distribution and settlement of the digital euro stresses the interdependencies between public and private actors. While it is fair to say that the central bank has made use of these synergies with the private sector via outsourcing, procurements and other cooperation arrangements on several occasions, the issue is slightly different, in the case of the digital euro, as it is precisely the central bank's "raw material" and core function.

The present chapter has also raised concerns, with regard to the regulatory approach adopted in the field of payments; the following paragraph summarises the critical aspects:

> *if the EU is going to continue to be market-leading and remain at the forefront of the regulatory framework for payment services and Open Finance then the focus of future legislation needs to address more than the deficits of PSD2 and bring together, in a holistic approach the vision of the Retail Payment Strategy, the Digital Finance Strategy and the overarching EU data strategy.*[37]

The criticism above is not just related to the claims raised by bank associations—mostly lack of clarity from the different projects and overlapping regulatory initiatives and potentially higher compliance costs. The question is much deeper and it is linked to the future-proof regulation referred to above. This concept of future-proof regulation, however, can be fuzzy and difficult to implement in practice. *To what extent can regulation be innovative?* In spite of the intellectual and policy challenges, there are two aspects that can provide a high-level guidance. First, piling up proposals and ad hoc legislation can backfire, as the coherence of the system is easily compromised. The digital domain does not follow a traditional institution or activity-based rationale, upon which regulation is meant to be enforced. Digitalisation is affecting different regulatory frameworks in a transversal way, thus rendering regulators and supervisors' tasks more complicated. Second, future-proof regulation can be developed from trial and error, from regulatory sandboxes that allow for the possibility to learn from mistakes in a more controlled way. Such a regulatory tool is not just a nice-to-have: if the public and private sectors' cooperation is to be taken seriously, then public authorities should be granted a certain degree of failure tolerance—especially in the digital euro and payments domain, characterised by legal uncertainty and high technological dynamism.

[37] Nilixa Devlukia, "PSD 1, 2, 3—we are out of the starting blocks with a marathon ahead," *The Paypers blogpost*, July 27, 2022, https://thepaypers.com/expert-opinion/psd-1-2-3-we-are-out-of-the-starting-blocks-with-a-marathon-ahead--1257721.

References

Bank for International Settlements. *Gaining momentum—results of the 2021 BIS survey on central bank digital currencies.* Paper no. 125, BIS, 2022. https://www.bis.org/publ/bppdf/bispap125.pdf.

Bank of England. *The digital pound: A new form of money for households and business?* Consultation Paper, February. BoE, 2023. https://www.bankofengland.co.uk/-/media/boe/files/paper/2023/the-digital-pound-consultation-working-paper.pdf.

Birne, Aurelia Philine, Christian Sillaber and Mirjam Eggen. "Principles for the transfer of retail CBDC." Recht Digital, December 15, 2022, 237–246. https://papers.ssrn.com/sol3/papers.cfm?abstract_id=4303955.

Board of Governors of the Federal Reserve System. *Money and payments: The U.S. dollar in the age of digital transformation.* Federal Reserve System, 2022. https://www.federalreserve.gov/publications/files/money-and-payments-20220120.pdf.

Carstens, Agustín. "Innovation and the future of the monetary system." *Keynote speech at the monetary authority of Singapore*, February 22. Singapore: BIS, 2023. https://www.bis.org/speeches/sp230222.htm (Accessed February 23, 2023).

Chorzempa, Martin. "How are central bank digital currencies different from other payment methods?" Peterson Institute for International Economics. April 21, 2021. https://www.piie.com/research/piie-charts/how-are-central-bank-digital-currencies-different-other-payment-methods (Accessed January 15, 2023).

Chorzempa, Martin. "Testimony before the US-China economic and security review commission." Panel 4: China's pursuit of leadership in digital currency, April 15, 2021. https://www.uscc.gov/sites/default/files/2021-04/Martin_Chorzempa_Testimony.pdf (Accessed January 15, 2023).

Deutsche Bundesbank. *Payment services in transition: Instant payments, PSD2 and new competitors.* Monthly report no. 51, June. Deutsche Bundesbank, 2019. https://www.bundesbank.de/resource/blob/800768/6fb2ab8dc1e6ce4a448a6f3271466c9a/mL/2019-06-zahlungsdienste-data.pdf.

Devlukia, Nilixa. "PSD 1, 2, 3—we are out of the starting blocks with a marathon ahead." *The Paypers blogpost*, July 27, 2022. https://thepaypers.com/expert-opinion/psd-1-2-3-we-are-out-of-the-starting-blocks-with-a-marathon-ahead--1257721.

European Banking Federation. *EBF response to the European commission's targeted consultation on a digital euro.* Consultation Paper, June 16. EBF, 2022. https://www.ebf.eu/wp-content/uploads/2022/06/FINAL-EBF-Response-to-EC-Consultation-on-a-Digital-Euro.pdf.

European Central Bank. "Opinion on a proposal for a regulation amending regulations (EU) No 260/2012 and (EU) 2021/1230 as regards instant credit transfers in euro." *Official Journal of the European Union (CON/2023/4) (2023/C 106/02)*, February 1, 2023. https://eur-lex.europa.eu/legal-content/EN/TXT/PDF/?uri=CELEX:52023AB0004.

European Central Bank. "Regulation of the European central bank (EU) No 795/2014 of 3 July 2014 on oversight requirements for systemically important payment systems (ECB/2014/28)." *Official Journal of the EU: L 217/16, 23/7/2014* (July 23, 2014). https://www.ecb.europa.eu/pub/pdf/other/ECB_Regulation_on_the_oversight_requirements_for_systemically_important_payment_systems.pdf?60670145e6f5d19765336f9658b05a9f.

European Central Bank. *Eurosystem oversight framework for electronic payment instruments, schemes and arrangements*. ECB, 2021. https://www.ecb.europa.eu/paym/pdf/consultations/ecb.PISApublicconsultation202111_1.en.pdf.

European Central Bank. *Progress on the investigation phase of a digital euro*. First report, 2022. https://www.ecb.europa.eu/paym/digital_euro/investigation/governance/shared/files/ecb.degov220929.en.pdf.

European Central Bank. *Progress on the investigation phase of a digital euro*. Second report, 2022. https://www.ecb.europa.eu/paym/digital_euro/investigation/governance/shared/files/ecb.degov220929.en.pdf.

European Central Bank. *Progress on the investigation phase of a digital euro*. Third report, 2023. https://www.ecb.europa.eu/paym/digital_euro/investigation/governance/shared/files/ecb.degov230424_progress.en.pdf.

European Central Bank. *Report on a digital euro*. ECB, 2020. https://www.ecb.europa.eu/pub/pdf/other/Report_on_a_digital_euro~4d7268b458.en.pdf.

European Central Bank. *Study on the payment attitudes of consumers in the euro area (SPACE)*. ECB, December 2022. https://www.ecb.europa.eu/stats/ecb_surveys/space/html/ecb.spacereport202212~783ffdf46e.en.html.

European Commission. *Proposal for a regulation of the European parliament and of the council amending regulation (EU) No 260/2012 and EU 2021/1230 as regards instant credit transfers in euro*. Proposal COM (2022) 546 final [2022/0341 (COD)], October. Brussels: European Commission, 2022. https://eur-lex.europa.eu/legal-content/EN/TXT/?uri=CELEX%3A52022PC0546.

European Securities and Markets Authority. *Financial stability and investor protection: BigTech—implications for the financial sector*. Report on Trends, Risks and Vulnerabilities no. 1, 2020. https://www.esma.europa.eu/sites/default/files/trv_2020_1-bigtech_implications_for_the_financial_sector.pdf.

German Banking Industry Committee. *Comments on the European commission's proposal for a regulation on instant credit transfers COM (2022) 546 final*. GBIC, 2022. https://die-dk.de/en/topics/article/comments-on-the-european-commissions-proposal-for-a-regulation-on-instant-credit-transfers-com-2022-546-final/.

House of Lords—Economic Affairs Committee. *Central bank digital currencies: A solution in search of a problem?* 3rd Report of Session 2021–22, 2022. https://committees.parliament.uk/publications/8443/documents/85604/defaul.

Iacomini, Costanza, and Simone Mezzacapo. "The transposition of the PSD2 in Italy: Policies and rules." In *The Payment Services Directive II*, edited by Gabriella Gimigliano and Marta Božina Beroš, pp. 386–405. Cheltenham, Northampton: Edward Elgar Publishing, 2021.

Khiaonarong, Tanai and David Humphrey. "Instant payments: Regulatory innovation and payment substitution across countries," Working Paper no. 22/228, International Monetary Fund, 2022. https://www.imf.org/en/Publications/WP/Issues/2022/11/18/Instant-Payments-Regulatory-Innovation-and-Payment-Substitution-Across-Countries-524032.

Padoa-Schioppa, Tommaso. "Shaping the payment system: A central bank's role." *Speech at bank of Korea's conference on payment systems in Seoul, May 13*. European Central Bank, 2004. https://www.ecb.europa.eu/press/key/date/2004/html/sp040513_1.en.html.

Panetta, Fabio. "Central bank digital currencies: Defining the problems, designing the solutions", *Speech at US Monetary Policy Forum in New York, February 18*. European Central Bank, 2022. https://www.ecb.europa.eu/press/key/date/2022/html/ecb.sp220218_1~938e881b13.en.html.

Pereira Pinto, Lara Sofia. "Digital euro project." Presentation, ESCB Legal counsels seminar, Frankfurt am Main, November 21–23, 2022 (unpublished).

Petrova, Savelina. "The new target framework: Presentation." ESCB Legal counsels seminar, Frankfurt am Main, November 21–23, 2022 (unpublished).

Sandner, Philipp and Jonas Gross. "The digital euro of the ECB: Do we need it?" *Digital euro association blog*, March 8, 2023. https://blog.digital-euro-association.de/the-digital-euro-of-the-ecb-do-we-need-it-article.

Tirole, Jean. "Digital payments and ecosystems." Keynote address, big techs in finance—implications for public policy, February, Basel, 2023. https://www.youtube.com/watch?v=-WVwrmU0v6A&t=13s.

Urbinati, Emanuele, Alessia Belsito, Daniele Cani, Angela Caporrini, Marco Capotosto, Simone Folino, Giuseppe Galano et al. *A digital euro: A contribution to the discussion on technical design choices*. Report no. 10, Bank of Italy, 2021. https://www.ecb.europa.eu/paym/digital_euro/investigation/profuse/shared/files/deexp/ecb.deexp211011.en.pdf.

Waller, Christopher J. "CBDC—A solution in search of a problem?" *Speech at Washington DC, August 5*. Bank for International Settlements, 2021. https://www.bis.org/review/r210806a.htm

CHAPTER 5

The Demand for CBDC in the Perspective of Existing (Retail) Payment Systems

Panagiotis N. Politsidis

1 Introduction

The prospective digital euro is a CBDC that would be accessible to all European citizens and firms as a complement to cash. In this regard, it purports to serve as a means for fostering the digitalisation of euro area payment systems, while addressing the payment needs and preferences of the public. This chapter provides an overview of the existing retail payments landscape in the euro area and discusses the issues arising from the potential introduction of the digital euro.

P. N. Politsidis (✉)
Audencia Business School, Nantes, Paris, France
e-mail: ppolitsidis@audencia.com; panagiotis.politsidis@ebi-europa.eu

European Banking Institute, Frankfurt, Germany

© The Author(s), under exclusive license to Springer Nature Switzerland AG 2025

F. Annunziata et al. (eds.), *Central Bank Digital Currency*, EBI Studies in Banking and Capital Markets Law,
https://doi.org/10.1007/978-3-031-80957-6_5

1.1 *Payment Methods of European Consumers*

Euro area consumers' self-reported preferences suggest a shift towards cashless payment instruments. According to a 2019 survey[1] from the ECB (see Fig. 1), approximately 49% of the respondents stated their preference for card usage or other cashless payment instruments (up from 43% in the 2016 survey[2]), while 27% expressed their preference for cash (down from 32% in the 2016 survey); the remaining 24% of the respondents stated that they were indifferent between the two payment methods. Finally, 55% of the respondents stated that it is important or very important for them to still have the option to pay with cash in the future.

Notably, consumers' actual payment behaviour differs from their self-reported preferences. Physical form of currency (coins and banknotes) is still the dominant means of payment in the euro area. Approximately 73% of the volume of physical point of sale (POS) and P2P transactions are carried out using cash as a payment instrument, while 27% are using non-cash payment instruments (card transactions).These estimates show a slight decrease in the use of cash from the previous survey in 2016, where cash usage comprised 79% of the overall number of transactions and card usage 19%. Taken together, these estimates suggest that euro area citizens have a preference for using cashless payment instruments, which stands in contrast with the actual high usage of cash (albeit decreasing) reported in the surveys.

The recent COVID-19 pandemic appears to have reinforced these preferences for some euro area consumers. Specifically, the results of a separate 2020 survey on the impact of the pandemic on cash trends in all euro area countries showed that 40% of the respondents replied that they have used less cash since the beginning of the pandemic.[3] Moreover, almost 90%

[1] The "Study on the Payment Attitudes of consumers in the euro area (SPACE)" was launched by the ECB in 2019 to investigate the payment behaviour of euro area citizens: European Central Bank, *Study on the payment attitudes of consumers in the euro area (SPACE)* (ECB, 2022), https://www.ecb.europa.eu/stats/ecb_surveys/space/html/ecb.spacereport202212~783ffdf46e.en.html).

[2] The "survey on the use of cash by households (SUCH)" analysed the payment behaviour of consumers in all 19-euro area countries at POS and P2P based on a survey consisting of a payment diary and a questionnaire: Henk Esselink and Lola Hernández, "The use of cash by households in the euro area" Occasional Paper 201 (ECB, 2017), https://www.ecb.europa.eu/pub/pdf/scpops/ecb.op201.en.pdf.

[3] The "IMPACT survey" was circulated by the ECB in July 2020 in all euro area countries in order to measure the impact of the pandemic on cash trends. The motivation

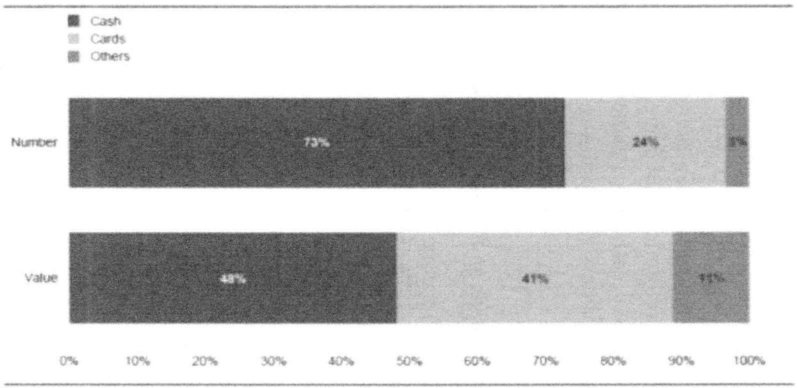

Fig. 1 Share of payment instruments used at the POS and P2P (in terms of the number and value of transactions). Data are for the euro area (all 19 countries). The category "Cards" includes credit and debit cards. The category "Others" refers to payments with mobile phones, bank cheques, credit transfers, direct debits and other (unidentified) payment instruments, and includes the answer "Don't know". Due to their low frequency of use, these instruments have been grouped into a single category. (*Source* European Central Bank's SPACE survey)

of the respondents revealed their intention to continue using cashless or online payment methods (46% certainly and 41% probably) after the end of the pandemic. Although the type and methodology of the 2020 survey is different than those of the 2016 and 2019 surveys (and thus not directly comparable), it nevertheless provides a view of potential changes in the payment attitude and behaviour of euro area consumers.[4]

This view is further confirmed for the post-pandemic period, as reflected in the key findings from the latest ECB's survey (SPACE 2022).[5] Specifically, 55% of respondents stated their preference for cashless means of payments (up from 49 and 43% in 2019 and 2016, respectively), while 22% prefer cash and 23% have no clear preference. Interestingly and despite their self-reported preferences, an increasing share of euro area consumers would like to have cash as a payment option (approximately 60% of consumers still considers the option to pay with cash to be important or very important).[6]

1.2 Payment Methods of European Companies

A similar survey on the use of cash payment methods by euro area companies reveals that companies have differing preferences.[7] Specifically, 24% of companies prefer consumers to pay with cash, 20% show preferences

for this survey was the concerns among the general public and retailers about the risks of being contaminated with the coronavirus via cash, and by the visibly higher card use, as many retailers asked their clients to pay (contactless) by card.

[4] The SPACE and SUCH surveys were consisting of a payment diary and a questionnaire, while the IMPACT survey was an online survey in most countries and interviews were not spread evenly over the days of the week. Moreover, it cannot be predicted how the changes in the methodology influence the results in terms of an over- or underestimation of cash usage (for more information, see ECB, 2022).

[5] The second "Study on the Payment Attitudes of consumers in the euro area (SPACE)" was conducted in 2022. Data for this study were collected through a survey of a random sample of the population in all euro area countries.

[6] It should be noted that although no major lockdowns have been in place in most euro area countries during the fieldwork periods, consumers' payment behaviour has still been affected by various pandemic-related measures (ibid.).

[7] The estimates are derived from the 2022 ECB's survey on the investigation of the use of cash by euro area companies. The survey was conducted between October and December 2021 and aimed at understanding companies' strategic view on the current and future use and acceptance. In total, 10,141 interviews were conducted for companies from all 19-euro area countries: European Central Bank, Use of cash by companies in

for contactless cards, while debit PIN cards and credit PIN cards follow with 17% and 16%, respectively (see Fig. 2).[8] The most important criteria according to which firms decide whether to accept a means of payment are security of payment (94%) and reliability of payment methods (92%).

Although cards as a whole (including contactless cards) account for 53% of overall preferences, companies still consider cash (albeit by a small margin) as the most popular means of payment. According to the survey, companies generally consider cash to be better in terms of overall costs, transaction speed and reliability relative to other payment methods. Moreover, cash preferences exhibit considerable variation across countries and industry sectors. The share of companies preferring cash ranges from as high as 36% and 45% in Denmark and Slovakia, respectively, to 4% in Cyprus or 8% in the Netherlands. Cash is considered as the most preferred payment method in restaurants and cafes, while in the remaining sectors (arts and entertainment, hotels, retail trade) ranges from 20–23%.

1.3 Future Trends in Payment Methods

Overall, the discussion in the previous sections reveals that European citizens and companies exhibit a preference for cash as a payment method, due to its convenience, speed and privacy features, however, alternative methods of payments continuously gain grounds. In fact, the number and volume of non-cash transactions (especially among consumers) worldwide are expected to experience a relatively slow, but steady, growth in the upcoming years (see Fig. 3).[9] In Europe, the average annual growth rate

the euro area (ECB, 2022), https://www.ecb.europa.eu/pub/pubbydate/2022/html/ecb.use_of_cash_companies_euro_area.06102022~2c3e7fba18.en.html.

[8] The results from the "Companies' Survey on Cash" were presented and discussed in the ECB's 2022 publication "Use of cash by companies in the euro area" (ibid). Although the survey included companies from all sectors, the analysis in the ECB's publication focused on four key sectors of interest that have the most private customers: the retail trade, hotels, restaurants and cafes, as well as the arts, entertainment and recreation sectors (7271 interviews in total).

[9] The analysis is included in the World Payments Report 2022 by Capgemini Research Institute for Financial Services: Capgemini

Research Institute for Financial Services, *World Payments Report 2022* (Capgemini, 2022).

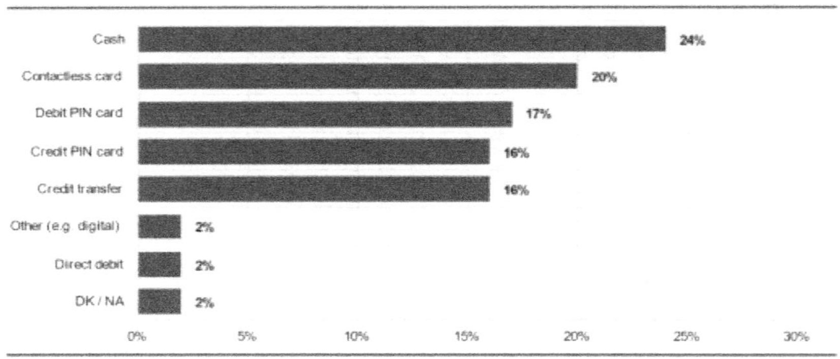

Fig. 2 Means of payments that euro area companies prefer to be paid with distribution of preferences across means of payment for the four sectors of interest: Retail trade, hotels, restaurants and cafes, and arts, entertainment and recreations. DK stands for "Don't know", while NA stands for "No answer". (*Source* European Central Bank [2022])

between 2021 and 2026 is expected to be 12.9%.[10] This is partially driven by new payments (such as instant payments, electronic money, mobile and digital wallets, etc.) that gain increasing prominence.

At the same time, public demand for cash remains steady, both as a means of payment and a safe haven.[11] Therefore, the consensus is that demand (primarily from consumers and secondarily from companies) for both cash and digital payments will remain strong. Depending on the profile of the user (consumers or companies), both means of payments will continue to serve a function in the retail payments landscape.[12]

2 Technological Developments and Digital Retail Payments

The advent of new technologies accommodates the increasing demand for immediacy from consumers, resulting in fundamental changes in the payment patterns of European citizens. The latter increasingly exhibit preferences for digital payments, as technological innovation, has been transforming the markets for retail payments, creating new payment methods, platforms and interfaces: these constitute a generally faster, cheaper and safer alternative, facilitating users' demands and expectations for payment products and developing the necessary conditions to facilitate adoption.[13]

The steady growth in digital payments is further driven by the emergence and consequent rise of cryptocurrencies. To this date, cryptocurrencies are generally perceived by European consumers as a supplementary payment method, rather than as a viable alternative for mainstream

[10] These calculations should be interpreted with caution, since they are based on forecasted figures for years 2022 to 2026 (ibid).

[11] Bank for International Settlements, *Digital payments make gains but cash remains* (Basel, 2023), 1.

[12] These are one of the conclusions of SPACE 2022 officially communicated by the ECB: European Central Bank. Cash remains the most frequently used means of payment in stores, but electronic payments grow further (ECB, 2022), https://www.ecb.europa.eu/press/pr/date/2022/html/ecb.pr221220~62a7c988ef.en.html.

[13] Bank for International Settlements, *Central bank digital currencies: User needs and adoption* (Basel, 2021), 2.

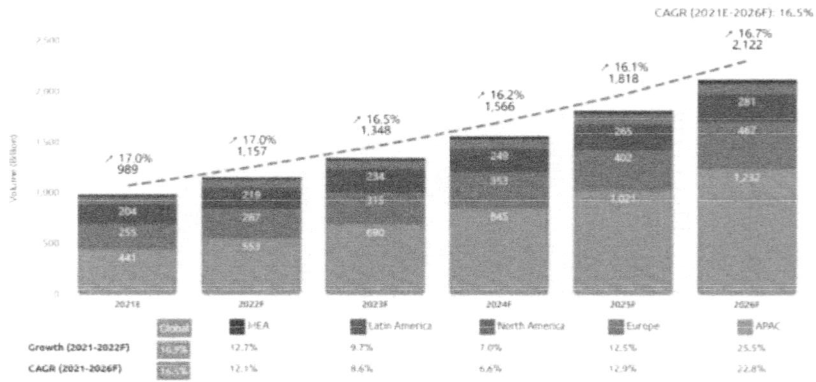

Fig. 3 Volume of worldwide non-cash transactions for years 2021–2026 (in USD billions). (*Source* Capegemini research institute for financial services, 2022; ECB statistical data warehouse, BIS statistical explorer, countries' central bank annual reports). (*Note* 2021 non-cash transaction data is sourced from central banks. Forecasted figures were used when data was unavailable. Figures are forecasted for 2022 and beyond)

methods.[14] However, acceptance rates are expected to increase, since young generations are more inclined towards digital currencies and payments, thus helping cryptocurrencies capturing higher market share. In this respect, an increasing number of companies across different industries provide customers with the option of using cryptocurrencies as an official payment method for their goods and services.

Currently, within the euro area setting, digital forms of money are provided only by private sector companies, as there is no equivalent digital form of money issued by the public sector (e.g., the ECB or the NCBs). Hence, should the expectations about the future growth of digital payments be realised, European consumers will inevitably favour the use of private digital currencies. On the same line, non-European digital payment solutions and technologies operated abroad might dominate the euro area retail payments market, a pattern already evident in some segments like cards and online payments.[15]

An increasing growth rate in the use of cryptocurrencies as alternative means of payment (and possibly, units of account), could reduce the demand for fiat currencies of central bank money; this diminishing demand, may further affect the ability of central banks to control short-term interest rates.[16] Arguably, this could result in central bank money losing its status as the dominant form of payment and consequently, being deprived of its capacity to ensure the complementarity and convertibility of public and private money; this complementarity is in turn a source of confidence for the central bank, facilitating the smooth and efficient operation of payment systems and commercial activities.[17,18] Moreover,

[14] Deutsche Bank, *Part III. Digital currencies: The ultimate hard power tool* (Deutsche Bank, 2020), 3.

[15] Fabio Panetta, "The digital euro and the evolution of the financial system" *Introductory statement at the committee on economic and monetary affairs of the European parliament,* European Central Bank, 2022, 4.

[16] Dong He, "Monetary policy in the digital age" *Finance & Development* (2018): 15.

[17] Fabio Panetta, "Central bank digital currencies: A monetary anchor for digital innovation" Bank for International Settlements, 2021, 6.

[18] In standard economic textbooks, central banks typically set short-term interest rates that they use for monetary policy purposes by manipulating the supply of banking system reserves (see Benjamin Friedman and Kenneth Kuttner, "Implementation of monetary policy: How do central banks set interest rates?" in *Handbook of monetary economics*, vol. 3 (Elsevier, 2010)). The change in short-term interest rates resulting from monetary authorities' exogenous policy actions is referred to as the liquidity effect (see Thornton, 2001).

this could compromise the ability of the monetary policy framework to provide a transparent nominal anchor that facilitates the private sector's economic and financial decisions.[19,20]

In this context, the absence of a CBDC contributes to financial instability and further undermines the role of the common currency in the Eurozone and globally.[21] The above arguments provide a rationale for central banks to foster a greater involvement in retail payments systems by building and keeping control of core components of these systems.[22] In the euro area setting, the introduction of the digital euro serves as an important opportunity to expand payment options for consumers (through the use of efficient and environment-friendly technologies), shield the European economy from alternative digital currencies (by central banks and private initiatives) and enhance the transparency and independence of the ECB's monetary policy framework.

An alternative view is that today, this process involves little or no variation in the supply of central bank liabilities; instead, banks set short-term interest rates through announcement effects, i.e., central bank statements (see, e.g., Graeme Guthrie and Julian Wright, "Open mouth operations" *Journal of Monetary Economics* 46, no. 2 (2000); Daniel Thornton, "Identifying the liquidity effect at the daily frequency" *Review—Federal Reserve Bank of Saint Luis 83*, no. 4 (2001); Alan Blinder et al., "Central bank communication and monetary policy: A survey of theory and evidence" *Journal of Economic Literature* 46, no. 4 (2008)). Therefore, the ultimate impact of cryptocurrencies on the effectiveness of monetary policy depends on whether the liquidity effect or the announcement effect dominates in the conduct of monetary policy.

19 Michael Bordo and Andrew Levin, *Central bank digital currency and the future of monetary policy* (National Bureau of Economic Research, 2017), 7.

20 In recent decades, central banks (including the ECB) achieved remarkable progress along these lines through the adoption of specific numerical inflation objectives (see, e.g., Bennett McCallum, "Inflation targeting in Canada, New Zealand, Sweden, the United Kingdom, and in General," In *Towards more effective monetary policy* (London: Palgrave Macmillan UK, 1997); Ben Bernanke and Frederic Mishkin, "Inflation targeting: A new framework for monetary policy?" *Journal of Economic perspectives* 11, no. 2 (1997); Ben Bernanke et al., *Inflation targeting:* In *Inflation Targeting* (Princeton University Press, 2018); Andrew Levin et al., "The macroeconomic effects of inflation targeting" *Review-Federal Reserve Bank of Saint Louis* 86, no. 4 (2004)).

21 Panetta, "The digital euro," 4.

22 Jorge Luis Ponce Moreno, "Digitalization, retail payments and Central Bank Digital Currency" *Financial stability review/Banco de España* 39 (2020): 8.

3 Retail Payments in Europe

The retail payments landscape in Europe has been subjected to substantial improvements in recent years, primarily due to the development of the Single Euro Payment Area (SEPA) and to the harmonisation of retail payments legislation.[23,24] Although these initiatives resulted in a decrease in cash usage, a distinctive feature of the European retail payments market is the dependence on international private entities, such as card schemes, privately owned retail payment systems[25] and financial technology companies. Furthermore, the market remains considerably fragmented along national borders, owing to the absence of a payment scheme (in the form of cards or instant payments) that operates cross-border.[26,27]

These conditions give rise to a competition between public money and alternative private instruments and schemes (such as cryptocurrencies) that operate outside the perimeter of monetary sovereignty; at the core of this competition, lies central bank money and its important role across the chain of the payment spectrum.[28] The protection of this role is essential for preserving public trust and confidence in the use of common

[23] The SEPA is an initiative of the European Union for the harmonisation of cashless euro payments across Europe. It allows European consumers, businesses and public administrations to conduct certain types of transactions (credit transfers, direct debit payments, card payments) under the same basic conditions. Detailed information is provided in the Regulation (EC) No 924/2009 and in the European Commission's proposal for cheaper euro transfers and fairer currency conversions everywhere in the Union (28 March 2018).

[24] European Commission, *Communication from the Commission to the European Parliament, the Council, the Economic and Social Committee and the Committee of the Regions on a Retail Payments Strategy for the EU*, COM(2020) 592 final, 2020, https://eur-lex.europa.eu/legal-content/EN/TXT/PDF/?uri=CELEX:52020DC0592, 9.

[25] These can include, for instance, the SEPA payment systems.

[26] Ibid., 9.

[27] A recent development is the proposal put forward by the European Commission for a regulation on instant credit transfers in euro across the EU and EEA (26 October 2022), which was subsequently supported by the Eurosystem (1 February 2023) and the Council of the European Union (22 May 2023). This amends the SEPA regulation of standard credit transfers in euro by allowing for instant credit transfers (see Council of the European Union, *Capital markets union: Council agrees its position on the instant payment's proposal* (Council of the EU, 2023)).

[28] Yannis Stournaras, "The Payments Landscape (EU—Greece)" Bank for International Settlements, 2022, 10.

currency (including in retail payments). To this end, a number of important initiatives have been put forward, with several of them pursued under the auspices of the Euro Retail Payments Board (ERPB) and the European Payments Council (EPC).[29] These aim at adopting common European schemes and rules, which are crucial in facilitating the emergence and interoperability of instant payment solutions in shops and electronic commerce.[30]

Despite the ongoing efforts for greater integration and harmonisation in the European retail payments market, this is currently only achieved for credit transfers and direct debits. However, we don't observe the same degree of market integration and harmonisation of business practices and rules, and technical standards, when we consider card payments.[31] The continuing increase in card transactions at the European level, has not been accompanied by a harmonised, competitive and innovative European cards payment area; this deprives certain users, such as cardholders and merchants from transacting under the same conditions as those under SEPA for cards, which is yet to be achieved.[32]

These relatively low levels of integration and harmonisation are also present when focusing on retail payments systems domestically. Although card transactions constantly gain market share, their usage varies across European countries, while the percentage of cross-border card payment transactions is relatively low in terms of overall volume.[33] Figure 4 shows the number of card payments per inhabitant for the 28 EU countries over the 2014–2017 period. Based on the graph, the number of card payments increases over time in all countries. However, the average number of card payments exhibits significant cross-country variations: in 2017, this

[29] Among them, is the European Payment Initiative (EPI), announced in 2020. Under the EPI, 31 European banks/credit institutions and 2 third-party acquirers aim to create a new pan-European payment solution for all types of retail transactions (in-store, online, cash withdrawal, peer-to-peer) in addition to existing international payment scheme solutions.

[30] European Commission, *Communication*, 9.

[31] European Central Bank, *Card payments in Europe—Current Landscape and Future Prospects: A Eurosystem Perspective* (ECB, 2019), 11.

[32] Ibid., 11.

[33] Ibid., 11.

number ranges from more than 250 (or marginally lower) in approximately a third of European countries to less (or marginally higher) than 50 in another third of countries.[34]

The preparations for the digital euro coincide with the strong pressure exerted by private, decentralised digital currencies and schemes. As such, the digital form of the common currency is expected to enhance the integration of the European retail payments market and strengthen consumers' confidence in the common currency. Moreover, by promoting digital cash payments, it is expected to mitigate cross-country differences in non-cash usage and further strengthen the efficiency and popularity of cross-border card payment transactions.

4 CBDC in Europe

The launch of a CBDC in Europe aims to provide European citizens with a simple, universally accepted and secure public means of (retail) payment. In this regard, the digital euro constitutes a fundamental tool in the effort of maintaining the integrity and stability of the financial system in Europe. However, the current nature of the European retail payments landscape, as well as specific socioeconomic and structural economic characteristics across and within euro area countries present certain challenges to the effectiveness of this pan-European initiative.[35]

These challenges pertain to the ability of the digital euro to protect user privacy and anonymity, the degree to which the digital euro interacts with financial inclusion and financial literacy and its association with informal economy. More specific:

> Privacy and security are identified as the most important features of the digital euro for both consumers and professionals: safety and security against fraud and hacking, as well as secure and reliable

[34] These large cross-country differences in the payment habits of consumers when purchasing goods or services at the POS are further evident in 2022. Based on SPACE 2022, in certain countries (Austria, Italy, Malta, Lithuania, Slovenia), a clear majority of POS payments (in number and value) were made in cash, whereas in others (Belgium, Finland, Luxembourg, the Netherlands) card payments were the most frequently used method (see ECB, *Cash remains*).

[35] This chapter is strictly meant to identify and discuss potential challenges regarding the adoption and use of the digital euro by the public, rather than to recommend or imply the most appropriate solutions to address these challenges.

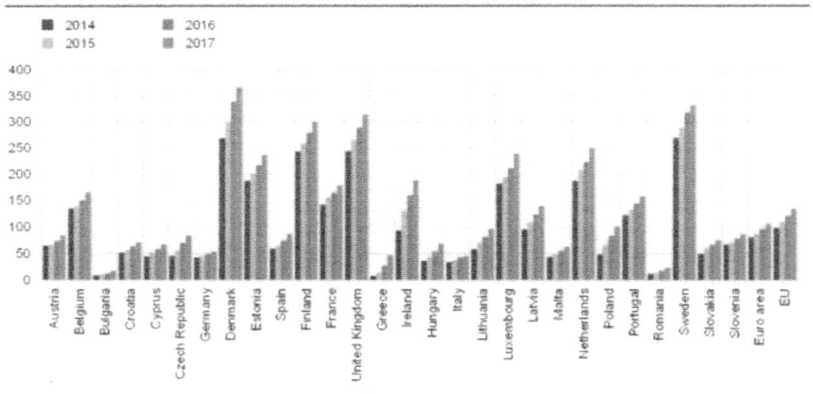

Fig. 4 Number of card payments per inhabitant (2014–2017). The chart shows card payments with cards issued by EU-resident payment service providers, except cards with an e-money function only. (*Source* European Central Bank [2019])

payment authentication methods represent important concerns for European citizens.[36]

- The extent of informal economy (shadow economy). The volume of informal economic activities and the consequent use of cash as primary payment method may affect the likelihood of retail CBDC adoption and usage. Given the association between informal economic activities and anonymity, this issue is closely linked to the CBDC's privacy and anonymity features.
- The current degree of financial inclusion at the national level. The introduction of the digital euro serves as an important complement to the existing initiatives to promote financial inclusion. As barriers to financial inclusion limit access to financial services for certain population groups, they can further constitute a barrier for the broad adoption of the digital euro. On the same line, the degree of financial literacy and digital literacy emerges as an additional factor driving citizens' attitudes towards CBDCs.

In the subsequent sections, these challenges are analysed in detail with a separate focus on the implications for the effectiveness of the digital euro as means for retail payments.

4.1 *Privacy and Security*

European citizens (public and professionals alike) value privacy and security most when considering the possibility of a digital euro in the future, as high safety and security standards are considered to be fundamental for digital payment methods. In fact, 8221 European citizens during a public consultation on the digital euro revealed their preferences for a digital euro that ensures user anonymity, while operating as a secure means of payment (see Fig. 5).[37] In this regard, the ability of the digital

[36] European Central Bank, *Eurosystem report on the public consultation on a digital euro* (ECB, 2021), 12. On 12 October 2020, the ECB launched the "Public consultation on a digital euro", which ran until 12 January 2021. The consultation included 18 questions in order to collect the views of both citizens and professionals.

[37] Ibid., 12. According to the consultation, privacy is cited as the most important feature of the digital euro by the public and professionals (ranked first by 43% of respondents), while security is cited as the second most important (ranked first by 18% of respondents).

euro to satisfy these preferences is one of the most important determinants of its wide adoption and use by European citizens. Historically, the popularity of cash as payment method can be explained in terms of its security and protection of user identity. Cash transactions do not require the involvement of a third party, therefore protecting user privacy and ensuring freedom and anonymity. Moreover, the security features of cash coins and banknotes render them resilient to fraud and counterfeiting.

The digital euro is expected to serve as complement to cash, by providing an alternative means for digital payments. Considering this, any digital form of currency should include some of the fundamental features of physical currencies in order to efficiently facilitate transactions between consumers and merchants. Among these features is the ability to protect user privacy and anonymity, as well as to ensure the security of transactions. In fact, consumers express legitimate concerns about privacy due to cybersecurity threats and vulnerabilities.

These vulnerabilities give rise to fears that consumer information could be employed for purposes not related to those underlying regular transactions. The decentralised collection of transaction data and the accumulation of large volumes of sensitive data raise security risk by increasing the payoff for cyber intruders; this in turn poses major privacy and security risks that are inherent in digital currencies.[38] Although data constitute a basic feature of the digitalisation process and may be socially useful to improve the efficiency and security of payments, potential anonymity concerns can prevent the wide adoption of the digital euro, which is crucial for the success of a retail payments system.[39,40]

To this end, the challenge for the ECB (and every central bank designing a digital currency) is the creation of an environment for protecting privacy (based on the separation between identity and transaction data) that could foster public confidence and trust in using the digital

[38] Giulia Fanti et al., "Central Bankers' New Cybersecurity Challenge" *Finance & Development* 59, no. 003 (2022): 13.

[39] Ponce, "Digitalization," 8.

[40] The issue of successful preservation of anonymity is contingent on the effective combatting of money laundering and the financing of terrorism. In fact, in April 2023, the European Parliament approved its negotiating mandates for proposals reforming the EU's policies on AML/CFT; the first meeting on the beginning of negotiations between Members of the European Parliament and the representatives of EU ministers was held in May 2023 (see European Parliament, *Stopping the flow of dirty money: Parliament ready for negotiations* (European Parliament, 2023)).

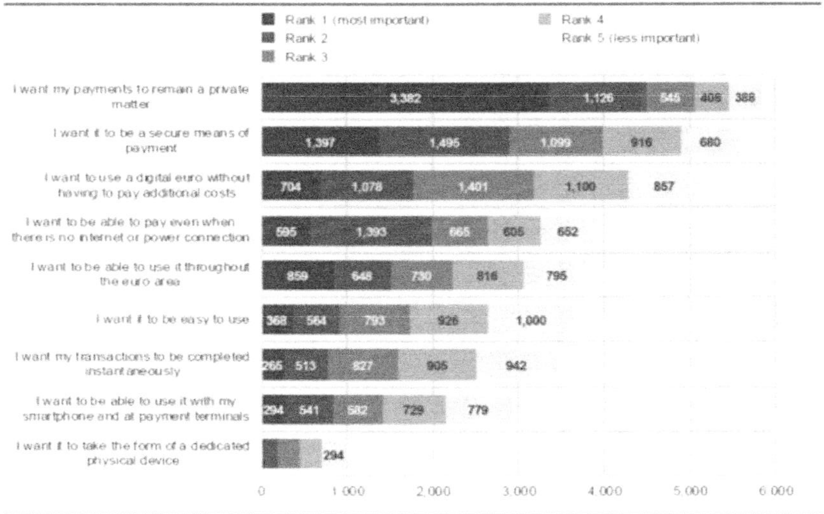

Fig. 5 Preference for some digital euro features based on top five rankings. The figure shows the number of respondents to a multiple-choice question about ranking in order of importance a list of specific features that a digital euro should offer (followed by a field to add comments). (*Source* European Central Bank [2021])

euro. An important decision that can determine this environment is with regard to the technical properties of the digital euro; among them, is the decision as to whether the digital euro will be token- or account-based. Under a token-based scheme, the distribution of the digital euro involves the transfer of an object of value from the virtual wallet of one user to the virtual wallet of another user.[41] Under an account-based scheme, the distribution of the digital euro involves a transfer from the account of one user to the account of another user.

An important distinction between token- and account-based digital currencies is the form of verification required during transaction: token-based currencies (or payment systems) depend on the ability of the payee to verify the validity of the payment object.[42] A key point of concern in the use of a tokenised digital currency is whether the token or "coin" is genuine or not (electronic counterfeiting) and whether it has already been spent; this is in turn equivalent to counterfeiting in the use of physical currency.[43] On the other hand, account-based digital currencies rely on the ability to verify the identity of the account holder: a key concern relates to identity theft, which can allow perpetrators to unauthorisedly transfer or withdraw money from accounts.[44]

In principle, a token-based digital currency can provide different degrees of anonymity (similarly to that provided by private digital tokens) by allowing players to indirectly impose their proprietary solution.[45] A token-based scheme increases the security of card-based payments by replacing the primary account number (PAN) with a value which can only be used in a controlled way (the token). However, under both schemes, a large amount of information would be available to the central bank or any other operator administering the scheme. This information could be used for reversing erroneous or fraudulent operations or identifying illegal

[41] Deloitte, *Central bank digital currencies: Building block of the future of value transfer* (Deloitte, 2022), 14.

[42] Charles Kahn and William Roberds, "Why pay? An introduction to payments economics" *Journal of Financial Intermediation* 18, no. 1 (2009): 15.

[43] Bank for International Settlements, *Central bank digital currencies* (BIS, 2018), 16.

[44] BIS, *Central bank digital currencies*, 16. This can be addressed by requiring account holder identification in order to correctly link payers and payees and to ascertain their respective account histories.

[45] ECB, *Card payments in Europe*, 11.

activities (e.g., money laundering, terrorism financing).[46] Arguably, a low degree of anonymity could prevent the wide adoption of digital euro by consumers (primarily) and merchants (to a lesser extent), while complete anonymity could encourage the financing of illegal activities.

This option could be designed in conjunction with additional security features, e.g., the introduction of limits; these limits may refer to the amount of digital euro that a given user can hold or the amount of transactions in a given period.[47,48] Such limits may benefit consumers by reducing the risk of losing large amounts of digital money (following a system failure). Moreover, they could further exert a societal impact by discouraging the use of digital euro for illegal activities. Finally, they could contribute to financial stability by controlling the use of the digital euro as a form of investment.

In fact, a number of euro area countries have adopted limits in the amount of physical cash payments.[49] Similar limits for digital cash payments can be adopted at the national level or can take the form of a common limit for all euro area countries. Importantly, these limits could be adjusted following the introduction of the digital euro and after the security features of this payment scheme are tested in practice.

Overall, the design of the digital euro requires achieving a balance between the degree of anonymity and privacy required for its broad adoption by the public (on the one hand) and the prevention of the digital currency to be employed for money laundering and the financing of illegal activities (on the other hand). If this balance is achieved, the digital euro could successfully address the privacy and security concerns of European citizens (consumers and merchants alike, as well as those of the authorities across all EU Member States).

[46] Ponce, "Digitalization," 8.

[47] Ibid., 8.

[48] Currently, the 5th Anti-Money Laundering Directive (AMLD) lays out certain risk-mitigating conditions for the use and treatment of anonymous electronic money in EU Member State (among others), a) the payment instrument is not reloadable, or has a maximum monthly payment transactions limit or EUR 150, which can be used only in a given Member State, b) the maximum amount stored electronically does not exceed EUR 150, c) redemption in cash or cash withdrawal of the monetary value of the electronic money the amount redeemed does not exceed EUR 50; for further information, see Directive (EU) 2018/843 of the European Parliament and of the Council.

[49] In this respect, as of 27 April 2019 the EUR 500 banknote is no longer being issued.

4.2 *Informal Economy*

Closely linked to the privacy and anonymity features of the digital euro is an additional factor that may affect the wide adoption and usage of the digital currency, namely the prevalence of informal economy. The informal economy comprises activities that are not taxed or registered by public authorities and therefore are difficult to measure; although the produced goods and services have market value, they do not contribute to Gross Domestic Product (GDP).[50] These activities can be legal, but are not recorded in order to avoid payment of taxes or complying with regulations, or can be illegal, referring to goods and services forbidden by law or that are unlawful when carried out by unauthorised producers.[51]

In principle, the size of informal activities is larger in developing economies relative to developed economies.[52] Moreover, within the EU context, there is significant cross-country variation in the size of informal activity as a share of GDP: this share ranges from approximately 10% (Austria, Luxembourg) to more than 35% (Lithuania, Bulgaria), with most countries being within the 15%–30% range (see Fig. 6).[53] As these activities involve cash payments, the anonymity associated with cash allows users to hide their transaction histories, with tax avoidance or tax evasion being one of the main reasons.

If digital currency schemes can be traced by public authorities, they create a disincentive for people to engage in informal economic activities. The strength of this disincentive depends on the technical features of the digital currency and especially on the decision between a token-based scheme and an account-based scheme; this ultimately determines

[50] Organisation for Economic Co-operation and Development, *Measuring the Non-Observed Economy—A Handbook* (OECD, 2002), 17.

[51] Generally, cash payments in the context of informal economic activities aggravate the tax enforcement problem (see Roger Gordon and Wei Li, "Tax structures in developing countries: Many puzzles and a possible explanation" *Journal of Public Economics* 93, no. 7–8 (2009)). However, informal legal activities do not necessarily exert a negative effect on the economy, in the presence of a well-designed consumption-based tax, given its self-enforcing nature (see Michael Keen and Ben Lockwood, "The value added tax: Its causes and consequences," *Journal of Development Economics* 92, no. 2 (2010)).

[52] Salvatore Capasso and Tullio Jappelli, "Financial development and the underground economy" *Journal of Development Economics* 101 (2013): 18.

[53] The estimates refer to the year 2016, see Kelmanson et al., *Explaining the shadow economy in Europe: size, causes and policy options* (International Monetary Fund, 2019).

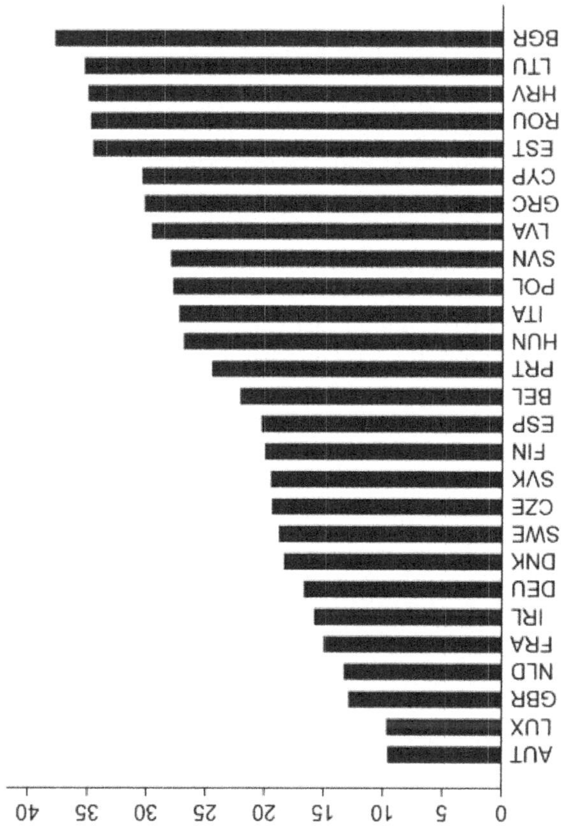

Fig. 6 Size of shadow economy in European countries in 2016 (percent of GDP). (*Data source* kelmanson, Kirabaeva, Medina, Mircheva and Weiss [2019])

the degree of anonymity during the transaction. Hence, the technological design of the digital euro constitutes an important determinant of people's perceptions of digital currency payments, in the setting of an informal economy.

The final core properties of the digital euro and the extent of digital surveillance suggest that the effectiveness of CBDC as an alternative retail payment option may differ depending on the size of the informal economy. In fact, countries with large informal sectors (as per cent of GDP) tend to have a smaller number of digital payment transactions (as per cent of overall transactions).[54] However, this can also exert the opposite effect; if in countries with sizeable informal economic activity authorities employ specific tax measures to promote cashless transactions and banking channels, thereby increasing digital currency payment adoption.[55]

However, the relationship between CBDC and the informal economy is not exhaustive. There are additional factors that determine the incentives to engage in informal economic activities. Among them, the level of direct and indirect taxation, the level and nature of social security contributions, the degree of labour market regulation and the quality of state institutions. Although the design of the digital euro will affect the motives of consumers and merchants to engage in informal legal activities and vice versa, the above factors should also be taken into consideration.

4.3 Financial Inclusion

One of the motives underlying the issuance of retail CBDCs is to serve as potential complement to existing tools and initiatives in promoting financial inclusion. Although there is no uniform definition of financial inclusion, it generally refers to access to financial services, such as the ability of firms and households to use financial products and services,

[54] Eun Young Oh and Shuonan Zhang, "Informal economy and central bank digital currency" *Economic Inquiry* 60, no. 4 (2022): 19.

[55] Rajul Awasthi and Michael Engelschalk, "Taxation and the shadow economy: how the tax system can stimulate and enforce the formalization of business activities" Policy Research Working Paper 8391 (World Bank, 2018), 20, https://doi.org/10.1596/1813-9450-8391.

given in particular the constraints of time and distance.[56] From a different perspective, financial inclusion often refers to the effective use of financial products and services, i.e., whether people actually use deposit accounts, payment services, microcredit schemes and insurance products.[57]

In this regard, the digital euro aims at providing European citizens with widespread access to central bank money (in digital form), while it constitutes an alternative payment method for the unbanked population (e.g., those that cannot meet minimum balance requirements). On the same line, it purports to provide consumers and merchants with low-cost payment solutions and financial services; all the above, should lead to an increase in the number of people participating in the digital economy.

However, current barriers to financial inclusion also present a challenge for the wide adoption of the digital euro. More specific, approximately 13.5 million people in the euro area are unbanked (i.e., have no bank account or access to financial services) and largely rely on cash to make payments independently.[58] More importantly, an even greater number of euro area citizens are underbanked, that is, although they have a bank account, they lack convenient access to financial services.

Furthermore, a divide already exists between people who are increasingly using digital payment methods and people who cannot use these methods or are reluctant to adopt them for any reason.[59] In this respect, an ECB-conducted survey on the specific issue of access to cashless means of payment is indicative: in 2019 around 2% of euro area citizens over 18 years old had no access to cashless payment methods and hence, relied

[56] Bruno Tissot, and Blaise Gadanecz, "Measures of financial inclusion—a central bank perspective" (Bank for International Settlements, 2017), 21, https://www.bis.org/ifc/publ/ifcb47q_rh.pdf.

[57] Ibid., 21.

[58] Alejandro Zamora-Pérez, "Guaranteeing freedom of payment choice: access to cash in the euro area" *Economic Bulletin Articles* 5 (2022), 22, https://www.ecb.europa.eu/pub/economic-bulletin/articles/2022/html/ecb.ebart202205_02~74b1fc0841.en.html. The number of unbanked adult EU citizens more than halved from approximately 31 million to 13.5 million (or 3.54% of the adult population) between 2017 and 2021, according to a European Savings and Retail Banking Group (ESBG) analysis of the World Bank's Global Findex Database 2021. For purposes of comparison, in the U.S., 22% of adults (63 million) were either unbanked or underbanked in 2018 (see Board of Governors, Federal Reserve System. *Report on the Economic Well-Being of U.S. Households in 2018* (Federal Reserve System, 2019)).

[59] Zamora-Pérez, "Guaranteeing," 22.

solely on cash or on other people to make payments.[60] This percentage increases for certain population groups, such as those aged 65 or over (3%), those with only primary or secondary education (4%), or those from certain countries, such as Cyprus, Greece or Malta (around 10%).

Therefore, if the introduction of the digital euro is accompanied by a shrinking cash infrastructure, it can affect the way citizens choose to pay and create barriers to the financial inclusion of vulnerable social groups. This in turn, may not only affect the effectiveness of the digital euro as retail payment method, but also preserve (and possibly aggravate) the financial exclusion of part of the population. This could further be the case for people more engaged with the informal economy, as these might be already financially excluded.

This issue is again related to the technological features of the digital euro and the choice between an account-based and a token-based digital scheme. The distribution of euro under an account-based scheme requires the existence of a digital account for every user. Although this constitutes an important path to financial inclusion, at the same time, it can pose problems for the wide adoption of the digital euro in the presence of financially excluded population groups. In contrast, under a token-based scheme only an internet connection is required for both users to complete the payment; theoretically, this facilitates better the CBDC's adoption by all population groups, while also contributing to financial inclusion goals (albeit to a lesser extent relative to an account-based scheme).

4.4 *Financial Literacy*

Special consideration should be given to the importance of financial literacy for CBDC adoption, as higher levels of financial knowledge are correlated with larger awareness of financial products; this in turn is considered an important step in removing demand-side barriers to

[60] Ibid., 22. The estimates are derived from the ECB's SPACE survey. SPACE 2022 does not include a similar question on access to any cashless means of payment. Instead, the question was whether Europeans have access to a) payment accounts and b) payment cards. On average, 91% of the respondents have an account for payment, while 94% have a payment card, although there is no information on the extent to which these figures overlap (conversely, respondents with no access to accounts or no access to cards are 9% and 6%, respectively).

financial inclusion.[61] Although financial literacy has varying conceptual definitions, it can be defined as "a combination of awareness, knowledge, skill, attitude and behaviour necessary to make sound financial decisions and ultimately achieve individual financial wellbeing".[62]

In our context, better understanding and usage of financial services is crucial to greater financial inclusion: these include, among other, knowledge on how to save and borrow, how to understand and compare financial offers and products or how to prepare for unexpected life events.[63] Limited knowledge of the above may give rise to a "cash mindset" among households, who perceive cash as easy to use and helpful for budgeting or controlling spending.[64] Along with financial literacy, digital literacy (the ability to read and navigate autonomously digital content)[65] is further identified as an important challenge for CBDC adoption from certain segments of society, such as older users.

In fact, a recent ECB-commissioned survey revealed that digital natives and the more technologically literate, in particular those who already use electronic payment methods, generally find it easier to comprehend the concept of the digital euro.[66] From the above, it is evident that in the presence of low levels of financial and digital literacy, access to financial services remains limited, especially for vulnerable groups; this may further prohibit part of the population from surrounding the digital euro with

[61] Organisation for Economic Co-operation and Development, *Financial literacy and inclusion: Results of OECD/INFE survey across countries and by gender* (OECD, 2013), 23.

[62] Ibid., 23.

[63] Raphael Auer et al., "Central bank digital currencies: A new tool in the financial inclusion toolkit?" FSI Insights on policy
implementation no. 41 (Bank for International Settlements and World Bank Group, 2022), 24,
https://www.bis.org/fsi/publ/insights41.pdf.

[64] Ibid., 24.

[65] Organisation for Economic Co-operation and Development, "Skills for a digital world" Background Paper for Ministerial Panel 4.2 (OECD, 2016), 25.

[66] European Central Bank, *Study on new digital payment methods* (Kantar Public, 2022), 26. The research was commissioned by the European Central Bank to investigate the citizens' payment habits and their attitudes towards digital payments. The research further found that the tech-savvy and the more technologically literate (mainly males aged 25–45) use digital wallets and mobile banking applications, while they are increasingly transitioning away from card-based payments.

the same level of trust currently enjoyed by other forms of central bank money.[67,68]

To address these issues and foster trust in the digital currency, central banks and government authorities should embark on wide-reaching policies aiming at enhancing financial and digital literacy and providing open and affordable access to digital infrastructure.[69] These can take the form of, among other, learning materials and campaigns on the use and advantages of certain payment instruments, while concentrating on the payment needs of older users, children and people with disabilities.

5 Conclusions and Further Considerations

The digital euro is a pan-European initiative that constitutes an important opportunity to expand payment options for consumers through a simple, universally accepted and secure public means of payment. It further aims at shielding the European economy from alternative digital currencies and enhancing the transparency and independence of the ECB's monetary policy framework.

However, the introduction and wide adoption of the digital currency from the public face certain challenges, owing to the current nature of the European retail payments landscape and to specific socioeconomic and structural economic characteristics across and within euro area countries. Prominent among these, are the ability of the digital euro to protect user privacy and anonymity, its association with informal economy and the degree to which the digital euro interacts with financial inclusion and financial literacy.

In addition to the above, a number of alternative issues should be considered for the effective implementation of the digital currency across the euro area and domestically. On the regulatory front, there is need for new laws and regulations, or adjustments to existing ones. On the financial inclusion front, there is need for the involvement of the private

[67] Auer et al., "Central Bank Digital Currencies" 24.

[68] According to the European Commission's Digital Economy and Society Index (DESI) 2022, only 54% of European have at least basic digital skills (see European Commission, *Digital economy and society index (DESI)* 2022 (European Commission, 2022)).

[69] G7 United Kingdom 2021, *Public policy principles public policy principles for retail central bank digital currencies (CBDCs)* (G7 UK, 2021), 27.

sector (i.e., banks, other payment service providers, merchants) to support the attractiveness of the digital currency to users and to ensure sufficient access points, even in remote areas.[70]

On the technology front, apart from the privacy and security issues, the design and operational features of the digital wallet may affect users' (consumers and merchants alike) experience and perceptions about the digital currency. Finally, on the financial stability front, an interest-bearing digitally euro may induce depositors to transfer funds from commercial banks towards digital currency, with consequences for the stability of financial institutions (although the likelihood of this event is relatively low).

Overall, the project of the digital euro is still under the investigation phase, where the Eurosystem constantly explores different possibilities and options for the design of the digital currency. In this regard, a number of further steps are still to be followed in order to help the digital euro achieve its objectives and facilitate a more competitive and resilient European retail payments system.

References

Auer, Raphael A., Holti Banka, Nana Yaa Boakye-Adjei, Ahmed Faragallah, Jon Frost, Harish Natarajan, and Jermy Prenio. "Central bank digital currencies: A new tool in the financial inclusion toolkit?" FSI insights on policy implementation no. 41, Bank for International Settlements and World Bank Group, 2022. https://www.bis.org/fsi/publ/insights41.pdf.

Awasthi, Rajul, and Michael Engelschalk. "Taxation and the shadow economy: How the tax system can stimulate and enforce the formalization of business activities." Policy Research working paper no. 8391, World Bank, 2018. https://doi.org/10.1596/1813-9450-8391.

Bank for International Settlements. *Central bank digital currencies*. Committee on payments and market infrastructures, March. BIS, 2018. https://www.bis.org/cpmi/publ/d174.pdf.

Bank for International Settlements. *Central bank digital currencies: User needs and adoption*. Report no. 3 in a series of collaborations from a group of central banks, September, 2021. https://www.bis.org/publ/othp42_user_needs.pdf.

[70] Auer et al., "Central bank digital currencies" 24.

Bank for International Settlements. *Digital payments make gains, but cash remains*. CPMI Brief no. 1, January. BIS, 2023. https://www.bis.org/statistics/payment_stats/commentary2301.pdf.

Bernanke, Ben S., and Frederic S. Mishkin. "Inflation targeting: A new framework for monetary policy?" *Journal of Economic perspectives* 11, no. 2 (1997): 97–116.

Bernanke, Ben S., Thomas, Laubach, Frederic, Mishkin, and Adam, Posen. *Inflation targeting: In inflation targeting*. Princeton University Press, 2018.

Blinder, Alan S., Michael Ehrmann, Marcel Fratzscher, Jakob De Haan, and David-Jan Jansen. "Central bank communication and monetary policy: A survey of theory and evidence." *Journal of Economic Literature* 46, no. 4 (2008): 910–945.

Board of Governors. *Report on the economic well-being of U.S. households in 2018*. Federal Reserve System, 2019. https://www.federalreserve.gov/publications/files/2018-report-economic-well-being-us-households-201905.pdf.

Bordo, Michael D., and Andrew T. Levin. *Central bank digital currency and the future of monetary policy*. No. w23711. National Bureau of Economic Research, 2017.

Capasso, Salvatore, and Tullio Jappelli. "Financial development and the underground economy." *Journal of Development Economics* 101, (2013): 167–178.

Capgemini Research Institute for Financial Services. *World Payments Report 2022*. Capgemini, 2022. https://www.capgemini.com/de-de/insights/research/world-payments-report-2022/.

Council of the European Union. *Capital markets union: Council agrees its position on the instant payment's proposal*. Press release, May 22. Council of the EU, 2023. https://www.consilium.europa.eu/en/press/press-releases/2023/05/22/capital-markets-union-council-agrees-its-position-on-the-instant-payments-proposal/.

Deloitte. *Central Bank Digital Currencies: Building block of the future of value transfer*. Deloitte, 2022. https://www2.deloitte.com/content/dam/Deloitte/in/Documents/financial-services/in-fs-cbdc-noexp.pdf.

Deutsche Bank. *Part III. digital currencies: The ultimate hard power tool*. Corporate Bank Research, January 2020. https://www.dbresearch.com/PROD/RPS_EN-PROD/PROD0000000000504589/The_Future_of_Payments_-_Part_III__Digital_Currenc.pdf?undefined&realload=pXew5F80fm6tMsf0esOpdaYbyUy03qCc3toLkiTwpKBuYbNb5Rl02~zwiCkS/bIE.

Esselink, Henk, and Lola Hernández. "The use of cash by households in the euro area." Occasional Paper 201, ECB, 2017. https://www.ecb.europa.eu/pub/pdf/scpops/ecb.op201.en.pdf.

European Central Bank. *Card payments in Europe – Current Landscape and Future Prospects: A Eurosystem Perspective*. ECB, April 2019. https://www.ecb.europa.eu/paym/intro/mip-online/2019/html/1904_card_payments_europe.en.html.

European Central Bank. *Cash remains the most frequently used means of payment in stores, but electronic payments grow further, ECB study shows*. Press release, December 20. ECB, 2022. https://www.ecb.europa.eu/press/pr/date/2022/html/ecb.pr221220~62a7c988ef.en.html.

European Central Bank. *Eurosystem report on the public consultation on a digital euro*. Report, April 2021. https://www.ecb.europa.eu/pub/pdf/other/Eurosystem_report_on_the_public_consultation_on_a_digital_euro~539fa8cd8d.en.pdf.

European Central Bank. *Study on new digital payment methods*. Kantar Public, March 2022. https://www.ecb.europa.eu/paym/digital_euro/investigation/profuse/shared/files/dedocs/ecb.dedocs220330_report.en.pdf.

European Central Bank. *Use of cash by companies in the euro area*. ECB, October 2022. https://www.ecb.europa.eu/pub/pubbydate/2022/html/ecb.use_of_cash_companies_euro_area.06102022~2c3e7fba18.en.html.

European Central Bank. *Study on the payment attitudes of consumers in the euro area (SPACE)*. ECB, December 2022. https://www.ecb.europa.eu/stats/ecb_surveys/space/html/ecb.spacereport202212~783ffdf46e.en.html.

European Commission. *Communication from the Commission to the European Parliament, the Council, the economic and social committee and the committee of the regions on a retail payments strategy for the EU*. COM (2020) 592 final, September 24, 2020. https://eur-lex.europa.eu/legal-content/EN/TXT/PDF/?uri=CELEX:52020DC0592.

European Commission. *Digital economy and society index (DESI) 2022*. European Commission, 2022. https://digital-strategy.ec.europa.eu/en/library/digital-economy-and-society-index-desi-2022.

European Parliament. *Stopping the flow of dirty money: Parliament ready for negotiations*. Press release, April 19. European Parliament, 2023. https://www.europarl.europa.eu/news/en/press-room/20230414IPR80123/stopping-the-flow-of-dirty-money-parliament-ready-for-negotiations.

Fanti, Giulia, Josh Lipsky, and Ole Moehr. "Central bankers' new cybersecurity challenge." *Finance & Development* 59, no. 003 (2022).

Friedman, Benjamin M., and Kenneth N. Kuttner. "Implementation of monetary policy: How do central banks set interest rates?" In *Handbook of monetary economics*, vol. 3, pp. 1345–1438. Elsevier, 2010.

G7 United Kingdom 2021. *Public policy principles for retail central Bank digital currencies (CBDCs)*. G7 UK, *2021*. https://assets.publishing.service.gov.uk/government/uploads/system/uploads/attachment_data/file/1025235/G7_Public_Policy_Principles_for_Retail_CBDC_FINAL.pdf.

Gordon, Roger, and Wei Li. "Tax structures in developing countries: Many puzzles and a possible explanation." *Journal of Public Economics* 93, no. 7–8 (2009): 855–866.

Guthrie, Graeme, and Julian Wright. "Open mouth operations." *Journal of Monetary Economics* 46, no. 2 (2000): 489–516.

He, Dong. "Monetary Policy in the digital age." *Finance & Development* (2018): 13–16. https://www.imf.org/external/pubs/ft/fandd/2018/06/central-bank-monetary-policy-and-cryptocurrencies/he.pdf.

Kahn, Charles M., and William Roberds. "Why pay? An introduction to payments economics." *Journal of Financial Intermediation* 18, no. 1 (2009): 1–23.

Keen, Michael, and Ben Lockwood. "The value added tax: Its causes and consequences." *Journal of Development Economics* 92, no. 2 (2010): 138–151.

Kelmanson, Ben, Koralai Kirabaeva, Leandro Medina, Borislava Mircheva, and Jason Weiss. *Explaining the shadow economy in Europe: Size, causes and policy options*. International Monetary Fund, 2019.

Levin, Andrew T., Fabio M. Natalucci, and Jeremy M. Piger. "The macroeconomic effects of inflation targeting." *Review-Federal Reserve Bank of Saint Louis* 86, no. 4 (2004): 51–58.

McCallum, Bennett T. "Inflation targeting in Canada, New Zealand, Sweden, the United Kingdom, and in General." In *Towards more effective monetary policy*, pp. 211–252. London: Palgrave Macmillan UK, 1997.

Oh, Eun Young, and Shuonan Zhang. "Informal economy and central bank digital currency." *Economic Inquiry* 60, no. 4 (2022): 1520–1539.

Organisation for Economic Co-operation and Development. "Skills for a digital world." Background paper for ministerial panel 4.2, DSTI/ICCP/IIS(2015)10/FINAL, OECD, 2016. https://one.oecd.org/document/DSTI/ICCP/IIS(2015)10/FINAL/En/pdf.

Organisation for Economic Co-operation and Development. *Financial literacy and inclusion: Results of OECD/INFE survey across countries and by gender*. OECD, 2013. https://www.oecd.org/daf/fin/financial-education/TrustFund2013_OECD_INFE_Fin_Lit_and_Incl_SurveyResults_by_Country_and_Gender.pdf.

Organisation for Economic Co-operation and Development. *Measuring the non-observed economy—a handbook*. OECD, 2002. https://www.wiego.org/sites/default/files/publications/files/OECD-MeasuringtheNon-ObservedEconomy.pdf.

Panetta, Fabio. "Central bank digital currencies: A monetary anchor for digital innovation." *Speech at the Elcano Royal Institute*, November 5. Bank for International Settlements, 2021. https://www.bis.org/review/r211123b.pdf.

Panetta, Fabio. "The digital euro and the evolution of the financial system." *Introductory Statement at the Committee on Economic and Monetary Affairs of the European Parliament*, June 15. European Central Bank,

2022. https://www.ecb.europa.eu/press/key/date/2022/html/ecb.sp220615~0b859eb8bc.en.html.

Ponce Moreno, Jorge Luis. "Digitalization, retail payments and central bank digital currency." *Financial stability review/Banco de España, 39 (Autumn 2020), pp. 127–155* (2020).

Stournaras, Yannis. 2022. "The payments landscape (EU—Greece)." *Speech at the Central Banks Payments Conference, Athens, June 28* (2022). https://www.bis.org/review/r220629f.htm.

Thornton, Daniel L. "Identifying the liquidity effect at the daily frequency." *Review—Federal Reserve Bank of Saint Luis* 83, no. 4 (2001): 59–78.

Tissot Bruno, and Blaise Gadanecz. "Measures of financial inclusion—a central bank perspective." Bank for International Settlements, 2017. https://www.bis.org/ifc/publ/ifcb47q_rh.pdf.

Zamora-Pérez, Alejandro. "Guaranteeing freedom of payment choice: Access to cash in the euro area." *Economic Bulletin Articles* 5 (2022). https://www.ecb.europa.eu/pub/economic-bulletin/articles/2022/html/ecb.ebart202205_02~74b1fc0841.en.html.

CHAPTER 6

Digital Euro and Financial Inclusion Considerations on Trust, the Digital Divide and Financial Literacy

Federico Riganti and Anne-Marie Weber

F. Riganti (✉)
University of Turin, Turin, Italy
e-mail: federico.riganti@unito.it

A.-M. Weber
University of Warsaw, Warsaw, Poland
e-mail: a.weber@wpia.uw.edu.pl

© The Author(s), under exclusive license to Springer Nature Switzerland AG 2025

F. Annunziata et al. (eds.), *Central Bank Digital Currency*, EBI Studies in Banking and Capital Markets Law,
https://doi.org/10.1007/978-3-031-80957-6_6

1 Introductory Remarks

The analysis of the growing legal and economic literature[1]—as well as of the countless institutional positions and reports on the subject matter[2]—suggests that the adoption of CBDCs, including the digital euro, is on the horizon. The policy reasons behind the recent surge in interest in CBDCs are numerous: they include the necessity to ensure the monetary sovereignty of central banks against the backdrop of the explosion (and fall?) of cryptocurrencies, central banks' resilience, as well as competitive considerations. In addition to these factors that bolster the urgency of adopting CBDCs, the advent of an institutionally backed digital currency is being advocated as a tool of social inclusion. In particular, CBDCs are acclaimed to foster financial inclusion through easier, more efficient and direct access to financial services.

This chapter aims to explore the policy premise of financial inclusion and intends to explain why the question of the digital euro's inclusiveness

[1] In relation to cryptocurrencies, see, Leopolodo Esposito and HajdúJózsef, "Cryptocurrencies, between money, currency, means of payment and financial product. An alternative financial tool?" *Open Review of Management, Banking and Finance* (2022), https://wp.me/p5r4Oe-qn; Robby Houben and Alexander Snyers, "Crypto-assets. Key developments, regulatory concerns and responses," Study requested by the ECON committee, European parliament, 2020. https://www.europarl.europa.eu/RegData/etudes/STUD/2020/648779/IPOL_STU(2020)648779_EN.pdf; Giovanni Rinaldi, "Approcci normativi e qualificazione giuridica delle criptomonete," *Contratto e Impresa* 35, no. 1 (2019); Federico Riganti et al., "The «wild west» of digital finance—do we need an(other) EU «sheriff»?," *Law and Economics Yearly Review*, 11 (2022); Daniele Masi, "Le criptoattività: Proposte di qualificazione giuridica e primi approcci regolatori," *Banca Impresa Società* 40, no. 2 (2021); Giovanni Maria Nori, "Bitcoin, tra moneta e investimento," *Banca Impresa Società* 40, no. 1 (2021); Andrea Monti, "Per un'analisi critica della natura giuridica delle criptovalute," *Ragion pratica*, 2 (2018). On the digital euro, see Giacomo Bosi, "Digital euro e dintorni giuridici." *Banca Impresa Società* 41, no. 2 (2022).

[2] See the Board of Governors, Federal Reserve System, *Money and payments: The U.S. dollar in the age of digital transformation,* Federal reserve system, 2022. It can be accessed on the institutional website. In Europe, see the Introductory statement by Fabio Panetta, Member of the Executive Board of the ECB, at the Committee on Economic and Monetary Affairs of the European Parliament, in 2023 (Fabio Panetta, "The digital euro: Our money wherever, whenever we need it," European Central Bank, 2023, https://www.ecb.europa.eu/press/key/date/2023/html/ecb.sp230123~2f8271ed76.en.html). For a constant updated of publications on digital euro, visit the following link: https://www.ecb.europa.eu/home/search/html/digital_euro.en.html. On the topic related to the digital pound see the following link: https://www.bankofengland.co.uk/the-digital-pound.

effects must be properly addressed and contextualized. The argument is that in the specific EU context, a CBDC would not function as a relevant instrument of financial inclusion. In fact, it is contended that the comparably low level of financial exclusion in the EU calls into question the entire stream of policy reasoning in favour of CBDCs that is supported by the "inclusiveness argument". Moreover, it is claimed that—beyond a trust issue—the EU's specific social fabric, characterized by an ageing society and financial exclusion emerging mostly in connection with the digital divide, in fact crucially undermines or even defies the "inclusiveness argument". To the contrary, it is found that in the EU context, the digital euro could actually increase financial exclusion or solidify its current occurrences. Consequently, the findings show that the EU's further pursuance of the development of the digital euro ought to be strongly supported by arguments other than financial inclusion in order to remain within the mandate of the ECB.

This chapter contains six parts. First, it is briefly delineated the ECB's mandate to adopt the digital euro (Sect. 2). Subsequently, it is portrayed the issue of financial inclusion in the EU context (Sect. 3). It is then discussed the issue of trust in relation to the contended inclusiveness of CBDCs (Sect. 4). In the next part, it is spotlighted the potential impact of the digital euro on the problem of the digital exclusion of the elderly from financial services (Sect. 5). Finally, the last part concludes with closing remarks (Sect. 6).

2 The Mandate of the ECB

The study of CBDCs in the EU context requires a short reference regarding the mandate of the ECB on the subject matter.[3] In particular, it is considered fundamental for the analysis to verify the ECB to pursue its

[3] On this topic, see Seraina Grünewald et al., "Digital euro and ECB powers," *Common Market Law Review* 58, no. 4 (2021); Pier Mario Lupinu, "Digital euro: Opportunity or (legal) challenge?" *Ianus, no.* 22 (2021): 38–62. https://papers.ssrn.com/sol3/papers.cfm?abstract_id=3957391; AnneliekeMooij, "European central bank digital currency: The digital euro. What design of the digital euro is possible within the European central bank's legal framework?" Working paper series 14 (BRIDGE Network, 2021), https://papers.ssrn.com/sol3/papers.cfm?abstract_id=3838729; Corinne Zellweger-Gutknecht et al., "Digital euro, monetary objects, and price stability: A legal analysis." *Journal of Financial Regulation* 7, no. 2 (2021), https://doi.org/10.1093/jfr/fjab009. Reference made to the link between Central Banks and non-financial sustainability, see David Ramos Muñoz et al., "Central banks and climate change. Fit, opportunity and suitability in the law and

endeavours regarding the digital euro issues under the applicable legal framework. In this chapter, we prefer not to revisit the vast comprehensive literature that addresses the quite clear connection between the subject matter and the first mandate of the ECB.[4] Instead, we spotlight the ECB's contentious secondary mandate[5] and focus on the interconnection between Article 128 of the TFEU, the classification of the digital euro and the topic of financial inclusion.

In that regard, it is crucial to point out that:

- *On the one hand*, Article 127 TFEU defines the main objective of the ESCB as to maintain price stability. It also clarifies the scope of the secondary mandate: the ECB shall support the general economic policies of the EU to contribute to the achievement of the broad objectives of the Union itself, as laid down in Article 3 of the TEU—including promoting well-being of Europeans, working for a highly competitive social market economy and sustainable development, and promoting technological advances. Article 127(2) TFEU, then, clarifies the basic tasks to be carried out through the ESCB. Among those, the promotion of the smooth operation of payment systems is of specific relevance in this chapter. It refers, for example, to the ECB's inclusivity considerations behind the digital euro adoption in reference to otherwise *unbanked* (see *infra*) citizens.
- *On the other hand*, Article 128 TFEU encompasses an issue of a structural nature. It specifies that in the European institutional architecture, the ECB has the exclusive right to authorize the issue of euro banknotes within the Union, given the power assigned to it

beyond," European banking institute, 2022, https://papers.ssrn.com/sol3/papers.cfm?abstract_id=4054908.

[4] A detailed analysis is offered by Christos Gortsos, "Legal aspects of the European Central Bank (ECB)—The ECB within the European System of Central Banks (ESCB) and the European System of Financial Supervision (ESFS)—Gortsos, Christos, Legal aspects of the European Central Bank (ECB)—The ECB within the European System of Central Banks (ESCB) and the European System of Financial Supervision (ESFS)—second (extended and updated) edition," *Available at SSRN 3162024 (2018)*: https://ssrn.com/abstract=3162024 or http://dx.doi.org/10.2139/ssrn.3162024.

[5] On the topic of the secondary mandate, even if related to the issue of sustainability, see Simon Dikau and Ulrich Volz, "Central bank mandates, sustainability objectives and the promotion of green finance," *Ecological Economics*, 184 (2021), https://doi.org/10.1016/j.ecolecon.2021.107022.

(as well as that to the NCBs) to issue banknotes that shall have the status of legal tender within the Union.

Another important piece of the regulatory framework relevant to this chapter is the Statute of the ESCB and of the ECB (Statute), which does not expressly grant the power to issue money in the broad sense,[6] but confirms the power outlined in Article 128 TFEU to issue euro banknotes, having obtained authorization in that sense from the ECB Governing Council.

It is in the face of the regulatory and statutory attribution hereabove mentioned that the phenomenon of the digital euro seems likely to lead to a separate series of considerations for the digital currency in question, which can change depending on the form and function of such a currency.[7]

Even if we do agree with the view that it is preferable for the ECB to be given an explicit legal mandate on which to issue the digital euro,[8] however, we know that distinct positions on this aspect have been taken in the literature. In fact:

- *On the one side*, some authors generally suggest a kind of evolutionary interpretation of the discipline noted above. In fact, being the formulation of the norms strictly linked to a specific period of time, it did not include within its scope of action a category of digital currencies, merely because they did not exist and were not, perhaps, even conceivable at that time;
- *On the second side*, some other authors envisage at least four interpretative options, to be graduated based on the purpose of a new digital tool and the counterparties to which it is addressed. This leads to referencing the following legislative provisions[9]:

[6] See Giacomo Bosi, "Digital Euro."

[7] European Central Bank, *Report on a digital euro* (ECB, 2020). https://www.ecb.europa.eu/pub/pdf/other/Report_on_a_digital_euro~4d7268b458.en.pdf; Ludovica Galotto and Maria Iride Vangelisti, "Designing an inclusive digital euro." *Journal of Payments Strategy & Systems* 16, no. 2 (2022).

[8] Digital Euro Association, "Ahead of the digital euro: Public digital euro working group recommendations," *Digital euro association blog*, August 16, 2022, https://blog.digital-euro-association.de/ahead-of-the-digital-euro.

[9] See ECB, *Report on a digital euro*, 7.

(a) Article 127(2) TFEU and Article 20 Statute, if the digital euro is seen as an instrument of monetary policy, comparable to central bank reserves and accessible "*only (…) to central bank counterparties*"[10];
(b) Article 127(2), TFEU and Article 17 Statute, if the digital euro is accessible "*to households and other private entities through accounts held with the Eurosystem*";
(c) Article 127(2) TFEU and Article 22 Statute, if the digital euro is "*issued as a settlement medium for specific types of payment*" and specifically designed for dedicated infrastructures and "*eligible participants*"; and
(d) Article 128 TFEU and Article 16 Statute, if the digital euro is issued as an instrument equivalent to banknotes.

The two sides mentioned above leave a broad margin of discretion to the ECB, but entail an additional problem regarding the possibility and opportunity of the digital euro being classifiable *ab origine* (i.e. from the beginning) as legal tender.[11] On this aspect, it must be underlined that having a "fully legal" digital euro may entail serious operational issues: in fact, such a digital euro would be subject to the rule of mandatory acceptance, but in a framework not yet ready—also because of the technological exclusion—to manage such a new tool. The above would also have consequences under a financial inclusion point of view, despite the wishes of the ECB.

In reference to this aspect, it must be underlined that the topic of financial inclusion appears to be intrinsically linked, although not firmly anchored, to the digital euro by the words of the ECB and due to an extensive (perhaps, forced) interpretation of both the objectives indicated in Article 3 TFEU—precisely, the cited social advancement—and Article 153(j) TFEU, where it is stated that, as part of the social policy measures, "*the Union*" and thus, its institutions, including the ECB according to Article 13 TEU, "*shall support and complement the activities of the Member States in the following fields: (..) combating of social exclusion*".

[10] Fabio Panetta, "Il presente e il futuro della moneta nell'era digitale," Intervention, December 10, European central bank, 2021, https://www.ecb.europa.eu/press/key/date/2021/html/ecb.sp211210~09b6887f8b.it.html.

[11] Vincenzo De Stasio, "Verso un concetto europeo di moneta legale: valute virtuali, monete complementari e regole di adempimento," *Banca borsa e titoli di credito*, 6 (2018).

In any case, we believe that even if allowed by the regulatory framework, the intention to adopt the digital euro for purposes of social inclusion is primarily a decision of political nature. It is not compulsory and is not actually being pursued in the same way in the various CBDC projects that can currently be mapped.[12] Therefore, it is crucial to properly analyse the problem of financial exclusion in Europe in order to better understand if the adoption of the digital euro is actually an adequate response.

3 Financial Inclusion in the EU: Understanding the Problem

Based on the data analysis provided below, it seems that there is not an urgent problem of financial inclusion in Europe, with the concept of financial inclusion being understood—differently from the broader and trendy concept of "inclusion"[13]—as "*the proportion of individuals and firms that can access and use financial services (…) a crucial element in driving business growth, with a positive impact on aggregate economic growth and on the reduction of income inequality and poverty. (…) Financial inclusion is a multifaceted concept, whose boundaries are difficult to define as they change depending on the level of economic and financial development*".[14] Moreover, we believe that the occurrences of financial exclusion in Europe are primarily tied to the problem of digital exclusion.

Taking a look at the empirics, the general rate of financial exclusion (identified as the problem of the so called unbanked) in Europe is low.

[12] Gabriel Soderberg et al., "Behind the scenes of central bank digital currency: Emerging trends, insights, and policy lessons," *Fintech Notes,* February 9, International Monetary Fund, 2022, https://www.imf.org/en/Publications/fintech-notes/Issues/2022/02/07/Behind-the-Scenes-of-Central-Bank-Digital-Currency-512174.

[13] Defined as "a complex and multi-dimensional process. It involves the lack of denial of resources, rights, goods and services, and the inability to participate in the normal relationships and activities, available to the majority of people in a society, whether in economic, social, cultural or political arenas. It affects both the quality of life of individuals and the equity and cohesion of society as a whole". See Ruth Levitas et al., "The multi-dimensional analysis of social exclusion," Department for Communities and Local Government, 2007, 246 plus additional Appendix 7 ed., https://dera.ioe.ac.uk/id/eprint/6853/1/multidimensional.pdf.

[14] See Magda Bianco et al., "Challenges for financial inclusion: The role for financial education and new directions," Questioni di economia e finanza (Occasional Paper) (Banca d'Italia, 2022), https://www.bancaditalia.it/pubblicazioni/qef/2022-0723/index.html.

According to this methodology of measuring financial exclusion, only around 3.6% of the population is financially excluded, an improvement from the 8.2% reported in 2017.[15]

Also, globally speaking, the level of financial inclusion consistently increased: in 2021, 76% of adults had an account at a bank or regulated institution, such as a credit union microfinance institution or mobile money service provider. Account ownership around the world increased by 50% in the 10 years spanning 2011 to 2021, from 51 to 76% of adults. From 2017 to 2021, the average rate of account ownership in developing economies increased by 8 percentage points, from 63 to 71% of adults. In sub-Saharan Africa, this expansion largely stems from the adoption of mobile money.[16]

However, for the assessment of the reasoning behind the adoption of the digital euro, the EU context is relevant. In this context, at least two points are interesting about financial exclusion in EU:

(a) about one-third of unbanked adults reported that they do not have a bank account because they distrust the banking system, and
(b) in certain parts of the EU, older generations often constitute the largest portion of the unbanked. On this aspect, it must also be noted that older adults are reluctant to adopt new ways of making financial transactions, particularly if these new methods

[15] World Savings and Banking Institute, *Number of unbanked adult EU citizens more than halved in the last four years*, analysis conducted by the European savings and retail banking group (WSBI, 2022), https://www.wsbi-esbg.org/number-of-unbanked-adult-eu-citizens-more-than-halved-in-the-last-four-years/. It is mentioned that "looking at some European countries in detail, Romania suffers the highest no-account rate at 30,9%, while neighbour Bulgaria faces the second highest financial exclusion rate at 16%. Following them are Hungary (11,8%), Croatia (8,2%) and Portugal (7,4%). Compared to the 2017 data, Bulgaria showed nearly an 11-percentage points improvement from 2017 when they reported 27,8% of the population remained unbanked. The Czech Republic and Lithuania significantly improved their unbanked rates over the reported period, dropping out of the top 5 list of EU countries with the highest no-account rates, as Croatia and Portugal replaced the pair. Best-in-class countries include Denmark, with hardly any unbanked people reported, followed by Germany (0,02% unbanked) and Austria (0,05%). These are followed by the Netherlands (0,3%) and Sweden (0,3%). Austria is the newcomer in this top 5, replacing Belgium. Nevertheless, Belgium, together with 10 other countries have more than 99% of their population participating in banking services".

[16] World Bank, *The global findex database 2021: Financial inclusion, digital payments, and resilience in the age of COVID-19* (World Bank, 2021), https://www.worldbank.org/en/publication/globalfindex.

require technologies, unfamiliar to them (digital distrust and digital divide).

Such last point—addressed in Sect. 5—seems to be crucial as the unbanked problem in Europe must be understood in the context of an economy where the demographic composition involves an unstoppable advance in the number of the over 80 s (whose share of the population almost doubled between 2001 and 2020) and a steady decline in the under 20 s.

In this context, a clear connection between financial exclusion, the digital divide and the belonging to the demographic group of older people exists. This problem is particularly relevant in some areas of Europe such as Italy, where recent evidence points to the fact that "*Italy ranks 18th out of 27 EU Member States in the 2022 edition of the Digital Economy and Society Index (DESI). As the third largest EU economy, Italy's progress in the digital transformation over the coming years is crucial to enable the EU as a whole to reach the 2030 Digital Decade targets. Italy is catching up and, looking at the progress of its DESI score over the past five years, it is advancing at a remarkable pace. In recent years, digital issues have gained political traction notably with the establishment of a ministry responsible for digital affairs, the adoption of several key strategies and the launch of many policy measures. That said, there are still gaps in the digital transformation to be overcome*".[17]

Given the above, digital euro seems not to be the right answer to the problem of financial inclusion in the EU context.

4 Better Not to Trust?

Given the context as designed above, one may question whether the digital euro would be easily and trustily welcomed by the EU population. Beyond the main problem of digital distrust and financial exclusion of the elderly, several reasons seem to support this view and affect both intermediaries and consumers. Concerning intermediaries, as already pointed

[17] European Commission, *Digital Economy and Society Index (DESI)*, Digital Economy and Society Index, 2022, https://www.astrid-online.it/static/upload/desi/desi_2022__italy__eng.pdf.

out in the literature,[18] the digital euro could have a disruptive effect on the banking system, since—depending on how the digital euro is designed[19]—it could also offer a kind of disintermediation of the system itself in favour of a direct communication mechanism between ECB and final consumers.[20]

With reference to consumers, the digital euro would be one of the outcomes of the same technological revolution that previously created crypto-assets and within such a category, cryptocurrencies, whether or not in their stabilized form. This implies perceiving the digital euro as a product that is: (i) sophisticated to explain and use, at least apparently (but appearances matter), and (ii) similar (in the eyes of non-experts) to cryptocurrencies and as such unfit to be easily managed by any economic player. On this point, we are fully aware that the design aspect of the digital euro will be a central element, given that, for example, the usability of the digital euro even off-line would make it more friendly (and therefore, more trustworthy) for consumers. In any case, at the present time we believe that the digital euro will remain, for a while, a sheer novelty whose macro-structural needs could also (and probably) not be clearly and entirely understood by the citizens of the EU and whose highly advanced technological nature would probably appear to a vast part of them a kind of "alchemy". In other words, a kind of unnecessary and esoteric re-propositioning of cash (the lack of which, at the end of the day, is the real problem of financial inclusion), with a stronger invasion into the banking system of the independent authorities, whose role of supervisors will be boosted by the digital approach.

In the end, as already mentioned above, the issues related to monetary governance that are likely to arise as a result of the adoption of the digital euro will have to contemplate the involvement of the banking system.

[18] Luigi Scipione, "Le valute digitali sovrane tra stabilità e concorrenza. Perno di un nuovo sistema finanziario o inganno demagogico?," *Innovazione e Diritto*, 3 (2019).

[19] On this topic—that is not the main focus of this chapter—please see European Central Bank, "Market research and prototyping exercise confirm feasibility of technical solutions and user interfaces for a digital euro," MIP News, May 26, 2023. https://www.ecb.europa.eu/paym/intro/news/html/ecb.mipnews230526.en.html.

[20] It must be underlined that such a possibility currently appears to be losing strength and relevance, even in the face of the supporting role played by individual banks in favour of the ECB. It is, in any case, a central element of the digital euro, which therefore if not carefully structured could negatively affect the credit intermediation system and also the inclusion of unbanked.

Consequently, we can imagine that the unbanked, which are out of the banking system, since they do not trust the system itself, will probably not be incentivized to take part in this "digital currency revolution".

5 Dredging Financial Exclusion of the Elderly?

As suggested above in Sect. 3, financial exclusion in the EU does not seem to be an urgent problem. Moreover, it primarily concerns a specific demographic group—i.e. society's older members. This stems from the fact that financial exclusion in the EU is tied to the digital divide and older people are a societal group particularly exposed to the risks of being digitally marginalized.[21] Certainly, the demographically limited extent to which EU societies are affected by financial exclusion does not imply the irrelevance of the topic for policymaking. To the contrary, the effective integration of the elderly in our society is being recognized as a pivotal component for creating a harmonious social fabric. The well-being of older people is embedded in goal No. 3 of the 17 Sustainable Development Goals in the United Nations (UN) Agenda 2030.[22] The tragic consequences of the COVID-19 pandemic, in terms of the elderly's vulnerability, have reminded society about the necessity to address the needs of the elderly population within our societies with the same diligence we devote to problems faced by younger generations. Consequently, any policy actions that could potentially contribute to marginalizing older people must be critically scrutinized. As mentioned above, it is therefore crucial to assess whether the digital euro could heighten the risks of financial exclusion of the elderly.[23]

[21] Organisation for Economic Co-operation and Development. International network on financial education. *International survey of adult financial literacy* (OECD/INFE, 2020). https://www.oecd.org/financial/education/launchoftheoecdinfeglobalfinancialliteracysurveyreport.htm. The authors are aware of the fact that there are other vulnerable groups in this respect; however, the reasons for vulnerability and respective remedies are diverse and are addressed elsewhere. See World Bank Group, *The impact of Covid-19 on digital financial* (World Bank, 2021).

[22] Department of Economic and Social Affairs, United Nations, *The 17 goals*, https://sdgs.un.org/goals.

[23] Pawel Kossecki and Artur Borcuch, "Digital, social and financial exclusion among elderly people," *Demographic problems of Europe—Polish example* (August 17, 2014), https://dx.doi.org/10.2139/ssrn.2482052.

Long before the emergence of the current debate on CBDCs, the financial industry commenced to move its activity online—predominantly, in search of efficiency savings and broader customer pools.[24] As a result, across the broad spectrum of financial services, participation in the "online world" is often no longer a result of choice but of necessity. Traditional person-to-person services, including commercial banking,[25] are increasingly disappearing, which forces consumers to adjust how they fulfil their basic everyday needs.[26] For example, empirical data sourced across the EU show that bank branches are steadily vanishing[27] and that the COVID-19 pandemic certainly expedited this trend.[28]

While the digital transformation of financial services seems inevitable, its impact upon the elderly has so far been only marginally analysed, as academic attention has been focused on the implications arising for the active participants in this process[29]—both on the sides of financial institutions and digitized customers. Similarly, the current debate on CBDCs' claimed financial inclusiveness effects seems to overlook this problem in its entirety.

While CBDCs could potentially increase the overall accessibility of financial services for the average consumer, in the case of countries with already high rates of financial exclusion, such an argument does not

[24] Emilios Avgouleas, "Regulating financial innovation: A multifaceted challenge to financial stability, consumer protection, and growth," in *The Oxford Handbook of Financial Regulation,* ed. Niamh Moloney, Eilís Ferran and Jennifer Payne (Oxford: Oxford University Press, 2015).

[25] Anne–Marie Weber et al., "Digitalizing the commercial banking business model—vanishing bank branches and the risks of financial exclusion of the elderly," in *Commercial Banking in Transition: A Cross-Country-Analysis*, ed. Gimigliano Gabriella, Marco Bodellini, and Dhillon Singh (Cham: Springer International Publishing, 2024).

[26] Eric Hilgendorf, "Introduction: Digitization and the law—a European perspective," in *Digitization and the LAW*, ed. Eric Hilgendorf and Jochen Feldle (Baden-Baden: Nomos Verlagsgesellschaft, 2018).

[27] Anne–Marie Weber et al., "Digitalizing."

[28] European Central Bank, "The banks are not complacent," Interview with Ana Botín, President of the European banking federation, February 16, 2022, https://www.bankingsupervision.europa.eu/press/publications/newsletter/2022/html/ssm.nl220216.en.html.

[29] European Commission, Building the European information society for us all, Final policy report of the high-level expert group of directorate-general for employment industrial relations and social affairs, 1997, https://op.europa.eu/en/publication-detail/-/publication/2aca04ac-7e7d-4eb4-b69d-1638ce0ddeb0.

hold in the EU context, where financial exclusion does not appear to be an urgent problem and it is tied to digital exclusion. Importantly, digital exclusion mostly affects the elderly. Older people are less confident regarding any online participation in economic activity and in particular in the area of financial services. For example, the use of online banking tools requires a basic proficiency in the use of electronic devices and essential knowledge regarding the nature of the financial services rendered.[30]

As existing research confirms, digital skills and financial literacy are lower among the elderly than for other age groups.[31] In particular, several studies suggest that cognitive abilities deteriorate with age which substantially affects the decline of the financial literacy index, especially in people over 60[32] (the age of 60 is the conventional limit of old age proposed by the World Health Organization and the OECD). Coupled with the elderly's lack of trust in digital financial services,[33] financial exclusion of the elderly is likely not going to be alleviated by the digital euro. On the contrary, the digital euro could potentially contribute to further the alienation of this demographic group regarding basic financial interaction (e.g. payments).

Against the backdrop of the EU's demographic structure, the abovementioned risks related to the financial exclusion of the elderly must be

[30] Niamh Moloney, "Financial market governance and consumer protection in the EU," in *Financial Regulation. A Transatlantic Perspective,* ed. Faia, E. et al. (Cambridge: Cambridge University Press, 2015).

[31] Fahad Asmi and Tanko Ishaya, "Understanding the behavior of the elderly towards internet banking in the UK," in *Proceeding of the 2nd International Conference on Social Eco-Informatics*, October, 2012, https://www.semanticscholar.org/paper/Understanding-the-Behavior-of-the-Elderly-towards-Asmi-Ishaya/008d8cf646cb25cebab2cc250dbf770d906ff4e2; Andreas Oehler and Stepan Wendt, "Good consumer information: The information paradigm at its (dead) end?," *Journal of Consumer Policy*, 40 (2017), https://doi.org/10.1007/s10603-016-9337-5; Michael Finke et al., "Old age and the decline in financial literacy," *Management Science* 63, no. 1 (2017).

[32] World Health Organization, "Ageing and health," October 1, 2022, https://www.who.int/news-room/fact-sheets/detail/ageing-and-health; Organisation for Economic Co-operation and Development, *Financial consumer protection and ageing populations* (OECD,2020), https://www.oecd.org/finance/financial-education/financialconsumerprotection.htm.

[33] Tony Greenham and Fionn Travers-Smith, "Cashing out. The hidden costs and consequences of moving to cashless society," Rivest, Shamir, Adleman, 2019, https://www.thersa.org/globalassets/pdfs/reports/rsa-cashing-out.pdf; Asmi and Ishaya, "Understanding," 27.

deemed a substantial policy consideration. The phenomenon of ageing or "graying" in EU society consists of an increase in the percentage of older people within society, while the share of people of working age in the total population decreases. It has been stipulated that by 2100, the percentage of the population in EU countries over 65 years of age will increase dynamically from 20.2% in 2019 and will account for nearly 31.3% of the total population of the EU, while the percentage of the oldest population, i.e. over 80 years of age, will increase from 5.8% to 14.6%.[34]‘ The share of people aged 80 years or above in the EU's population is projected to increase between 2021 and 2100 from 6% to 14.6%.[35]

While the effects of digital transformation could naturally marginalize the elderly in multiple ways, the implications of digital exclusion regarding financial services seem to be especially fierce.[36] In particular, the capacity to execute payments for goods and services is instrumental to the elderly. Financial exclusion affects the possibility of satisfying basic needs in all areas of the elderly's societal interactions. Therefore, any EU policy actions that expedite the digitalization of financial services bear the risks of aggravating the financial exclusion of older people. Since financial exclusion in the EU mostly affects the elderly, particularly due to their lower digital proficiency and capacities, the implementation of a digital tool, as a policy remedy, appears misplaced. Consequently, the adoption of the digital euro will not be able to effectively contribute to the financial inclusion of the elderly in the EU. Therefore, the "financial inclusiveness" argument, which is being advocated in the CBDC debate, does not hold in the EU context.

[34] The Statistical Office of the EU, *Population structure and ageing* (Eurostat, 2023), https://ec.europa.eu/eurostat/statistics-explained/index.php?title=Population_structure_and_ageing; The Statistical Office of the EU, *Aging Europe. Looking at the lives of older people in the EU* (Eurostat, 2020), https://ec.europa.eu/eurostat/documents/3217494/11478057/KS-02-20-655-EN-N.pdf.

[35] Ibid.

[36] Vassilakopoulou, P., and E., Hustad. 2021. Bridging digital divides: A literature review and research agenda for information systems research. *Information system frontiers*. https://doi.org/10.1007/s10796-020-10096-3.

6 Final Remarks

According to the analysis in this chapter, we consider that in the EU context the digital euro cannot be primarily understood and legitimized as an instrument of financial inclusion. The problem of financial exclusion in the EU is marginal, tied to the problem of digital exclusion and mostly concerns the demographic group of elderly citizens. Consequently, the situation of those currently excluded from financial systems in the EU would most probably not be impacted by the adoption of the digital euro. On the contrary, in a policy scenario, which is based upon the idea of a digital tool that would encompass a steady decline in the use of cash, the digital euro could, in fact, become a means of furthering financial exclusion in the EU. Consequently, we argue that in the EU context, the adoption of a CBDC policy by the ECB must be based on arguments other than its alleged financial inclusivity effects.

References

Asmi, Fahad, and Tanko Ishaya. "Understanding the behavior of the elderly towards internet banking in the UK." In *Proceeding of the 2nd international conference on social eco-informatics, October*, pp. 21–26. 2012. https://www.semanticscholar.org/paper/Understanding-the-Behavior-of-the-Elderly-towards-Asmi-Ishaya/008d8cf646cb25cebab2cc250dbf770d906ff4e2.

Avgouleas, Emilios "Regulating financial innovation: A multifaceted challenge to financial stability, consumer protection, and growth." In *The oxford handbook of financial regulation,* edited by Moloney Niamh, Eilís Ferran, and Jennifer Payne, pp. 660–688. Oxford: Oxford University Press, 2015.

Bianco, Magda, Daniela Marconi, Angela Romagnoli, and Massimiliano Stacchini. "Challenges for financial inclusion: The role for financial education and new directions." Questioni di economia e finanza (Occasional Paper), Banca d'Italia, 2022. https://www.bancaditalia.it/pubblicazioni/qef/2022-0723/index.html.

Board of Governors. Federal reserve system. *Money and payments: The U.S. dollar in the age of digital transformation.* Federal reserve system, 2022. https://www.federalreserve.gov/publications/money-and-payments-discussion-paper.htm.

Bosi, Giacomo. "Digital euro e dintorni giuridici." *Banca Impresa Società* 41, no. 2 (2022): 219–250.

De Stasio, Vincenzo. "Verso un concetto europeo di moneta legale: Valute virtuali, monete complementari e regole di adempimento." *Banca borsa e titoli di credito*, 6 (2018): 747–761.

Department of Economic and Social Affairs, United Nations. *The 17 goals*. Web site, https://sdgs.un.org/goals.

Digital Euro Association. "Ahead of the digital euro: Public digital euro working group recommendations." *Digital euro association blog*, August 16, 2022. https://blog.digital-euro-association.de/ahead-of-the-digital-euro.

Dikau, Simon, and Ulrich Volz. "Central bank mandates, sustainability objectives and the promotion of green finance." *Ecological Economics*, 184 (2021): 107022. https://doi.org/10.1016/j.ecolecon.2021.107022.

Esposito, Leopoldo, and Hajdú József. "Cryptocurrencies, between money, currency, means of payment and financial product. An alternative financial tool?" *Open Review of Management, Banking and Finance*, (2022). https://wp.me/p5r4Oe-qn.

European Central Bank. "The banks are not complacent," *Interview with Ana Botín*, President of the European banking federation, February 16, 2022. https://www.bankingsupervision.europa.eu/press/publications/newsletter/2022/html/ssm.nl220216.en.html.

European Central Bank. *Market research and prototyping exercise confirm feasibility of technical solutions and user interfaces for a digital euro.* MIP News, May 26, 2023. https://www.ecb.europa.eu/paym/intro/news/html/ecb.mipnews230526.en.html.

European Central Bank. *Report on a digital euro.* ECB, 2020. https://www.ecb.europa.eu/pub/pdf/other/Report_on_a_digital_euro~4d7268b458.en.pdf.

European Commission. *Digital Economy and Society Index (DESI).* Digital Economy and Society Index, 2022, https://www.astrid-online.it/static/upload/desi/desi_2022__italy__eng.pdf.

European Commission. *Building the European information society for us all.* Final policy report of the high-level expert group of Directorate-General for employment industrial relations and social affairs, 1997. https://op.europa.eu/en/publication-detail/-/publication/2aca04ac-7e7d-4eb4-b69d-1638ce0ddeb0.

Finke, Michael S., John S. Howe, and Sandra J. Huston. "Old age and the decline in financial literacy." *Management Science* 63, no. 1 (2017): 213–230.

Galotto, Ludovica, and Maria Iride Vangelisti. "Designing an inclusive digital euro." *Journal of Payments Strategy & Systems* 16, no. 2 (2022): 137–147.

Gortsos, Christos. "Legal aspects of the European Central Bank (ECB): The ECB within the European System of Central Banks (ESCB) and the European System of Financial Supervision (ESFS)—Gortsos, Christos, legal aspects of the European Central Bank (ECB)—The ECB within the European System of Central Banks (ESCB) and the European System of Financial Supervision (ESFS)—second (extended and updated) edition." *Available at SSRN 3162024 (2018)*. https://ssrn.com/abstract=3162024.

Greenham, Tony, and Fionn Travers-Smith. "Cashing out. The hidden costs and consequences of moving to cashless society." Rivest, Shamir, Adleman (RSA), 2019. https://www.thersa.org/globalassets/pdfs/reports/rsa-cashing-out.pdf.

Grünewald, Seraina Neva, Corinne Zellweger-Gutknecht, and Benjamin Geva. "Digital euro and ECB powers." *Common Market Law Review* 58, no. 4 (2021): 1029–1055.

Hilgendorf, Eric. "Introduction: digitization and the law–a European perspective." In *Digitization and the law*, edited by Eric Hilgendorf, and Jochen Feldle, pp. 9–20. Baden—Baden: Nomos Verlagsgesellschaft, 2018.

Houben, Robby, and Alexander Snyers. *Crypto-assets. Key developments, regulatory concerns and responses*. Study requested by the ECON Committee, European Parliament, 2020. https://www.europarl.europa.eu/RegData/etudes/STUD/2020/648779/IPOL_STU(2020)648779_EN.pdf.

Kossecki, Pawel, and Artur Borcuch. *Digital, social and financial exclusion among elderly people. Demographic problems of Europe–Polish example*. Demographic Problems of Europe–Polish Example (August 17, 2014) (2014). https://doi.org/10.2139/ssrn.2482052.

Levitas, Ruth, Christina Pantazis, Eldin Fahmy, David Gordon, Eva Lloyd-Reichling, and Demy Patsios. *The multi-dimensional analysis of social exclusion*. Department for Communities and Local Government (DCLG), 2007. https://dera.ioe.ac.uk/id/eprint/6853/1/multidimensional.pdf.

Lupinu, Pier Mario. "Digital euro: Opportunity or (legal) challenge?" *Ianus no*. 22 (2021): 38–62. https://papers.ssrn.com/sol3/papers.cfm?abstract_id=3957391.

Masi, Daniele. "Le criptoattività: Proposte di qualificazione giuridica e primi approcci regolatori." *Banca Impresa Società* 40, no. 2 (2021): 241–270.

Moloney, Niamh. "Financial market governance and consumer protection in the EU." In *Financial regulation. A transatlantic perspective*, edited by Faia, E. et al., pp. 221–244. Cambridge: Cambridge University Press, 2015.

Monti, Andrea. "Per un'analisi critica della natura giuridica delle criptovalute." *Ragion pratica*, 2 (2018): 361–378.

Mooij, Annelieke AM. "European central bank digital currency: The digital euro. What design of the digital euro is possible within the European central bank's legal framework?" Working Paper Series no. 14, BRIDGE Network, 2021. https://papers.ssrn.com/sol3/papers.cfm?abstract_id=3838729.

Nori, Giovanni Maria. "Bitcoin, tra moneta e investimento." *Banca Impresa Società* 40, no. 1 (2021): 157–185.

Oehler, Andreas, and Stefan Wendt. "Good consumer information: The information paradigm at its (dead) end?" *Journal of Consumer Policy*, 40 (2017): 179–191. https://doi.org/10.1007/s10603-016-9337-5.

Organisation for Economic Co-operation and Development. *Financial consumer protection.* OECD, 2020. https://www.oecd.org/finance/financial-education/financialconsumerprotection.htm.

Organisation for Economic Co-operation and Development. *International network on financial education. International survey of adult financial literacy.* OECD/INFE, 2020. https://www.oecd.org/financial/education/launchofttheoecdinfeglobalfinancialliteracysurveyreport.htm.

Panetta, Fabio. "Il presente e il futuro della moneta nell'era digitale." Intervention, December 10. European Central Bank, 2021. https://www.ecb.europa.eu/press/key/date/2021/html/ecb.sp211210~09b6887f8b.it.html.

Panetta, Fabio. *The digital euro: Our money wherever, whenever we need it. Introductory statement at the committee on economic and monetary affairs of the European parliament, January 23.* European Central Bank 2023. https://www.ecb.europa.eu/press/key/date/2023/html/ecb.sp230123~2f8271ed76.en.html.

Ramos Muñoz, David, Antonio Cabrales, and Anxo Sánchez. *Central banks and climate change. Fit, opportunity and suitability in the law and beyond.* European Banking Institute, 2022. https://papers.ssrn.com/sol3/papers.cfm?abstract_id=4054908.

Riganti, Federico, Rodríguez de las Heras Ballell Teresa, and Weber Anne-Marie. "The «wild west» of digital finance–do we need an (other) EU «sheriff»?" *Law and Economics Yearly Review*, 11 (2022): 88–107.

Rinaldi, Giovanni. "Approcci normativi e qualificazione giuridica delle criptomonete." *Contratto e impresa* 35, no. 1 (2019): 257–296.

Scipione, Luigi. "Le valute digitali sovrane tra stabilità e concorrenza. Perno di un nuovo sistema finanziario globale o inganno demagogico?" *Innovatione e Diritto*, 3 (2019): 1–44.

Soderberg, Gabriel, Marianne Bechara, Wouter Bossu, Sonja Davidovic, John Kiff, Inutu Lukonga, Tommaso Mancini Griffoli, Tao Sun, and Akihiro Yoshinaga. *Behind the scenes of central bank digital currency: Emerging trends, insights, and policy lessons.* Fintech Notes, February 9. International Monetary Fund, 2022. https://www.imf.org/en/Publications/fintech-notes/Issues/2022/02/07/Behind-the-Scenes-of-Central-Bank-Digital-Currency-512174.

The Statistical Office of the EU. *Aging Europe. Looking at the lives of older people in the EU.* Eurostat, 2020. https://ec.europa.eu/eurostat/documents/3217494/11478057/KS-02-20-655-EN-N.pdf.

The Statistical Office of the EU. *Population structure and ageing.* Eurostat, 2023 https://ec.europa.eu/eurostat/statistics-explained/index.php?title=Population_structure_and_ageing.

Vassilakopoulou, Polyxeni, and Eli Hustad. "Bridging digital divides: A literature review and research agenda for information systems research." *Information*

Systems Frontiers 25, no. 3 (2021): 955–969. https://doi.org/10.1007/s10796-020-10096-3.

Weber, Anne-Marie, Anne-Christin Mittwoch, Weronika Herbet-Homenda, and Weronika Stefaniuk. "Digitalizing the commercial banking business model: Vanishing bank branches and the risks of financial exclusion of the elderly." In *Commercial banking in transition: A cross-country analysis*, edited by Gimigliano Gabriella, Marco Bodellini, and Dhillon Singh, pp. 87–107. Cham: Springer International Publishing, 2024.

World Bank Group. *The global findex database 2021: Financial inclusion, digital payments, and resilience in the age of Covid-19*. World Bank, 2021 https://www.worldbank.org/en/publication/globalfindex.

World Bank Group. *The impact of Covid-19 on digital financial*. World Bank, 2021 https://www.gpfi.org/sites/gpfi/files/sites/default/files/5_WB%20Report_The%20impact%20of%20COVID-19%20on%20digital%20financial%20inclusion.pdf.

World Health Organization. "Ageing and health." October 1, 2022. https://www.who.int/news-room/fact-sheets/detail/ageing-and-health.

World Savings and Banking Institute. *Number of unbanked adult EU citizens more than halved in the last four years*. Analysis conducted by the European savings and retail banking group. WSBI, 2022. https://www.wsbi-esbg.org/number-of-unbanked-adult-eu-citizens-more-than-halved-in-the-last-four-years/.

Zellweger-Gutknecht, Corinne, Benjamin Geva, and Seraina Neva Grünewald. "Digital euro, monetary objects, and price stability: A legal analysis." *Journal of Financial Regulation* 7, no. 2 (2021): 284–318. https://doi.org/10.1093/jfr/fjab009.

PART IV

Mechanics: Governance, Form of Issuance, Impact on Banking System

CHAPTER 7

Governance Issues Concerning the Issuer of CBDC, Who Supervises and Controls the CBDC Scheme?

Ioannis E. Linaritis

1 Introduction: Relevance and Importance of Governance in CBDC Schemes

International central banks' research, consultation and planning, with regard to the issuance of different kinds of sovereign digital currencies (hereinafter "CBDC"), have progressed at an even faster pace in the

This book Chapter benefited from presentations at the European Banking Institute ARG seminar on Central Bank Digital Currencies (Athens, September 29, 2022). For valuable comments and discussions on the subject matters, the author would like to thank particularly Christina Livada, Associate Professor of Law, National and Kapodestrian University of Athens, Member of the EBI ARG, Angeliki Makri, Attorney-at-law, LL.M. and Mariela Tiliakou, Attorney-at-law, M.Sc. The thoughts and opinions expressed in this Chapter reflect only the author's views and not the views or positions of any of the academic or professional affiliations or employers of the author.

© The Author(s), under exclusive license to Springer Nature Switzerland AG 2025

F. Annunziata et al. (eds.), *Central Bank Digital Currency*, EBI Studies in Banking and Capital Markets Law,
https://doi.org/10.1007/978-3-031-80957-6_7

post-COVID-19 era.[1] What started as an experimental consideration and strategic reaction to the emergence and growth of "crypto-currencies" and similar assets generated by the private sector (including Fintech and big tech companies),[2] has undergone thorough review and analysis from various perspectives, to consider its potential utility and alignment with the multiple central banks' objectives. Monetary policy, financial, legal and technical aspects, drivers, possible impact and consequences of this prospective new form of currency have been examined and subjected

I. E. Linaritis (✉)
Assistant Professor, Democritus University of Thrace, Faculty of Law, Komotini, Greece
e-mail: ILINARIT@law.duth.gr

[1] See International Monetary Fund, "Digital Money Across Borders: Macro-Financial Implications," Policy Paper no. 050 (IMF, 2020), https://www.imf.org/en/Publications/Policy-Papers/Issues/2020/10/17/Digital-Money-Across-Borders-Macro-Financial-Implications-49823, considering CBDC as next milestone in the evolution of money; Bank for International Settlements, *Central Bank Digital Currencies: Foundational Principles and Core Features*, Report no. 1 in a series of collaborations from a group of central banks, 2020, https://www.bis.org/publ/othp33.pdf, contrasting extensively CBDC with existing types of money; Raphael Auer et al., "Rise of the central bank digital currencies: drivers, approaches and technologies," Working Papers 880 (Bank for International Settlements, 2020), 9, https://www.bis.org/publ/work880.htm; On the CBDC classification in the taxonomy of money, see Bank for International Settlements, *Central Bank Digital Currencies* (BIS, 2018), 4, https://www.bis.org/cpmi/publ/d174.htm.

[2] On the evolving taxonomy and terminology of different categories of crypto-assets, see Article 3(1) of European Parliament and Council of the European Union, "Regulation (EU) 2023/1114 of the European Parliament and the Council of 31 May 2023 on markets in crypto-assets, and amending Regulations (EU) No 1093/2010 and (EU) No 1095/2010 and Directives 2013/36/EU and (EU) 2019/1937 (MICA regulation)," *Official Journal of the EU L 150/40* (2023), https://eur-lex.europa.eu/legal-content/EN/TXT/PDF/?uri=CELEX:32023R1114; Claude Brown et al., "Cryptoassets and initial coin offerings," in *Fintech: law and regulation*, ed. Jelena Madir, (Northampton: Edward Elgar Publishing, 2021), 90, 92; Dirk Zetzsche et al., "Regulating LIBRA: The transformative potential of facebook's cryptocurrency and possible regulatory responses," Working Paper Series 2019/44 (European Banking Institute, 2019), https://papers.ssrn.com/sol3/papers.cfm?abstract_id=3414401; Phoebus Athanassiou, "Impact of digital innovation on the processing of electronic payments and contracting: an overview of legal risks," Legal Working Paper Series 16 (European Central Bank, 2017), 8, https://www.ecb.europa.eu/pub/pdf/scplps/ecb.lwp16.en.pdf. On the policy risks involved, see indicatively Financial Stability Board, *Crypto-asset markets, Potential channels for future financial stability implications* (FSB, 2018), 3, https://www.fsb.org/wp-content/uploads/P101018.pdf.

to extensive assessment and public discussion.[3] At the European level, the "digital euro" project investigation has progressed in the last years,[4] along with major legislative developments, forming part of the greater

[3] At the EU level, see European Commission, *A digital euro for the EU*, call for evidence for an impact assessment (European Commission, 2022), https://ec.europa.eu/info/law/better-regulation/have-your-say/initiatives/13392-A-digital-euro-for-the-EU_en. Reference is made there to the initial European Central Bank, *Report on a digital euro* (ECB, 2020), https://www.ecb.europa.eu/pub/pdf/other/Report_on_a_digital_euro~4d7268b458.en.pdf; European Central Bank, public consultation on a digital euro (October 2020-January 2021) and ECB Governing Council decision to start an investigation phase on a digital euro project (October 2021); Fabio Panetta, "More than an intellectual game: exploring the monetary policy and financial stability implications of Central Bank Digital Currencies," *Opening speech at the IESE Business School Banking Initiative Conference on Technology and Finance*, Frankfurt am Main, April, 8, 2022; Phoebus Athanassiou, Digital innovation in financial services: legal challenges and regulatory policy issues, Kluwer Law International BV, 2018: 203, 210. For the global assessment and up to date developments, see Bank for International Settlements, *BIS Innovation Hub research on Central Bank Digital Currency (CBDC)* (BIS, 2021), https://www.bis.org/about/bisih/topics/cbdc.htm, with reference to the BIS survey (2021) (according to which 86% of central banks surveyed were actively researching the potential for Central Bank Digital Currencies (CBDCs), 60% were experimenting with the technology and 14% were deploying pilot projects), 43; Kiff et al., "A survey of research on retail Central Bank Digital Currency," Working Paper no. 104 (International, Monetary Fund, 2020), https://www.imf.org/en/Publications/WP/Issues/2021/04/23/Central-Bank-Risk-Management-Fintech-and-Cybersecurity-50278. Saule Omarova, "The people's ledger: How to democratize money and finance the economy," *Vanderbilt Law Review 74* (2021), 1250, https://papers.ssrn.com/sol3/papers.cfm?abstract_id=%203715735, focusing on the U.S. Federal Reserve System; Nicola Bilotta and Fabrizio Botti, *The (Near) Future of Central Bank Digital Currencies Risks and Opportunities for the Global Economy and Society*, Peter Lang International Academic Publishers, 2021, 27.

[4] "Digital euro" is understood as a central bank liability offered in digital form for use by individuals and businesses, which would complement cash and private payment means. The "digital euro" project is steered by the High-Level Task Force on Central Bank Digital Currency, composed by representatives from the ECB and the national central banks of the euro area. See European Central Bank, *Digital Euro project governance and stakeholder management* (ECB, 2022), https://www.ecb.europa.eu/paym/digital_euro/investigation/governance/shared/files/ecb.degov220608_governance.en.pdf; European Central Bank, *Progress on the investigation phase of a digital euro,* First report, 2022, 2, https://www.ecb.europa.eu/paym/digital_euro/investigation/governance/shared/files/ecb.degov220929.en.pdf. On the prospect of the Eurosystem issuing a digital currency, as significant novel element in the euro area and the advanced developments of Monetary Union, see Christos Gortsos, "Future of the Economic and Monetary Union," Working Paper Series no. 129 (European Banking Institute, 2022), https://ssrn.com/abstract=4212947.

EU digital finance package.[5] In such dynamic international context, thorough assessments led to a tentative positive inference: that implementing CBDC initiatives can indeed contribute to the financial markets' integration and innovation, while also serving efficiently public interest and contemporary needs of the society.[6]

From the very beginning, leading authorities and academic literature have promptly emphasized the significant role of CBDC issuers and schemes' governance, among the critical factors which would influence the outcome of the central banks' digital currencies' endeavours. Governance issues have always been critical in the financial sector's sub-industries and markets, given the existence of manifold diverging interests of public and private stakeholders.[7] In the CBDC landscape, it is no wonder that governance concerns attract special attention, because of the challenging interplay between, on the one side, the traditional central banks' institutional mandate, competences and structural characteristics and on the other side, the innovative features and challenges posed by the envisioned new form of currency. That fundamental complexity leads to a set of key inter-related questions that this chapter aims to examine and propose some preliminary answers: Are the conventional central bank governance mechanisms suitable, adequate and readily available, in the prospective run-up to the CBDC issuance, distribution and

[5] On the broader EU digital finance package, see the aforementioned Markets in Crypto-Assets Regulation (EU) (footnote 2), establishing EU's harmonized crypto-assets' regime, the Regulation (EU) 2022/2554 on digital operational resilience for the financial sector (DORA), and the Regulation (EU) 2022/858 on a pilot regime for market infrastructures based on distributed ledger technology, and amending Regulations (EU) No 600/2014 and (EU) No 909/2014 and Directive 2014/65/EU ("DLT Pilot Regime").

[6] See Euro Summit call for a stronger and more innovative digital finance sector and more efficient and resilient payment systems at *Statement by the Members of the Euro Summit, meeting in an inclusive format* (Brussels: March 25, 2021), https://www.consilium.europa.eu/media/48975/25-03-21-eurosummit-statement-en.pdf, DigEuro-Reg and the Proposal for a Regulation of the European Parliament and of the Council on the provision of digital euro services by payment services providers incorporated in Member States whose currency is not the euro and amending Regulation (EU) 2021/1230 of the European Parliament and the Council, COM(2023) 368 final.

[7] On the different priorities and objectives pursued by central banks, commercial banks, other financial intermediaries, including payment service providers, merchants, sophisticated investors, wholesale or retail depositors, and general public, see below II.1, II.3. On the potentially gigantic implications of opening central bank deposit services to the public, and relevant academic literature long before CBDC entered the scene, see indicatively Omarova, "The People's ledger," 1254.

cross-border use? Or is there a need for complementary institutional and on-the-ground safeguards? What are the key concepts of CBDC governance, audit and supervision? Who (which entity, which bodies) should be given the regulatory and supervisory role and competence(s) with respect to identifiable CBDC activities? Which legal bases might be employed? Should part of relevant responsibilities and actual tasks be shared with, supported by, or even outsourced to experienced private sector specialists (and to what extent)? Will, ultimately, the CBDC issuer and supervisor be capable to control the digital currency scheme? What additional controls and mechanisms should they set in motion to ensure the safety and efficiency of their scheme? And would the current governance within the Central Bank (particularly that of the ECB), be a suitable framework once the central bank commences deploying this new activity as issuer of CBDC?

The above intriguing points are discussed in the subsequent sub-chapters. Section 2 portrays the main challenges and risks, originating from sovereign digital currency issuance and use, since those are the influential factors calling for all CBDC issuers' efficient governance. Section 3 closely reviews the governance of the digital euro scheme, as it is currently envisaged, and offers recommendations. At first, the ESCB, the ECB and the Eurosystem's institutional mandates and multiple competences are depicted, in relation to the prospective issuance of digital euro, to highlight the significance of establishing an effective own governance framework. Central banks' (with emphasis in ECB's) conventional governance pillars are described in brief, to introduce the main discussion over the necessary additional governance mechanisms and safeguards. At that point, the important question concerning the private sector's potential co-participation in the governance of the digital euro is dealt with, presenting both the persuasive arguments for it, along with the legal constraints and profounder institutional concerns, opposing such a possibility. Building on the latter opinion, the following sub-chapters of this chapter are devoted to the interpretation, adaptation and enhancement of the existing ECB governance framework to rise up to the demands of the digital euro. Particular thoughts, remarks and proposals are submitted, in relation to the digital euro issuer and scheme's supervisor's mandate, autonomy, internal organization (including its decision-making bodies, committees, internal functions and a potential advisory body with private sector co-participation), transparency and accountability. Section 4 focuses on the specific matters of concern and puts forward proposals for additional governance safeguards to ensure the Eurosystem control over the digital euro scheme. Section 5 concludes, summarizing the main answers of the preceding analysis.

2 Challenges and Risks Stemming from CBDC Issuance and Cross-border Use

2.1 Challenges

The potential issuance of digital currency by central banks has raised significant challenges both for themselves and the international financial system. It is seen as an expansion of central banks' traditional role, which has long focused mainly on monetary policy operations and preservation of financial stability. Such expansion has become necessary and was accelerated due to a number of concurrent causes and under the influence of certain drivers (as discussed in Chapter 2 of this book),[8] including technological developments, merchants' expectations for state-of-the-art means of payment, diverse end users' needs and demands, private sector developments (digital payment solutions, crypto-assets) and growing offers.[9] Under such demanding circumstances, CBDC issuance is questioning multiple integral parts of the established financial regime, as exemplified below.[10]

At the outset, central banks need to confirm their legitimacy (in other words, their legal competence and authority), to proceed to the issuance of digital currency. Such legitimacy should be explored in the light of the applicable policy objectives and function(s) and on the final CBDC design characteristics. Multiple different legal bases could be relied upon depending on whether the CBDC is a means of payment and a storage of value (akin to a digital form of a banknote), or a monetary policy

[8] See Chapter 2, Macchiavello, Objectives, rationale and opportunities of a CBDC, 27; Kiff et al., "A Survey."

[9] On the introduction of digital euro aims, in order to preserve the role of public money in a rapidly digitalized economy and evolving user expectations, see also IMF, "Digital," 10.

[10] On the substantial horizons offered by CBDC in the conduct of monetary policy, still considered to be restricted legally by the Article 128(1) TFEU rationale and objective, see in particular Seraina Neva Grünewald et al., "Digital Euro and ECB powers," *Common Market Law Review* 58, no. 4 (2021), 1036, https://papers.ssrn.com/sol3/papers.cfm?abstract_id=3807855 and below under III.1, III.4.

function or operation, or an instrument promoting the policies pursued by competent authorities in relation to the stability of the financial system, or all of the above. Relevant analysis should also consider CBDC typically desired function as legal tender in each respective jurisdiction.[11]

Apparently, CBDC issuance and use need to be subjected to additional regulation, to deal with its unique features, while serving existing currency purposes. Central banks themselves need to consider whether they already possess (or need to acquire speedily) necessary knowledge and capacity, in terms of human and technology resources, as well as appropriate internal procedures and mechanisms.[12] Those are required to implement CBDC operations, effectively, including digital currency distribution to financial services intermediaries, up to end users if decentralized distribution is the chosen model. It may be difficult to assess in advance actual technology requisites and CBDC-use efficiency, given that future digital currency

[11] See Wouter Bossu et al., "Legal aspects of Central Bank Digital Currency: Central bank and monetary law considerations," Working Paper no. 254 (International Monetary Fund, 2020), 31 et seq., https://www.imf.org/en/Publications/WP/Issues/2020/11/20/Legal-Aspects-of-Central-Bank-Digital-Currency-Central-Bank-and-Monetary-Law-Considerations-49827; Kiff et al., "A Survey," 37; Athanassiou, *Digital innovation,* 203; The European Commission considered whether granting legal tender status to the digital euro has implications for the legal tender of euro cash, that would warrant the option of a binding EU legislative proposal defining the meaning of legal tender for euro cash, in line with CJEU case law, to ensure coherence and safeguard the role of euro cash as a complement to the digital euro. Any such piece of secondary legislation would need to respect and not interfere with the powers of the ECB/Eurosystem (Article 133 TFEU). See indicatively European Commission, *A digital euro for the EU*; European Commision, "Commission Recommendation of 22 March 2010 on the scope and effects of legal tender of euro banknotes and coins (2010/191/EU)," *Official Journal of the EU L 83/70* (March 30, 2010), https://eur-lex.europa.eu/legal-content/EN/TXT/PDF/?uri=CELEX:32010H0191; Court of Justice of the EU, *Judgment in Joined Cases C-422/19 and C-423/19: Johannes Dietrich and Norbert Häring v Hessischer Rundfunk* (CJEU, 2021), https://eur-lex.europa.eu/legal-content/EN/TXT/PDF/?uri=ecli:ECLI%3AEU%3AC%3A2021%3A63; Grünewald et al., "Digital euro and ECB powers," 19 et seq. According to the latter Judgment (see par. 36-38), "*the broad concept of 'monetary policy' is not limited to its operational implementation, which, under the first indent of Article 127(2) TFEU, is one of the basic tasks of the ESCB, but also entails a regulatory dimension intended to guarantee the status of the euro as the single currency*". On the proposed legal tender status of the digital euro, entailing inter alia its mandatory acceptance by payees and set of exceptions, see DigEuro-Reg, art. 7 et seq., and Legal Tender-Reg, art. 15.

[12] See in detail regarding Fintech-related operational challenges International Monetary Fund, *The Bali Fintech Agenda*, Policy Paper (IMF, 2018), 60.

transactions' volumes and respective throughput requirements are complicated to estimate. Relevant challenges are intensified, since most central banks' plans also involve the creation of digital tokens for retail transactions settlement,[13] even offline. At the same time, they need to ensure all CBDC systems uppermost resilience against cyber-attacks, which will inevitably occur.

The success of CBDC endeavours requires their smooth integration within the existing international financial system. Thus, central banks' digital currency systems are faced with the challenge to ensure fast interoperability with the existing payment systems and arrangements.[14] While fostering financial innovation, the same endeavours are aimed to increase competition, without jeopardizing the viability of established financial sector intermediaries.[15] In addition, they should be designed in a way that they can adapt to the future demands of the financial community and end users. Finally, digital currencies are expected to be designed by the issuing central banks as available (at least in the medium-term future) for cross-border use.[16] In that respect, their efficient launch requires the cooperation of numerous actors, including international central banks and payment systems. Such actors need to gradually converge and agree on

[13] See Hubert De Vauplane, "Cryprocurrencies and central banks," in *Fintech: Law and regulation*, ed. Jelena Madir (Northampton: Edward Elgar Publishing, 2021), 138; Kiff et al., "A Survey," 29; Bossu et al., "Legal aspects," 11.

[14] See for instance the prototyping exercise of the investigation phase for the digital euro, which includes a test to assess how well potential back-end solutions developed by the Eurosystem could be integrated with front-end prototypes (European Central Bank, *FAQ on a digital euro, n.d.,* https://www.ecb.europa.eu/paym/digital_euro/faqs/html/ecb.faq_digital_euro.en.html).

[15] On CBDC and the risks of bank balance sheet disintermediation and financial instability, see indicatively Ulrich Bindseil et al., "Central Bank Digital Currency: Functional scope, pricing and controls," Occasional Paper Series no. 286 (European Central Bank, 2021), https://www.ecb.europa.eu/pub/pdf/scpops/ecb.op286~9d472374ea.en.pdf; Ramón Adalid et al., "Central Bank Digital Currency and bank intermediation—Exploring different approaches for assessing the effects of a digital euro on euro area banks," Occasional Paper Series no. 293 (European Central Bank, 2022), 29, https://www.ecb.europa.eu/pub/pdf/scpops/ecb.op293~652cf2b1aa.en.pdf; Lorenzo Burlon et al., "The optimal quantity of CBDC in a bank-based economy," Working Paper Series no. 2689 (European Central Bank, 2022), https://www.ecb.europa.eu/pub/pdf/scpwps/ecb.wp2689~846e464fd8.en.pdf.

[16] On the current central bank thinking on cross-border CBDC, see Bank for International Settlements, *Central Bank Digital Currencies for cross-border payments*, Report to the G20, 2021, https://www.bis.org/publ/othp38.pdf.

common standards and rules, especially in areas such as data sharing, foreign currency exchange and capital controls, to prevent the dominance of one digital currency over the others,[17] or their collective efforts proving futile, due to the materialization of significant risks, as explained in the next paragraph.

2.2 Risks

The above observations on CBDC challenges point out clearly that the envisioned new digital currency presents not only opportunities for central banks and the public, but also significant risks. From an operational perspective, it is widely observed that relevant initiatives are expected to motivate criminal activity against (what is to be perceived as) the greatest "digital treasures" of the world. While central banks have managed to handle successfully (minimize) counterfeiting of paper currency, they, as well as the public, are now faced with substantial cyber-security and digital fraud risks.[18] Indeed, digital world fraudsters constantly innovate and perfect, at an alarmingly increasing pace, methods of remote attacks against international financial institutions' IT systems. Their fraudulent schemes are often directed against digitally active corporates and consumers, employing malicious software and techniques such as phishing, ransomware attacks and insecure remote access threats.[19] In

[17] On a potential multipolar world featuring intense competition between a few major CBDCs and GSCs (among future hypothetical scenarios), and on potential restrictive measures on both domestic and cross-border use of CBDCs and GSCs, requiring adequate technological support, see IMF, "Digital," 17, 29.

[18] See Ashraf Khan and Majid Malaika, "Central Bank Risk Management, Fintech, and Cybersecurity," Working Paper no. 105, (International Monetary Fund, 2021); Tabrez Ahmad, "Corona virus (COVID-19) pandemic and work from home: Challenges of cybercrimes and cybersecurity," Available at SSRN 3568830 (2020), http://dx.doi.org/10.2139/ssrn.3568830; BIS, *Central Bank Digital Currencies*, 10. On susceptibility to system-wide fraud of the decentralized networks recording transactions in digital currencies, see Athanassiou, "Impact of digital innovation," 16.

[19] On the foremost relevant EU legislative initiative, regarding the adopted Regulation on digital operational resilience for the financial sector (op. cit., footnote 5), see https://www.europarl.europa.eu/doceo/document/TA-9-2022-0381_EN.html#title2. The Regulation ("DORA") sets uniform requirements for the security of network and information systems of companies and organizations operating in the financial sector as well as critical third parties which provide Information Communication Technologies-related services to them, such as cloud platforms or data analytics services. DORA purports to create a

addition, given that CBDC operational challenges are to be managed through complex systems and burdensome specifications of IT requirements, the risk arises that those may result in impaired functionality of digital currency issuance and transactions, or even worse, they may compromise the computational functionalities and lead to errors and disruptions of clearing and settlement processes. Consequently, they pose a major threat for the reliability of the issued digital currency.

In essence, the expansion of central banks traditional activity into the wider digital ecosystem will inevitably bring about additional risks associated with assigning important parts or projects of their digital currency infrastructure interfacing with that of private third parties. Apparently, central banks will rely to cloud computing, data storage, IT hardware and specialized software, payment systems and messaging providers and vendors, to a greater degree than ever before. Inadequate project management of the relevant outsourcing activities could jeopardize the sovereign digital currency initiative. Potential utilization of distributed ledger technology architecture renders the desired accountability of the involved third parties vis-à-vis central banks even more uncertain.

Needless to stress that the central banks will, directly or indirectly, internalize the impact of any default of CBDC system participating parties, especially at the initial period of the scheme operation. In case of insolvency or provisional (liquidity) problems of digital currency distributors, including commercial banks, exchanges, "e-wallets" and other payment service providers, the central banks may not only suffer financial losses, but also, at the same time, critical damage or loss of the essential public confidence on the scheme. From a public policy perspective, relevant micro-financial risks have the potential to transform—due to the existing financial system structure, interdependence and contagion effects—into macro financial issues, risks and constraints. It has been observed that CBDCs have the potential to induce changes in the retail, wholesale and cross border payments, which have negative spillover effects on monetary policy, through their effects on money velocity, bank deposit

regulatory framework on digital operational resilience whereby all firms need to make sure they can prevent, withstand, respond to, mitigate and recover from all types of ICT-related disruptions and threats. European Supervisory Authorities (ESAs), such as the European Banking Authority (EBA), the European Securities and Markets Authority (ESMA) and the European Insurance and Occupational Pensions Authority (EIOPA), are to develop technical standards for all financial services institutions to abide by.

disintermediation, volatility of bank reserves, currency substitution and capital flows.[20] Volatile instant digital capital flows between central bank, payments service providers', e-money institutions' and commercial banks' accounts, pose, then, a direct threat to financial stability, a cornerstone central bank objective. International circumstances may further propel those risk incidents into spillover on other jurisdiction(s) monetary policy or financial stability, thus amplifying repercussions.

2.3 Alternative CBDC Systems Designs and Initial Implications for Governance

Full understanding of the CBDC-embedded risks described above allows the deduction of some useful initial observations and offers some first thoughts on appropriate governance for relevant schemes. First, it is now evident that "within the CBDC world", many conflicting incentives and interests are met, in the short or long term. Central banks are the protagonists, not least as issuers of the digital currency, pursuing specific public policy objectives, but also as co-regulators and main supervisors of the scheme (to be illustrated below). Yet, a large number of private participants perform different roles, seeking different economic benefits. Financial industry players, including commercial banks, e-money institutions, payment service providers, will engage to maintain and

[20] See Inutu Lukonga, "Monetary policy implications of Central Bank Digital Currencies: Perspectives on jurisdictions with conventional and Islamic banking systems," Working Paper no. 60 (International Monetary Fund, 2023), 20, 28. 5, https://www.imf.org/en/Publications/WP/Issues/2023/03/17/Monetary-Policy-Implications-Central-Bank-Digital-Currencies-Perspectives-on-Jurisdictions-531074. David Andolfatto, "Assessing the impact of Central Bank Digital Currency on private banks," *The Economic Journal* 131, no. 634 (2021), 525. On the macroeconomics of central bank issued digital currencies and financial stability issues, especially the universally accessible and interest-bearing central bank liability, implemented via distributed ledgers, competing with bank deposits as medium of exchange, see indicatively John Barrdear and Michael Kumhof, "The macroeconomics of central bank issued digital currencies." Staff Working Paper no. 605 (Bank of England 2016), 13, https://www.bankofengland.co.uk/-/media/boe/files/working-paper/2016/the-macroeconomics-of-central-bank-issued-digital-currencies.pdf?la=en&hash=341B602838707E5D6FC26884588C912A721B1DC1; IMF, "Digita," 21.

improve their business position, offering additional services to their clientele.[21] Different categories of digital currency end users, including large (corporate) businesses, small & medium enterprises and consumers, will accumulate and dispense such form of currency, as a liquidity alternative and to facilitate transactions, or even in the context of (very limited) risk-free investment.[22] Major and niche technology providers, including Fintech companies, will seek flourishing opportunities into outsourcing, R&D or joint-cooperation mandates assigned mainly by central banks, as well as other financial intermediaries.[23] At the same time, CBDC initiatives and relevant schemes' implementation do raise the concern of additional public stakeholders, notably sovereign States, supranational unions and international organizations' bodies and various industry sectors' competent Authorities.

The above observations lead to a second preliminary remark that the governance model applying to CBDC issuers is associated with the key (high-level) features of each digital currency scheme that is being assessed. In effect, given the possibility of multiple (forms of) interactions of all above "actors" in various international schemes (currently under consideration or development),[24] the effective governance of each CBDC scheme, also for its issuer, necessarily requires to be structured in accordance with that scheme's actual preferred principal design. A distinctive example of an implemented model relates to the issue of central bank digital currency by the Chinese central bank (People's Bank of China—PBOC).

[21] On the architecture of retail payments environment, non-bank payment service providers (NBPSPs) and digital payment and electronic money services provided, see Johannes Ehrentraud et al., "Fintech and payments: Regulating digital payment services and e-money," Financial Stability Institute Insights on policy implementation no. 33 (Bank for International Settlements, 2021), 5 et seq, https://www.bis.org/fsi/publ/insights33.htm.

[22] Any investment consideration would presuppose a (competitively) remunerated CBDC. On the proposed limitation of digital euro's storage function and use as a form of investment (to avoid adverse impact on the funding structure of banks, with potential implications for financing conditions), see Panetta, "More than an intellectual game." According to DigEuro-Reg, the digital euro should not bear interest (art. 16 par. 8).

[23] See BIS, *Central Bank Digital Currencies*, describing the wider ecosystem, currently evolving, to support the underlying system required for CBDC provision and distribution.

[24] On no universal case yet for CBDC adoption and the differentiated design forms, see IMF, "Digital"; De Vauplane, "Cryprocurrencies," 139; Kiff et al., "A Survey"; BIS, *Central Bank Digital Currencies,* 11 et seq.; Bossu et al., "Legal aspects," 10; Auer et al., "Rise," 21; Lukonga, "Monetary policy implications," 6, 8.

In this scheme, electronic Chinese yuan (e-CNY) issuance follows a highly centralized model, in reality. In this context, the issuer of the digital currency, the PBOC, acts as central ledger administrator, wallet provider and manager of the wallet ecosystem, as well as core entry and clearing centre for the digital currency. It is responsible for the CBDC infrastructure, including "inter-institution" support. E-CNY is distributed to selected banks or payment platforms. PBOC as regulator is authorized to set rules and standards for the whole CBDC system, also empowered to organize payment systems and license main system participants, including commercial banks. PBOC is supervising e-CNY exchange and circulation, as well as authorized operators, including all system participants' anti-money laundering and risk management activities. Concurrently, the PBOC monitors CBDC transactions, runs the centres of authentication, registration, personal and financial data analysis, which have been established by making use of POBC technology and information management solutions.[25]

On the other hand, other central banks (including ECB) have considered differentiated (multi-tier) CBDC design models.[26] In the latter

[25] On the digital yuan as a systemic catalyst and its architecture, see Anton Didenko et al., "After Libra, digital Yuan and COVID-19: Central Bank Digital Currencies and the new world of money and payment systems," Working Paper Series no. 65 (European Banking Institute 2020), 28, https://papers.ssrn.com/sol3/papers.cfm?abstract_id=3622311. According to The People's Bank of China, "E-CNY: Main objectives, guiding principles and inclusion considerations," in *CBDCs in emerging market economies*, ed. Bank for International Settlements Papers no. 123 (BIS, 2022), 47, https://www.bis.org/publ/bppdf/bispap123.pdf, the e-CNY system follows the principle of "anonymity for small-value and trace ability for high-value transactions", attaches great importance to protecting personal information, and aims to meet the public demand for anonymous small-value payment services based on the risk features and information processing logic of current electronic payment systems. See also Heng Wang, "China's approach to Central Bank Digital Currency: Selectively reshaping international financial order?" *University of Pennsylvania Asian Law Review* 18 (2022), http://dx.doi.org/10.2139/ssrn.4036466.

[26] See indicatively Bank for International Settlements, *Central Bank Digital Currencies: system design and interoperability*, Report no 2 in a series of collaborations from a group of central banks (BIS, 2021), https://www.bis.org/publ/othp42_system_design.pdf; Kiff et al., "A Survey," 21 et seq.; ECB, *Progress,* fist report, 5; Hossein Nabilou, "Central Bank Digital Currencies: Preliminary Legal Observations," *Journal of Banking Regulation* (2019), 17. European Commission has also consulted on alternative digital euro's design choices, as regards more detailed functions, including: (a) account or bearer-based models (e.g. verification), (b) access to digital euro and usability (e.g. obligation for intermediaries to ensure the access to and usability of digital euro for their clients), (c) identifying appropriate identity solutions including the possibility of using the European

contexts, it is expected that an increasingly high involvement of private market participants in implementing many of the above functions and tasks, on a competitive basis, will foster innovation and efficiency of the scheme, thereby enhancing its attractiveness. In addition, the digital currency ledger may, as well, be structured in decentralized form, employing DLT technological solutions.[27] In such set up, a central bank is expected to be exclusively responsible for the digital currency issuance and redemption, but its distribution and payment services are to be delegated fully to private sector entities. System participants remain subject to their typical sectoral licensing and supervision regime, including competent authorities' supervision, while central bank is to retain critical oversight competence over payment systems.[28] In contrast to the e-CNY, digital euro is intended to be designed in a way so as to minimize

digital identity wallet, (d) offering the possibility of a common certified infrastructure including a secure and trustworthy solution for on-boarding and for online and offline payments, (e) distribution (centralized, decentralized involving intermediaries), (f) financial inclusion (easy onboarding and use), (g) the payment solutions (online, offline, micro and programmable payments), (h) the store of value functions (potential limits or disincentives to mitigate risks to financial stability and impact on the financial sector), (i) business model (fee structure for intermediaries), and (j) legal tender status (e.g. acceptance requirements for merchants providing digital payment services). See European Commission, *A digital euro*, 5. On the envisaged distribution model of the digital euro, and the various tasks and functions of the involved payment services providers, see DigEuro-Reg, art. 13 and 14.

[27] See in particular Rolf Weber, "Global Financial Architecture and Decentralised CBDC Regimes," in *Central Bank Digital Currencies, colloquium,* ed. Christos V. Gortsos and Rolf Sethe, (EIZ Publishing, 2023) by Collegium Helveticum in cooperation with the URPP Financial Market Regulation, May 9, 2023; Athanassiou, *Digital innovation in financial services*, 199, 210. On the comparison between conventional or DLT-based central bank infrastructure, see Raphael Auer and Rainer Böhme, "The technology of retail Central Bank Digital Currency," *Quarterly Review* (Bank for International Settlements, 2020), 91. On self-executing smart contracts, in the context of a DLT-based CBDC platform, providing for automation functionalities (incl. direct payment of taxes to tax authorities at point of sale, distribution of economic relief measures, etc.) and, more generally, programmable money functionality on the core ledger, see Kiff et al., "A Survey," 34. On the probability that CBDCs-to-be- implemented will use neither DLT nor blockchain, see Didenko et al., "After Libra," 45.

[28] On the strict licensing, regulatory and supervising measures for commercial banks, as a form of establishing sovereign control over them, as "private franchisees" (administrators) of the sovereign credit-money (since they have been empowered to create private liabilities (deposits) by means of extending loans), see indicatively Omarova, "The People's ledger," 1239.

Eurosystem involvement in the processing of user data, while allowing it to perform its tasks.[29]

Intrinsically, the first above model raises most serious concerns over the central bank's amplified wide-ranging powers and thus, it postulates the existence of increased *internal* governance requirements. The second aforementioned model raises the question as to which of the central bank's powers can be legitimately delegated to the private sector, which not and how the central bank will coordinate its supervision with other partially responsible authorities. In addition, such model(s) might be associated with a comparatively higher default risk of system participants (including DC exchanges to cash or other fiat or digital currencies, or assets). In that sense, such design model may appear, at first sight, as requiring less stringent digital currency issuer's internal governance rules. Yet, those rules should set clear responsibilities of CBDC system participants and promote an increased oversight of the supervised entities, to minimize probability of digital currency loss incidents, which could damage end users (businesses and consumers) confidence. In practice, effective governance of central banks, as issuers of the digital currency, is a primary requisite to be resolved upon (and follow the due implementation of) the foremost decisions on CBDC system architecture. The latter include decisions on issues such as, who (if not only the central bank) is to have access in the system core ledger, who (up to what extent the central bank) is to be responsible for the authentication of payers and payees and the integrity of CBDC payment transactions, who (whether central bank) may access which part of each payment transactions personal data

[29] On the evolution of key choices regarding design and distribution of a digital euro, see the ECB, *Progress*; ECB, *Progress on the investigation phase of a digital euro*, Second Report, 2022, https://www.ecb.europa.eu/paym/digital_euro/investigation/governance/shared/files/ecb.degov221221_Progress.en.pdf; ECB, *Progress on the investigation phase of a digital euro*, Third Report, 2023, https://www.ecb.europa.eu/paym/digital_euro/investigation/governance/shared/files/ecb.degov230424_progress.en.pdf; Seraina Grünewald, *A legal framework for the digital euro*, An assessment of the ECB's first three progress reports (European Parliament, 2023), https://www.europarl.europa.eu/RegData/etudes/IDAN/2023/741518/IPOL_IDA(2023)714518_EN.pdf. Ultimately, it has been made clear that the prevailing principle is that Eurosystem would not be able to infer how much digital euro any individual end user holds nor to infer end users' payment patterns. See also ECB, *Progress*. According to DigEuro-Reg, art. 35, personal data processing should build on the use of state-of-the-art security and privacy preserving measures, such as pseudonymization or encryption, to ensure that data is not directly attributed to an identified digital euro user by the ECB and national central banks.

(and under which circumstances), who decides which payment systems will be interconnected, how CBDC costs and revenues are to be allocated across the system. Central banks' governance is aimed to address the digital form currency challenges, mentioned earlier in this chapter (such as own operational capacity, due functioning of the system, fulfilment of duties of third-party service providers, including supervised financial service providers, systematically important technology providers, etc.), and avoid relevant crucial risks (including financial industry competition distortion, financial instability, criminal activities and economic losses).

3 Establishing Effective Governance of the Digital Euro Issuer

3.1 The Foundations of ESCB, ECB & Eurosystem Multiple Competences

Central banks, prospective issuers of CBDC, have been recognized wisely as sophisticated institutions, combining sovereign, public policy-making, objectives, with complex balance sheets and several functions, which resemble commercial credit institutions.[30] In the case of ESCB, those objectives and tasks are laid down in Article 127–128 TFEU.[31] Maintenance of price stability is cited as the primary, overarching objective,

[30] Wouter Bossu and Arthur Rossi, "The role of board oversight in central bank governance: Key legal design issues," Working Paper no. 293 (International Monetary Fund, 2019), 2, https://www.imf.org/en/Publications/WP/Issues/2019/12/27/The-Role-of-Board-Oversight-in-Central-Bank-Governance-Key-Legal-Design-Issues-48906.

[31] On the institutional foundations of European Monetary Union (EMU) and, in particular, the multi-layered complexity and objectives of the European System of Central Banks, see indicatively Lastra and Louis, "European Economic and Monetary Union: History, Trends, and Prospects," *Yearbook of European Law* 32, no. 1 (2013), 72 et seq.; Christos Hadjiemmanouil, "Economic and Monetary Union," in *European Union Law*, ed. Damian Chalmers, Christos Hadjiemmanuil, Giorgio Monti and Adam Tomkins (Cambridge: Cambridge University Press, 2006), 551; Christos Gortsos, *European central banking law, the role of the European central bank and national central banks under European law* (Palgrave Macmillan, 2020), 185 et seq.; Chiara Zilioli and Phoebus Athanassiou, "The European Central Bank," in *Oxford principles of European Union Law: The European union legal order: Volume I: The European union legal order*, ed. Robert Schütze and Takis Tridimas, (Oxford: Oxford University Press, 2018), 625, 50; Claudia Wutscher, "Artikel 127–132 des AEUV," in *EU-Kommentar,* 4th Edition, Jürgen Schwarze, Ulrich Becker, Armin Hatje, & Johann Schoo (Baden-Baden: Nomos Verlagsgesellschaft, 2019), 2045.

while ESCB is also supporting the general economic policies in the EU, to contribute to the objectives of the latter, as laid down in Article 3 TFEU. In accordance with Article 127 (1) TFEU, ESCB acts in line with the principle of an open market economy with free competition, favouring an efficient allocation of resources, in compliance with the principles set out in Article 119 TFEU (stable prices, sound public finances and monetary conditions, sustainable balance of payments).

In the context of the aforementioned mandate, the basic tasks to be carried out through the ESCB, as per. Article 127 (2),[32] are to define and implement the monetary policy of the Union, to conduct foreign-exchange operations (consistent with the provisions of Article 219 TFEU), to hold and manage the official foreign reserves of the Member States and promote the smooth operation of payment systems.[33] Those tasks are complemented with additional advisory functions, contribution to prudential supervision,[34] safeguard of financial stability, promotion of European financial integration, collection of statistics and international cooperation.[35]

In particular, with regard to the European single currency, the ECB has been vested, by virtue of Article 128 (1) TFEU, with the exclusive right to authorize the issue of euro banknotes within the EU. ECB, along with the NCBs of the Member States whose currency is the euro, form the Eurosystem, which is the monetary authority of the euro area.[36] The ECB and those NCBs may themselves issue such notes, which are the only

[32] On the division of ESCB functions to basic and non-basic tasks, and additional functions, see indicatively Lastra and Louis, "European Economic," 79; Gortsos, *European Central Banking Law*, 281; Wutscher, "Artikel," 2049.

[33] On the three main central banks' functions in payment and settlement systems, involving their management, settlement of payments and their oversight, in order to safeguard their stability and efficiency, see Gortsos, *European Central Banking Law*, 22.

[34] On the separation of monetary policy from banking supervision tools and the reversal of relevant trend, in the aftermath of financial crisis see also Gortsos, *European Central Banking Law*, 22 and more analytically on the Single Supervisory Mechanism below under 2.2 and 4.2.

[35] See Article 6 of the Statute of ESCB/ECB.

[36] On the institutional ground, primary and secondary objectives, basic tasks and operation of the Eurosystem, as part of the European System of Central Banks, see in particular art 14.3 of the Statute of ESCB/ECB, Mission Statement of the Eurosystem, 2005; Gortsos, "Future"; Lastra and Louis, "European Economic," 72.

notes enjoying the status of legal tender within the EU.[37] In essence, the legitimacy (competence) of ECB, regarding the envisaged issuance of the digital euro is considered to be founded on multiple provisions of the Treaty and the Statute of the ESCBs and of the ECB (the "Statute of the ESCB/ECB") provisions.[38] Such interpretation ensures the continuity of publicly issued, risk-free money of the euro area, on the basis that "*is needed as an anchor to maintain the quality of deposits and the stability of the banking system in the medium to long term*".[39]

Following issuance, the distribution of prospective digital currency is to be relayed through payment systems and financial intermediaries. Individual payment systems are complemented with sets of electronic payment instruments, allowing end users (payers and payees) to transfer value or discharge their payment obligations. Relevant schemes ("payment schemes") define standardized procedures for such electronic payment instruments, while relevant arrangements ("payment arrangements") provide functionalities, supporting the use of electronic payment instruments, as well as the services of payment service providers.[40] Both safety and efficiency of the euro area payment systems are, indeed, essential[41] for a stable and well-functioning financial system and contribute jointly to confidence in the single currency. For this main reason, payment

[37] On the legal tender aspects of money see De Vauplane, "Cryprocurrencies," 124 et seq. and Grünewald et al., "Digital euro," 20 et seq., considering that it would not be legally necessary for the digital euro to possess formal legal tender status, given ECB's guaranteeing the conversion of digital euros to tangible cash promptly, in all instances.

[38] See below under III.4. On the exclusive right of the European Central Bank to authorize the issue of the digital euro (which may be issued by itself and the national central banks), see DigEuro-Reg, art. 4.

[39] On the powers (and even obligation) of ECB to issue a digital euro under the EU's existing constitutional framework, see Grünewald et al., "Digital euro," 3, 9 et seq., considering that the relevant provision limits the issuance of ECB digital banknotes to a functional design that mimics tangible banknotes (i.e. without own monetary policy instrument features).

[40] See in particular European Central Bank, *Eurosystem oversight framework for electronic payment instruments, schemes and arrangements* (ECB, 2021); Athanassiou, "Impact of digital innovation," 8, also referring to hybrids between payment and remittance-type money transfer schemes.

[41] On the safety (incorporating stability, integrity, customer and data protection concerns) and the efficiency (including cost efficiency, competition and innovation), as the joint recurring policy objectives and challenges of the payment systems design and regulation, see Didenko et al., "After Libra," 10.

systems' due operation is promoted by the Eurosystem, which is held responsible for their oversight, in accordance with the fourth indent of Article 127(2) TFEU referred above and the fourth indent of Article 3.1 of the Statute of the ESCB/ECB.[42] On the basis of such competence, ECB has introduced special rules and minimum requirements for the systemically important payment systems, following the Principles for financial market infrastructures. The latter were developed by the Committee on Payment and Settlement Systems (CPSS) of the BIS and the Technical Committee of the International Organization of Securities Commission's (IOSCO) (the "CPSS-IOSCO principles"), with the goal to harmonize and strengthen the payment systems' oversight standards.[43]

At the same time, ECB exercises additional prudential supervisory functions, which were conferred to it through secondary EU legislation. Article 127(6) TFEU prescribes that specific task, concerning policies relating to the prudential supervision of EU credit institutions, may be conferred on the ECB by the Council, by means of regulations adopted in accordance with a special legislative procedure. Relevant tasks were conferred, in effect, by virtue of Council Regulation (EU) 1024/2013, while ECB Regulation (EU) 468/2014,[44] subsequently, established the framework for cooperation within the SSM between the ECB

[42] See Article 22 of the Statute of ESCB/ECB; analytically Tom Kokkola, "The Payment System: Payments, Securities and Derivatives, and the Role of the Eurosystem," European Central Bank, 2010, https://www.ecb.europa.eu/pub/pdf/other/paymentsystem201009en.pdf; Wutscher, "Artikel," 2056; Gortsos, *European Central Banking Law*, 307. On ECB possible indirect action, through its regulatory, supervisory and oversight powers over banking and payment systems, to influence the cryptocurrency markets, see Nabilou, "Central Bank Digital Currencies."

[43] See in particular Regulation ECB (EU) 795/2014 on oversight requirements for systemically important payment systems (ECB/2014/28); ECB Decision (EU) 2019/1349 on the procedure and conditions for exercise by a competent authority of certain powers in relation to oversight of systemically important payment systems (ECB/2019/25); Guido Ferrarini and Paolo Saguato, "Regulating Financial Market Infrastructures," Law Working Paper no. 259, European Corporate Governance Institute, 2014, 20 et seq., https://ssrn.com/abstract=2450095; Gortsos, *European Central Banking Law*, 308.

[44] The SSM Framework Regulation (ECB/2014/17). On the establishment of the European Banking Union and the adopted institutional framework, see extensively Gortsos, *European Central Banking Law*, 144 et seq., 153 et seq.

and national competent authorities and with national designated authorities.[45] Granting of authorization to and supervision of electronic money institutions and payment institutions has been assigned to and exercised by the national competent authorities.[46,47]

On the basis of the competences described above, it is evident that ECB will not act solely as the issuer of digital euro. Additionally, it will exercise its powers in the context of establishing the digital currency and regulating its various legal and technical issues[48]; it will also supervise, directly or indirectly, some critical private sector's (licensed or non-licensed) entities and systems, which will be participating or be involved, respectively, in the process of digital currency distribution and use by businesses and individual market participants[49]; ECB will also closely cooperate with national competent authorities, in order for them to

[45] On the specific supervisory tasks of the ECB in relation to credit institutions and other supervised entities incorporated in Member States, see ibid., 334 et seq. On the dichotomy between significant and less significant supervised entities, and discussion of the appropriateness of full underlying substantive bank regulatory framework indifferently to all, see also Bart Joosen and Matthias Lehmann, "Proportionality in the Single Rule Book," in *The Palgrave Handbook of European Union Banking Law, ed.* Mario Chiti, and Vittorio Santoro (Palgrave Macmillan, 2019), 86 et seq.

[46] See Article 11 and 15 of Directive (EU) 2015/2366 on payment services in the internal market (PSD2), also referring to the central registry of those institutions established by the EBA.

[47] On the treatment of the so-called "fintech banks", as credit institutions, in terms of their licensing, regulatory and supervision regime and relevant remarks, see Louis Barroso, "Fintechs: concept, level playing field and the supervisory approach," in *Fintech Regulation and the Licensing Principle*, ed. Dário Moura Vicente, Diogo Pereira Duarte and Catarina Granadeiro, eBook Series 2 (European Banking Institute, 2023), 38; European Central Bank, *Guide to assessments of fintech credit institution licence applications* (ECB, 2018).

[48] In that sense, Eurosystem digital euro legal acts are expected to include acts on its design features (including technical specifications), setting up and operation of settlement infrastructure, governance of distribution scheme, approval and allocation of volume of issue, accounting guidelines and decision on the ECB annual Accounts.

[49] On the ECB's additional tasks, regarding its contribution to the smooth conduct of policies, pursued by the national competent authorities, relating to the prudential supervision of credit institutions and the stability of the financial system, according to Article 127(5) TFEU and the macro-prudential oversight of the EU financial system in the context of functioning of the European Systemic Risk Board, on the ground of Article 2 Council Regulation (EU) 1096/2010, see Christos Gortsos, "Chinese Walls within the European Central Bank after the Establishment of the Single Supervisory Mechanism," *Paper presented at the conference of the University of Siena on "The Europeanisation of the Payment System, II Edition"* (October 22-24, 2015), 3.

accomplish their assigned role of compliance oversight and enforcement on the adopted Regulation on digital operational resilience for the financial sector.[50] This is the foremost reason the governance of ECB itself,[51] performing such multiple roles, while facing the distinct challenges and risks associated with the issuance of a central bank digital currency, attracts special attention and interest. These circumstances may, actually, suggest particular enhancements of the typical central banks' governance frameworks, including ECBs, as presented below.

3.2 Typical Central Banks' Governance Framework and ECB

From a formal perspective, the governance of central banks, as public institutions, is always established pursuant to national primary laws and supplementary or secondary legal instruments. The latter (such as central banks' statutes, internal regulations, codes of conduct, etc.) often provide for more detailed or procedural aspects, of their decision-making processes. From a substantive perspective, central bank governance has been aptly characterized, as a multifaceted concept, composed of four constitutive and interrelated components, the central bank's: mandate, autonomy, decision-making structures, as well as accountability and transparency.[52]

In general, mandate refers to the objectives, functions and tasks, which have been delegated to *any* central bank according to the applicable administrative law provisions. In effect, central banks, as creation of a State (or a union of sovereign states), are only authorized to perform the acts which the (domestic or international) law requires and allows them

[50] See DORA Regulation, Recital (97).

[51] On the inherent conflict of interest arising from ECB concurrently pursuing the objectives of price stability maintenance and prudential supervision of credit institutions, as the reason behind the introduction of "Chinese walls", separating its monetary and supervisory functions, in accordance with Article 25 SSM Regulation, see Gortsos, "Chinese Walls," 2.

[52] See Bossu and Rossi, "The Role," 9 et seq. 44; Ashraf Khan, "Central Bank Governance and the Role of Nonfinancial Risk Management," Working Paper no. 34 (International Monetary Fund, 2016), 4; Seraina Grünewald, "CBDCs and Central Bank Independence/Accountability," in *Central Bank Digital Currencies*, colloquium hosted by the Collegium Helveticum and the University of Zurich's Priority Research Program on Financial Market Regulation (URPP Financial Market Regulation, 2023).

to perform, explicitly or implicitly.[53] In that respect, the ESCB/ECB/Eurosystem mandate has been set to include (exclusively) the competences mentioned above, including authorization to adopt legislative and administrative measures to carry out the tasks conferred to them and to opine on matters in its field of competence, on the basis of TFEU and Statute of the ESCB/ECB provisions referred earlier.[54]

3.2.1. Autonomy

The second component (autonomy) refers to the independence of a central bank from political institutions and private economic interests. Such autonomy is further exemplified with regard to its institutional, functional, personal and financial attributes. ECB and Member States' NCBs independence is enshrined in primary EU law (TFEU and Statute of the ESCB/ECB). In particular, institutional independence of ESCB/ECB is established by virtue of Article 130 TFEU and Article 7 of the Statute of the ESCB. Those provisions prohibit the ECB, the NCBs and the members of their decision-making bodies from seeking or taking instructions from EU institutions or bodies, from any Member State government or from any other body, when exercising the powers and carrying out the tasks and duties conferred upon them by the Treaties.[55] They also stipulate that EU and national authorities must respect this independence and not seek to influence the members of the ECB's or the NCBs' decision-making bodies in the performance of their tasks.[56]

Functional (or operational) independence refers to the capability of the central bank to implement its functions without governmental interference. The ECB has been given the autonomy to determine which policy tools to use to achieve its primary objective of price stability. It possesses sole competence to decide which means and instruments are most appropriate to enable the achievement of its goals (such as outright

[53] Bossu and Rossi, "The Role."

[54] On the basis of Article 12 (1) of Statute of ESCB/ECB, ECB has recourse, to the extent deemed possible and appropriate to the national central banks to carry out operations which form part of the tasks of the ESCB/Eurosystem.

[55] On the ECB institutional independence, see indicatively Gortsos, *European Central Banking Law*, 264 et seq.

[56] On the additional requirement for institutional autonomy, that the central bank should not be influenced by private third parties, in decision-making in the context of the performance of the central bank functions, see below under 4.1.

purchases, the establishment of the collateral framework, the designation of its counterparties, etc.).[57]

Personal autonomy ensures that key decision-makers of the central bank are independent from government, political parties or other private sector entities' interests. Article 283 (2) TFEU and Article 11 (2) and (4) of the Statute of ESCB/ECB safeguard the capacity of the members of the ECB's decision-making bodies to take decisions without external influence. The members of the ECB Executive Board are appointed for a non-renewable term of eight years and can only be removed from office by the Court of Justice in two cases.[58] Article 14 (2) of the Statue of the ESCB requires that the NCB statutes provide for a minimum term of office of five years for the NCB governors, who also may only be relieved from office in the aforementioned cases. Finally, the treaties provide a powerful judicial remedy against arbitrary dismissals allowing the ECB and the governors to refer a dismissal to the Court of Justice of the European Union (CJEU).

Financial autonomy relates to the capability of central banks to pursue and fulfil their mandate with own adequate financial means. Indeed, it is observed that ECB possesses also financial independence, since it is free to manage its own finances and ensure that it has sufficient capital, staff and income to perform its tasks independently.[59]

3.2.2. Decision-Making

Decision-making structures of central banks involve, firstly, the stipulation of their relevant responsibilities and powers which are to be exercised. They commonly include public policy formulation, issuance of regulations to implement policies, enactment of individual decisions, executive management actions and oversight of the bank. Decision-making involves typically two to three distinct central bank's decision-making bodies,

[57] See Yves Mersch, "International trends in central bank independence: the ECB's perspective," *Remarks in roundtable Discussion on Central Bank Independence* (European Central Bank, 2019); Gortsos, *European Central Banking Law*, 265, 287. See analytically Bossu and Rossi, "The Role," 12, for the differentiation of level of the autonomy of the central bank, vis-à-vis the State, depending in its various functions.

[58] If they no longer fulfil the conditions required for the performance of their duties or if they have been guilty of serious misconduct.

[59] On the particular manifestations of ECB financial independence, see Gortsos, *European Central Banking Law*, 187. NCBs, as well, may not be deprived by their governments of sufficient financial resources to carry out their tasks.

including the Governor or Executive Board, the Board of Directors or Supervisory Board and specialized policy formulating Committees. Their actions and resolutions are supported by the central bank organization resources' work, research and proposals. Decision-making procedures refer to the modalities pursuant, to which the competent bodies of the central bank are executing their decision-making responsibilities.

ECB decision-making bodies, their composition, nomination, term and responsibilities allocation, are laid down in Article 283 TFEU and Article 10–14 of the Statute of ESCB/ECB.[60] The Governing Council is the main decision-making body, consisting of the six members of the Executive Board, plus the governors of the NCBs of the 20 euro-area countries. It is assigned with the prime task of monetary policy formulation (especially defining key ECB interest rates and liquidity terms), as well as to adopt guidelines and decisions to ensure the performance of the tasks of the Eurosystem.[61] The Executive Board is the operational decision-making body, consisting of the President of the ECB, the Vice-President and four other members. Its main tasks include the implementation of the ECB monetary policy, the preparation of meetings of the Governing Council and the conduct of the day-to-day business of the ECB. The General Council of ECB comprises the President of the ECB, the Vice-President and the governors of the NCBs of the 27 EU Member States.[62] It reports on convergence and contributes to several functions of the ECB, among others, its advisory functions, its reporting activities, the collection of statistical data and the layering of the conditions of employment of the ECB staff.[63] The aforementioned ECB bodies are supported

[60] See indicatively Lastra and Louis, "European Economic," 76; Zilioli and Athanassiou, "The European," 619.

[61] On the ECB regulatory powers and competence of ECB bodies to issue categories of legal instruments (Regulations, Decisions, Recommendations and Opinions), by virtue of TFEU and Statute of ESCB/ECB, see in detail Gortsos, *European Central Banking Law*, 247, 252.

[62] On the representation of NCBs in the Governing Council (and the General Council) and the principle of decentralization of operations, especially the power of NCBs to act independently, see ibid., 190.

[63] On the basis of Article 1, 26 SSM Regulation, the ESCB prudential banking supervision competence has been assigned to the ECB Supervisory Board, comprising a Chair, a Vice-Chair, four ECB representatives and representatives of national supervisors. Supervisory Board plans and carries out the ECB's supervisory tasks and proposes complete draft decisions to the Governing Council. See Gortsos, *European Central Banking Law*, 194,

by the ESCB/Eurosystem Committees. The latter are formed with regard to each one of central bank main task,[64] and their members are nominated by NCBs and chaired by ECB. Committees act as advisory bodies to ECB decision-making bodies and particularly, contribute to the Eurosystem's integration.[65]

It has been also commented that Eurosystem's human resources are deployed in a way to achieve centralized decision-making, as well as a high degree of operational decentralization. In that sense, ECB is considered as the decision-making centre, which owes regulatory powers, conducts euro area-wide analysis to prepare decisions and ensures consistent implementation of policies. NCBs perform many operational tasks, such as conduct of most operations (monetary policy and foreign exchange), provision of payment and securities settlement facilities, procurement, issue and post-issue handling of euro banknotes, collection of statistics, conduct of national analysis and research and communication at the national level, while undertaking additional non-Eurosystem tasks.

3.2.3. Accountability and Transparency

Accountability and transparency are considered as critical legal counterbalances (ex-post explanation and justification) to the central banks' high degree of multiform autonomy enjoyed.[66] In effect, central banks are required to be accountable for the execution of their mandate to both the State's (and international Union's) institutions (executive, legislative

249, also for the Supervisory Board resolution-making in such "no objection" -procedure with the Governing Council.

[64] Accounting and Monetary Income Committee (AMICO), Banknote Committee (BANCO), Committee on Controlling (COMCO), Eurosystem/ESCB Communications Committee (ECCO), Eurosystem IT Steering Committee (EISC), Financial Stability Committee (FSC), Information Technology Committee (ITC), Internal Auditors Committee (IAC), International Relations Committee (IRC), Legal Committee (LEGCO), Market Operations Committee (MOC), Monetary Policy Committee (MPC), Organizational Development Committee (ODC), Payment and Settlement Systems Committee (PSSC), Risk Management Committee (RMC), Statistics Committee (STC), Budget Committee (BUCOM), Human Resources Conference (HRC).

[65] Michael Sturm, "The ECB and the Eurosystem: Institutional structure and governance," *Presentation* (European Central Bank, July 1, 2019).

[66] Tomasso Padoa—Schioppa, "An institutional glossary of the Eurosystem," *Speech at the conference The Constitution of the Eurosystem: the Views of the EP and the ECB* (March 2, 2000); International Monetary Fund, "Update the monetary and financial policies transparency code," Policy Paper no. 011 (IMF, 2019).

and judiciary), as well as to the public at large, reflecting the broader constitutional, political and societal parameters of respective State (or Union). TFEU establishes several mechanisms through which the ECB is held accountable for the performance of its monetary policy function. Those include the submission of annual reports to the EU's political bodies (the European Parliament, the Council, the Commission and the European Council), financial controls, the regular consultation and other forms of cooperation of ECB with the above-mentioned EU institutions,[67] as well as the publication of quarterly reports on ECB activities and financial statements.[68] ECB individual decisions remain also subject to judicial review.[69] The European Court of Auditors' remit covers the examination of any revenue or expenditure accounts of the EU or any EU body and relevant reporting, thus contributing to improvement of EU financial management. Transparency requirements allow the stakeholders' prompt access to information and reinforce the central bank's accountability ultimately to the general public (society). Transparency entails the communication in real time (or even in advance) of the central bank's policies and financial position, thereby facilitating public understanding of the central bank's objectives, conduct and decisions.[70] For

[67] See Article 284 TFEU, 15.1–15.4, 26.2–26.3, 27.1–27.2 of Statute of ESCB/ECB; René Smits, "Central bank independence and accountability in the light of EMU," in *International monetary law: Issues for the New Millennium*, ed. Mario Giovanoli (Oxford: Oxford University Press, 2000); Zilioli and Athanassiou, "The European," 619.

[68] ECB regular appearance at public hearings before the European Parliament, oral discussions between representatives of EU institutions (even "behind closed doors"), quarterly dialogue between the President of the ECB and the Economic and Monetary Affairs Committee of the European Parliament also contribute to upholding the principle of accountability. See in detail Nicole Fraccaroli et al., "The evolution of the ECB's accountability practices during the crisis," ECB Economic Bulletin no. 5 (European Central Bank, 2018); Interinstitutional Agreement between the European Parliament and the European Central Bank on the practical modalities of the exercise of democratic accountability and oversight over the exercise of the tasks conferred on the ECB within the framework of the Single Supervisory Mechanism (2013/694/EU).

[69] On the ECB sanctioning powers and the judicial audit of ECB (and NCBs) individual binding acts (for review and interpretation), along with relevant legal grounds (Article 263 TFEU, Article 35 Statute of ESCB/ECB), see Gortsos, *European Central Banking Law*, 258 and 275, respectively.

[70] On the reasonableness and proportionality of the level of transparency imposed upon a central bank, so as to avoid hindering the fulfilment of its mandate, see Manuel Monteagudo, "Central banks and ethics: The virtual paradox of transparency and confidentiality mandates," in *Research handbook on law and ethics in banking and finance*, eds.

this purpose, ECB holds press conferences immediately after Governing Council monetary policy meetings and releases monetary policy accounts four weeks after each monetary policy meeting. It also publishes the Economic Bulletin, articles, interviews and speeches online, and answers questions from the general public. Moreover, it applies a legal framework for handling public access requests for its documents, which, in principle, entitles every EU citizen to access them.[71]

3.3 Significance of Private Sector Role—Should It Co-participate in the Governance of Digital Euro?

3.3.1. The Case for Private Sector Participation in the Digital Euro Governance

Private sector is considered to undertake a crucial role in the implementation of central banks' digital currencies' initiative. According to the digital euro project model currently envisaged, private entities (financial intermediaries) will cooperate with the Eurosystem not only in the business side, i.e., in the distribution of digital euro,[72] but also on the operational side, i.e., in the course of important functional activities, such as those related to the user management, liquidity management and processing of digital euro payments, acting on behalf of ECB/NCBs.[73] User management involves management of digital euro accounts and wallets of wholesale and retail users. Liquidity management includes funding and defunding digital euro holdings, i.e., converting end users' commercial bank money or cash into digital euro and vice versa, respectively. Users will choose to fund or defund their digital euro wallets manually (as in the existing cash world) or automatically (via predetermined orders or repeated actions). In both cases, financial intermediaries shall cooperate to ensure that

Costanza Russo, Rosa Lastra, and William Blair (Northampton: Edward Elgar Publishing, 2019).

[71] See ECB Decision 4.3.2004 on public access to European Central Bank documents, OJEU, L 80, p. 42; Mersch, "International trends."

[72] On the CBDC efficient distribution, especially through on boarding, funding and payment services, as important condition for its success, see Bindseil et al., "Central Bank Digital Currency," 20.

[73] Grünewald, *A legal framework*, 15.

users can receive a payment that exceeds their digital holding limits[74] (ceiling to be set by the Eurosystem).[75] Conversely, financial intermediaries shall cooperate to facilitate users to make a payment that exceeds their digital holding funds, through their other available accounts and payment services.[76]

Transaction management, particularly with regard to transaction initiation and authentication, will very likely depend additionally on private intermediaries. On the contrary, settlement of digital euro transactions (without any direct user contact) will most probably be validated and recorded by the Eurosystem central banks. This results from the fact that the digital euro shall be central bank liability, thus its holdings would be recorded on the Eurosystem ledger. On the same rationale, Eurosystem should have full control over clearing and settlement, in

[74] On central banks adapting CBDC design features and utilizing effective ways of mitigating risks, including tiered remuneration or holding limits, and other techniques to prevent excessive holdings of CBDC, see Bindseil et al., "Central Bank Digital Currency," 11; Panetta, "More than an intellectual game"; On the dissenting opinion that imposing limits on the holdings of digital euros (in order also to decrease competitive pressure on commercial banks) conflict with a legal tender concept, because the latter encompasses limitless use of cash as a store of value, see Grünewald et al., "Digital euro," 19, who consider that such limits can only serve as a safeguard during an adjustment period for the banking sector, while tangible cash is still in use.

[75] On the currently proposed limit to digital euro holdings ("*of around 3000 to 4000 digital euro per capita*") and criticism from the perspective of it prohibiting digital euro's usability and hindering its "store of value" function, see Grünewald, *A legal framework*, 11; Chiara Zilioli, "The perspective of the European Central Bank (ECB): Towards a digital euro," in *Central Bank Digital Currencies*, colloquium jointly hosted by the collegium Helveticum and the University of Zurich's Priority Research Program on Financial Market Regulation (URPP Financial Market Regulation, 2023). According to DigEuro-Reg, art. 16, the European Central Bank should develop instruments to limit the use of the digital euro as a store of value, including holding limits. The legislative proposal defines a set of criteria that the parameters and use of the instruments developed by the ECB should meet with the view of safeguarding financial stability. Subject to the relevant criteria, the decision on whether and when to use such instruments, as well as their calibration, should rest entirely with the ECB.

[76] ECB, *Progress*, second report. and DigEuro-Reg, art. 14 par. 3 and 4. On the challenging conflicting interests of the financial intermediaries, especially banks attracting deposits for their balance sheet vs. attracting digital euros, on which they would presumably earn a fee, and their address through proper compensation, see Angeloni (2023). Digital Euro: When in doubt, abstain (but be prepared), In-depth analysis requested by the ECON Committee, 11.

order to maintain control on its balance sheet.[77] To that effect, the ECB/NCBs will provide all those supervised intermediaries with centralized accounts. Nevertheless, the digital euro project is currently evolving as technology-neutral (technology agnostic). It is implied that transaction settlement could be designed based on DLT technology, which is driven fully out of the Eurosystem's control.[78] In addition, settlement of offline digital euro payments will take place via local storage devices, which, again, given their quantity and geographical dispersity, will probably neither be owned, nor operated by the Eurosystem, but rather by financial technology intermediaries.

The above observations raise the issue of potential partial or joint participation of private sector in the governance of the digital Eurosystem. Such participative role might be further proposed, on the basis of current level of possession of knowledge and experience necessary for the functioning of similar systems.[79] In fact, the development of digital currencies was brought about by innovative private, non-bank entities, which utilized the distributed ledger technology commercially. In the first era of private digital assets and tokens, banks avoided to contract and interact directly with the digital currencies' intermediaries, due to

[77] See ECB, *Progress*, second report. Indeed, the validation of claim to the CBDC is an important step in the further execution of the transactions, and settlement thereof. It requires the confirmation as to whether or not the holder of the CBDC is an authorized and legitimate holder of the CBDC, and upon validation of such claim, settlement can be effected.

[78] On the views of Banque de France regarding the different levels of appropriateness of DLT for wholesale vs. retail CBDC, see De Vauplane, "Cryprocurrencies," 139.

[79] It is noted that ECB searched for private-sector support to develop potential user interfaces for the digital euro and eventually appointed a quintet of companies to build front-end prototypes. Working with the ECB's in-house CBDC team, each of the companies is to focus on one specific digital euro use case. According to the relevant announcement (16.9.2022), CaixaBank is to focus on peer-to-peer online payments; Worldline will look at peer-to-peer offline payments; the European Payments Initiative (EPI) company will look at point-of-sale payments initiated by the payer; Nexi will undertake point-of-sale payments initiated by the payee; and Amazon will focus on e-commerce payments (ECB, *ECB selects external companies for joint prototyping of user interfaces for a digital euro*, MIP News, September 16, 2022, https://www.ecb.europa.eu/paym/intro/news/html/ecb.mipnews220916.en.html).

legal uncertainty, as well as anti-money laundering considerations.[80] Today, both large and niche businesses in the financial and technology sector, including Fintech entities, have substantially invested and acquired resources and expertise in dealing efficiently with most of the substantive matters, in relation to the sound functioning of the envisaged CBDC system, such as money transactions settlement, data authentication and storage.[81] Such existing resources and nurtured expertise, arguably, have the potential to accelerate and materially benefit the public sector (central bank) initiatives, should the private sector be granted a complementary role in the governance of the digital currency.

3.3.2. Legal Constraints and Institutional Concerns

Nevertheless, according to the fundamental rules of European public law discussed, it is observed that the Eurosystem is generally not entitled to transfer, even part of its competences and responsibilities to the private sector. The established governance framework of the ECB, as summarized above, does not provide for private entities (including specialized or leading companies) becoming involved jointly in the decision-making regarding any of central bank's assigned competences and functions, including in this case the prospective issuance and functional management of the digital euro.[82] Therefore, relevant companies' representatives

[80] See Bank for International Settlements, *Digital Currencies* (BIS, 2015), 7. On the early legislated extension of AML/CFT requirements to "virtual currency exchange" platforms and certain custodial e-wallet providers see Directives 2018/843/EU and 2018/1673/EU; Brown et al., "Cryptoassets," 105.

[81] See indicatively Society for Worldwide Interbank Financial Telecommunication Reports: Connecting digital islands a) Results of SWIFT experiments interlinking CBDC networks and existing payments systems to achieve global interoperability and b) Results of SWIFT's collaborative experiments interlinking multiple tokenization platforms to achieve global interoperability (Society for Worldwide Interbank Financial Telecommunication, *CBDCs and Tokenized Assets Can Integrate into International Financial Ecosystem*, Report, October 12, (SWIFT, 2022), https://ca.practicallaw.thomsonreuters.com/w-037-2021?transitionType=Default&contextData=(sc.Default)&firstPage=true). It is argued that experimental findings "*solve the significant challenge of interoperability in cross-border transactions by bridging between different distributed ledger technology (DLT) networks and existing payment systems, allowing digital currencies and assets to flow smoothly alongside, and interact with, their traditional counterparts.*"

[82] On the proposed distinction between ECB decision-making and implementation powers and its implications, see Grünewald et al., "Digital euro," 14. According to that opinion, strategy and the definition of all essential features ("design") of the core digital euro infrastructure cannot be delegated, while tasks that merely execute the decisions

or other private consultants cannot be granted membership of the ECB or Eurosystem Committees, in accordance with the internal ECB rules of procedure.[83]

Alternatively, private sector expertise could be utilized if respective representatives or consultants participated as observers in selected ECB Committees, or if they assisted, by means of accomplishing technical documents or preparing and compiling documentation relevant to the digital euro system operation. These documents might even extend to analytical CBDC rulebooks and guidelines, which would then be reviewed, amended and ultimately enacted by the ECB decision-making bodies.[84] However, even such lighter forms of private–public sector cooperation in the governance of digital euro do raise institutional concerns. In case the central bank simply withholds the decision powers while being deprived of necessary knowledge, substantively, its relevant decision-making will not be genuine. Therefore, respective regulatory and administrative acts would entail severe legal risk. In essence, if the ECB bodies were not to be able to examine themselves and materially assess the technical policies, rules, standards or decisions, which are to be adopted, the latter would rather resemble "fictitious" public authority acts.

Furthermore, any significant dependence of the digital euro issuer on the private sector (even if it were not to result directly to administrative actions' legal deficiencies), may well have negative impact on the central bank oversight and supervisory functions. Especially with regard to IT and operational systems in use, central banks, given their prominent role in the due function of the economy, have typically implemented strongest security and performance specifications and requirements. Yet, as discussed in the previous chapter, CBDC initiative still involves unique challenges, uncertainties and risks in that domain. Notably, some of the private technology initiatives regarding the issuance and management of digital currency have not been exhaustively experimented in demanding extended use circumstances.[85] Consequently, in order to secure firstly the

taken, or utilize the core infrastructure to facilitate the use of the digital euro (such as "production", "distribution", "storage", transfer") may be delegated to the market.

[83] Decision of the European Central Bank of 19 February 2004 adopting the Rules of Procedure of the European Central Bank (ECB/2004/2), OJEU L 80, pp. 33–41 as currently in force.

[84] See below under 4.2.

[85] BIS, *Central Bank Digital Currencies*.

resilience and safety and at the same time the efficiency of the digital Eurosystem, it appears reasonable that it adopts a cautious approach in internal governance mechanisms and arrangements with third parties. In that context, it is worth mentioning that the Digital Operations Resilience Act has established the Oversight Forum as a sub-committee to ensure Information and Communication Technology third-party risk across financial sectors is monitored.[86] It is also advisable to introduce additional layers of control of the envisaged system, to ensure compliance with additional applicable rules (including data protection and confidentiality, free competition, anti-money laundering), as well as to minimize own potential liability in cases of undesirable incidents.[87]

3.4 *Analytical CBDC-Related Governance Framework Proposals for ECB*

In the light of the above, ECB governance framework is proposed to be complemented, as regards its respective four pillars, with particular legal enhancements, measures and procedures, in order to improve the prospects of success, security, acceptance and efficiency of its CBDC scheme.

At the outset, the mandate of the Eurosystem, regarding specifically the issuance and distribution of the digital euro, as well as the operation of its scheme, has been discussed extensively in Chapter 3 of this volume.[88] Three credible legal bases have been identified, being also associated with the ultimate design choices of the scheme to be actually implemented.

[86] See Article 32 DORA Regulation. This Forum is tasked with providing draft joint positions to the Joint Committee, referred in Article 54 of Regulations (EU) no. 1093/2010, (EU) no. 1094/2010 and (EU) no. 1095/2010, and undertaking collective assessment of results and findings of oversight activities, as well as compiling benchmarks for critical ICT third-party service providers. The Forum is composed of representatives from the European Supervisory Authorities, the Commission, the ESRB, the ECB, and ENISA, as well as one high-level representative from each Member State and, where applicable, one additional representative of a competent authority. The ESAs will also establish guidelines for cooperation between authorities and ESAs and submit a report on the application of the Act each year to the European Parliament, Council and Commission.

[87] See above footnote 80, on the recent ECB commissioning of certain development tasks to major technology providers, which effectively necessitates the establishment of additional layers of control applying to the envisaged system.

[88] See Chapter III Christy Ann-Petit, Central Bank Digital Currency and the Treaty Mandate of the European Central Bank, 27, 30.

At first, Article 128(1) TFEU and Article 16 of the Statute of ESCB/ECB do allow for the interpretation that ECB is entitled to issue the euro currency also in digital format, drawing on the analogy with the banknotes.[89] Then, Article 127(2), first indent TFEU and Article 17 of the Statute of ESCB/ECB can also establish ECB competence, given the recent financial and technological evolutions discussed above (under I). That stems from the factual expectation that digital euro is expected to play significant role in implementing the monetary policy of the Union, which has been exclusively assigned to ECB for the Member States whose currency is the euro, as per Article 3(1)(c) TFEU.[90] At the same time, Article 127(2) fourth indent TFEU and Article 22 of the Statute of ESCB/ECB, deploying ECB basic task to promote the smooth operation of payment systems,[91] appear particularly attractive to establish its remit in deciding on the technical features and in distributing a digital euro, since they focus on its inherent nature as settlement medium[92] and on the relevant dominant payment system-feature of the scheme.[93] The application

[89] See Grünewald, "CBDCs," 71; Anneelike Mooij, "A digital euro for everyone: Can the European System of Central Banks introduce general purpose CBDC as part of its economic mandate?," *Journal of Banking Regulation* 24, no.1 (2023), 89; Nabilou, "Central Bank Digital Currencies," 15 et seq. On the prevalence and exclusivity of the Eurosystem's powers to issue a digital euro over the remaining competence of Member States to issue coins, i.e. prohibiting the latter from issuing a parallel digital euro on the basis of Article 128 (2) TFEU, in the light of the need to preserve the euro's singleness, see Grünewald et al., "Digital euro," 10. On the broad interpretation that the concept of "issue" encompasses not only the circulation (of banknotes), but also all other actions related to circulation (including their withdrawal), see Gortsos, *European Central Banking Law*, 320.

[90] See also Grünewald, *A legal framework*, 15.

[91] As per Article 22 of Statute of ESCB/ECB on clearing and payment systems, the ECB and national central banks may provide facilities, and the ECB may make regulations, to ensure efficient and sound clearing and payment systems within the Community and with other countries. The application of such provision should not be restricted to the existing wholesale (interbank) large value payment systems providing settlement services, such as TARGET(2) system services. See Benjamin Geva, "TARGET2 Transfer of Funds and Harmonization of EU Payment Law," *Uniform Commercial Code Law Journal* 41, no. 2 (2008), 113.

[92] On the gradual departure from reference to the Euro banknotes and apparent specialization of the digital euro to a public means of payment see Grünewald, *A legal framework*, 10.

[93] In that sense, Article 22 of Statute of ESCB/ECB covers the formation and the operation of a scheme (digital euro "primary distribution" scheme) that will allow for

of the latter ground appears consistent also with the recent extension (due to the technological developments) of Eurosystem oversight of payment instruments to all electronic payment instruments, enabling transfer of value between end users.[94] Cumulation of the above legal bases can be validly considered, to the extent that digital euro will pursue all above different objectives, each of manifold importance.[95]

It has been the prevailing view that, while the amendment of TFEU or Statute of the ESCB/ECB may not be absolutely necessary, secondary EU legal acts are required to elaborate on and implement ECB competence to manage the digital euro issuance, distribution, functioning and redemption. The Commission has undertaken a legislative proposal on the essential aspects of the digital euro, in the form of a European Regulation. The latter is expected to be adopted by the European Parliament and the Council, after consultation with the ECB, on the grounds of Article 133 TFEU, providing for the laying down of "*measures necessary to the use of the euro as the single currency*".[96] Such Regulation will clarify the terms

the central bank money to be made available, ultimately, to EU households in digital form, so that also retail payments be initiated and executed among participating financial institutions. According to a different opinion, Article 127(2) TFEU, in conjunction with Article 22 of the Statute of ESCB/ECB, could serve as legal basis for the establishment of a facility (i.e., an infrastructure for the issuance of CBDC), but not provide legal basis for the issuance of CBDC itself. Relevant concern has been expressed particularly with regard to the issuance of *retail CBDC*, on the interpretation Article 127(2) TFEU would not allow the Eurosystem to directly provide facilities to households and other private entities. It has been also considered whether a targeted amendment to Article 22 of the Statute could reinforce the legal basis for the Eurosystem to issue a digital euro, by explicitly extending its scope to encompass the settlement of digital euro transactions, a competence auxiliary to the competence of issuing such a digital euro.

[94] In essence, the fundamental provisions founding ESCB competence for promoting payment systems' safe and efficient operation and their oversight have already been interpreted to extend the Eurosystem oversight scope (apart from the transfer of euro funds) also to transfer of representations of value backed by claims or assets denominated in euro or redeemable in euro, or other digital assets, that are accepted under the rules of a scheme for payment purposes, or to discharge payment obligations in euro. See in detail, the new Eurosystem oversight framework for electronic payment instruments, schemes and arrangements (November 2021) (the PISA framework).

[95] On the CJEU jurisprudence on acceptable cumulation of legal bases, and exceptional non-adherence to the established "centre of gravity" theory, see Judgment of the Court of 22 May 1990, European Parliament v Council of the European Communities, ECLI:EU:C:1990:217 Case C-70/88; Grünewald, "CBDCs."

[96] See European Commission, *A digital euro for the EU*, 4, European Council recommendation of January 2022 on the economic policy of the euro area for 2022 and

of engagement and the boundaries of the central bank role, including the involvement of other financial or digital services intermediaries.[97] It will also rule on some foremost legal features of the digital euro, including the eligibility of its users, fundamental privacy issues, the digital euro tokens' regime,[98] protection from counterfeiting, fees, compensation and legal tender. Moreover, it will provide reference to additional public policy

DigEuro-Reg. On new TFEU provisions (Article 133, 136) conferring upon EU institutions the power to issue legal acts of secondary law, see Gortsos, *European Central Banking Law*, 92. On the opinion that the single issuance of digital euro banknotes by the Eurosystem would not require any prior legislative act authorizing the Eurosystem to utilize its powers, see Grünewald et al., "Digital euro," 12. On the realistic view that issuance of CBDC necessitates respective central bank law reform, see Bossu et al., "Legal aspects"; Roland Broemel, "20 Jahre Euro – bald auch digital?," *Europäische Zeitschrift für Wirtschaftsrecht* 33 (2022), 393, observing that classifying a digital euro legally in the category of physical banknotes reflects only partially the objectives, functionality and requirements of a digital sovereign currency.

[97] On the envisaged European legislation acts and their indicative elements, see European Commission, *Targeted consultation on a digital euro*, Consultation document, Directorate General for Economic and Financial Affairs (European Commission, 2022); Zillioli, "The Perspective"; Grünewald, *A legal framework*, 22.

[98] On the issuance of token-based CBDC in the context of international central banking law, see particularly Bossu et al., "Legal aspects," 16 et seq. Depending on the digital euro tokens exact different characteristics (including ECB account reference, convertibility, reversibility or even programmability), some of those might be interpreted as falling into, or relating with, selected provisions of existing E-money legislation, potentially to be amended. See in detail below IV.2, Article 2(2) of Directive 2009/110/EC as in force ("*'electronic money' means electronically, including magnetically, stored monetary value as represented by a claim on the issuer which is issued on receipt of funds for the purpose of making payment transactions .... and which is accepted by a natural or legal person other than the electronic money issuer*"); Court of Justice of the EU, *Judgment in case C-264/14: Skatteverket v David Hedqvist* (CJEU, 2015), par. 52; De Vauplane, "Cryprocurrencies," 133 et seq. On the international regulation of e-money, see Ehrentraud et al., "Fintech," 12. With regard to the hypothetical submission of similar tokens to the Markets in Crypto-Assets legislation (EMTs), the Article 3(2), (4) and (3a) of MiCAR, op. cit., are initially noted. Yet, according to Article 2 par. 3 (a) MiCAR, the ECB and the NCBs, when acting in their capacity as monetary authority or other public authorities, are expressly excluded from MiCAR scope. Therefore, ECB and NCBs are not subjected to the distinct supervision regime applying to the issuers of "significant e-money tokens", nor involved with the registration of broadest crypto-asset service providers (See on those, Article 98 et seq. MiCAR; Ehrentraud et al., "Fintech," 37; issuers of significant e-money tokens are set to be subject to dual supervision by both national competent authorities and the EBA given the risks they can pose to financial stability, while European Securities and Markets Authority (ESMA) will establish a register of crypto-asset service providers, which should include information on the entities authorised to provide those services across the EU).

objectives to be served by the digital euro, such as support of the European economy's digitalization, development of state of the art, safe and efficient pan-European payments, financial integrity, financial inclusion and transaction data protection. Still, additional solid governance safeguards appear necessary, due to the aforementioned digital euro scheme challenges and risks and the substantial regulatory powers of ECB, not least since the latter's oversight role to (retail) payment systems may seem as extending, in effect, to its "own" digital Eurosystem.

3.4.1. Autonomy

In the context of both CBDC challenges and the rising significance of the private sector in the digital environment (as outlined in earlier chapters), the generally established autonomy of ECB within the Eurosystem, deserves some additional attention. Further to the arguments discussed earlier, against the potential interference of private sector in the central bank decision-making, it is also suggested that personal independence of the digital euro issuer will be preserved to the extent that not only the members of its decision-making bodies and Committees, but also all central bank operations' resources are not concurrently engaged (even on provisional or project-oriented basis), by private (information technology) industry stakeholders.

An additional question arises, as to whether the central bank may seek recourse to third parties' services, in relation to the evaluation of, or to obtain advice on, the performance of its own functions. For example, it is discussed whether Eurosystem own digital euro infrastructure, including its resilience and cybersecurity posture, could be verified, through a specialized independent third party, namely a private assurance services provider. In the author's opinion, such independent ad-hoc verification could be implemented through transparent procedures and effective measures, which would not allow the above third-party provider to interfere with or control any critical parameters of the scheme following the verification exercise. In that sense, that verification would neither compromise the central bank functional or operational autonomy, nor bring its independence in jeopardy, but would rather contribute to the enhancement of its aimed digital euro objectives.[99]

[99] See Khan and Malaika, "Central Bank," 55.

On a distinct autonomy point, it was noted earlier that full implementation of the digital euro project will require significant—and most importantly—repetitive (on a regular basis) capital expenditure on the side of the central bank. To preserve its financial independence, then, ECB should take into account all those long-term costs involved, while undertaking significant resolutions on the cost allocation structure of the digital euro payment scheme. It is admitted that such resolutions may ultimately affect the potential remuneration structure and levels of both wholesale and retail digital euro accounts, to be held with the central bank.[100] In essence, critical ECB decisions are to be made with regard to the central bank affording, or not, interest payable to digital euro holdings, at which interest rate (pegged or not to one of the ECB applicable rates).[101] Relevant decisions also cover the possibility of imposing fees to digital euro accounts, or even the possibility of applying negative interest rate, in certain monetary circumstances.

Importantly, the decision about how and from whom the above digital euro project recurrent capital costs are to be recovered, will have implications for ECB own budget and CBDC ecosystem's efficiency, competition, innovation and inclusiveness.[102] Primarily, relevant resolutions must respect the Economic and Monetary Union (EMU) Treaty, in the sense that they ultimately relate to the monetary policy and common currency-liability of all EMU-Member States.[103] It might be argued, particularly,

[100] On the sovereignty of central bank to determine the level of any (CBDC) interest rate, in accordance with any public order rules aimed at protecting end users, particularly consumers, see De Vauplane, "Cryprocurrencies," 145. According to Grünewald et al., "Digital euro," 24, the Article 128(1) TFEU, Article 16 Statute of ESCB/ECB preclude digital euro design as an instrument of monetary policy (incl. interest (positive or negative)-bearing)). On interest payments and transaction fees considerations, with regard to modulate CBDC demand, restricting anonymity and elimination of the effective lower bound on interest-rate policy, see Kiff et al., "A Survey," 33.

[101] Zillioli, "The Perspective."

[102] See BIS, *Central Bank Digital Currencies*, 13, pointing out that directly recovering costs from the public users would be transparent, but could be a disincentive to CBDC adoption. On the consideration of alternative principles, regarding the design of CBDC costs recovery and relevant fee/compensation structures, see also Bindseil et al., "Central Bank Digital Currency," 31.

[103] See on the fundamentals of ECB role, Court of Justice of the EU, *Judgment in Case C-62/14: Gauweiler et al. v Deutscher Bundestag* (CJEU, 2015), para. 50 et seq. On the opinion that a system of negative remuneration (penalizing digital euro holdings) would appear problematic from legal point of view, from the perspectives of Article 1

that remuneration should not be offered to, nor sought, from the individual users, but rather to/from the financial intermediaries to be involved in digital euro distribution. According to additional views, other proposed means and measures appear more apt to achieve wide availability and usability of the digital euro.[104] Remarkably, according to DigEuro-Reg, art. 16 par. 8 and 15 par. 2, the digital euro shall not bear interest, while the level of charges or fees to be paid by natural persons or merchants to payment service providers, or between payment service providers, shall be subject to limits (as exemplified further in art. 17). Eurosystem is envisaged to bear its own costs, including those related to scheme management and settlement processing.[105]ECB may also attribute "seigniorage" (as the income currently afforded to the central bank, from the distribution of banknotes to the banks) to the supervised intermediaries, from issuing the digital euro.[106] In that context, all resolutions related to potential remuneration and compensation or fees concerning the digital euro scheme will require the ECB decision-making body to exercise constant cautiousness, in order to balance stakeholders' conflicting expectations and keep the CBDC scheme competitive and viable altogether.

3.4.2. Internal Organization

Decision-Making Bodies

Elaborating on the remarks made in earlier sections, it is evident that central bank organizational proficiency is critical for ECB to successfully discharge its mandate, without undermining its independency. Existing research on central bank governance frameworks has emphasized the

of Protocol No. 1 of the European Convention of Human Rights and EU Treaties, see Grünewald, *A legal framework*, 13. On the currently prevailing international view of discarding CBDC remuneration, see Lukonga, "Monetary policy implications."

[104] Such as sufficiently high holding limits, attractive privacy features, legal tender status and mandatory distribution, see Grünewald, *A legal framework*, 12; Grünewald, "CBDCs."

[105] That option follows a similar logic to euro cash and reflects the nature of digital euro as a public good. See ECB (2023). A stocktake on the digital euro. Summary report on the investigation phase and outlook on the next phase.

[106] Grünewald, *A legal framework*, 17.

growing need that their collective decision-making bodies possess perceptive skills and multiple expertise.[107] The education and/or earlier professional experience of (some of) those bodies' members in the technology sector will be highly beneficial in their roles in the digital currency environment, where they will need to assess and handle, equally demanding IT infrastructure and cybersecurity issues and risks. Specifically for the ECB, these proposals seem to be of rather limited direct value, in view of its main decision-making bodies' (Executive board & Governing Council) institutional composition and nomination, which are predetermined.[108] Nevertheless, it is still advisable for the Eurosystem's collective bodies to include a broad and diverse expertise and skillsets, ranging from economics, finance, risk, legal and audit, to engineering, computer science and information technology, in order to boost the efficiency of their oversight responsibilities.

Committees

Obviously, the above characteristics of ECB's decision-making bodies make the role of its special Committees even more prominent, as they will be required to handle issues and formulate proposals with regard to the digital euro initiative. Notably, the high-level Audit Committee (established by the Governing Council pursuant to Article 9b of the Rules of Procedure of the ECB) can provide advice and opinions, also regarding the oversight of internal controls for the digital euro and the compliance with applicable laws, regulations and codes of conduct.[109] Eurosystem's Risk Management Committee (RMC), assisting the ECB decision-making

[107] Bossu and Rossi, "The Role," 41, referring to (international) central banks' non-executive board members' eligibility criteria, bringing expertise (citing fintech and cyber security) that usefully complements that of the central bank's executive management.

[108] See above 2.2. In accordance with Article 283 (2) TFEU, the President, the Vice-President and the other (four) members of the Executive Board of ECB shall be appointed by the European Council, acting by a qualified majority, from among persons of recognised standing and professional experience in monetary or banking matters, on a recommendation from the Council after it has consulted the European Parliament and the Governing Council.

[109] As per Article 5(2) of its Mandate (https://www.ecb.europa.eu/ecb/shared/pdf/corgov/202012_audcomman.en.pdf), that Committee is composed partly by (up to three) external members, chosen from among high-ranking officials with experience in central banking, banking supervision and/or financial matters, as well as from among recognized experts from academia and/or the audit profession, provided they do not simultaneously hold positions in the financial sector.

bodies in attaining an appropriate level of protection for the Eurosystem, by managing and controlling the risks originating from ECB's monetary policy operations, would be expected to be involved actively in the design and implementation of the digital currency. The Information Technology Committee can undertake a principally advisory role concerning digital euro information systems architecture and security policies, transactions' data governance, CBDC scheme applications' implementation and interoperability. Nevertheless, given the importance of the Eurosystem digital euro initiative, it is hereby proposed that a new dedicated "Digital Euro Committee" is formed, which would be best suited to handle the miscellaneous, as well as complex relevant matters and shape proposals for the decision-making bodies, as it will be discussed in the next section.

Internal functions

In general, it would be advisable for ECB's internal organization to continue efforts to hire and retain specialized personnel for its units (Directorates) which are most relevant to functions required to address the various digital currency challenges discussed. Focus is on the operational risk management activities, to deal with cybersecurity and third-party involvement, which are creating procurement and outsourcing risk for the Eurosystem.[110] Attention should also be given to the payment markets infrastructure, information systems infrastructure and operations services, data analytics, business continuity management and settlement systems to-be-developed. Operational level staff needs to acquire knowledge and training, so as to build their capacity and understanding of all key issues, as well as develop expertise in operational, cyber, payment, fintech, data governance and settlement risks' areas. The formation of multidisciplinary teams could help ECB exploit the potential of new technologies, new payment methods, techniques and data, while at the same time handling any risks involved efficiently.[111] A unique CBDC (digital

[110] See Kiff et al., "A Survey," 43; Khan and Malaika, "Central Bank," 13, 47. On the importance, event categories of central bank operational risks, and ECB relevant taxonomy, see Khan, "Central Bank," 17, 37.

[111] On ECB projects combining expertise from different fields (e.g. economists, financial stability experts, statisticians, data scientists and IT experts) to jointly work on concrete questions, by leveraging on the different skill sets and expertise, see Emily Witt and Jannick Blaschke, "ECB data for analysis and decision-making: data governance and technology," *9th IFC Conference on "Are post-crisis statistical initiatives completed?*," Bank for International Settlements, 2018, 12.

euro) internal regulation is expected to be formulated and lay out clear allocation of competences, tasks and checkpoints within the Eurosystem (ECB and national euro-area central banks) organizations.[112]

In the same context, ECB internal audit and internal control roles are reasonably expected to be expanded, to accommodate digital euro issuance and use challenges. The increased standards of new digital currency will call for additional, more frequent and comprehensive audits. These will be necessary, in order to verify the systems' resilience,[113] promptly identify potential system violations, misuse or malfunction and minimize the probability of adverse pecuniary or reputational consequences. Depending on internal auditors' qualities and capacity, same units may also offer, in the long run, internal assurance services of IT and cybersecurity management. If ECB opts for extensive use of DLT techniques, where the "nodes" may be the NCBs and/or selected external commercial parties, then the ECB internal audit and control functions will need to be granted access and power to audit the relevant public and private entities, in order to verify their IT infrastructure's equivalent resilience.

Depending on the final digital euro scheme design, ECB Data Committee and Eurosystem Data Protection Officers' responsibilities and tasks may be expanded. That development would be expected, especially, if substantial personal data collection and storage were to take place in the Eurosystem.[114] Nevertheless, according to the "hybrid" system,

[112] On the importance of clear policies about CBDC responsibilities (for wrong and redress) allocation, see Bank of England, *Central Bank Digital Currency: Opportunities, Challenges and Design* (BoE, 2020). On the organizational separation of ECB staff, including their reporting lines, from the staff involved in carrying out ECB tasks conferred to it by virtue of the SSM Regulation, see European Central Bank, *Decision 2014/723/EU of the European Central Bank of 17 September 2014 on the implementation of separation between the monetary policy and supervision functions of the European Central Bank (ECB/2014/39)* (ECB, 2014), https://eur-lex.europa.eu/legal-content/EN/TXT/?uri=CELEX%3A32014D0039%2801%29; Gortsos, "Chinese Walls," 8. The conclusion of intra-ESCB cooperation agreements has been also considered, to provide for flexible secondments from the NCBs.

[113] See BIS, *Central Bank Digital Currencies for cross-border payments*, 6.

[114] On CBDC privacy considerations arising from the fact that even in a digital token-based system, transaction-level financial data reveal sensitive personal data, see Auer and Böhme, "The technology," 94; ECB, *Progress*.

currently promoted by the ECB, the functions of initial users' identification ("onboarding"), digital transactions' (above certain threshold)[115] authentication and AML are to be typically carried out by the intermediaries.[116] Yet even such design choice will still call for increased internal data governance safeguards and supervision of all respective private entities, especially if the latter are enabled to use personal and transactional data for their business purposes.[117] For ECB itself, without access to individual user data, it may prove challenging (legally, operationally and reputationally) to be able to monitor compliance with holding limits by individual users of the digital euro.[118]

Apart from the aforementioned compliance, Eurosystem will need to have access anyway to aggregate (or even pseudoanonymized) data, so as to perform ancillary digital euro related tasks, including statistics, research and oversight of the payment systems. The objectives of establishing robust data governance, across all involved organizations, focus on mitigation of significant data management risks, through meeting legislative requirements, preserving data confidentiality and preventing unauthorized exploitation.[119] By applying appropriate data management policies, ECB units' resources will still be able to analyse the underlying forces driving economic behaviour on the digital euro use. In that sense, they will also promptly assess the interconnectedness between the institutions

[115] On current ECB views regarding identification of thresholds for "low-value transactions" and overall spending limits over a specified time period, to be clarified in case it decides to adopt a higher degree of privacy for low-value transactions to increase the attractiveness of digital euro, see ECB, *Progress*, second report, 8.

[116] On latest ECB commitment to minimize the Eurosystem's involvement in the processing of users' data, so that Eurosystem would not be able to infer how many digital euro any individual end user held, not to infer end users' payment pattern, see Ibid., 7.

[117] See in more detail below under IV.2.

[118] See Grünewald, *A legal framework*, 14, also on the potentially available (sub-optimal) options of pseudo-anonymization or outsourcing this critical task entirely to private intermediaries.

[119] On the view that imposing higher levels of privacy and data restrictions beyond those required by the jurisdiction's data regulation may impact negatively CBDC intermediaries' revenue streams and their ability to add new innovative products, potentially reducing the diversity of participants in the system, see BIS, *Central Bank Digital Currencies,* 7.

involved, so as to better calibrate policy measures and timely undertake any course of action required.[120]

A Eurosystem dedicated committee on digital Euro

Taking into account the complexity and significance of the digital euro project implementation, ECB may seriously consider the establishment of a dedicated governance body, being responsible for the technical and operational management tasks in the field of digital euro infrastructure. Alternatively, the existing Market Infrastructure Board could undertake relevant tasks and responsibilities. The latter ensures that the Eurosystem's market infrastructures, platforms, applications and related services in the fields of cash settlement, securities settlement and collateral management are maintained and further developed, as well as that projects in the above fields are developed, in line with the Treaty objectives of the ESCB, its business needs, technological advances, as well as regulatory and oversight requirements, as applicable from time to time.[121]

Should a dedicated body eventually be established, that would be responsible for the preparation of proposals for decision by the Governing Council on the most important digital euro matters, services and arrangements. Those issues would include the actual digital euro strategy and scope of services, including their timely realignment and potential differentiation for certain subcategories of digital euro users, according to the actual digital euro market and use future evolutions.[122] They would also include project governance issues, digital euro scheme financing, risk management framework, service level agreements with relevant parties,

[120] Witt and Blaschke, "ECB data," 4. On the opportunities to use the data generated through the use of the digital euro, to broaden the information base for monetary policy or supervisory measures, as well as to decrease the market power of digital platforms, see Broemel, "20 Jahre Euro," 393.

[121] See European Central Bank, "Decision (EU) 2019/166 of the ECB on the Market Infrastructure Board and repealing Decision ECB/2012/6 on the establishment of the TARGET2-Securities Board (ECB/2019/3)," *Official Journal of the EU L 32/14* (Febrouary 2, 2019), https://eur-lex.europa.eu/legal-content/EN/TXT/?uri=CELEX%3A32019D0003%2801%29.

[122] On the possible differentiation between individual users, on the one hand, and merchants and governments, on the other, regarding even the entitlement of the latter entities to hold digital euros at all (i.e. zero-holding limit) as well as additional differentiation with regard to transaction limits, see Grünewald, *A legal framework*, 12.

network connectivity, crisis management and business continuity strategies, information security strategy and frameworks, liability and other claims, eligibility criteria and compliance requirements for the participants of the Eurosystem digital euro platform.

Such dedicated body would be primarily responsible to compile the digital euro detailed rulebooks, including rules and guidelines addressed to all digital euro scheme participants.[123] It would also support the management activities in respect of the digital euro services. Its orderly performance would ensure that the Eurosystem digital euro infrastructure and services meet both the wholesale and retail markets' needs. It would implement and manage the overall aforementioned strategies (after them being resolved upon by the Governing Council). At the same time, it would implement and manage (within the parameters set by the Governing Council) the governance arrangements, financial arrangements, risk management frameworks, operational frameworks, including the incident and crisis management strategy, cyber resilience and information security strategy, etc. It would, thus, ensure the proper functioning and quality of the Eurosystem digital euro infrastructure services, as well as compliance with regulatory and oversight requirements. Same Committee's tasks would include overseeing the scheme's financial affairs, ranging from collection of digital euro scheme fees to the extent applicable, up to allocation and reimbursement of such fees to each of Eurosystem central banks. It would also be involved in handling relations with the national euro-area central banks and Eurosystem governance bodies and external stakeholders.

Relevant committee's membership selection criteria should involve, certainly, expertise in the electronic money, digital payments, IT industry, as well as long exposure (experience) to the financial services industry and project management. In that sense, the members of the committee would have the mix of skills and integrity needed to perform their roles and fulfil their operational and risk management responsibilities. The objectives of such committee (hypothetically a "Digital euro infrastructure Board") should be to ensure the highest safety, efficiency and prudent management of the digital euro scheme. In the course of preparation of analytical rulebooks documentation, it should lay out clear and direct lines

[123] On the central position of CBDC core rulebook outlining the legal basis, governance, risk management, access and other requirements of participants, in any CBDC ecosystem, see BIS, *Central Bank Digital Currencies*, 2.

of responsibilities and accountability, as illustrated in the next chapter. In that context, it should also document procedures for identifying, addressing and managing potential conflicts of interest within the digital euro scheme.

In that direction, the Eurosystem's High-Level Task Force on Central Bank Digital Currency (HLTF-CBDC) established in January 2023 the digital euro scheme Rulebook Development Group (RDG). The first phase objective of this Group has been specified to develop a draft digital euro rulebook, building on the design decisions taken by the Governing Council of the Eurosystem. Such work entails investigating rules, practices and standards that could support the distribution and operation of a digital euro. The members of the group are senior professionals from the private and public sectors with experience in finance and payments. In addition to the representatives from the Eurosystem, other representatives are nominated by different European stakeholder associations in the European retail payments market. According to its mandate, the digital euro RDG will reflect on a future governance model for the digital euro scheme once it is in full operational mode.[124]

An advisory body on digital Euro

The above proposed dedicated governance body is thought to be best suited to accomplish its demanding tasks and objectives, if assisted by an advisory body bringing together public and private industry knowledge and the capacity to provide specialized advice on material matters related to digital euro issuance, distribution and cross-border use. Drawing valuable inferences from the two advisory groups established to counsel the Eurosystem and provide advice on market infrastructures for payments, and on market infrastructures for securities and collateral, it can be argued that a similar advisory body could benefit the digital euro issuer substantially. It could facilitate an active interaction with all different financial markets and technology systems participants, fostering and further promoting the objectives of the digital euro project.

The main responsibility of such an advisory body would be to exchange views and advise the Eurosystem decision-making bodies (through the dedicated committee on digital euro), in all material aspects of the digital euro scheme. Particular focus should be with regard to technological and

[124] See https://www.ecb.europa.eu/paym/digital_euro/investigation/shared/files/digital_euro_mandate_rulebook_development_group.pdf.

digital assets developments, financial system evolution and their potential impact. This advisory body would be expected to convey the actual needs, demands and desires of prospective digital euro users, in both wholesale and retail segments. It would access and consider any innovative cases, technologies, international developments or proposed applications and arrangements that could be potentially utilized (or simply tested) to enhance the digital euro scheme. It could concurrently provide advice to the Eurosystem on the interrelation of the envisaged CBDC scheme with the existing payment systems infrastructure, with a view to facilitate their integration and minimize embedded operational risks. In the context of discussing various potential digital euro stakeholders' concerns and exploring alternative practical solutions, such advisory body could address important operational issues and make suggestions of strategic nature, in order to increase the safety and efficiency of the CBDC scheme.

The ultimate value-added and effectiveness of such an advisory body would obviously depend on the composition and engagement of its members. Its meaningful contribution to the digital euro issuer would presuppose the active joint involvement of the dedicated digital euro committee, along with further critical ECB Units (Directorates) of the ECB (incl. Directorate General Market Infrastructure and Payments, Directorate General Information Systems, Directorate Risk Management), through their leading Directors (General). The advisory body from the private sector should be comprised of multiple senior executive managers, representing different types of banks, electronic money institutions and payment service providers, active in the EU, with emphasis on the euro area. Those could be complemented by selected senior executive managers, representing leading financial technology or information technology companies, who would be able to contribute specialized knowledge and experience to these advisory body deliberations. NCBs should also be represented (on a rotating basis), via their senior managers. Finally, financial services industry associations, other financial market services providers and other EU institutional Authorities (including European Commission, Eurosystem oversight function and European Data Protection Supervisor—EDPS) could be granted observer status, at least on ad-hoc basis. Such a role would allow them to be informed and participate in the dialogue, even before advice and reports are formulated and circulated to the Eurosystem dedicated committee and decision-making bodies for their competent evaluation and resolutions.

Notably, a Digital Euro Market Advisory Group has been formed to advise the Eurosystem on the design and potential roll-out of the digital euro. It also explores how a digital euro could be beneficial to those involved in the euro area's network of payments systems. The group is chaired by a senior manager in the ECB's Directorate General Market Infrastructure and Payments, while its members are market practitioners. Those members are active in the retail payments market, yet they do not represent their institutions, but act in a personal capacity. European Commission services also participate, as observer, in that Group sessions.[125]

3.4.3. Transparency and Accountability

The digital euro issuance and scheme operation, to the extent they involve marginal redesign of ECB balance sheet, could themselves be considered complementary tools optimizing and increasing ECB's operational transparency.[126] They are expected (as sovereign state functions delegated to EU central banks) to be subjected, along with such currency cross-border use, to the established limited external oversight mechanisms, exercised by the EU Executive (European Commission), Legislature (European Parliament) and Judiciary. Although Member States should not directly interfere, nor issue directives to the Eurosystem on digital currency issues, they may still address enquiries, remarks on the scheme operation and raise potential matters of concern. Those can be relayed also via National Parliaments, at the EU Council or Eurogroup level, or by individual Member State officials. ECB's external auditors and the European Court of Auditors may serve, additionally, as significant external layers of control.

In essence, the governing body of the digital euro scheme should ensure that its design, overall strategy, rules and major decisions reflect

[125] See https://www.ecb.europa.eu/paym/digital_euro/investigation/shared/files/digital_euro_mandate_mag.pdf.

[126] On the CBDC-related possible differentiation of central bank assets and liabilities, as enabling central bank to formulate and dynamically adjust its key monetary policy priorities and choices in a more targeted and publicly accountable manner, see Omarova, "The People's ledger," 1258.

appropriately the legitimate interests of EU citizens and other relevant stakeholders.[127] The latter include the digital euro scheme participants, credit institutions, payment service providers, industry specialists, IT infrastructure and financial technology providers, developers of payment solutions, merchants, merchant associations, consumer associations, etc. Ex-ante consultation with members of the broadest digital euro ecosystem, through market contact groups, surveys and calls for expression of interest on the technical design features of a digital euro, has proved beneficial to take timely account of their expectations.[128] In parallel, the agenda and minutes of the established Rulebook Development Group's meetings are published on the ECB's website, along with regular updates on the progress made on the digital euro project. Once a first draft of the Rulebook is ready, ample public consultation is to be organized to collect feedback from all interested parties. In that context, drafting process should be sufficiently flexible to accommodate potential adjustments based on the outcome of the public consultation.

It has been announced that the recent resolution of the Governing Council of the ECB (dd. 18.10.2023) to move to the preparation phase of the digital euro project is not a decision on whether to issue a digital euro. That latter resolution will only be considered by ECB once the EU's aforementioned legislative process has been duly completed. Yet,

[127] On the view that risks associated with the introduction of CBDC as well as the new powers and tools that it makes available to central banks may require higher levels of central bank accountability, appropriate safeguards, and standards of judicial scrutiny, see Nabilou, "Central Bank Digital Currencies," 21.

[128] During the investigation phase, this approach has been followed through regular exchanges between ECB Member of the Executive Board, Dr. F. Panetta and the ECON Committee of the European Parliament, as well as targeted public consultation and focus groups in the euro area Member States, since October 2020 (Panetta, Fabio, "A digital euro for the digital era," *Introductory statement at the ECON Committee of the European Parliament*, European Central Bank, 2020, https://www.ecb.europa.eu/press/key/date/2020/html/ecb.sp201012_1~1d14637163.en.html). See Grünewald, "CBDCs," also commenting on limited further public outreach, except for the joint ECB-EC conference on the digital euro (7.11.2022). On the European Parliament parallel evaluation of the digital euro prospects and on the ECB support of the democratic debate on the digital euro, see Angeloni (2023), op, cit. (footnote 76), 11. (broadly positive of the preparatory work of EU institutions, yet casting doubt on the wisdom of eventually launching a digital euro) and www.ecb.europa.eu/paym/digital_euro/investigation/governance/shared/files/ecb.degov231006_Letter_from_Fabio_Panetta_to_several_MEPs_on_request_to_postpone_the_decision_on_the_digital_euro.en.pdf?ffba66151e533bfab912c2d52742263f, respectively.

it should be emphasized that ECB will need to take into account any adjustments to the design of the digital euro that may become necessary as a result of the legislative deliberations and public debate. During the preparation and the implementation phases, major decisions on the system architecture should be clearly and orderly disclosed and justified to the above stakeholders and the public, given the broad market impact of the digital euro project.[129] According to DigEuro-Reg, art. 40, the European Central Bank will report on the digital euro as part of its regular reporting obligations. Furthermore, it will specifically report to the Parliament, to the Council and to the European Commission on the instruments to limit the use of the digital euro as a store of value as well as their parameters, in relation to the objective to safeguard financial stability, no later than 6 months before the planned issuance of the digital euro, and at regular intervals afterwards. The Commission should also report on the impact of the parameters and the use of the instruments in particular on the role of financial intermediaries in the financing of the economy.

Transparency is to be further bolstered, by means of efficient coordination and cooperation of the Eurosystem bodies and committees, on clear terms, with other domestic and international agencies and Authorities outside the financial sector, which have been granted (entrusted) legal responsibility to resolve upon, or opine, on specific matters related to, or marginally affected by, the operation of the digital euro system. Those include, in particular, tax authorities, anti-money laundering authorities, data protection authorities, communications security authorities and competition authorities. In our view, they should be consulted on major developments and have access to necessary information in order to perform their mandates. Notably, according to DigEuro-Reg, the European Central Bank should consult the European Data Protection Supervisor regarding any measures, rules and standards, that may be adopted by the ECB which have an impact on the protection of individual's rights and freedoms with regard to the processing of personal data, as well as prior to developing the details on the operational elements of the broad fraud detection and prevention mechanism. They should also be entrusted to organize assessments and regular audits of ECB, NCBs and digital euro scheme participants, to verify compliance with relevant

[129] On the CBDC programmability feature, and its offered ability to central banks to impose negative rates, as additional factors justifying even higher levels of central bank public accountability, see also Nabilou, "Central Bank Digital Currencies," 22.

EU and domestic legislation. It is also proposed that the Eurosystem undertakes initiatives to foster transparency of the digital euro system operation. To this respect, disclosure of ECB and NCBs internal audits' potential material findings, illegal activity incidents[130] and the enhanced internal and external communication[131] would be particularly meaningful. Indeed, ECB is expected to engage actively with the society to promote the adoption and use of the new digital currency, to maximize its envisaged benefits and minimize inherent risks, through targeted reports, speeches, parliamentary hearings, as well as by providing relevant educational programs for financial sector representatives, merchants and the general public.[132]

4 Additional Governance Safeguards for Eurosystem Control over Its CBDC Scheme

The above proposed governance framework for the issuer of digital euro (Eurosystem) may be further enhanced through application of additional selected mechanisms, aimed at securing its substantive control over the CBDC scheme. They relate mainly to risk management, selection of "primary system" participants and technology providers, supervision of distribution platforms and interoperability of digital currency with the private world.

4.1 Digital Euro Risk Management Framework and Policies

The Eurosystem decision-making bodies should consider introducing additional material components to the applicable ECB risk management framework. Drawing on the challenges and risks examined previously in 2,

[130] On the compulsory reporting of major ICT–related incidents and voluntary notification of significant cyber threats, see particularly DORA Regulation, Article 19.

[131] On the suggested improvement of ECB (and SRB) accountability by means of making the findings of their internal quality assurance and review bodies publicly available (subject to constraints on professional secrecy), also allowing the European Parliament to use these findings to scrutinize and stimulate public debate about the operations and effectiveness of those institutions, see Jonathan Zeitlin and Filipe Brito Bastos, "SSM and the SRB accountability at European level: room for improvements?," European Parliament, 2020, 26.

[132] Kiff et al., "A Survey," 36.

the amended framework should include a distinct digital euro scheme risk tolerance policy, assign responsibility and accountability for risk decisions (including regarding remuneration, compensation, selection of intermediaries, procurement, outsourcing) and address decision-making related to the scheme features during crises and emergencies.[133] Such CBDC-related risk management framework components should be subject to frequent review.

Additionally, a specific digital euro risk management policy should be in place, along with procedures and systems that will enable competent Eurosystem officials to identify, measure, monitor and manage the range of risks that arise out of, or are borne by, the CBDC scheme. It will involve developing CBDC crisis playbooks, laying down contingency and business continuity measures to manage serious operational digital euro scheme disruptions, instances of financial system instability or inadequacy to meet regulatory requirements.[134] The relevant governance analysis needs to also consider the most disruptive form of CBDC carefully, which encompasses token-based, potentially programmable and reversible (digital euro) to other private digital assets (and vice versa).[135] With the assistance of the advisory body and dedicated committee, the ECB Governing Council should regularly review the material risks that the Eurosystem bears from and poses to other entities (including but not limited credit institutions, e-money and payment service institutions, digital assets exchanges,[136] or other settlement systems), as a result of

[133] See also ibid., 40; Khan and Malaika, "Central Bank," 28. On the efficient management of non-financial risks of central banks through the organizational functions of risk management and internal audit, see Khan, "Central Bank," 14.

[134] Kiff et al., "A Survey," 36; see also European Central Bank, *Eurosystem assessment methodology for electronic payment instruments, schemes and arrangements* (ECB, 2021), 18, 34, https://www.ecb.europa.eu/paym/pdf/consultations/ecb.PISApublicconsultation202111_2.en.pdf. On the unprecedented risk that, in case of banking crises or runs , the ECB may come under political pressure (due to public savings put at risk) to relax the upper limit of prospective digital euro holdings, thus contributing to financial instability, see Angeloni (2023), op. cit. (footnote 76), 15.

[135] See supra footnote 98, Article 2(2) of Directive 2009/110/EC, Article 3(1) MiCAR; Filippo Annunziata, "Speak, If You Can: What Are You? An alternative approach to the qualification of tokens and initial coin offerings," *European Company and Financial Law Review* 17, no. 2 (2020), http://dx.doi.org/10.2139/ssrn.3332485; Athanassiou, "Impact of digital innovation," 34.

[136] On CBDC importance in continuing to provide the reference value for all forms of private money in the economy, thus protecting the value of money and monetary

interdependencies, and it should develop appropriate management tools to address those risks.[137]

4.2 *Strict Regulatory Technical Standards and Interoperability with Private Digital "Currencies" and Tokens*

Security of the prospective digital euro scheme comes through the consistent application of strict technical standards for the CBDC-related system, services and participating parties. Those standards are expected to be set by the Eurosystem decision-making bodies with the assistance, consultation and advice of internal resources, committee and advisory body mentioned earlier. Developing common relevant technical standards, in cooperation with other major international central banks, international authorities and organizations,[138] will be essential to facilitate the cross-border use of the sovereign digital currency of the euro area.[139] These standards would cover multiple methods, procedures and technical

sovereignty, see Panetta, "More than an intellectual game." According to the DigEuro-Reg's Impact Assessment, a digital euro could support European businesses for future use cases in "industry 4.0" and "web 3 (i.e. decentralised internet)" by giving them a public alternative to programmable payments potentially offered by CBDCs of foreign countries and stablecoins from technology companies. Yet, as per the relevant DigEuro-Reg, art. 24, payment service providers and users will be able to use conditional digital euro payment transactions, but the digital euro should not be programmable money (i.e. not be used to limit its spending to or direct it at specific goods or services); in essence, as a digital form of the single currency, the digital euro should be fully fungible.

[137] See ECB, *Eurosystem*, 22.

[138] On the international dimension and user/use categories of envisaged CBDCs, see also Bindseil et al., "Central Bank Digital Currency," 20, emphasizing the need for an international consensus and a set of rules, and probably also safeguards against facilitating large and fast capital flows. Notably, according to DigEuro-Reg, art. 32, the European Central Bank may establish a general fraud detection and prevention mechanism to support fraud management activities performed by payment service providers on online digital euro payment transactions. The transfer of information between PSPs and the fraud detection and prevention mechanism should be subject to state-of-the-art security and privacy-preserving measures to ensure that individual digital euro users are not identified by the central fraud detection and prevention mechanism. Additionally, it has been proposed that the European Central Bank should provide payment service providers and digital euro users with technical and functional support for dispute resolution, related at least to technical and fraud (pre) disputes.

[139] See in detail Panos Papapaschalis, "Legal interoperability of retail CBDCs: Initial considerations," in *ESCB Legal Conference 2022*, ed. European Central Bank (Frankfurt: ECB, 2022), 117.

aspects related to digital euro issuance, distribution and use. Indicatively, they will govern digital identity repositories, AML/CFT and fighting financial fraud checks, transactional and personal data protection, cross-border access to domestic CBDC, payment system access, settlement finality, etc.[140] In that respect, Eurosystem may need to consider delaying launch of its own CBDC until a higher degree of consensus is reached internationally on those standards.

At the operational level, the system should ensure that users are able to exchange digital euro for cash and commercial bank deposits, and vice versa, at all times, without friction. In that sense, ECB may obligate the intermediaries that will eventually fulfil the criteria to participate in the scheme to provide funding and defunding services as a core digital euro service.[141] In the context of its significant resolutions regarding the rules of parallel issuance of the unique, token-based (or even ever programmable) form of the digital euro, Eurosystem will have to provide cautiously for relevant tolerable technical standards.[142] In essence, they should not hinder convertibility, but rather allow for interoperability of the latter challenging form of digital euro, not simply with the account-based CBDC of the euro area, but more importantly, also with the international major private tokens' world, including stablecoins.[143]

[140] On the protection of transactional and other data in a DLT environment, see Athanassiou, *Digital innovation in financial services*, 32.

[141] See Grünewald, *A legal framework*, 17, and below IV.3. See also the proposed use of the European Digital Identity Wallets to onboard and make digital euro payments, as per DigEuro-Reg, art. 25.

[142] In the case of potential future use of programmable form of the digital euro (which would allow the central bank to impose restrictions on how users' funds could be spent), Eurosystem would need to provide, additionally, moral ethical considerations. On the current decisively negative stance of ECB, regarding such feature, see Coindesk, website, https://www.coindesk.com/policy/2023/01/23/digital-euro-will-never-be-programmable-ecbs-panetta-says/.

[143] See Weber, "Global"; Zillioli, "The Perspective"; BIS, *Central Bank Digital Currencies,* 9. On inclusivity and interoperability as central pillars of the financial ecosystem, see Annunziata, "Speak.". On stablecoins' evolution, see Douglas Arner et al., "Stablecoins: risks, potential and regulation", BIS Working Papers no. 905 (Bank for International Settlements, 2020), https://www.bis.org/publ/work905.pdf; Didenko et al., "After Libra," 27; IMF, "Digital," 17.

4.3 Selection of "Primary System" Participants and Increased Supervision of Distribution and Tokenization Platforms

The Eurosystem has already established that supervised intermediaries are best placed to provide user-facing services and to build new business models for the actual implementation of the digital euro scheme.[144] In essence, the prospective digital currency should be made available on an equal basis in all euro countries through supervised intermediaries. Recently, ECB has confined the set of supervised intermediaries that would be eligible to qualify as participants in the digital euro scheme to payment service providers, according to the PSD2.[145] In addition to the banks, then, e-money and payment institutions would be possibly allowed to distribute the digital euro and provide related services.

Nevertheless, it may be still debatable which of all supervised intermediaries will be eligible to form part of the "core" or "primary digital euro system" (i.e., hold accounts with the ECB)[146] and perform functional tasks on ECB/NCBs behalf, as exemplified above. The objectives and competition concerns of all relevant credit institutions, electronic money

[144] See Eurosystem report on a digital euro (2020), also Grünewald et al., "Digital euro," 16, on the extraordinary possibility of delegation of functions to private firms being outside the Eurosystem's direct or indirect supervisory remit, such as telecommunication firms that design and provide cell phone applications for the distribution, transfer, and storage of the digital euro, and relevant obligation of ECB to lay out general requirements for those delegees, or approve the use of delegees in individual cases. Notably, according to DigEuro-Reg, art. 26, the European Central Bank shall seek to ensure to the extent possible the interoperability of standards governing digital euro payment services with relevant standards governing private digital means of payment. ECB shall seek to enable, to the extent possible and where appropriate, private digital means of payment to use rules, standards and processes governing the digital euro payment services, while interoperability may be supported inter alia by the use of open standards.

[145] See ECB, *Progress*, third report, 2023. According to DigEuro-Reg, all payment services providers authorised in the EU may provide digital euro payment services, including additional digital euro payment services, in addition to basic digital euro payment services. It is envisaged that payment service providers will not need an additional authorization from their competent authorities to provide digital euro payment services.

[146] On the scholarly view that a central bank might not (does not have to) "own" such primary CBDC system, but reserve to itself (monopolizing) certain essential functions (such as key operations, account balancing and consent for material redesigns), while the legal ownership of the system might be spread across the participants of such system, so that the information flow to the central bank and the supervision are assured, see Didenko et al., "After Libra," 48, referring to the established participation of central banks in network-like critical market infrastructure as "a nationalization in function".

institutions and payment service providers need to be weighed against the need for a most secure and controllable digital euro issuance environment.[147] The digital euro scheme's rulebook will specify the relevant criteria of access, yet legislative action may be needed to support ECB proposal.[148] Actually, ECB has not communicated yet whether all supervised intermediaries will get direct access to its balance sheet or whether this access will continue to be confined to banks, while the access of other PSPs would be only indirect.[149] It may be the case, then, that direct participation in the "primary" system is entrusted, at least at the first phase of implementation, to the institutions meeting highest objective standards and prudential requirements.[150] Although such ECB option might attract criticism, acting as a "market maker", i.e., distorting free market competition,[151] it could still be justified, for a transitional period, in the author's opinion, in order to ensure the overarching public interest of financial stability. At any rate, ECB would maintain the right to exclude participants, in case they pose major threat to the scheme infrastructure.

At any rate, all third parties engaged in the CBDC ecosystem and relevant private system arrangements, including distribution platforms as well

[147] On the comparable, to some extent, considerations, as regards the selection of "eligible counterparties" for the conduct of Eurosystem monetary policy operations, which is made dependent on their fulfilment of present (by virtue of relevant ECB Guideline) eligibility criteria, to minimize embedded risks, see Gortsos, *European Central Banking Law*, 295.

[148] See Grünewald, *A legal framework*, 15, 19 referring to ECB broad discretion, on the basis of Article 22 of the Statute of ESCB/ECB, to determine criteria for access to the digital euro scheme and distribute the roles and functions between scheme participants, as well as to potential amendments to the scope of Settlement Finality Directive 98/26/EC, the Payment Accounts Directive 2014/92/EU and the Payment Services Directive II.

[149] Grünewald, *A legal framework*, 15.

[150] On the opposing matter, whether ECB may consider that certain intermediaries (due to their market position) might be required to distribute the digital euro (i.e. participation in the scheme not be voluntary in all circumstances), and/or provide core digital euro services to their clientele: ibid., 15.

[151] See above under III.1 on Article 127(1) TFEU and Article 2 of the Statute of ESCB/ECB. In essence, the Eurosystem, while pursuing its public tasks (ensuring availability of digital euro, promoting smooth operation of payment systems, etc.), is not subject to Article 101-102 TFEU; yet it must act in accordance with the principle of an open market economy with free competition.

as tokenization networks, should be subjected to robust regulatory oversight and supervision by the involved authorities.[152] ECB (through both its monetary and supervisory functions), NCBs and national competent authorities (supervisors of EU electronic money, payment institutions, etc.) shall need to cooperate closely, through consultation and information exchange, to ensure consistent interpretation of applicable rulebooks and avoid supervised entities' opportunities for arbitrage,[153] also internationally.[154] According to the express provision of art. 6 DigEuro-Reg, the competent authorities responsible under Directive (EU) 2015/2366 for supervising the provision of payment services should also cooperate with the European Central Bank for the purposes of supervising the application of payment-related obligations laid down in the proposed Regulation. Supervisory assessments and potential disciplinary actions would be particularly directed to relevant entities' market conduct (including vis-à-vis consumers), anti-money laundering,[155] personal data protection and cybersecurity. It has been advised that private entities offering CBDC transfer, storage or custody should be held to equivalent standards as firms offering similar services for cash or existing private digital "money".[156] Same should stand as well for CBDC exchange. Notably, MiCAR provides

[152] Kiff et al., "A Survey," 26. On the accomplishment of potentially compound ECB supervisory roles, see broadly Gortsos, "Chinese Walls." On the power of ECB to impose sanctions in case of infringement of the Regulation on oversight requirements for systemically important payment systems, see Gortsos, *European Central Banking Law*, 309. On the risk that, absent sufficient compensation for their role in the distribution of digital euro, banks may expect an implicit compensation in the form of easier financing or more lenient supervision, see Angeloni (2023), op. cit. (footnote 76), 11.

[153] On the discussion and justification regarding lighter touch regulatory regime applicable to (fintech) payment and electronic money institutions in comparison to credit institutions, see Barroso, "Fintechs," 38.

[154] On the importance of a well-functioning, mutual supervisory cooperation among international financial sector (in our case CBDC systems and stablecoins) supervisors, see Dirk Zetzsche et al., "The Markets in Crypto-Assets Regulation (MICA) and the EU digital finance strategy," Working Paper Series no. 77 (European Banking Institute, 2020), 27, https://ssrn.com/abstract=3725395.

[155] In the AML area, cooperation of NCBs and NCAs with national judicial authorities and national AML authorities will be required as well, since relevant concerns tend to result to criminal investigations, or even at higher-level national security concerns, if it concerns combating terrorism financing, which is typically dealt with by the member state internal affairs authorities.

[156] See De Vauplane, "Cryprocurrencies."

for specific requirements on the offer of e-money tokens, as defined above.[157] More importantly, it establishes uniform regulatory, authorization and supervision regime for the providers of services of crypto-assets (including e-money tokens).[158] That regime shall indeed prove relevant, especially in the prospective development of digital euro tokens, levelled for retail transactions' offline settlement.[159]

Yet, it seems reasonable, that given the systemic dimension and innovative features of the digital euro, the entities involved in the aforementioned activities and services should be required to meet even more sophisticated (stricter) operational (technical) requirements. These intensified requirements may indeed prove valuable in the context of the limited anonymity, which is envisaged to-be-granted for the low value

[157] Those may only be issued by credit institutions and electronic money institutions, while a large number of regulations from the E-Money Directive will also apply. A white paper must be drafted for e-money tokens issuance and notified to the competent authority.

[158] See Filippo Annunziata, "The licensing rules in MiCA," in *Fintech regulation and the licensing principle*, eds. Dário Moura Vicente, and Diogo Pereira Duarte Catarina Granadeiro, EBI eBook Series 2 (Frankfurt: European Banking Institute, 2023), 115; Zetzsche et al., "The Markets," 10. Only legal persons that are established in the EU and have received the relevant authorization or certain financial institutions (for example, credit institutions, investment firms and alternative investment fund managers) may provide such services. The authorization is to be issued by the national competent authorities and is to be valid for the entire EU ("pass porting"). In addition to the capital requirements, depending on the type of service, requirements are established regarding the management body (good repute and possess sufficient knowledge, skills and experience, committing sufficient time) and shareholders. The service providers also have obligations towards conflicts of interest, information obligations and provisions on outsourcing. A grandfathering process will be available to e-money institutions, under which a simplified procedure for obtaining an authorization will be offered rather than having to undergo the full authorization process. Each national competent authority shall provide relevant information on the largest service providers to ESMA on a regular basis. On the preceding policy discussion of how virtual currencies should fit into the European legal and regulatory framework, see Athanassiou, "Impact of digital innovation," 19.

[159] Notably, the MiCAR exemption regarding crypto-assets issued by central banks, acting in their monetary authority capacity, does not extend to private intermediaries acting in the issuance of CBDCs, or providing services to CBDCs. See Zetzsche et al., "The Market," 26, who recommend that, subject to further rules stipulated by the respective central bank, the private entities acting on behalf of a central bank, or in cooperation with a central bank, in the context of a CBDC system, be exempted from MiCA. Yet, with regard to the latter proposed exemption case, some concerns might be raised, regarding potential distortion of competition in the relevant market.

digital currency holdings and transactions, to ensure CBDC public acceptance.[160] The rationale is that such requirements have the potential to control and ensure, more efficiently, the end users' compliance with the existing AML and anti-fraud legislation.[161] Ultimate objective of supervision would be no other than to protect customers, build confidence in the new digital currency and avoid risks to financial stability.

4.4 Selection of IT Resources and Technology Providers

The issuer of digital euro will be necessary to adopt measures and techniques mitigating the risk of potential overdependencies on Information Technology (IT) resources and technology providers. That would imply careful, broader than the existing, diversification of systems, providers and data storage, as well as frequent audit attestation of the third party (including cloud providers') systems, procedures and infrastructure. Indeed, due to resource and other constraints inside the central banks, certain IT deliverables would need to be outsourced to the private sector.[162] Relying subsequently on specific providers (mostly US-based conglomerates) would create dependencies, which could have serious implications in terms of resilience and autonomy, and ultimately the safety of the currency and the smooth transmission of monetary policy.[163] It has already been noted that ECB and NCBs will need to continuously run rigorous own cybersecurity activities and appropriate prevention controls, to be assessed regularly by independent cybersecurity assurance specialists

[160] On related CBDC traceability, pseudonymity and anonymity concerns and alternatives for central banks, see De Vauplane, "Cryprocurrencies," 143; Kiff et al., "A Survey," 30; ECB, *Progress*, 7 (considering full anonymity not a viable digital euro option from a public policy perspective, and presenting alternatives ("selective privacy" and offline functionality" options).

[161] IMF, "Digital," 31.

[162] See for instance the cloud strategy paths that most EUIs, including the EC and the ECB have adopted: European Commission, *European Commission cloud strategy: Cloud as an enabler for the European commission digital strategy* (European Commission, 2019), https://commission.europa.eu/system/files/2019-05/ec_cloud_strategy.pdf.

[163] On the dependence on the technology firms' intermediaries, in distributing CBDC as a new challenge to institutional independence of central banks, also Grünewald, "CBDCs." On the Big Tech companies as "an increasingly indispensable component of the financial sector" and prospective collaborator and supplier of innovations to ECB, see Angeloni (2023), op, cit. (footnote 76), 11.

(both in design & full operation phases) and have their own resilience verified.[164] An additional material operation risk is identified, in the cases where Eurosystem will cooperate with one of the largest ("too big to ignore") private technology-software providers for critical digital euro functionalities.[165] In each of those cases, Eurosystem should apply special measures to address respective risk by imposing specific onerous contractual obligations to, or even demand particular structural requirements by, the respective counterparty. Those requirements may involve highest resilience controls, compulsory utilization of diversified IT resources and data centres, geographic segregation of services provided, thorough data protection management controls, special purpose reserves and facilities along with constant availability. More broadly, best procurement practices should be employed on technology selection and project management. As already advised, they are expected to involve open and transparent procedures,[166] comprehensive selection criteria, evaluation of proposed solutions first through series of proof of concepts against the Eurosystem's design, risk management framework and adoption criteria.[167]

5 Concluding Remarks

Among the challenges associated with the issuance of a sovereign digital currency, the implementation of relevant schemes raises substantial interest in respect of their supervision and control, including issuers' governance. The latter development is attributed to the fact that in the international CBDC ecosystem central banks are called to serve multiple roles. At the European level, particularly, ECB within the Eurosystem is expected to delineate the digital euro scheme's operational design model,

[164] On relevant technology considerations and proposals, see BIS, *Central Bank Digital Currencies,* 14; Khan and Malaika, "Central Bank," 46. On the financial cross–sector crisis management and contingency exercises, see also DORA Regulation, Article 48.

[165] See above footnote 77, on ECB recent choice to cooperate with largest software and services providers to develop front-end prototypes for the digital euro.

[166] From the procurement law perspective, on the non-exclusion of bidders based outside of the EEA, yet operating via a European affiliate, see Judgment dated 13.2.2023 (VK 2–114/22) of the Bundeskartellamt's Procurement Chamber. As a further example, it is noted that according to DigEuro-Reg, art. 32, the general fraud detection and prevention mechanism may be operated directly by the ECB or by the (third party) providers of support services designated by the ECB.

[167] See eloquently Kiff et al., "A Survey," 35 et seq.

to regulate on some of its legal and technical issues and at the same time, along with national competent Authorities, to supervise the most important of the private sector's entities and systems, participating and involved, respectively, in the process of digital currency distribution and use by wholesale and market participants.

According to the design model currently envisaged, Eurosystem is set to cooperate closely with the private sector, not only in the business side (i.e., in the distribution of digital euro), but also on the operational side (i.e., in the course of important functional activities, such as those related to the user management, liquidity management and processing of digital euro payments). Nevertheless, when it comes to the governance of the scheme, potential private–public sector cooperation (even if it were to involve common preparation of documentation relevant to the system operation, or ultimately, compilation of analytical CBDC rulebooks and guidelines), is confronted with severe institutional concerns. In the author's view, a central bank should not simply retain the decision powers, while being substantively deprived of necessary knowledge. In contrast, ECB bodies should be able to ascertain themselves and appraise materially the technical policies, rules, standards or decisions, which are to be adopted. In the same context, any significant dependence of the digital euro issuer on the private sector (even if it were not to result directly to administrative actions' legal deficiencies), may well have negative impact on the central bank oversight and supervisory functions. Thus, it is proposed that Eurosystem adopts a cautious approach in internal governance mechanisms and arrangements with third parties and also, introduces additional layers of control of the envisaged system. Those shall ensure compliance with additional applicable rules (including data protection and confidentiality, free competition, anti-money laundering processes) and minimize potential issuer's liability, in cases of undesirable incidents.

Building on the traditional central banks' governance framework (involving their mandate, autonomy, decision-making, accountability and transparency), particular enhancements have been proposed with regard to the ECB, as issuer, regulator and, in many respects, supervisor of the digital euro scheme. While the ECB mandate can be grounded in multiple legal bases (Article 128(1) TFEU/16 Statute of ESCB/ECB, Article 127(2), first indent TFEU/17 Statute of ESCB/ECB and 127(2) fourth indent TFEU/22 Statute of ESCB/ECB), secondary EU legislation has been considered necessary to clarify the terms of ECB engagement, as well as to provide reference to additional public policy objectives to be served by digital euro, such as financial integrity, financial inclusion and transaction data protection. The relevant EU Regulation, to be adopted by the European Parliament and the Council, after consultation with the ECB, on the grounds of Article 133 TFEU, will define more clearly the boundaries of central bank's role, with regard to the involvement of other financial or digital services intermediaries and rule on critical matters affecting the scheme.

Personal and functional independence of the digital euro issuer will be preserved, provided that all central bank's resources are not concurrently engaged (even on provisional or project-oriented basis) by private industry (incl. information technology) stakeholders. Yet, the verification of Eurosystem own digital euro infrastructure (including its resilience and cybersecurity posture) can be appraised regularly through a specialized private assurance services provider. To safeguard its financial independence, ECB should reflect the capital expenditure and the considerable recurring costs of the full-scale implementation of the digital euro project, in its resolutions on the cost allocation structure of the digital euro payment scheme. Those might affect, ultimately, the compensation offered to the financial intermediaries to proactively support the diffusion of the digital euro, the potential remuneration levels of digital euro and/ or fees or "seigniorage" to-be-attributed to the financial intermediaries involved in digital euro distribution. All relevant resolutions will require constant attention of ECB decision-making body, in order to safeguard its budget, balance the stakeholders' conflicting expectations and keep the CBDC scheme competitive and viable altogether.

Notwithstanding the restrictions originating from primary EU law rules on the composition of ECB decision-making bodies, it has been proposed that Eurosystem's collective organs procure a broad and diverse expertise and skillset (covering economics, finance, risk, legal, audit, as well as engineering and information technology), to be able to exercise their digital euro scheme oversight responsibilities most effectively. In addition to the existing ECB Audit Committee, Risk Management Committee, Information Technology Committee, Data Committee, Internal audit and Internal control expanded responsibilities, the formation of a new dedicated "Digital Euro Committee" has been proposed. That committee would be held responsible for the shaping of proposals for decision by the Governing Council on most important and complex digital euro matters, services and arrangements. Those issues include the actual digital euro strategy and scope of services, project governance issues, digital euro scheme financing, risk management framework, service-level agreements with third parties, network connectivity, crisis management and business continuity strategies, information security strategy and frameworks, liability and other claims, eligibility criteria and compliance requirements for the participants of the Eurosystem digital euro platform. Same dedicated body could be also assigned to compile the digital euro detailed rulebooks, including rules and guidelines addressed to all digital euro scheme participants. Building on the example in the area of market infrastructures for payments, it has been proposed that the above dedicated governance body be assisted by a separate advisory body. The latter could bring together public and private industry knowledge and specialized advice on material matters related to digital euro issuance, distribution and cross-border use. While conveying the actual needs, demands and desires of prospective digital euro (wholesale and retail) users, such advisory body would be positioned to access expeditiously innovative cases, technologies, international developments or proposed applications and arrangements that could be potentially utilized to enhance the scheme.

In parallel, Eurosystem should hire, promote knowledge, train and retain specialized personnel for the units (Directorates) most relevant to addressing the digital currency challenges discussed, with focus on operational (in particular cybersecurity, procurement and outsourcing) risk management activities, information systems infrastructure and operations services. By means of a unique digital euro internal regulation, clear allocation of competences, tasks and checkpoints within the Eurosystem (ECB and national euro-area central banks) should be established. In addition to the long-established central banking transparency and accountability mechanisms, the digital euro scheme's transparency can be bolstered further, by means of efficient coordination and cooperation of the Eurosystem bodies and committees, on clear terms, with several other domestic and international agencies and Authorities outside the financial sector. Reference has been made to the authorities granted partial responsibility for matters related to (or affected by) the operation of the digital euro system, including tax authorities, competition authorities, anti-money laundering authorities, data protection authorities and communications security authorities. Particularly meaningful, towards the same objective, will be the disclosure of ECB and NCBs internal audits' potential significant findings, illegal activity incidents and the enhanced internal and external communication. Especially, ESCB/ECB are expected to engage actively with the society, to encourage the adoption and use of the new digital currency, to maximize its envisaged benefits and minimize inherent risks, through targeted reports, speeches, parliamentary hearings, educational activities to financial sector representatives, merchants and the general public.

The envisioned governance framework for the issuer of digital euro has been proposed to be enhanced further, by means of Eurosystem applying additional selected mechanisms, aimed to preserve its substantive *control* over the CBDC scheme. At first, an amended risk management framework should include a digital euro scheme risk tolerance policy, assign responsibility and accountability for risk decisions and address decision-making related to digital euro and scheme features during crises and emergencies. A corresponding digital euro risk management policy should be in place, along with procedures and systems that will enable competent Eurosystem officials to identify, measure, monitor and manage the range of risks that arise in the CBDC scheme. Relevant analysis should consider carefully the most disruptive form of CBDC, which encompasses token-based, potentially programmable and reversible (digital euro) to other private digital assets (and vice-versa).

Second, the safety of the prospective digital euro scheme is to be achieved through the consistent application of austere technical standards for the system services and participating parties. Those standards would cover multiple methods, procedures and technical matters related to digital euro issuance, distribution and use, indicatively digital identity repositories, AML/CFT and fighting financial fraud checks, personal data protection, cross-border access to domestic CBDC, payment system access and settlement finality. Given the systemic dimension and innovative features of the new form of sovereign currency, the entities offering digital euro transfer, storage, custody or exchange to crypto-assets can be required to meet sophisticated operational (including interoperability) requirements (even stricter than those imposed on firms offering similar services for cash or existing private digital assets). MiCAR regime may also prove relevant with regard to the prospective widespread development of digital euro tokens (by the involved supervised financial intermediaries), levelled for retail transactions' offline settlement. Intensified requirements are to prove valuable in the context of the limited anonymity, which is envisaged to-be-granted for the small digital currency holdings and transactions, to ensure CBDC public acceptance.

Third, Eurosystem should carefully select which of all supervised intermediaries will be eligible to form part of the "core" or "primary digital euro system" (hold accounts with the ECB). Notwithstanding the competition concerns of numerous credit institutions, electronic money institutions and payment service providers, it has been considered that participation in the above system can be entrusted, at the first phase of implementation, to selected institutions meeting objective highest standards and prudential requirements, in order to maintain a most secure and controllable digital euro issuance environment. On the other hand, all entities engaged in the CBDC ecosystem and relevant private system arrangements, including distribution platforms and tokenization networks, have to be subjected to robust regulatory oversight and supervision by the competent authorities. ECB (through both its monetary and supervisory functions), NCBs and national competent authorities (supervisors of EU electronic money, payment institutions, etc.) shall need to cooperate closely, to ensure consistent interpretation of applicable rulebooks and avoid supervised entities' opportunities for arbitrage. Relevant assessments would be particularly directed to their market conduct (including vis-à-vis consumers), anti-money laundering processes, personal data protection and cybersecurity.

Last but not least, the digital euro scheme should be complemented with effective processes mitigating the risk of potential overdependencies on private IT resources and technology providers. In addition to technological neutrality, diversification of systems, rigorous own cybersecurity activities and appropriate prevention controls, best procurement practices have been suggested to be employed on technology selection and project management. Eurosystem may even need to consider special contractual safeguards, or even structural remedies, in case it elects to assign critical digital euro system IT functionalities to one of the largest ("too big to ignore") private technology-software providers.

In essence, respective central bank governance enhancements, persistent supervision and proposed effective control mechanisms will enable the European CBDC scheme to meet its multiple, well-framed public policy objectives.[168] Not only they will contribute meaningfully, but they are actually to prove indispensable, to the efficient conduct of euro monetary policy and preservation of access to public money in the digital era, by

[168] See in detail Panetta, "More than an intellectual game."

means of promoting confidence in the digital euro and relevant infrastructure, protecting the legitimate interests of all categories of users, financial and technology intermediaries, while avoiding risks to financial stability.

References

Adalid, Ramón, Álvaro Álvarez-Blázquez, Katrin Assenmacher, Lorenzo Burlon, Maria Dimou, Carolina López-Quiles, Natalia Martín Fuentes et al. "Central bank digital currency and bank intermediation." Occasional Paper 2022/293, European Central Bank, 2022. https://www.ecb.europa.eu/pub/pdf/scpops/ecb.op293~652cf2b1aa.en.pdf.

Ahmad, Tabrez. "Corona virus (covid-19) pandemic and work from home: Challenges of cybercrimes and cybersecurity." *Available at SSRN 3568830* (2020). https://doi.org/10.2139/ssrn.3568830.

Andolfatto, David. "Assessing the impact of Central Bank Digital Currency on private banks." *The Economic Journal* 131, no. 634 (2021): 525–540.

Angeloni, Ignazio. 2023. Digital euro: When in doubt, abstain (but be prepared), in-depth analysis requested by the ECON Committee. https://www.europarl.europa.eu/RegData/etudes/IDAN/2023/741507/IPOL_IDA(2023)741507_EN.pdf.

Annunziata, Filippo. "Speak, if you can: What are you? An alternative approach to the qualification of tokens and initial coin offerings." *European Company and Financial Law Review* 17, no. 2 (2020): 129–154. https://doi.org/10.2139/ssrn.3332485.

Annunziata, Filippo. "The licensing rules in MiCA." In *Fintech regulation and the licensing principle*, edited by Dário Moura Vicente, Diogo Pereira Duarte and Catarina Granadeiro, 107–125. Frankfurt: European Banking Institute, Centro de Investigaçao de direito privado, 2023. https://ebi-europa.eu/wp-content/uploads/2023/02/eBook-22Fintech-Regulation-Licensing-Principle-2-2023.pdf.

Arner, Douglas, Raphael Auer and Jon Frost. "Stablecoins: risks, potential and regulation." Working Papers no. 905, Band for International Settlements, 2020. https://www.bis.org/publ/work905.pdf.

Athanassiou, Phoebus. *Digital innovation in financial services: legal challenges and regulatory policy issues*. Kluwer Law International BV, 2018.

Athanassiou, Phoebus. "Impact of digital innovation on the processing of electronic payments and contracting: an overview of legal risks." Legal Working Paper Series 16, European Central Bank, 2017. https://www.ecb.europa.eu/pub/pdf/scplps/ecb.lwp16.en.pdf.

Auer, Raphael, Giulio Cornelli, and Jon Frost. "Rise of the Central Bank Digital Currencies: drivers, approaches and technologies." Working Paper no. 880,

Bank for International Settlements, 2020. https://www.bis.org/publ/work880.htm.

Auer, Raphael, and Rainer Böhme. "The technology of retail Central Bank Digital Currency." *BIS Quarterly Review, March* (2020). https://www.bis.org/publ/qtrpdf/r_qt2003j.htm.

Bank of England. *Central Bank Digital Currency: Opportunities, Challenges and Design*. Discussion Paper, March 12. BoE, 2020. https://www.bankofengland.co.uk/paper/2020/central-bank-digital-currency-opportunities-challenges-and-design-discussion-paper.

Bank for International Settlements. *Digital Currencies*. BIS, 2015. https://www.bis.org/cpmi/publ/d137.pdf.

Bank for International Settlements. 2018. *Central Bank Digital Currencies*. BIS, 2018. https://www.bis.org/cpmi/publ/d174.htm.

Bank for International Settlements. *Central Bank Digital Currencies: Foundational Principles and Core Features*. Report no. 1 in a series of collaborations from a group of central banks, 2020. https://www.bis.org/publ/othp33.pdf.

Bank for International Settlements. *Central Bank Digital Currencies: System Design and Interoperability*. Report no. 2 in a series of collaborations from a group of central banks, 2021. https://www.bis.org/publ/othp42_system_design.pdf.

Bank for International Settlements. *Central Bank Digital Currencies for cross-border payments*. Report to the G20, 2021. https://www.bis.org/publ/othp38.pdf.

Barrdear, John, and Michael Kumhof. "The macroeconomics of central bank issued digital currencies." Staff Working Paper no. 605, Bank of England, 2016. https://www.bankofengland.co.uk/-/media/boe/files/working-paper/2016/the-macroeconomics-of-central-bank-issued-digital-currencies.pdf?la=en&hash=341B602838707E5D6FC26884588C912A721B1DC1.

Barroso, Louis. "Fintechs: concept, level playing field and the supervisory approach." In *Fintech Regulation and the Licensing Principle*, edited by Dário Moura Vicente, Diogo Pereira Duarte and Catarina Granadeiro, 25–43. European Banking Institute eBook Series 2/2023, 2023. https://ebi-europa.eu/wp-content/uploads/2023/02/eBook-22Fintech-Regulation-Licensing-Principle-2-2023.pdf.

Bilotta, Nicola, and Fabrizio Botti. *The (near) future of Central Bank Digital Currencies: Risks and opportunities for the global economy and society*. Peter Lang International Academic Publishers, 2021.

Bindseil, Ulrich, Fabio Panetta, and Ignacio Terol. "Central Bank Digital Currency: functional scope, pricing and controls." Occasional Paper no. 286, European Central Bank, 2021. https://www.ecb.europa.eu/pub/pdf/scpops/ecb.op286~9d472374ea.en.pdf.

Bossu, Wouter, Masaru Itatani, Catalina Margulis, Arthur Rossi, Hans Weenink, and Akihiro Yoshinaga. "Legal aspects of Central Bank Digital Currency: Central bank and monetary law considerations." Working Paper no. 254, International Monetary Fund, 2020. https://www.imf.org/en/Publications/WP/Issues/2020/11/20/Legal-Aspects-of-Central-Bank-Digital-Currency-Central-Bank-and-Monetary-Law-Considerations-49827.

Bossu, Wouter, and Arthur Rossi. "The role of board oversight in central bank governance: Key legal design issues." Working Paper no. 293, International Monetary Fund, 2019. https://www.imf.org/en/Publications/WP/Issues/2019/12/27/The-Role-of-Board-Oversight-in-Central-Bank-Governance-Key-Legal-Design-Issues-48906.

Broemel, Roland. "20 Jahre Euro—bald auch digital?." *Europäische Zeitschrift für Wirtschaftsrecht*, 33 (2022): 9, 393–394.

Brown, Claude, Tim Dolan, and Karen Butler. "Cryptoassets and initial coin offerings." In *FinTech*, edited by Jelena Madir, pp. 90–120. Northampton: Edward Elgar Publishing, 2021.

Burlon, Lorenzo, Carlos Montes-Galdon, Manuel A. Munioz, and Frank Smets. "The optimal quantity of CBDC in a bank-based economy." Working Paper Series, no. 2689, European Central Bank, 2022. https://www.ecb.europa.eu/pub/pdf/scpwps/ecb.wp2689~846e464fd8.en.pdf.

Court of Justice of the EU. *Judgment in Case C-264/14: Skatteverket v David Hedqvist*. CJEU, 2015. https://curia.europa.eu/juris/document/document.jsf?docid=170305&mode=lst&pageIndex=1&dir=&occ=first&part=1&text=&doclang=EN&cid=220157.

Court of Justice of the EU. *Judgment in case C-62/14: Gauweiler et al. v Deutscher Bundestag*. CJEU, 2015. https://curia.europa.eu/juris/document/document.jsf?docid=165057&mode=lst&pageIndex=1&dir=&occ=first&part=1&text=&doclang=EN&cid=224779.

Court of Justice of the EU. *Judgment in Joined Cases C-422/19 and C-423/19: Johannes Dietrich and Norbert Häring v Hessischer Rundfunk*. CJEU, 2021. https://eur-lex.europa.eu/legal-content/EN/TXT/PDF/?uri=ecli:ECLI%3AEU%3AC%3A2021%3A63.

De Vauplane, Hubert. "Cryprocurrencies and central banks." In *Fintech: Law and regulation*, edited by Jelena Madir, pp. 121–146. Northampton: Edward Elgar Publishing, 2021.

Didenko, Anton, Dirk Zetzsche, Douglas Arner, and Ross Buckley. "After Libra, digital Yuan and COVID-19: Central Bank Digital Currencies and the new world of money and payment systems." Working Paper Series no. 65, European Banking Institute, 2020. https://papers.ssrn.com/sol3/papers.cfm?abstract_id=3622311.

Ehrentraud, Johannes, Jermy Prenio, Codruta Boar, Mathilde Janfils, and Aidan Lawson. "Fintech and payments: Regulating digital payment services and e-money." Financial Stability Institute Insights on policy implementation no. 33, Bank for International Settlements, 2021. https://www.bis.org/fsi/publ/insights33.htm.

European Central Bank. *FAQ on a digital euro.* N.d. https://www.ecb.europa.eu/paym/digital_euro/faqs/html/ecb.faq_digital_euro.en.html.

European Cental Bank. 2023. A stocktake on the digital euro summary report on the investigation phase and outlook on the next phase.

European Central Bank. *Decision 2014/723/EU of the European central bank of 17 September 2014 on the implementation of separation between the monetary policy and supervision functions of the European Central Bank (ECB/2014/39).* ECB, 2014. https://eur-lex.europa.eu/legal-content/EN/TXT/?uri=CELEX%3A32014D0039%2801%29.

European Central Bank. *Guide to assessments of Fintech credit institution licence applications.* ECB, 2018 https://www.bankingsupervision.europa.eu/ecb/pub/pdf/ssm.201803_guide_assessment_fintech_credit_inst_licensing.en.pdf.

European Central Bank. "Decision (EU) 2019/166 of the ECB on the market infrastructure board and repealing decision ECB/2012/6 on the establishment of the TARGET2-Securities Board (ECB/2019/3)." *Official Journal of the EU L 32/14*, February 2, 2019, https://eur-lex.europa.eu/legal-content/EN/TXT/?uri=CELEX%3A32019D0003%2801%29.

European Central Bank. *Report on a digital euro.* ECB, 2020. https://www.ecb.europa.eu/pub/pdf/other/Report_on_a_digital_euro~4d7268b458.en.pdf.

European Central Bank. *Eurosystem assessment methodology for electronic payment instruments, schemes and arrangements.* ECB, 2021. https://www.ecb.europa.eu/paym/pdf/consultations/ecb.PISApublicconsultation202111_2.en.pdf.

European Central Bank. *Eurosystem oversight framework for electronic payment instruments, schemes and arrangements.* ECB, 2021. https://www.ecb.europa.eu/paym/pdf/consultations/ecb.PISApublicconsultation202111_1.en.pdf.

European Central Bank. *Digital euro project governance and stakeholder management.* ECB, 2022. https://www.ecb.europa.eu/paym/digital_euro/investigation/governance/shared/files/ecb.degov220608_governance.en.pdf.

European Central Bank. *ECB selects external companies for joint prototyping of user interfaces for a digital euro.* MIP News, September 16. ECB, 2022. https://www.ecb.europa.eu/paym/intro/news/html/ecb.mipnews220916.en.html.

European Central Bank. *Progress on the investigation phase of a digital euro.* First Report, 2022. https://www.ecb.europa.eu/paym/digital_euro/investigation/governance/shared/files/ecb.degov220929.en.pdf.

European Central Bank. *Progress on the investigation phase of a digital euro.* Second Report, 2022. https://www.ecb.europa.eu/paym/digital_euro/investigation/governance/shared/files/ecb.degov221221_Progress.en.pdf.

European Central Bank. *Progress on the investigation phase of a digital euro.* Third Report, 2023. https://www.ecb.europa.eu/paym/digital_euro/investigation/governance/shared/files/ecb.degov230424_progress.en.pdf.

European Central Bank. *Study on new digital payment methods.* Kantar Public, 2022. https://www.ecb.europa.eu/paym/digital_euro/investigation/profuse/shared/files/dedocs/ecb.dedocs220330_report.en.pdf.

European Commision. "Commission recommendation of 22 March 2010 on the scope and effects of legal tender of euro banknotes and coins (2010/191/EU)." *Official Journal of the EU L 83/70*, March 30, 2010. https://eur-lex.europa.eu/legal-content/EN/TXT/PDF/?uri=CELEX:32010H0191.

European Commission. *European commission cloud strategy: Cloud as an enabler for the European commission digital strategy.* European Commission, 2019. https://commission.europa.eu/system/files/2019-05/ec_cloud_strategy.pdf.

European Commission. *A digital euro for the EU.* Call for Evidence for an impact assessment. European Commission, 2022. https://ec.europa.eu/info/law/better-regulation/have-your-say/initiatives/13392-A-digital-euro-for-the-EU_en.

European Commission. *Targeted consultation on a digital euro.* Consultation document, directorate general for economic and financial affairs. European Commission, 2022. https://finance.ec.europa.eu/system/files/2022-06/2022-digital-euro-consultation-document_en.pdf.

Ferrarini, Guido, and Paolo Saguato. "Regulating financial market infrastructures." Law Working Paper no. 259, European Corporate Governance Institute, 2014. https://ssrn.com/abstract=2450095.

Financial Stability Board. *Crypto-asset markets, Potential channels for future financial stability implications.* Report, 2018. https://www.fsb.org/wp-content/uploads/P101018.pdf.

Fraccaroli, Nicole, Alessandro Giovannini, and Jean-François Jamet. "The evolution of the ECB's accountability practices during the crisis." ECB Economic Bulletin no. 5, European Central Bank, 2018. https://www.ecb.europa.eu/press/economic-bulletin/articles/2018/html/ecb.ebart201805_01.en.html.

Geva, Benjamin. "TARGET2 Transfer of Funds and Harmonization of EU Payment Law." *Uniform Commercial Code Law Journal* 41, no. 2 (2008): 113-123.

Gortsos, Christos. "Chinese walls within the European Central Bank after the establishment of the single supervisory mechanism." *Paper presented at the conference of the University of Siena on "The Europeanisation of the Payment System, II Edition."* Siena: October 22–24, 2015. https://ssrn.com/abstract=2700176.

Gortsos, Christos. *European central banking law: The role of the European central bank and national central banks under European law*. Palgrave Macmillan Studies in Banking and Financial Institutions Series: Palgrave Macmillan, 2020.

Gortsos, Christos. "Future of the Economic and monetary union." Working Paper Series no. 129, European Banking Institute, 2022. https://ssrn.com/abstract=4212947.

Grünewald, Seraina Neva, Corinne Zellweger-Gutknecht, and Benjamin Geva. "Digital euro and ECB powers." *Common Market Law Review* 58, no. 4 (2021): 1029–1055. https://papers.ssrn.com/sol3/papers.cfm?abstract_id=3807855.

Grünewald Seraina. *A legal framework for the digital euro*. An assessment of the ECB's first three progress reports, Economic Governance and EMU Scrutiny Unit. European Parliament, 2023. https://www.europarl.europa.eu/RegData/etudes/IDAN/2023/741518/IPOL_IDA(2023)714518_EN.pdf.

Grünewald, Seraina. "CBDCs and Central Bank Independence/Accountability." In *Central Bank Digital Currencies (CBDCs)*, Colloquim jointly hosted by the Collegium Helveticum and the University of Zurich's priority research program on financial market regulation, May 9, 2023.

Hadjiemmanuil, Christos. "Economic and monetary union." In *European Union law*, edited by Damian Chalmers, Christos Hadjiemmanuil, Giorgio Monti and Adam Tomkins. Cambridge: Cambridge University Press, 2006.

Joosen, Bart, and Matthias Lehmann. "Proportionality in the single rule book." In *The Palgrave Handbook of European Banking Union Law*, edited by Mario Chiti and Vittorio Santoro, 65–90. Palgrave Macmillan, 2019.

International Monetary Fund. *The Bali Fintech agenda*. Policy Paper, 2018. https://www.imf.org/en/Publications/Policy-Papers/Issues/2018/10/11/pp101118-bali-fintech-agenda.

International Monetary Fund. "Update the monetary and financial policies transparency code." Policy Paper no. 011. IMF, 2019. https://www.imf.org/en/Publications/Policy-Papers/Issues/2019/05/13/Update-The-Monetary-And-Financial-Policies-Transparency-Code-46885.

International Monetary Fund. "Digital money across borders: Macro-Financial implications." Policy Paper no. 050, IMF, 2020. https://www.imf.org/en/Publications/Policy-Papers/Issues/2020/10/17/Digital-Money-Across-Borders-Macro-Financial-Implications-49823.

Khan, Ashraf. "Central bank governance and the role of nonfinancial risk management." Working Paper no. 16/34, International Monetary Fund, 2016. https://papers.ssrn.com/sol3/papers.cfm?abstract_id=2737528.

Khan, Ashraf, and Majid Malaika. "Central Bank Risk Management, Fintech, and Cybersecurity." Working Paper no. 105, International Monetary

Fund, 2021. https://www.imf.org/en/Publications/WP/Issues/2021/04/23/Central-Bank-Risk-Management-Fintech-and-Cybersecurity-50278.

Kiff, John, Jihad Alwazir, Sonja Davidovic, Aquiles Farias, Ashraf Khan, Tanai Khiaonarong, Majid Malaika, Hunter Monroe, Nobu Sugimoto, Hervé Tourpe and Peter Zhou. "A Survey of Research on Retail Central Bank Digital Currency." Working Paper no. 104, International Monetary Fund, 2020. https://www.imf.org/en/Publications/WP/Issues/2020/06/26/A-Survey-of-Research-on-Retail-Central-Bank-Digital-Currency-49517.

Kokkola, Tom. "The payment system: Payments, Securities and Derivatives, and the Role of the Eurosystem." European Central Bank, 2010. https://www.ecb.europa.eu/pub/pdf/other/paymentsystem201009en.pdf.

Lastra, Rosa M., and Jean-Victor Louis. "European Economic and Monetary Union: history, trends, and prospects." *Yearbook of European Law* 32, no. 1 (2013): 57–206. https://ssrn.com/abstract=2244764.

Lukonga, Inutu. "Monetary policy implications of Central Bank Digital Currencies: Perspectives on jurisdictions with conventional and Islamic banking systems." Working Paper no. 60, International Monetary Fund, 2023. https://www.imf.org/en/Publications/WP/Issues/2023/03/17/Monetary-Policy-Implications-Central-Bank-Digital-Currencies-Perspectives-on-Jurisdictions-531074.

Mersch, Yves. "International trends in central bank independence: the ECB's perspective." *Remarks at the roundtable discussion on central bank independence, ECB speeches, November* (2019).

Monteagudo, Manuel. "Central banks and ethics: The virtual paradox of transparency and confidentiality mandates." In *Research handbook on law and ethics in banking and finance*, edited by Costanza Russo, Rosa Lastra and William Blair, pp. 351–367. Edward Elgar Publishing, 2019.

Mooij, Anneelike. "A digital euro for everyone: Can the European system of central banks introduce general purpose CBDC as part of its economic mandate?" *Journal of Banking Regulation* 24, no. 1 (2023): 89–104.

Nabilou, Hossein. "Central Bank Digital Currencies: Preliminary legal observations." *Journal of Banking Regulation* (2019). https://papers.ssrn.com/sol3/papers.cfm?abstract_id=3329993.

Omarova, Saule T. "The People's ledger: How to democratize money and finance the economy." *Vanderbilt Law Review 74* (2021). https://papers.ssrn.com/sol3/papers.cfm?abstract_id=%203715735.

Padoa Schioppa, Tomasso. "An institutional glossary of thè Eurosystem." *Speech at the conference The Constitution of the Eurosystem: The Views of the EP and the ECB*, March 2, 2000.

Panetta, Fabio. "A digital euro for the digital era." *Introductory statement at the ECON Committee of the European Parliament*, October 12. European Central

Bank, 2020. https://www.ecb.europa.eu/press/key/date/2020/html/ecb.sp201012_1~1d14637163.en.html.

Panetta, Fabio. "More than an intellectual game: Exploring the monetary policy and financial stability implications of Central Bank Digital Currencies." *Opening speech at the IESE Business School Banking Initiative Conference on Technology and Finance*, Frankfurt am Main, April 8, 2022.

Panetta, Fabio. "The digital euro and the evolution of the financial system." *Introductory statement at the committee on economic and monetary affairs of the European parliament*, June 15. European Central Bank, 2022. https://www.ecb.europa.eu/press/key/date/2022/html/ecb.sp220615~0b859eb8bc.en.html.

Papapaschalis, Panos. "Legal interoperability of retail CBDCs: Initial considerations." In *ESCB Legal Conference 2022*, edited by European Central Bank, 117–126. Frankfurt: ECB, 2022. https://www.ecb.europa.eu/pub/pdf/other/ecb.escblegalconferenceproceedings2022~1646d63f3e.en.pdf.

The People's Bank of China. "E-CNY: Main objectives, guiding principles and inclusion considerations." In *CBDCs in emerging market economies*, BIS Papers no. 123, 45–48. Bank for International Settlements, 2022. https://www.bis.org/publ/bppdf/bispap123.pdf.

Smits, René. "Central bank independence and accountability in the light of EMU." In *International Monetary Law: Issues for the New Millennium*, edited by Mario Giovanoli, 245–266. Oxford: Oxford University Press, 2000.

Statement by the Members of the Euro Summit, meeting in an inclusive format (Brussels: March 25, 2021), https://www.consilium.europa.eu/media/48975/25-03-21-eurosummit-statement-en.pdf.

Sturm, Michael. "The ECB and the Eurosystem: Institutional structure and governance." *Presentation*, European Central Bank, 2019. https://www.ecb.europa.eu/pub/conferences/shared/pdf/20190701_CBS2019/ecb.CBS2019_Sturm_The_ECB_and_the_Eurosystem_institutional_structure_and_governance_presentation.en.pdf.

Society for Worldwide Interbank Financial Telecommunication (SWIFT). *CBDCs and tokenized assets can integrate into international financial ecosystem.* Report, October 12, 2022. https://ca.practicallaw.thomsonreuters.com/w-037-2021?transitionType=Default&contextData=(sc.Default)&firstPage=true.

Wang, Heng. "China's approach to Central Bank Digital Currency: Selectively reshaping international financial order?" *University of Pennsylvania Asian Law Review* 18 (2022): 77. https://doi.org/10.2139/ssrn.4036466.

Weber, Rolf. "Global Financial Architecture and Decentralised CBDC Regimes." *In Central Bank Digital Currencies Proceedings of the colloquium*, edited by Christos V. Gortsos, and Rolf Sethe, 13–33. EIZ Publishing, 2023. https://eizpublishing.ch/wp-content/uploads/2023/10/Central-Bank-Digital-Currencies-CBDCs-Digital-V1_03-20231023.pdf.

Witt, Emily and Jannick Blaschke. "ECB data for analysis and decision-making: data governance and technology." *9th IFC Conference on "Are post-crisis statistical initiatives completed?"* Basel, August, 30–31. Bank for International Settlements, 2018. https://www.bis.org/ifc/publ/ifcb49_36.pdf.

Wutscher, Claudia. "Artikel 127–132 des AEUV." In *EU-Kommentar*, 4th Edition, Jürgen Schwarze, Ulrich Becker, Armin Hatje, and Johann Schoo, 2042–2080. Baden-Baden: Nomos Verlagsgesellschaft, 2019.

Zetzsche, Dirk, Ross Buckley, and Douglas Arner. 2019. "Regulating LIBRA: The Transformative Potential of Facebook's Cryptocurrency and Possible Regulatory Responses." Working Paper Series no. 44, European Banking Institute, 2019. https://papers.ssrn.com/sol3/papers.cfm?abstract_id=3414401.

Zetzsche, Dirk, Filippo Annunziata, Douglas Arner, Ross Buckley. "The Markets in Crypto-Assets Regulation (MICA) and the EU Digital finance strategy." Working Paper Series no. 77, European Banking Institute, 2020. https://ssrn.com/abstract=3725395.

Zilioli, Chiara and Phoebus Athanassiou. "The European Central Bank." In *Oxford principles of European Union law: The European union legal order: Volume I: The European Union legal order*, edited by Robert Schütze and Takis Tridimas, 610–650. Oxford: Oxford University Press, 2018.

Zilioli, Chiara. "The Perspective of the European Central Bank (ECB): Towards a digital euro." In *Central Bank Digital Currencies (CBDCs)*, Colloquim jointly hosted by the Collegium Helveticum and the University of Zurich's priority research program on financial market regulation, May 9, 2023.

Zeitlin, Jonathan, and Filipe Brito Bastos. "SSM and the SRB accountability at European level: room for improvements?" Economic governance support unit, directorate-general for internal policies of the union. European parliament, 2020. https://op.europa.eu/en/publication-detail/-/publication/9238570a-2e02-11eb-b27b-01aa75ed71a1/language-en.

CHAPTER 8

Exploring the Impact of the Digital Euro on Euro Area Banks

Nikos Maragopoulos

1 Introduction

The monetary system is based on the complementarity of public money with private money. In modern economies, central banks issue two types of public money, central bank reserves and banknotes,[1] and provide infrastructure to support the provision of a third (non-public) type of money, bank deposits (otherwise called "private money") that form the bulk of total money in the economy. Central banks support private money by (i) allowing banks to settle interbank payments using public money, (ii) enabling convertibility between public and private money through banknote provision; and (iii) offering emergency liquidity assistance to

[1] In this chapter the term "banknotes" is used interchangeably with the term "cash".

N. Maragopoulos (✉)
European Banking Institute, Frankfurt, Germany
e-mail: nikos.maragopoulos@ebi-europa.eu

© The Author(s), under exclusive license to Springer Nature Switzerland AG 2025

F. Annunziata et al. (eds.), *Central Bank Digital Currency*, EBI Studies in Banking and Capital Markets Law,
https://doi.org/10.1007/978-3-031-80957-6_8

banks under the lender of last resort function.[2] Whereas the public has full access to banknotes, central bank reserves are available only to commercial banks that carry out transactions with central banks. Households and companies cannot have deposits at central banks, but instead they can at commercial banks.

Confidence in private money is based on the ability to convert, at par, private money into public money. Public money is a risk-free form of money guaranteed by the sovereign.[3] Private money pertains to banks' liabilities to customers, backed by assets that typically include loans, bonds, central bank reserves and other financial assets. Under the so-called maturity transformation process, banks convert deposits into long-term illiquid assets (e.g., loans). Bank deposits are based on banks' soundness and underpinned by the promise of one-to-one convertibility with public money upon request from depositors. In the absence of confidence in the convertibility of private money, bank-runs would be more frequent and people would have to constantly monitor the soundness of banks.

Banknotes are used less and less for payments in the modern economy, as people are increasingly paying digitally instead of using cash. In a digital world cash could become marginalized as a means of payment.[4] Against this backdrop, central banks explore the possibility of introducing retail CBDCs aiming to preserve the role of public money as a monetary anchor and address potential threats arising from initiatives for a new type of money (i.e., commercial digital currencies).[5] Central banks across the world are exploring CBDCs in order to maintain public access to and full

[2] Bank for International Settlements, Central bank digital currencies: Foundational principles and core features, Report no.1 in a series of collaborations from a group of central banks, 2020, https://www.bis.org/publ/othp33.pdf (accessed May 27, 2023).

[3] Fabio Panetta, "Central bank digital currencies: defining the problems, designing the solutions," *Contribution to a panel discussion on central bank digital currencies at the US Monetary Policy Forum*, European Central Bank, 2022, https://www.ecb.europa.eu/press/key/date/2022/html/ecb.sp220218_1~938e881b13.en.html (accessed June 2, 2023).

[4] European Central Bank, *The case for a digital euro: key objectives and design considerations* (ECB, 2022), https://www.ecb.europa.eu/pub/pdf/other/key_objectives_digital_euro~f11592d6fb.en.pdf (accessed May 15, 2023).

[5] A currency not issued by a central bank having the role of conventional payment method would negatively impact the ability of central banks to execute their monetary policy tasks.

usability of central bank money in a world where consumers and firms are turning more and more to electronic payments. In accordance with a survey carried out by the BIS in 2021, 86% of central banks were actively researching the potential for CBDCs, 60% were experimenting with the technology and 14% were deploying pilot projects.[6] More than two-thirds of central banks consider it likely to issue a retail CBDC in the short or medium term.[7]

In this context, the Eurosystem's initiative to explore the possibility of introducing its own CBDC, called "digital euro", would be a turning point for the EU monetary system. A digital euro could be a new form of central bank money allowing households and businesses for the first time to use central bank money to make electronic payments. The digital euro would function as an electronic means of retail payments complementing, rather than replacing cash.

2 Factors Affecting the Take-Up of the Digital Euro

To date, no major developed economy has introduced a CBDC, making it very challenging to estimate its demand and to adopt the appropriate design options to control its take-up.[8] In this context, the Eurosystem should design a digital euro in a way to strike the right balance between ensuring a substantial level of usage, which is necessary to achieve its policy objectives, and mitigating the risks for bank disintermediation and financial stability from a large and rapid take-up.[9] The Eurosystem should

[6] For more details, see Bank for International Settlements, *BIS Innovation Hub Work on Central Bank Digital Currency (CBDC)* (BIS, 2021), https://www.bis.org/about/bisih/topics/cbdc.htm.

[7] European Central Bank, *Digital euro—our future money* (ECB, 2022), https://www.ecb.europa.eu/paym/digital_euro/investigation/profuse/shared/files/dedocs/ecb.dedocs221017_ecbatsibos.en.pdf?447523fb3a77c4c58413c7f3870340da (accessed June 5, 2023).

[8] European Central Bank, "Central Bank Digital Currency and bank intermediation," Occasional Paper Series no. 293 (ECB, 2022), https://www.ecb.europa.eu/pub/pdf/scpops/ecb.op293~652cf2b1aa.en.pdf (accessed May 14, 2023).

[9] Fabio Panetta, "Designing a digital euro for the retail payments landscape of tomorrow," *Introductory remarks at the ECON Committee of the European Parliament*, European Central Bank, 2021, https://www.ecb.europa.eu/press/key/date/2021/html/ecb.sp211118~b36013b7c5.en.html (accessed May 15, 2023).

establish a digital euro as a widespread means of payment and prevent it from becoming a form of investment. An easy-to-use, low-cost, efficient means of payment that is widely accepted by businesses and merchants is the key for an attractive digital euro. What also matters for users is an option for offline payments and a higher level of privacy compared to the existing payment solutions.[10] In addition, safety and remuneration are two critical characteristics for the attractiveness of the digital euro vis-à-vis cash and bank deposits.

In contrast to private money that bears the risk of issuer/counterparty (bank risk), by definition, central bank money is risk-free given that the sovereign guarantees it. Individuals with low trust in banks or individuals particularly risk-averse, including those having deposit balances spread across several banks to take full advantage of the deposit guarantee schemes (DGSs), would find the digital euro very attractive from a safety perspective. The same applies to businesses with (high) deposit balances exceeding the deposit guarantee threshold (i.e., 100.000 euro per depositor per bank), which would have every incentive to convert their deposits into the digital euro, particularly in times of stress.

A key decision for the Eurosystem to take is whether interest will be paid on the digital euro balances. The digital euro could be either unremunerated, as is the case for banknotes, or remunerated, similar to central bank reserves and bank deposits. Remuneration is a key determinant for the attractiveness of the digital euro to households and businesses affecting the extent of bank disintermediation and the impact on financial stability and transmission mechanism of monetary policy.[11] From a financial stability perspective, a remunerated digital euro could foster deposit substitution limiting the role of banks in the financing of the economy.[12] The amount that users would convert into the digital euro

[10] Bank for International Settlements, *Central bank digital currencies: user needs and adoption,* Report no. 3 in a series of collaborations from a group of central banks, 2021, https://www.bis.org/publ/othp42_user_needs.pdf (accessed May 20, 2023).

[11] Ibid.

[12] Banks could limit deposit substitution if they adopt an appropriate approach to disincentivize depositors from shifting to the digital euro, including through an upwards adjustment of deposit rates and/or an offer of more attractive lending products to customers-depositors.

depends, among others, on the level of interest rate paid and the interest rate environment at each period of time.[13]

Non-remuneration of the digital euro could be an option. Cash already offers a non-interest-bearing alternative to deposits. However, storage costs and risks for cash entail that deposit rates can be below zero without triggering a large-scale substitution into cash. In the absence of such risks, the digital euro would be a more attractive option than holding cash. In an environment of positive interest rates, an unremunerated digital euro would function mostly for payment purposes, being unattractive to households and businesses as a form of investment. Thus, the Eurosystem would run the risk of a low appetite from households and businesses for the digital euro affecting its take-up. In that case, the shift to the digital euro would stem mostly from banknotes used for payments rather than from bank deposits. Considering that only 20% of cash is used for payment transactions in the euro area, with the remaining used as a store of value,[14] it is plausible to assume that the digital euro take-up would be low, making the achievement of the objectives set by the Eurosystem difficult.

By contrast, in a negative interest environment, an unremunerated or positive interest-bearing digital euro could induce a deposit substitution of larger scale, as users would earn a higher return compared to deposits or other low-risk investments (e.g., short-term sovereign notes). Under a remuneration-based digital euro scenario, a variable interest rate linked to other central bank rates could apply. The interest rate could be adjusted in parallel or independently of ECB's policy rates changes. Indicatively, the Eurosystem could set the variable interest rate as a spread over other central bank interest rates.[15] Lastly, as mentioned below (under sub-chapter 4), a two-tiered remuneration approach could apply, where balances up to a threshold would earn a higher interest rate compared

[13] Michiel Bijlsma et al., "What triggers consumer adoption of CBDC?," Working Paper no. 709 (De Nederlandsche Bank, 2021), https://www.dnb.nl/media/amwfjgey/working_paper_no-_709.pdf (accessed May 12, 2023).

[14] Ulrich Bindseil et al., "Central Bank Digital Currency: functional scope, pricing and controls," Occasional Paper Series no. 286 (European Central Bank, 2021), https://www.ecb.europa.eu/pub/pdf/scpops/ecb.op286~9d472374ea.en.pdf (accessed May 15, 2023).

[15] European Central Bank, *Report on digital euro* (ECB, 2020), https://www.ecb.europa.eu/pub/pdf/other/Report_on_a_digital_euro~4d7268b458.en.pdf (accessed June 2, 2023).

to the balances exceeding that threshold, which would earn a lower or no interest rate at all. Tiered remuneration could incentivize users to limit their holdings in the digital euro by making it less attractive to hold amounts exceeding the threshold. In this way, the Eurosystem could meet its objective of a digital euro used primarily for transactions, preventing its use as a form of large-scale store of value.

3 Exploring the Potential Impact of the Digital Euro on the Eurosystem and Euro Area Banks

3.1 Potential Effects Under a Mild Scenario of a Digital Euro Take-Up

The digital euro will be a new form of liability on the Eurosystem's balance sheet. Households and businesses could obtain the digital euro through a conversion from banknotes or bank deposits. The impact of the digital euro on the Eurosystem and the euro area banking sector will both hinge on the level of take-up and whether this will come from a conversion of banknotes or bank deposits. In the first case, users could convert, through private intermediaries (e.g., banks), banknotes to digital euro. Both banknotes and the digital euro would be an asset for users and a liability for the Eurosystem. Conversion from banknotes to digital euro affects the composition of balance sheets of households and Eurosystem, but not the size thereof. Replacing banknotes with a digital euro has no implications for banks' balance sheets, as banks would act solely as distributing agents. On the contrary, switching from deposits to the digital euro would affect the euro area banking sector. Depositors would have the incentive to convert their deposits into digital euro given that a digital euro, being on a par with deposits with regard to liquidity and convenience, would be preferred as a safe haven asset.[16] Substitution of deposits with the digital euro would result in banks using their excess reserves at the Eurosystem to accommodate deposit reduction. Acting as intermediaries between the public and the Eurosystem, banks would use

[16] Bank of International Settlements, *Central bank digital currencies: financial stability implications*, Report no. 4 in a series of collaborations from a group of central banks, 2021, https://www.bis.org/publ/othp42_fin_stab.pdf (accessed May 22, 2023); Jesús Fernández-Villaverde et al., "Central Bank Digital Currency: Central Banking For All?", Working Paper no. 26753 (National Bureau of Economic Research, 2020), https://www.nber.org/system/files/working_papers/w26753/w26753.pdf (accessed April 25, 2023).

excess reserves held at the Eurosystem to acquire a digital euro in order to pass it on to their customers in exchange for deposits. Given the unequal distribution of excess reserves across banks and any potential difference in customers' demand for the digital euro across banks, there might be a need for banks to engage in interbank borrowing to cover any liquidity needs. In the short run, a bank could address a potential liquidity shortfall through interbank (secured) borrowing.

As long as the take-up of the digital euro stems from: (i) a swap with banknotes and/or (ii) a moderate substitution with bank deposits, a mild impact on the banking system should be anticipated (mild scenario). Where the digital euro is exchanged for banknotes, the impact on the Eurosystem's balance sheet will be neutral resulting in a swap between these two liabilities. The same applies in case of a manageable substitution with bank deposits, which could be offset by banks through a reduction of excess reserves held at the Eurosystem. Thus, as shown in the table below, under this mild scenario there will be no change in the size of the Eurosystem's balance sheet, but rather in the composition of its liability side (i.e., the digital euro take-up is offset by a reduction in banknotes and excess reserves) (Table 1).[17]

Table 1 Impact on the Eurosystem's balance sheet (mild scenario)

Assets		*Liabilities*	
Loans to banks	–	Banknotes	↓
Securities	–	Reserves	↓
Foreign reserves, gold and other	–	Digital euro	↑
		Capital and other	–
TOTAL	–	TOTAL	–

[17] Fabio Panetta, "More than an intellectual game: Exploring the monetary policy and financial stability implications of central bank digital currencies," *Opening speech at the IESE Business School Banking Initiative Conference on Technology and Finance*, April 8. European Central Bank, 2022, https://www.ecb.europa.eu/press/key/date/2022/html/ecb.sp220408~980e39957b.en.html (accessed May 25, 2023).

Table 2 Impact on banks' balance sheets (mild scenario)

Assets		*Liabilities*	
Reserves at the Eurosystem	⇩	Deposits	⇩
Loans	–	Central bank funding	–
Securities	–	Market funding	–
Other	–	Capital	–
TOTAL	–	TOTAL	–

Based on the mild scenario described above, the reduction in excess reserves held at the Eurosystem will compensate for the (manageable) deposit reduction triggered by the digital euro take-up. Hence, the size of banks' balance sheets will remain unchanged, as shown in the table below (Table 2).

3.2 *Potential Effects Under an Adverse Scenario of a Digital Euro Take-Up*

Overview of Potential Measures

The introduction of the digital euro is expected to bring some degree of deposit reduction, particularly if the digital euro was introduced in absence of any mitigation measure. Whereas conversion of banknotes into the digital euro would not have any implications for banking intermediation and financial stability, material risks are expected to arise if a significant substitution of bank deposits with the digital euro takes place, which would be an adverse scenario for the banking sector. In that case, the digital euro would trigger a significant long-term reduction in customer deposits.

Once banks have exhausted their excess reserves held at the Eurosystem and retain only the minimum required reserves, they will have to take other structural measures to address the deposit reduction and continue meeting regulatory liquidity requirements, while at the same time maintaining an efficient funding cost.[18] In response to that loss of deposits, banks could take any of the following measures:

[18] In the short run, banks could address any liquidity shortfall through the interbank market, either by selling assets or borrowing.

Table 3 Impact on banks' balance sheets (adverse scenario)

Assets		*Liabilities*	
Reserves at the Eurosystem	⇩	Deposits	⇩
Loans	⇩	Central bank funding	⇧
Securities	⇩	Market funding	⇧
Other	–	Capital	–
TOTAL	⇩	TOTAL	⇩

(i) increase in deposits rates in order to disincentivize depositors from converting deposits into a digital euro, (ii) replacement of lost deposits with more central bank funding,[19] (iii) increase in long-term market funding to cover the liquidity outflows or (iv) decrease in lending to economy (deleverage).[20] It is very likely that banks would have to implement all the above measures in order to compensate for the negative effects of the introduction of the digital euro. The table below provides an overview of the impact from the implementation of the aforementioned structural measures taken as a result of the significant take-up of the digital euro (Table 3).

Increase in Deposit Rates

In normal conditions, a key driver behind the demand for the digital euro would be its remuneration rate. It is reasonable to assume that sight deposits with low interest rates would shift to the risk-free digital euro, leading to an equal funding loss for banks. A digital euro would introduce more competition by setting an interest rate floor for bank deposits. In the case of banks having market power in the deposit market, the digital euro could increase competition incentivizing banks to offer

[19] Fabio Panetta, "The digital euro and the evolution of the financial system," *Introductory statement at the Committee on Economic and Monetary Affairs of the European Parliament,* June 15, European Central Bank, 2022. https://www.ecb.europa.eu/press/key/date/2022/html/ecb.sp220615~0b859eb8bc.en.html (accessed May 13, 2023).

[20] ECB, *Report on digital euro.*

better services and/or higher deposit rates.[21] In an imperfectly competitive deposit market, a digital euro would force banks to increase deposit rates to retain their deposit base, which would eventually have a crowd-in effect of encouraging saving.[22] Thus, banks would attract more deposits and offer more loans, provided that the digital euro rate lies in some intermediate range (i.e., neither too low, nor too high where disintermediation occurs).

Hence, in response to the introduction of the digital euro, banks could adjust their deposit rates to a level at least equal, if not higher, to the remuneration rate of the digital euro aiming to make deposits more attractive to depositors and minimize deposit outflows. Nonetheless, in this scenario banks' funding cost would increase even if no deposit outflows took place.[23]

Increase in Central Bank Funding

As mentioned above, if the demand for the digital euro exceeds the amount of excess reserves held by banks at the Eurosystem, banks may have to resort to the Eurosystem to meet their customers' demand for the digital euro and to mitigate the negative effects on their funding capacity.[24] In response to deposit outflows, central bank funding is an alternative source of funding provided that either banks have adequate collateral in terms of both quantity and quality to borrow, or the Eurosystem is willing to lend with less strict collateral requirements.

[21] Ulrich Bindseil et al., "Central."

[22] Chiu et al., "Bank market power and central bank digital currency: Theory and quantitative assessment," Staff Working Paper/ Document de travail du personnel 2019-20 (Bank of Canada, 2019), https://www.bankofcanada.ca/wp-content/uploads/2019/05/swp2019-20.pdf (accessed April 25, 2023); Michael Kumhof and Clare Noone, "Central bank digital currencies—design principles and balance sheet implications," Staff Working Paper no. 725 (Bank of England, 2020), https://www.bankofengland.co.uk/-/media/boe/files/working-paper/2018/central-bank-digital-currencies-design-principles-and-balance-sheet-implications (accessed May 14, 2023).

[23] Ulrich Bindseil, "Tiered CBDC and the financial system," Working Paper Series no. 2351 (European Central Bank, 2020), https://www.ecb.europa.eu/pub/pdf/scpwps/ecb.wp2351~c8c18bbd60.en.pdf (accessed May 9, 2023).

[24] Markus Brunnermeier and Jean-Pierre Landau, "The digital euro: policy implications and perspective," Study requested by the ECON Committee, European Parliament, 2022, https://www.europarl.europa.eu/RegData/etudes/STUD/2022/703337/IPOL_STU(2022)703337_EN.pdf (accessed June 3, 2023).

The substitution of bank deposits with a digital euro could force the Eurosystem to establish an offsetting liquidity-providing operation to ensure that the liquidity situation of the euro area banking sector is kept intact.[25] Alternatively, banks could sell (part of) their own assets (e.g., securities) to the Eurosystem to obtain a digital euro for their customers. In addition, the Eurosystem could carry out outright purchases of securities from investors (i.e., quantitative easing). Asset purchases would lead to the creation of new central bank reserves, as the Eurosystem would have to pay for the assets purchased and the consideration paid would increase the deposit balances of investors-sellers.

As shown in the below Table 4, the execution of the aforementioned measures (i.e., increase in lending to banks, asset purchases) would create new central bank reserves, resulting in the expansion of the Eurosystem's balance sheet.[26] This policy would increase the Eurosystem's role both in the financial markets and the euro area economy in normal periods, let alone in times of stress, aiming to address the liquidity shortfall of banks and avoid the risk of contraction in bank credit to the economy.

Table 4 Impact on Eurosystem's balance sheet (adverse scenario)

Assets		*Liabilities*	
Loans to banks	⇧	Banknotes	⇩
Securities	⇧	Reserves	⇩
Foreign reserves, gold and other	–	Digital euro	⇧
		Capital and other	–
TOTAL	⇧	TOTAL	⇧

[25] ECB, "Central."

[26] Tommaso Mancini Griffoli et al., "Casting Light on Central Bank Digital Currency," Staff Discussion Note SDN/18/08 (International Monetary Fund, 2018), https://www.imf.org/en/Publications/Staff-Discussion-Notes/Issues/2018/11/13/Casting-Light-on-Central-Bank-Digital-Currencies-46233 (accessed May 8, 2023).

Increase in Market Funding
Banks could also respond to deposit outflows by leveraging further on market-based sources of funding, mostly of long-term maturity, either secured (e.g., covered bonds, securitizations), or unsecured (e.g., senior preferred/non-preferred bonds). This option is more suitable for large banks with long-standing access to wholesale markets, while it seems barely feasible for small (non-listed) banks with limited (if any) presence in capital markets. This funding source is less stable compared to deposit funding and more expensive. Increased demand for market funding by euro area banks is likely to increase further the cost of wholesale funding, given that the investors' capacity and appetite to meet increased demand would remain unchanged. The Eurosystem could contribute to alleviating the implications from the increased demand for market funding by increasing its outright holdings of securities (i.e., quantitative easing), including banks' issuances. In this way, the Eurosystem would expand its role in the economy, as well as its risk exposure.

Alternatively, banks could borrow in the short-term interbank market to address the lost liquidity from deposit outflows, but this option would be temporary and could not address the structural problem of the reduced deposit base. Also, it would make it very challenging for banks to comply with the regulatory liquidity requirements, i.e., Liquidity Coverage Ratio (LCR) and Net Stable Funding Ratio (NSFR) that penalize reliance on short-term funding sources.

3.3 Impact on Banks' Funding Capacity and Profitability

A digital euro replacing banknotes would merely entail the transformation of one type of public money into another with no broader impact on the banking system. On the contrary, a digital euro replacing bank deposits would imply a shift from private money to public money, reducing a cheap and stable funding source for banks.[27] Funding through customer deposits lies at the heart of the banking business of maturity transformation. In the absence of any safeguard, the introduction of a digital euro is

[27] Fabio Panetta and Ulrich Bindseil, *Central bank digital currency remuneration in a world with low or negative nominal interest rates* (Centre for Economic Policy Research, 2020), https://cepr.org/voxeu/columns/central-bank-digital-currency-remuneration-world-low-or-negative-nominal-interest (accessed May 18, 2023).

expected to crowd out bank deposits, interfering with the way in which lending and deposit-taking complement each other.[28]

Under the adverse scenario described above, banks' funding would become more unstable and costly, affecting both their profitability and their lending capacity towards the economy.[29] Any of the measures mentioned above to compensate for the deposit reduction would increase the funding cost of banks, hampering their competitiveness relating to other forms of funding for households and businesses.[30] Higher deposit rates would worsen banks' profitability if not passed fully on lending rates. The outflow of cheap deposits would increase banks' funding cost if that outflow were compensated by an increase in more expensive funding sources, such as central bank funding and/or market funding. Deposits are the cheapest source of funding, followed by central bank funding and market funding.[31] The aforementioned options available to banks to respond to deposit reduction are expected to increase the overall cost of funding for banks, though not to the same extent, with a greater impact on deposit-funded banks. However, even among those banks, the increase in the cost of deposit funding will be disproportionate. Large banks with a high share of low-cost transactional deposits most likely would be affected to a larger extent, compared to small banks that offer higher deposit rates.

Aiming to counterbalance the profitability effects, banks might prefer secured funding or interbank borrowing with a short-term horizon. Typically, secured funding is cheaper than unsecured funding and short-term funding is cheaper than long-term funding. However, these options do not come at no cost in terms of liquidity risk, since banks' dependence on central bank funding and/or wholesale funding would increase. As mentioned above, central bank funding requires a sufficient amount of high-quality collateral, while the same applies for secured market funding (e.g., covered bonds) where overcollateralization is needed (i.e., the amount of collateral should significantly exceed the received funding). Also, interbank borrowing is sensitive to market developments, increasing the risk for a bank not to cover its liquidity needs, particularly in times of (system-wide or idiosyncratic) stress.

[28] Panetta, "More than an intellectual game."

[29] Brunnermeier and Landau, "The digital euro."

[30] Ulrich Bindseil et al., "Central."

[31] Bindseil, "Tiered."

The introduction of the digital euro would affect banks also from a regulatory perspective. The LCR,[32] which is the key regulatory liquidity ratio, treats (retail) deposits as a stable source of funding with the assignment of a lower outflow rate compared to other short-term sources of funding. Hence, banks are required to hold a smaller amount of High-Quality Liquid Assets (HQLAs) to withstand potential liquidity outflows.[33] The substitution of deposits with the digital euro would result in the increase of the LCR denominator (net liquidity outflows), driving down the LCR. Also, a potential replacement of lost deposits with short-term interbank borrowing would, also, drive LCR lower, due to a higher outflow rate applied to interbank borrowing and a fall in the pool of HQLAs held given that interbank borrowing is typically secured with HQLAs.[34] Furthermore, the use of excess reserves, also treated as HQLAs, would reduce the pool of HQLAs with a negative effect on LCR. Therefore, banks should strike the right balance between mitigating the impact on profitability and ensuring sustainable liquidity ratios above the respective regulatory thresholds.

Under the adverse scenario, the introduction of the digital euro is likely to trigger bank disintermediation and curtail the volume of bank credit to the economy, both directly and indirectly.[35] As regards the former, the

[32] The LCR aims to ensure that banks hold a sufficient reserve of High-Quality Liquid Assets (HQLA) to allow them to survive a period of significant liquidity stress lasting 30 calendar days. It is defined as the stock of HQLAs held by a bank over its total net cash outflows over the next 30 calendar days.

[33] The introduction of a digital euro might change the outflow rate applied to deposits given that the digital euro could be considered a credible alternative for deposits in case of crisis. Thus, prudential regulation might have to adapt to the increased outflow rate of deposits under stressed conditions affecting banks' LCR as well.

[34] ECB, "Central". Central bank funding can be secured both with HQLAs and non-HQLAs. Unsecured long-term funding and long-term central bank funding secured with non-HQLAs, such as additional credit claims, do not have negative effects on LCR and NSFR.

[35] Although the widespread view is that the digital euro would trigger bank disintermediation, there are views suggesting that an interest-bearing digital euro could foster bank intermediation. An increase in the remuneration of the digital euro would force banks to increase interest rates on deposits leading to higher deposit balances (ECB, *Report on digital euro*). A digital euro could function as a floor on deposit rates limiting banks' profits in the deposit market and driving them to increase lending to economy. Some studies note the potential for increased competition in the deposit market resulting in an increase of the overall depositor base and lending expansion. Indicatively, a study argues that higher deposit rates could increase the deposit base and lower borrowing rates

substitution of deposits with the digital euro would reduce the banks' core funding source, affecting their capacity to provide loans to the economy. In the short term, banks could cope with any liquidity mismatch by resorting to other funding sources, though at a higher cost, or reducing their liquid assets (e.g., securities). However, in a medium- to long-term horizon, banks most likely will have to deleverage by adjusting downwards the amount of loans provided to the economy. In this way, banks would reduce their loan balances and overall their balance sheets. In addition to the amount of lending, banks would have to change the mix of lending by adapting their lending policy to assets that can be securitized. For instance, banks could draw liquidity from covered bonds and/or securitizations, which could be either sold to investors for liquidity purposes or retained and used as eligible collateral in central bank borrowing.[36]

Increased funding cost could also indirectly affect bank lending. A heightened cost of funding would translate into a significant hit on banks' profitability. This is particularly relevant for banks with a negative risk profile (e.g., bad asset quality, low profitability, problematic business model), where investors price the increased riskiness and charge higher rates for market funding. Should banks intend to retain the same interest margins (i.e., the difference between lending and funding rates), they will have to raise their lending rates.[37] Banks' reaction to the digital euro hinges on their market power. Banks with sufficient market power can better protect their interest margin and profitability by passing the increase in deposit rates to lending rates.[38] An increase in the cost of

thus expanding banks' lending (David Andolfatto, "Assessing the Impact of Central Bank Digital Currency on Private Banks," Working Paper Series 026B (Economic Research Federal Reserve Bank of St. Louis, 2018), https://doi.org/10.20955/wp.2018.026 (accessed April 28, 2023)). Similarly, a study concludes that under imperfect bank competition in the deposit market, higher deposit rates can increase lending by increasing deposit demand (Chiu et al., "Bank"). They argue that, even when CBDC is not used in equilibrium, its introduction provides a lower bound on deposit rates, limiting monopoly profits of banks in the deposit market and inducing them to lend more.

[36] Reimo Juks, "Central bank digital currencies, supply of bank loans and liquidity provision by central banks," in *Second special issue on the e-krona*, ed. Marianne Nessén and Ulf Söderström, Economic Review 2 (Sveriges Riksbank, 2020), https://www.riksbank.se/globalassets/media/rapporter/pov/engelska/2020/economic-review-2-2020.pdf (accessed May 25, 2023).

[37] Kumhof and Noone, "Central."

[38] Griffoli et al.,"Casting"; BIS, *Central bank digital currencies*.

credit is likely to come at the cost of loan demand resulting in a lower volume of lending to households and businesses, since some projects that are profitable at a lower cost of funding will fail to secure cost-efficient bank financing.[39] Banks could absorb a share of the increase in funding cost and not pass this fully to borrowers. There are natural limits on how much banks can increase lending rates to compensate for increased funding cost.[40] Banks with immaterial reliance on deposit funding, as well as other non-bank sources of funding (e.g., corporate bond market), could take advantage of this development and act as a substitute for lending, primarily to corporates, setting the cap for the lending rates applied by deposit-funded banks.

The magnitude of the macroeconomic impact from the above (direct and indirect) channels depends on several factors, including: (i) the level of the lending adjustment banks have to make, once other funding options have been used, (ii) the length of the adjustment period given that the longer is the time frame for banks to adjust, the lower adverse impact would arise; and (iii) the monetary policy response from the Eurosystem, considering that an accommodative monetary policy could contain the negative impact from the substitution of deposits with the digital euro.

In addition to the aforementioned effects, banks' profitability is likely to suffer from additional implications triggered by the introduction of the digital euro.[41] Firstly, banks' fee and commission income would be reduced, since payments between digital euro users would be free of charge.[42] Secondly, recourse to central bank funding would increase the demand for collateral (e.g., sovereign bonds). In an era of excess liquidity, the implications might be manageable. However, in periods of

[39] BIS, *Central bank digital currencies*.

[40] Reimo Juks, "When a central bank digital currency meets private money: The effects of an e-krona on banks," in *Special issue on the e-krona*, ed. Jesper Lindé and Marianne Nessén, Economic Review 3 (Sveriges Riksbank, 2018), https://www.riksbank.se/globalassets/media/rapporter/pov/engelska/2018/economic-review-3-2018.pdf (accessed May 6, 2023).

[41] In general, the digital euro implies negative effects for banks' profitability. An exception to that refers to lower cash usage, benefitting banks with reduced costs associated with cash handling.

[42] Fabio Panetta, "A digital euro: widely available and easy to use," *Introductory statement at the Committee on Economic and Monetary Affairs of the European Parliament*, European Central Bank, 2023, https://www.ecb.europa.eu/press/key/date/2023/html/ecb.sp230424_1~f44c7ac164.en.html (accessed June 2, 2023).

tight liquidity conditions, this could drive down the interest rates of those assets. Considering that typically banks invest in those assets, a drop in their market interest rates would significantly affect their return from such investments.

3.4 Potential Effects in Times of Stress

During times of financial stress, depositors move their deposits away from banks perceived as risky towards safer banks. Typically, under bank-runs money flows from weakly capitalized banks to strongly capitalized ones, from private banks to state-controlled ones and from domestically owned banks to foreign-owned ones (i.e., subsidiaries or branches of foreign banks).[43] In case of a bank-specific crisis, depositors can transfer their money digitally and very rapidly from a troubled bank to a strong one, triggering an individual bank-run.[44] The failure of Silicon Valley Bank in March 2023 demonstrated how digital banking applications enable depositors to transfer easily and fast their money outside troubled banks, triggering bank runs.[45] In a systemic crisis, an aggregate bank-run can materialize if depositors withdraw their funds from banks in the form of cash or invest in low-risk financial assets.[46] Nonetheless, none of these options is free of costs and risks. A run from deposits into cash is constrained by the risks of storing large amounts of cash (e.g., risk of theft) and transaction costs associated with cash withdrawals (e.g., going to the ATM, waiting in line). Investment in low-risk financial assets (e.g., gold, highly rated sovereign bonds) also entails some disincentives for prospective buyers, including: (i) upward price adjustment due to the increased demand resulting in a drop of the expected returns, (ii) costs relating to the fees paid for the execution of the transaction; and (iii) exposure to (market and liquidity) risks.

[43] Agustin Carstens, “The future of money and payments,” *Speech at the Central Bank of Ireland*, Dublin, March 22, Bank for International Settlements, 2023, https://www.bis.org/speeches/sp190322.pdf (accessed June 5, 2023).

[44] Ibid.; Kumhof and Noone, “Central.”

[45] Ignazio Angeloni, “Digital Euro: When in doubt, abstain (but be prepared),” In-depth analysis requested by the ECON Committee, European Parliament, 2023, https://www.europarl.europa.eu/RegData/etudes/IDAN/2023/741507/IPOL_IDA(2023)741507_EN.pdf (accessed June 6, 2023).

[46] Also, depositors can transfer their deposits abroad to foreign banks.

Today, bank-runs are less likely to happen, given the rigorous regulatory and supervisory regime to which banks are subject and the existence of DGSs and bank resolution frameworks that protect (covered) depositors. Under the existing Union regulatory framework, upon the failure of a bank, the resolution authority may decide to place the bank concerned either in resolution or in normal insolvency proceedings. Under the former case, covered deposits[47] are fully protected (i.e., excluded from the scope of resolution), while uncovered deposits might suffer losses if other subordinated to them liabilities (i.e., shares, capital instruments, senior bonds/liabilities) are not sufficient for the loss absorption and recapitalization of the failed bank.[48] In case of insolvency, the national DGS shall compensate covered depositors for their deposits up to 100,000 euro held at the bank concerned. However, the robust Union regulatory framework limits rather than eliminates the risk of depositors withdrawing their deposits from troubled banks and triggering bank-runs. Unsophisticated depositors, particularly those having limited (if any) trust in banks and public authorities, would be more prone to move their money away from commercial banks in times of financial distress, triggering a self-fulfilling bank crisis. In this context, whereas bank-runs triggered from conversion of deposits into cash are constrained by the risks and costs of storing large amounts of cash, no such limitations would exist if households and businesses could hold a risk-free, fully liquid asset with no holding costs.

Against this backdrop, the introduction of a digital euro could make bank-runs more likely to happen, since it would provide users with access to a safe asset that can be held in large volumes and at no cost. This is particularly relevant for a systemic crisis, where all banks are deemed risky. In that case, a digital euro would be a credible alternative as a safe, fully liquid-run asset that would allow depositors to move their money away from banks at no cost and hold unlimited amounts of public money. Even if the digital euro is designed primarily for payment purposes, in periods of stress a flight towards the safety provided by the Eurosystem may occur on a fast and large scale.[49] The digital euro could be preferred over other

[47] Covered deposits, which can be up to €100,000 per depositor per bank, are guaranteed by the DGS of the country in which the bank is located.

[48] The extent of losses that might fall upon uncovered deposits is related to the extent of losses and the ranking of deposits (e.g., uncovered deposits from corporates absorb losses in priority to uncovered deposits from natural persons and SMEs).

[49] Ulrich Bindseil et al., "Central."

deposits or other low-risk assets. In the absence of safeguards, it could amplify deposit outflows and trigger a bank-run, or better called "digital run",[50] which would be destabilizing for the banking sector, putting in danger the EU financial stability.[51]

4 Safeguards to Control the Digital Euro Take-Up

4.1 Potential Quantity-Based and Remuneration-Based Safeguards

The digital euro might disrupt the bank intermediation model by increasing the cost of funding and reducing the availability of bank lending. The extent of the disruption depends on the scale of the digital euro's take-up and the speed of substitution of bank deposits, once the digital euro is introduced. Based on an analysis performed by the BIS, the introduction of CBDCs would have limited impact on banking intermediation for many plausible levels of CBDC take-up if the system had the time and flexibility to adjust.[52] Therefore, careful design and implementation is needed to control the adoption of the digital euro. To this end, the literature recommends some safeguards to moderate the impact of the digital euro and to limit bank disintermediation: (i) quantity-based safeguards, (ii) remuneration-based safeguards or (iii) a combination of quantity-based and remuneration-based safeguards.[53] These measures could mitigate risks both in the transition to the digital euro and in the long run.[54]

Quantity-based safeguards would restrict the take-up of the digital euro by imposing strict limits on the holdings and/or transfer of the digital euro. In particular, such limits could be either stock-based (i.e., limitation of the amount held by each user) or flow-based (i.e., restriction of

[50] Ibid.

[51] Juks, "Central."

[52] Bank for International Settlements, et al., *Central bank digital currencies: executive summary* (BIS, 2021) https://www.bis.org/publ/othp42.pdf_ (accessed May 27, 2023). This assessment is subject to uncertainties in relation to the future structure of the financial system, the design of a CBDC and its underlying system, the size and scale of user adoption of CBDC and differences between jurisdictions.

[53] BIS, *Central bank digital currencies.*

[54] BIS et al., *Central.*

the amount that can be transferred by a user within a specific period, as for example, a day).[55] Differentiated limits could apply to accounts held by households and corporates (non-bank financial companies and non-financial companies). Tight limits on the use of the digital euro by corporates would moderate the overall take-up, while ensuring that the digital euro is used as a means of retail payment. The calibration of holding limits for corporates is quite puzzling, considering the large variation in their size and presumed cash needs.[56] To this end, a holding limit could be proportional to the size of corporates or could be set to zero for the sake of simplicity (i.e., only Tier 2 holdings available, as described in more detail below).

The limits could apply either on a permanent or on a transitional basis. The first option would apply if the Eurosystem intended to structurally limit the take-up of the digital euro. The second option could be the preferred one during the transition phase to allow the banking system to adjust to that development, as well as in times of stress to avoid massive deposit outflows and potential bank-runs. Setting limits on the amount of the digital euro held by each individual or business could minimize the risk of deposit outflows, reducing the extent of bank disintermediation. However, the implementation of such holding limits could be challenging from an operational perspective. For instance, what would happen if a user had reached the digital euro limit and had some incoming payments? A proposed solution to overcome this problem is the so-called waterfall mechanism. This mechanism would enable the digital euro holdings exceeding the threshold limit (i.e., excess amount arising from incoming payments) to be automatically transferred to an account held by the payee concerned in a commercial bank or another financial intermediary. The adoption of the "waterfall" approach ensures that a user can always receive a payment, while no information on current individual holdings is disclosed to other users.[57] Otherwise, if such a mechanism were not in place, the settlement of the digital euro transactions would not be always possible and this could allow other users to realize that the amount of

[55] Riccardo De Bonis and Giuseppe Ferrero, "Technological progress and institutional adaptations: the case of the Central Bank Digital Currency (CBDC)," Occasional Paper no. 690 (Banca D'Italia, 2022), https://www.bancaditalia.it/pubblicazioni/qef/2022-0690/QEF_690_22.pdf?language_id=1 (accessed April 25, 2023).

[56] Ulrich Bindseil et al., "Central"; Panetta and Bindseil, *Central bank digital currency*.

[57] ECB, *Report on digital euro*.

the digital euro held by the payee is close to the applicable threshold. However, this mechanism has certain drawbacks. Firstly, it requires monitoring and retaining information on both holdings and transactions.[58] Secondly, all payees will have to hold a bank account, while for those without a bank account or unwilling to open one the single limit could apply.[59]

The remuneration-based safeguards aim to disincentivize users from holding large amounts of the digital euro or performing large payments in that. In this context, a single-tier or two-tiered remuneration approach might apply. Under the former, the digital euro would be remunerated at a rate irrespective of the amount held. The digital euro could bear uncompetitive interest rates, including a zero-remuneration rate in the context of positive interest rates environment.[60] Under the two-tiered remuneration approach, a digital euro up to a predefined threshold (Tier 1 holdings) would earn a specific return, while the amount exceeding that threshold (Tier 2 holdings) would earn a lower interest rate. In this way, a two-tiered remuneration structure would allow the assignment of the payment function of money to Tier 1 holdings and penalize the holdings exceeding that threshold (soft rate disincentive). Hence, a two-tiered remuneration approach ensures that the digital euro is used solely for payments and not as a form of investment, preventing both excessive structural and cyclical bank disintermediation and any undermining of monetary policy.[61]

As regards the level of remuneration rates, the Tier 1 rate could be set at a relatively attractive level, namely below or up to the ECB's Deposit Facility Rate (i.e., remuneration rate of excess reserves held by banks) floored at zero in case of negative interest rate policy applied by the Eurosystem.[62] Thus, the Tier 1 remuneration would provide households with a means of payment at least as attractive as cash, including non-negative remuneration, for an amount that covers the payment needs of

[58] BIS, *Central bank digital currencies*. On the contrary, transfer-based safeguards (e.g., fees/limits on the transferable amount) do not require such level of information, as they could be applied at transaction level.

[59] Ulrich Bindseil et al., "Central."

[60] ECB, "Central."

[61] Ulrich Bindseil et al., "Central."

[62] Although today the Eurosystem applies a positive interest rate policy, this does not preclude the possibility of the re-introduction of a negative interest rate policy, as were the case until mid-2022.

the average household, ensuring that the normal payment function of money is covered.[63] On the contrary, the Tier 2 remuneration rate could be set at such a level to be unattractive as a store of value, which means less attractive than bank deposits or other short-term financial assets, even including risk premia.[64] In case of the application of a negative interest rate policy, the Tier 2 rate could fall below zero. Moving the rates would simply serve to keep a similar spread over time to other ECB's policy rates and thus, to other market rates, with an additional special provision for the Tier 1 rate, when the zero lower bound territory is approached.[65] For instance, as mentioned by Fabio Panetta, a member of the ECB's Executive Board, the Tier 1 rate could be set at $\max\{0, i_{dfr}-2\%\}$, while the Tier 2 rate could be set at $\min\{0, i_{dfr}-0.5\%\}$. The Eurosystem would have the right to lower the Tier 2 rate in a financial crisis, while it would be bound to not worsen the formula for Tier 1 rate, particularly in relation to zero lower bound.[66]

4.2 *The ECB's Key Principles for the Safeguards to Control the Amount of the Digital Euro in Circulation*

In September 2022, the ECB published the first progress report on the investigation phase of the digital euro,[67] while two additional progress reports followed in December 2022[68] and April 2023.[69] As per the latest progress report, the Eurosystem proposes the digital euro to be available

[63] For instance, an amount of 3,000 euro for Tier 1 holdings could cover the average monthly net income of euro area households.

[64] Bindseil, "Tiered."

[65] Panetta and Bindseil, *Central bank digital currency*.

[66] Ibid.

[67] European Central Bank, *Progress on the investigation phase of a digital euro* (ECB, 2022), https://www.ecb.europa.eu/paym/digital_euro/investigation/governance/shared/files/ecb.degov220929.en.pdf (accessed May 19, 2023).

[68] European Central Bank, *Progress on the investigation phase of a digital euro*, Second Report (ECB, 2022), https://www.ecb.europa.eu/paym/digital_euro/investigation/governance/shared/files/ecb.degov221221_Progress.en.pdf?f91e0b8ff8cbd6654d7e6b071a8f7071 (accessed May 8, 2023).

[69] European Central Bank, *Progress on the investigation phase of a digital euro,* Third Report (ECB, 2023), https://www.ecb.europa.eu/paym/digital_euro/investigation/governance/shared/files/ecb.degov230424_progress.en.pdf (accessed May 25, 2023).

to euro area residents, merchants[70] and governments in its initial releases. Non-resident euro area citizens could also have access to the digital euro, provided they have an account relationship with a euro area PSP, while access for consumers in the wider European Economic Area (EEA) and selected third countries could be part of subsequent releases of the digital euro.

The above progress reports set out, among others, the key principles to control the digital euro take-up in order to avoid a structural substitution of bank deposits, which could trigger undesirable consequences for financial stability and the real economy. In particular, the Eurosystem is moving towards the introduction of both quantity-based and remuneration-based tools in the design of the digital euro to restrict its use as a form of investment. Thus, the Eurosystem intends to adopt quantitative limits on the amount of the digital euro held by users to control individual take-up and to limit the speed at which bank deposits are converted into a digital euro.[71] Individuals should be subject to uniform holding limits (not defined yet), which would cover day-to-day payments in euro area Member States. On the contrary, merchants and governments in the euro area should have zero-holding limits (i.e., cannot hold digital euro), at least for the initial releases of the digital euro, with deviations limited to what needed for the technical implementation of the "waterfall" and "reverse-waterfall"[72] functionalities (i.e., exceeding holding limits only for a few seconds).[73] The fact that merchants and governments will not hold digital euro reduces the risk for deposit outflows from banks and the resulting risk for banking disintermediation described above. Also, remuneration-based tools could be incorporated into the design of the digital euro in order to disincentivize users from holding large amounts. In this way, the digital euro holdings exceeding a threshold would be unattractive compared to other highly liquid low-risk assets.

[70] Merchants outside the euro area could offer digital euro acceptance, but should not hold digital euro, as will be the case of euro area merchants as well. They would obtain the equivalent in private money through a collecting euro area PSP.

[71] ECB, *Progress*.

[72] A "reverse-waterfall" functionality would ensure that users can make a payment even if the amount exceeds their current digital euro funds. Additional liquidity would be pulled from the linked private money account.

[73] ECB, *Progress*, third report.

The Eurosystem will decide on the combination and calibration of the aforementioned tools closer to the possible introduction of the digital euro, considering also the economic and financial conditions prevailing at that point in time (e.g., interest rates, level of excess reserves held by banks, potential availability of alternative digital means of payment). To date, the Governing Council has decided: (i) a specific limit for offline holdings to apply within the overall limit, (ii) to permit different limits for online and offline use, as well as temporary deviations from the holding limit; and (iii) the use of the "waterfall" functionality tool under which funds exceeding the holding limit would be transferred automatically to a linked commercial bank account of the payee.

5 Concluding Remarks

The impact of the digital euro on the euro area banking system is linked to the level of its take-up. The key determinants of the digital euro take-up pertain to: (i) the attractiveness of the digital euro to users based on its design features, (ii) the banks' reaction to the introduction of the digital euro, (iii) the prevailing economic and financial conditions at the time of issuance; and (iv) the safeguards applied by the Eurosystem to control its take-up. Based on an ECB's analysis, keeping the total digital euro holdings below €1.5 trillion euro would avoid material negative consequences for financial stability and monetary policy. This amount would be comparable with the current holdings of banknotes in circulation. Taking into account that the population of the euro area is around 340 million, this would allow for holdings of 3,000 to 4000 digital euro per capita.[74]

A significant substitution of bank deposits with the digital euro could have an adverse impact on the role of banks in maturity transformation with significant implications for the amount and cost of credit that banks provide to the economy.[75] If the digital euro becomes too successful (i.e., very large take-up), it is likely to lead to bank disintermediation, affecting the existing financial market structures and bank business models. In addition, risks for the EU financial stability could arise, particularly in times of stress. What literature shows is that maintaining bank profitability at the current levels will be quite challenging and the magnitude of the impact

[74] Panetta, "The digital euro."

[75] Kumhof and Noone, "Central."

will be affected by key determinants, such as the substitutability between deposits and the digital euro, the level of competition in the banking sector, the functioning of the market for loans from non-banks and the willingness of central banks to provide liquidity to banks.[76] Central bank funding is expected to play a critical role in a more permanent and structural manner, as an alternative funding source for banks through the establishment of permanent liquidity facilities.

A digital euro should neither be too broad to crowd out private sector solutions and threaten the bank intermediation model, nor too narrow to be of limited use. Particular emphasis should be placed on the safeguards to control the take-up of the digital euro, particularly in the transition to the digital euro. The safeguards should be calibrated in such a manner to strike the right balance between mitigating the risks from a large and rapid take-up of the digital euro and ensuring a substantial level of usage, which is necessary to achieve the policy objectives of the digital euro.[77] The safeguards should ensure that the digital euro is only used as a means of payment and not as a store of value. The Eurosystem should adopt safeguards that are not too restrictive to prevent users from having access to a safe means of payment in central bank money. Rigid constraints or disincentives (e.g., low remuneration rate), applied above a relatively low threshold, would make the digital euro less attractive as a means of payment for households and businesses.[78] In addition, the Eurosystem should monitor the take-up of foreign CBDCs, particularly from households and businesses in the euro area, and adjust the safeguards of the digital euro in order to prevent a widespread adoption of a foreign CBDC that would increase the risk of financial transactions being managed and supervised elsewhere, with limited oversight by domestic authorities.

In any case, the digital euro should be carefully designed so that it is not used as a form of investment that would trigger the risk of large shifts from bank deposits to the digital euro. A combination of quantity-based and remuneration-based safeguards seems the most suitable approach to mitigate the attractiveness of the digital euro as a means of investment reducing, thus, the scale of bank disintermediation. Most likely the adoption of the new digital euro will be gradual and is expected to take several

[76] BIS, *Central bank digital currencies*.

[77] Ibid.

[78] ECB, *Report on digital euro*.

years before a majority of the euro area population hold a digital euro.[79] Aiming to ensure the financial stability and the orderly functioning of the monetary transmission mechanism, the Eurosystem should adopt a cautious approach as regards the calibration of the safeguards, at least in the initial phase of the digital euro and then adjust based on experience and the take-up of the digital euro over time.[80]

References

Andolfatto, David. "Assessing the impact of central bank digital currency on private banks." Working paper series 026B, Economic Research Federal Reserve Bank of St. Louis, 2018. https://doi.org/10.20955/wp.2018.026 (accessed April 28, 2023).

Angeloni, Ignazio. "Digital Euro: When in doubt, abstain (but be prepared)." In-depth analysis requested by the ECON Committee, April. European Parliament, 2023. https://www.europarl.europa.eu/RegData/etudes/IDAN/2023/741507/IPOL_IDA(2023)741507_EN.pdf (accessed June 6, 2023).

Bank for International Settlements. *Central bank digital currencies: Foundational principles and core features*. Report no.1 in a series of collaborations from a group of central banks, 2020. https://www.bis.org/publ/othp33.pdf (accessed May 27, 2023).

Bank for International Settlements. *BIS innovation hub work on Central Bank Digital Currency (CBDC)*. BIS, 2021. https://www.bis.org/about/bisih/topics/cbdc.htm.

Bank for International Settlements. *Central bank digital currencies: User needs and adoption*. Report no. 3 in a series of collaborations from a group of central banks, 2021. https://www.bis.org/publ/othp42_user_needs.pdf (accessed May 20, 2023).

Bank for International Settlements. *Central bank digital currencies: Financial stability implications*. Report no. 4 in a series of collaborations from a group of central banks, 2021. https://www.bis.org/publ/othp42_fin_stab.pdf (accessed May 22, 2023).

Bank for International Settlements, Bank of Canada, European Central Bank, Bank of Japan, Sveriges Riksbank, Swiss National Bank, Bank of England, and Board of Governors Federal Reserve System. *Central bank digital currencies: Executive summary*. BIS, 2021. https://www.bis.org/publ/othp42.pdf (accessed May 27, 2023).

[79] Panetta, "The digital euro."

[80] Ibid.

Bijlsma, Michiel, Carin van der Cruijsen, Nicole Jonker, and Jelmer Reijerink. "What triggers consumer adoption of CBDC?" Working Paper no. 709, De Nederlandsche Bank, 2021. https://www.dnb.nl/media/amwfjgey/working_paper_no-_709.pdf (accessed May 12, 2023).

Bindseil, Ulrich. "Tiered CBDC and the financial system." Working Paper Series no. 2351, European Central Bank, 2020. https://www.ecb.europa.eu/pub/pdf/scpwps/ecb.wp2351~c8c18bbd60.en.pdf (accessed May 9, 2023).

Bindseil, Ulrich, Fabio Panetta, and Ignacio Terol. "Central Bank Digital Currency: Functional scope, pricing and controls." Occasional Paper Series no. 286, European Central Bank, 2021. https://www.ecb.europa.eu/pub/pdf/scpops/ecb.op286~9d472374ea.en.pdf (accessed May 15, 2023).

Brunnermeier, Markus, and Jean-Pierre Landau. "The digital euro: policy implications and perspective." Study requested by the ECON Committee, January. European Parliament, 2022. https://www.europarl.europa.eu/RegData/etudes/STUD/2022/703337/IPOL_STU(2022)703337_EN.pdf (accessed June 3, 2023).

Carstens, Agustin. "The future of money and payments." *Speech at the Central Bank of Ireland, Dublin*, March 22. Bank for International Settlements, 2019. https://www.bis.org/speeches/sp190322.pdf (accessed June 5, 2023).

Chiu, Jonathan, Mohammad Davoodalhosseini, Janet Jiang, and Yu Zhu. "Bank market power and Central Bank Digital Currency: Theory and quantitative assessment." Staff Working Paper/Document de travail du personnel 2019–20, Bank of Canada, 2019. https://www.bankofcanada.ca/wp-content/uploads/2019/05/swp2019-20.pdf (accessed April 25, 2023).

De Bonis, Riccardo, and Giuseppe Ferrero. "Technological progress and institutional adaptations: The case of the Central Bank Digital Currency (CBDC)." Occasional Paper no. 690, Banca D'Italia, 2022. https://www.bancaditalia.it/pubblicazioni/qef/2022-0690/QEF_690_22.pdf?language_id=1 (accessed April 25, 2023).

European Central Bank. *Report on a digital euro.* ECB, 2020. https://www.ecb.europa.eu/pub/pdf/other/Report_on_a_digital_euro~4d7268b458.en.pdf (accessed June 2, 2023).

European Central Bank. "Central Bank Digital Currency and bank intermediation." Occasional Paper Series no. 293, ECB, 2022. https://www.ecb.europa.eu/pub/pdf/scpops/ecb.op293~652cf2b1aa.en.pdf (accessed May 14, 2023).

European Central Bank. *Digital euro – our future money.* ECB, 2022. https://www.ecb.europa.eu/paym/digital_euro/investigation/profuse/shared/files/dedocs/ecb.dedocs221017_ecbatsibos.en.pdf?447523fb3a77c4c58413c7f3870340da (accessed June 5, 2023).

European Central Bank. *Progress on the investigation phase of a digital euro*. First Report, 2022. https://www.ecb.europa.eu/paym/digital_euro/investigation/governance/shared/files/ecb.degov220929.en.pdf (accessed May 19, 2023).

European Central Bank. *Progress on the investigation phase of a digital euro*. Second Report, 2022. https://www.ecb.europa.eu/paym/digital_euro/investigation/governance/shared/files/ecb.degov221221_Progress.en.pdf (accessed May 8, 2023).

European Central Bank. *The case for a digital euro: key objectives and design considerations*. ECB, 2022. https://www.ecb.europa.eu/pub/pdf/other/key_objectives_digital_euro~f11592d6fb.en.pdf (accessed May 15, 2023).

European Central Bank. *Progress on the investigation phase of a digital euro*. Third Report, 2023. https://www.ecb.europa.eu/paym/digital_euro/investigation/governance/shared/files/ecb.degov230424_progress.en.pdf (accessed May 25, 2023).

Fernández-Villaverde, Jesús, Daniel Sanches, Linda Schilling, and Harald Uhlig. "Central Bank Digital Currency: Central Banking For All?." Working Paper no. 26753, National Bureau of Economic Research, 2020. https://www.nber.org/system/files/working_papers/w26753/w26753.pdf (accessed April 25, 2023).

Griffoli, Tommaso Mancini, Maria Soledad Martinez Peria, Itai Agur, Anil Ari, John Kiff, Adina Popescu, and Celine Rochon. "Casting Light on Central Bank Digital Currency." *IMF Staff Discussion Note SDN/18/08*, International Monetary Fund, 2018. https://www.imf.org/en/Publications/Staff-Discussion-Notes/Issues/2018/11/13/Casting-Light-on-Central-Bank-Digital-Currencies-46233 (accessed May 8, 2023).

Juks, Reimo. "Central bank digital currencies, supply of bank loans and liquidity provision by central banks." In *Second special issue on the e-krona*, edited by Marianne Nessén and Ulf Söderström, 62–79. Economic Review 2: Sveriges Riksbank, 2020. https://www.riksbank.se/globalassets/media/rapporter/pov/engelska/2020/economic-review-2-2020.pdf (accessed May 25, 2023).

Juks, Reimo. "When a central bank digital currency meets private money: The effects of an e-krona on banks." In *Special issue on the e-krona*, edited by Jesper Lindé and Marianne Nessén, 79–99. Economic Review 3: Sveriges Riksbank, 2018. https://www.riksbank.se/globalassets/media/rapporter/pov/engelska/2018/economic-review-3-2018.pdf (accessed May 6, 2023).

Kumhof, Michael, and Clare Noone. "Central bank digital currencies—design principles and balance sheet implications." Staff Working Paper no. 725, Bank of England, 2020. https://www.bankofengland.co.uk/-/media/boe/files/working-paper/2018/central-bank-digital-currencies-design-principles-and-balance-sheet-implications (accessed May 14, 2023).

Panetta, Fabio and Ulrich Bindseil. *Central bank digital currency remuneration in a world with low or negative nominal interest rates*. Centre for Economic Policy Research (CEPR), 2020. https://cepr.org/voxeu/columns/central-bank-digital-currency-remuneration-world-low-or-negative-nominal-interest (accessed May 18, 2023).

Panetta, Fabio. "Designing a digital euro for the retail payments landscape of tomorrow." *Introductory remarks at the ECON Committee of the European Parliament*, November 18. European Central Bank, 2021. https://www.ecb.europa.eu/press/key/date/2021/html/ecb.sp211118~b36013b7c5.en.html (accessed May 15, 2023).

Panetta, Fabio. "Central bank digital currencies: Defining the problems, designing the solutions." *Contribution to a panel discussion on central bank digital currencies at the US Monetary Policy Forum*. European Central Bank, 2022. https://www.ecb.europa.eu/press/key/date/2022/html/ecb.sp220218_1~938e881b13.en.html (accessed June 2, 2023).

Panetta, Fabio. "More than an intellectual game: Exploring the monetary policy and financial stability implications of central bank digital currencies." *Opening speech at the IESE Business School Banking Initiative Conference on Technology and Finance*, April 8. European Central Bank, 2022. https://www.ecb.europa.eu/press/key/date/2022/html/ecb.sp220408~980e39957b.en.html (accessed May 25, 2023).

Panetta, Fabio. "The digital euro and the evolution of the financial system." *Introductory statement at the Committee on Economic and Monetary Affairs of the European Parliament*, June 15. European Central Bank, 2022. https://www.ecb.europa.eu/press/key/date/2022/html/ecb.sp220615~0b859eb8bc.en.html (accessed May 13, 2023).

Panetta, Fabio. "A digital euro: widely available and easy to use." *Introductory statement at the Committee on Economic and Monetary Affairs of the European Parliament*, April, 24. European Central Bank, 2023. https://www.ecb.europa.eu/press/key/date/2023/html/ecb.sp230424_1~f44c7ac164.en.html (accessed June 2, 2023).

CHAPTER 9

Anti-Money Laundering (AML) Implications of Central Bank Digital Currencies (CBDC)

Andrea Minto

1 Introduction

Over the last years the anti-money laundering and countering terrorist financing (AML/CTF) regulatory frameworks have been reshaping globally as to keep up with the developments of modern finance.[1] In a world

[1] Technological innovation is changing the way financial service providers and financial users interact, to meet their evolving financial and payment needs in the digital age. See, *e.g.*, See the recent surveys conducted by the European Banking Authority (EBA, *Report on the use of digital platforms*, September 2021) and by the Bank of Italy, *Indagine* fintech *nel sistema finanziario italiano*, 22 November 2021, which show an upward trend especially with regard to the adoption of artificial intelligence and machine learning systems. See also ESAs, *Joint opinion on the use of innovative solutions by credit and financial institutions the customer due diligence process*, 23 January 2018 and the EBA *Guidelines on customer due diligence and the factors credit and financial institutions should consider when assessing the money laundering and terrorist financing risk associated with individual business relationships and occasional transactions («The ML/TF Risk Factors Guidelines») under Articles 17 and 18(4) of Directive (EU) 2015/849*, 2021.

A. Minto (✉)
Department of Economics, Ca' Foscari University of Venice, Venice, Italy
e-mail: andrea.minto@unive.it

© The Author(s), under exclusive license to Springer Nature Switzerland AG 2025

F. Annunziata et al. (eds.), *Central Bank Digital Currency*, EBI Studies in Banking and Capital Markets Law,
https://doi.org/10.1007/978-3-031-80957-6_9

increasingly layered and dominated by technology (despite common wisdom advocating for dis-intermediation[2]), policy- and law-makers were called upon to appraise the effectiveness of the regulatory and supervisory architectures.[3]

This holds true in particular for the European Union, where a long line of legislative acts—in the form of directives, so far—kept updating the AML legislation, ever since Directive 91/308/ECC (the so-called first AML directive) laid the foundation, as a milestone, of the EU policy and regulatory strategy to curb the risk of money laundering.[4]

Every new piece of EU legislation—from the first to the fifth AML directive—was in fact projected at adapting the "regulatory net" in the quest to capture all potential means through which the proceeds of

UiS School of Business and Law, University of Stavanger, Stavanger, Norway

[2] On this topic see, *e.g.*, A. Minto, M. Voelkerling, M. Wulff, *Separating apples from oranges: identifying threats to financial stability originating from FinTech*, in *Capital Markets Law Journal*, 2017, 12(4), p. 428 ss. In general, with regard to critical issues related to "*layering*" see T.C. Lin, *Infinite Financial Intermediation*, in *Wake Forest Law Review*, 2015, 50, p. 643 ss.

[3] D.W. Arner, J.N. Barberis, R.P. Buckley, *The Evolution of Fintech: A New Post-Crisis Paradigm?* in *University of Hong Kong Faculty of Law Research Paper No. 2015/047* and in *UNSW Law Research Paper No 2016/62*; H.Y. Chiu, *Regulating the Crypto Economy. Business Transformation and Financialisation,* New York, Bloomsbury Publishing Plc, 2021, p. 85 ss.; P. Chirulli, *FinTech, RegTech and SupTech: Institutional challenges to the supervisory architecture of the financial markets*, in H.Y. Chiu, G. Diepenbrock (edited by) *Routledge Handbook of Financial Technology and Law*, New York, Routledge, 2021, p. 645 ss.; Leigh-Alexandra Basha, Overview on recent developments for the legislation, regulatory and anti-money laundering US update, Trusts & Trustees, Volume 25, Issue 1, February 2019, Pages 138–148, https://doi.org/10.1093/tandt/tty173.

[4] Directive 91/308/ECC ("AMLD1") indeed set out a regulatory framework based on the three pillars that still underpin—as adequately revised and updated over time—the current EU AML legislation, and namely (i) identification (ii) record-keeping and (iii) reporting of suspicious transactions. While directive 2001/97/EC ("AMLD2") was mostly concerned with the breadth of the AML subjective and in fact it integrated the "credit and financial institutions" (the only ones subject to "AMLD1") with a much wider list of "obliged entities", Directive 2005/60/EC ("AMLD3") made quite a paradigmatic shift by, among other things, (i) expanding the goals of the AML framework to the "prevention of the use of the financial system for the purpose of money laundering and terrorist financing" ("AML/CFT") (ii) formalising the *risk-based approach* as overarching principle that guides the AML architecture of rules and checks (iii) substituting the "identification" pillar with a full-fledged "customer due diligence" obligation.

criminal activities could be laundered.[5] This was done in several ways, and namely—among other things—by progressively expanding the list of obliged entities (the recipients of the AML legislation), remoulding the obligations imposed on such obliged entities as a form of "active" cooperation rather than a "passive" contribution,[6] elaborating important principles which tried to introduce checks and balances and to tailor the AML requirements to the actual money laundering risks the obliged entity is exposed to (such as the risk-based approach or the principle of proportionality).[7]

[5] In this respect, see the recent "Basel AML index 2022", October 2022, prepared by the Basel Institute on Governance comparing the AML regulatory frameworks worldwide in an attempt to appraise their effectiveness (data on the effectiveness of AML/CFT systems is drawn from the FATF reports). The Report is available here https://index.baselgovernance.org/api/uploads/221004_Basel_AML_Index_2022_72cc668efb.pdf.

[6] Indeed, over the years the EU AML legislation has evolved in the direction of asking more compelling efforts in carrying out the obligations and discharging the requirements and checks enshrined in the AML Directives. In this respect, noticeable is the evolution of the so-called first pillar of the AML regulatory framework, which moved from "identification" to "customer due diligence" introduced by the AMLD3 and then further developed thanks to AMLD4 as amended by AMLD5. In fact, while art. 3, par. 11 AMLD1 simply imposed on obliged entities to proceed with the identification of the client, whereas art. 13, par. 1 AMLD4 sets out a quite articulated set of activities within the customer due diligence obligations (in the perspective of the active cooperation, think for example at the circumstance that CDD comprises "assessing and, as appropriate, obtaining information on the purpose and intended nature of the business relationship").

[7] The risk-based approach in the AML legislation in fact refers to the approach whereby competent authorities and obliged entities identify, assess and understand the money laundering and terrorist financing risks to which subjects of assessment are exposed and take AML/CFT measures that are proportionate to those risks. AMLD3 is the first AML directive codifying the "risk-based approach": beginning with recital 22, which outlines the basic rationale for the careful approach to modulate compliance on the basis of risk exposure, and moving on to articles 8, 9 and 13 concerning customer due diligence, the AMLD3 is studded with references to the need to take the risk of money laundering as the benchmark for implementing the AML requirements. In literature, see, *e.g.*, L. Dalla Pellegrina, D. Masciandaro, *The Risk-Based Approach in the New European Anti-Money Laundering Legislation: A Law and Economics View*, in *Review of Law & Economics*, vol. 5, no. 2, 2009, p. 940, who underline that «with the RBA [Risk-Based Approach], the discretion of the FIs [Financial Intermediaries] in designing their own AML model is complete. In this way, the social outcome of the regulation becomes clearer, that is maximizing the number of true suspicious transactions, increasing the FIs discretion in organizing the AML internal controls». See also P. Costanzo, *The risk-based approach to anti-money laundering and counter-terrorist financing in international and EU standards: What it is, what it entails*, in B. Unger e D. van der Linde (eds.), *Research Handbook on Money Laundering*, Edward Elgar, Cheltenham, 2013, p. 349; L. dalla Pellegrina, G.

Along the way of strengthening the AML legislation, one of the major drivers for change has most certainly been financial innovation lately.

There is little doubt, in fact, that the advent of new portals and platforms (with the rapid increase of clients' remote onboarding) as well as the "crypto rise" had challenged the effectiveness of the AML regulatory framework (along with raising many other questions pertaining to other pieces of law) and prompted legislators to take adequate care of such innovative technology-driven solutions.[8]

Despite policy-makers and regulators animatedly discussing the introduction of enabled-technology currencies with legal tender status (the Central Bank Digital Currencies, CBDCs), the AML legislation has not been recast to adapt to their potential use yet, and it is currently lacking any specific reference to such new form of central bank money.

Thc aim of this contribution is to examine CBDCs *vis-à-vis* the current and upcoming European AML regulatory frameworks. In this respect, the analysis will account for the recent developments of the AML legislation, which will be essential in navigating its requirements, provisions and principles and their potential application to CBDCs. It will then explore whether and how the AML legislation can intercept digital central bank money, by studying the notion of "virtual currency", "crypto-assets", "cash" and "currency" enshrined in the fourth AML directive (AMLD4), as amended by the fifth directive (AMLD5), as well as in the EC proposal

Di Maio, D. Masciandaro, M. Saraceno, *Organised crime, suspicious transaction reporting and anti-money laundering regulation*, in *Regional Studies*, 2020, 54(12), p. 1761; R.M. Axelrod, *Criminality and suspicious activity reports*, in *Journal of Financial Crime*, 2017, 24(3), p. 461; R.J. Lowe, *Anti-money laundering—The need for intelligence*, in *Journal of Financial Crime*, 2017, 24(3), p. 472; M. Pellegrini, *Anti-Money Laundering Legislation in the light of the Proposal of the Third EC Directive*, in *European Business Law Review*, 2005, p. 1181; D. Siclari, *The New Anti-Money Laundering Law. First Perspectives on the 4th European Union Directive*, London, 2016.

[8] The process of digitalisation and, more broadly, the new market dynamics that characterise the provision of financial services are causing regulators and supervisors to drastically rethink the paradigms underpinning financial law: See, *e.g.*, W. S. Frame—L. J. White, *Technological Change, Financial Innovation, and Diffusion in Banking* in A.N. Berger, P. Molyneux, J.O.S. Wilson (eds.), *The Oxford Handbook of Banking*, Oxford, p. 271; H.Y. Chiu, *The disruptive implications of FinTech—Policy themes for financial regulators*, in *Journal of Technology Law & Policy*, 2017, p. 55 ss.; G. A. Walker, *Financial Technology Law—A New Beginning and a New Future*, in *The International Lawyer*, 2017, 50(1), pp. 137–216; D. Awrey, *Complexity, Innovation and the Regulation of Modern Financial Markets*, in *Oxford Legal Studies Research Paper* No. 49/2011 and in *Harvard Business Law Review*, 2012, 2 (2), p. 235 ss.

for the AMLR. The research extends also to the standards elaborated at the international level by the FAFT.

In the light of the recent EC proposal for the DigEuro-Reg, the contribution then delves into the specific characteristic and uses of the digital form of this currency to clarify whether and how AML rules and requirements apply to it. In doing this, it will carefully distinguish between "online digital euro transactions" and "offline digital euro transactions".

Finally, the analysis focuses on how the regulatory engagement with cash (i) has been designed over time according to the EU AML Directives, and (ii) will be developing by virtue of the changes envisaged in the EC proposal for the AMLR. In the light of the ECJ case-law and considering that the proposal for an AMLR introduces a Union-wide cash payment limit of EUR 10,000, the contribution deals with the thorny topic of the potential application of cash limits to the digital euro.

2 Financial Innovation and the EU AML "Multistage" Reforms

The EU AML framework is under an unprecedented process of restructuring, mainly due to the new financial paradigms and innovative market dynamics enabled by technological advancement.[9] The tokenisation and the emergence of new technological ways to cryptographically transfer value and/or rights raised in fact general fundamental questions on the nature and legal qualification of such digital representations, first, and consequently on the applicability (and thus the effectiveness) of the existing regulatory regimes.

The debate regarded all the several compartments of EU financial markets regulation and the extension of their regulatory nets vis-à-vis crypto-assets and, most importantly, their relevant licensing regimes vis-à-vis the business activities based on such crypto-assets (*e.g.* the MiFID II and the licensing regime provided for herein), bringing EU legislators

[9] On this topic, see B. Kelly, *The Bitcoin Big bang: How Alternative Currencies Are About to Change the World*, New Jersey, John Wiley & Sons, 2015; N. Mancini, *Bitcoin: rischi e difficoltà normative*, in «*Banca, impresa, società*», 2016, I, p. 127 ss.; H. Halaburda – M. Sarvary, *Beyond Bitcoin: The Economics of Digital Currencies*, New York, Palgrave Macmillan, 2016; M. T. Chimienti, U. Kochanska, A. Pinna, *Understanding the crypto-asset phenomenon, its risks and measurement issues*, ECB *Economic Bullettin*, 2019; ECB *Crypto-Assets Task Force, Crypto-Assets: implications for financial stability, monetary policy, and payments market infrastructures, Occasional Paper Series* no. 223, 2019.

to realise that there exist "blind spots". The circumstance that certain crypto-assets and the activities based on such crypto-assets currently escape existing legislation called for a tailored regulatory strategy. As well known, this caused legislators to intervene with the ambitious "Digital Finance Package"[10] that recently culminated in the publication in the MiCAR.[11]

Not only did EU legislators realise that substantive legislation on issuance, offering, admission to trading (as well as provision of services) of certain types of crypto-assets was missing.[12] They also accounted for the need to revise AML legislation as to keep up with the new pace of digital finance.

[10] The Digital Finance Package branches out in three specific regulatory actions: (i) DORA (Regulation (EU) 2022/2554 "on digital operational resilience for the financial sector"); (ii) DLT (Regulation (EU) 2022/858 on "a pilot regime for market infrastructures based on distributed ledger technology"); and, (iii) MICA (Regulation (EU) 2023/1114 "on markets in crypto-assets"). The Package could be said to amount to the policy "reaction" to the warnings raised towards the end of 2018 by the European Securities and Markets Authority (ESMA) on the critical issues related to those tokens that do not qualify as «financial instruments» and, therefore, escaping the scope of application of the financial market law (*i.e.* MiFID) (see ESMA, The Distributed Ledger Technology Applied to Securities Markets, 2017; ESMA, Advice-Initial Coin Offerings and Crypto-Assets, 2019). For more details, see, *e.g.*, F. Annunziata, *Speak, If You Can: What Are You? An Alternative Approach to the Qualification of Tokens and Initial Coin Offerings*, in *European Company and Financial Law Review*, 2020, vol. 17, no. 2, p. 129; D. A. Zetzsche, F. Annunziata, D. W. Arner, R. P. Buckley, *The Markets in Crypto-Assets Regulation (MICA) and the EU Digital Financial Strategy*, in *EBI Working Paper Series*, 2020.

[11] Indeed, the MiCAR aims to create a legal regime capturing what escapes the scope of application of the existing financial market regulations (in particular, the MiFID2).

[12] Financial innovation is also raising problems of consistency between sector-specific pieces of legislation. It is essential in fact to adopt common definition, notions and languages that enable different regulatory areas to be properly coordinated in order to avoid loopholes, legal uncertainty and the much-feared opportunities for regulatory arbitrage. The most recent survey conducted by Thomson Reuters *Special Report. Cryptos on the rise 2022. A complex regulatory future emerges*, dated 5 April 2022 available at https://www.thomsonreuters.com/en-us/posts/wp-content/uploads/sites/20/2022/04/Cryptos-on-the-Rise-2022.pdf, shows the «*regulatory fragmentation*» surrounding crypto activities in Europe. On the general subject of regulatory arbitrage, see, *e.g.*, A. Minto, S. Prinz, M. Wulff, *A Risk Characterisation of Regulatory Arbitrage in Financial Markets* in *European Business Organisation Law Review*, 2021, p. 719.

As soon as cryptocurrencies grew in popularity, in fact, international, European and national policy makers issued a wide set of soft-law documents which expressed a common concern about the potential infiltration of economic crime through the folds of the "crypto ecosystem".[13]

The build-up of warnings issued by the European supervisory authorities led law-makers to enact Directive 2018/843/EU ("AMLD5"), which amended Directive 2015/849/EU ("AMLD4") in order to introduce, among other things, a definition of "virtual currency", along with a new list of obliged entities which has been broadened to include cryptocurrency service providers.

Article 3, par. 1, n. 18 of the AMLD5 indeed refers to "a digital representation of value that is not issued or guaranteed by a central bank or a public authority, is not necessarily attached to a legally established currency and does not possess a legal status of currency or money, but is accepted by natural or legal persons as a means of exchange and which can be transferred, stored and traded electronically".[14] This definition

[13] At the international level, the first steps in this regard have been taken by the *Financial Action Task Force* (FATF-GAFI), which, in June 2014, published a Report entitled *Virtual Currencies: Key Definitions and Potential AML/CFT Risks* in response to the emergence of virtual currencies and associated payment mechanisms aimed at providing new methods of value transfer through the Internet: specifically, the possibility of anonymous transactions through the use of decentralised systems, together with the development of non-face-to-face customer relationships, have been considered vulnerability factors in terms of the potential criminal use of virtual currencies. In June of the following year, the FATF then published a set of Guidelines concerning the money laundering and terrorist financing (ML/TF) risks associated with payment products and services based on virtual currencies (*Guidance for a Risk-Based Approach to Virtual Currencies*). Differently from the international legislator, from the very first soft regulation documents, the aim of the European legislator has been not so much to protect market stability or financial integrity (from a "macroeconomic" perspective, as emerged from the FATF documents), but to protect the individual investor. Again, in July 2014, the European Banking Authority (EBA) tried to define cryptocurrencies through an *Opinion on virtual currencies* (EBA/Op/2014/08), inviting the European legislator to take a position on the potential risks involved. This Opinion was followed by other documents and *Discussion Papers*, inviting the European Commission to include cryptocurrencies within the scope of anti-money laundering regulations (EBA/Op/2016/14; EBA/Op/2021/04), or alerting investors to risks related to them (ESMA, EBA, EIOPA *Joint Warning on Virtual Currencies*, 12 February 2018).

[14] Quite interestingly the definition of "virtual currency" enshrined in the AMLD5 has been implemented differently in some EU jurisdictions. For instance, the Italian AML legislation adopted a more detailed definition than the European one. Art. 1, par. 2, let. qq) of Legislative Decree 231/2007 (the Italian AML legislation) in fact defines virtual

is functional to frame the category of cryptocurrency service providers, which includes: (a) Virtual Asset Service Providers ("VASPs"), defined as "any natural or legal person who provides third parties, on a professional basis, with services (including online services) for the use, exchange and storage of 'virtual currencies', as well as their change from or into fiat currencies or digital assets, [...] as well as the issuance, offer, transfer, clearing and any other service functional to the acquisition, trading or intermediation in the exchange of such currencies"; and (b) custodian wallet providers, defined as any natural or legal person who provides, on a professional basis, to third parties, including online, cryptographic key custody services on behalf of its clients, for the purpose of holding, storing and transferring virtual currencies (see art. 3 AMLD5).

Beyond the updates brought by the AMLD5, however, the European anti-money laundering framework is destined to undergo a complete overhaul in the coming years, which will bring about an innovative institutional and substantive setting.

In this perspective, on 20 July 2021, the European Commission presented its proposal for the reform of the anti-money laundering and counter-terrorism system, which is articulated in a series of legislative

currency as a "digital representation of value, not issued or guaranteed by a central bank or public authority, not necessarily linked to a legal tender, used as a means of exchange for the purchase of goods and services or for investment purposes and transferred, stored and traded electronically". Indeed, Legislative Decree No. 125/2019, in amending the Italian AML legislation due to the implementation of the AMLD5 formulated the definition specifying, *inter alia*, that virtual currencies are used as a "medium of exchange *for the purchase of goods and services*" (emphasis added) or for "investment purposes". This may cast some doubts as to whether certain crypto-assets that, for example, could be limited to be used as a means of exchange for fiat currencies only come within the definition of virtual currencies for the purposes of Italian AML legislation. Since such cryptocurrencies are envisaged to be used as a means of exchange that is different from the one explicitly stated by the legislation (*i.e.*, purchase of good/service or investment), it could be argued that they escape the qualification of "virtual currency" for the purposes of Italian AML rules. However, despite the letter of the law, a broader interpretation seems to be preferred, especially in light of the goals of anti-money laundering legislation. In particular, it should be considered that: (a) the correspondent notion of virtual currency under the AMLD5 refers merely to the use of the virtual currency as a "means of exchange"; (b) Recital 10 of AMLD5 states that "the objective of this Directive is to cover all the potential uses of virtual currencies"; and (b) the illustrative report of the Italian Decree implementing AMLD5 clarifies that the notion has the aim to take not account all the possible uses of the virtual currency, also in light of the FAFT international standards.

proposals, being: (*i*) the sixth-anti-money laundering directive[15]; (*ii*) the regulation establishing a European Anti-Money Laundering and Anti-Terrorist Financing Authority (AMLA)[16]; (*iii*) the AMLR referred to before; and finally (*iv*) a revision of the 2015 regulation on funds transfers for the purpose of tracking cryptocurrency transactions.[17]

Those measures "refine the existing EU regulatory framework, *adapting it to new and emerging challenges related to technological innovation, such as virtual currencies*, the increased integration of financial flows in the single market and the global nature of terrorist organisations. These proposals will help create a much more coherent framework to facilitate compliance for operators subject to AML/CFT rules, in particular those operating across borders" (*emphasis added*, author).[18] This is echoed in recital n. 6 of the Proposal for the AMLR that quite significantly emphasises that "technology keeps evolving, offering opportunities to the private sector to develop new products and systems to exchange funds or value. While this is a positive phenomenon, it may generate new money laundering and terrorist financing risks, as criminals continuously manage to find ways to exploit vulnerabilities in order to hide and move illicit funds around the world".

The Proposal for the AMLR goes in the direction of abandoning the concept of "virtual currency" and VASPs that are today in use—rightly so—in favour of referring to the definitions of "crypto-asset" and "crypto-assets service providers" that are provided for in the MiCAR (see art. 2(1) nn. 13 and 14, respectively, of the AMLR proposal). Despite the two legislative texts pursue their own specific goals, the decision to increase their coordination and consistency in depicting the same phenomena will most certainly have positive consequences on the effectiveness of each of them.

According to art. 3, par. 1, n. 5 of the MiCAR, crypto-asset means "a digital representation of a value or of a right that is able to be transferred and stored electronically using distributed ledger technology or similar technology". As explained in recital n. 16, "any legislative act

[15] COM(2021) 423 *final*.

[16] COM(2021) 421 *final*.

[17] Regulation (UE) 2015/847.

[18] Thus, European Commission Press Release, *Beating financial crime: Commission overhauls anti-money laundering and countering the financing of terrorism rules*, 20 July 2021, available at https://ec.europa.eu/commission/presscorner/detail/it/ip_21_3690.

adopted in the field of crypto-assets should be specific and future-proof, be able to keep pace with innovation and technological developments and be founded on an incentive-based approach. The terms 'crypto-assets' and 'distributed ledger technology' should therefore be defined as widely as possible to capture all types of crypto-assets that currently fall outside the scope of Union legislative acts on financial services. Any legislative act adopted in the field of crypto-assets should also contribute to the objective of combating money laundering and terrorist financing. For that reason, entities offering services falling within the scope of this Regulation should also comply with applicable anti-money laundering and counter-terrorist financing rules of the Union, which integrate international standards".

The final text of the MiCAR confirms how important the dialogue between this piece of legislation and the AMLR is,[19] without ending up

[19] The tight relationship between the MiCAR and the AML regulatory framework is confirmed by the fact that in the MiCAR the term "anti-money laundering" is repeated 38 (!) times. More than that, it is worth noticing that relevant provisions—from a substantive point of view—contain important references to AML legislation. For example, Article 60 of MiCA on the «Provision of crypto-asset services by certain financial entities» provides that a regulated entity (e.g., a credit institution, an investment firm, ...) may offer crypto-asset services if it notifies the competent authority of its home Member State with a specific set of information (see par. 1 and 7). Among the relevant pieces of information to be provided, par. 7 (i) refers to "a description of the internal control mechanisms, policies and procedures to ensure compliance with the provisions of national law transposing Directive (EU) 2015/849; (ii) the risk assessment framework for the management of money laundering and terrorist financing risks". In parallel, for the application for authorisation as a crypto-asset service provider art. 62(2)(i) requires that: "the application referred to in paragraph 1 shall contain [...] a description of the applicant crypto-asset service provider's internal control mechanisms, policies and procedures to identify, assess and manage risks, including money laundering and terrorist financing risks". From the opposite angle, art. 64(1)(f) provides that "Competent authorities shall withdraw the authorisation of a crypto-asset service provider if the crypto-asset service provider [...] fails to have in place effective systems, procedures and arrangements to detect and prevent money laundering and terrorist financing in accordance with Directive (EU) 2015/849". It seems quite interesting to note that the AML organisational requirements—that are provided for in the IV AML directive at art. 8—are overtly mentioned in the MiCAR as requirements necessary to access the activity or licensing requirements. Indeed, even without this explicit reference made by MiCAR, it goes without saying that the CASPs and the regulated entities that carry out crypto-asset's services are obliged to implement the internal controls, process and procedures to manage AML risk according to the relevant AML rules. Furthermore, the Proposal for an AML regulation seems to confirm this trend that emphasises the relevance of the organisational measures vis-à-vis AML risk. The Proposal in fact requires obliged entities to carry out a "stricter" risk assessment and put

endorsing the attempt of the Parliament to integrate MiCAR's goals also with "measures to prevent the misuse of crypto-assets for illicit purposes and to protect the internal market from the risks relating to money laundering, terrorist financing and other criminal activities".[20]

Despite the overhaul of the AML regulatory framework is predominantly justified by the technology-enabled opportunities to develop new products and systems to exchange funds or value,[21] no reference is currently made to CBDCs and to whether and how the AML requirements should apply to the digital central bank money.

3 CBDCs vis-à-vis the Current and Upcoming EU AML Frameworks and the FATF Standards

There is currently no single definition of what a CBDC is. In fact, in exploring around the world the different CBDC initiatives and Central Banks' white papers, one realises that there is not a unique type of CBDCs

in place proportionate risk management measures (e.g., internal controls), which have to account for the "new products and systems to exchange funds or value" (see art. 8 in conjunction with recitals nn. 6 and 21).

[20] See European Parliament, Report on the proposal for a regulation of the European Parliament and of the Council on markets in crypto-assets and amending Directive (EU) 2019/1937 (COM(2020)0593 – C9-0306/2020 – 2020/0265(COD)) Committee on Economic and Monetary Affairs, 17 March 2022. Despite the relevance of making an overall consistent "regulatory framework" that embraces all aspects pertaining to the crypto ecosystem, the choice to intervene at the level of the MiCAR's goals and objectives cast some serious doubts. In fact, there exists already a piece of law projected at preventing money laundering (the current AMLD4 and the upcoming AML regulation) which should not be intersected by any other piece of legislation. Legal certainty calls for clear-cut regulatory areas and regulatory goals that are incorporated in *ad hoc* regulatory frameworks. Overlapping the objectives of the AML directive and the MiCAR might have caused interpretative uncertainties and ultimately threatened the effectiveness of the overall regulatory framework surrounding cryptos.

[21] See recital n. 6 of the Proposal for an AML regulation. According to A. Schmidt, Virtual assets: compelling a new anti-money laundering and counter-terrorism financing regulatory model, in International Journal of Law and Information Technology, Volume 29, Issue 4, Winter 2021, Pages 332–363, https://doi.org/10.1093/ijlit/eaac001, virtual assets' potential as a new way to exchange value presents unique Anti-Money Laundering and Counter-Terrorism Financing (AML/CTF) risks that have been overlooked by global regulation in the past.

but different designs, solutions and forms which could vary from each other quite drastically.[22]

According to Committee on Payments and Market Infrastructures and Markets Committee, a central bank digital currency (CBDC) amounts to a "digital form of central bank money that is different from balances in traditional reserve or settlement accounts" and it is possible to distinguish three types of CBDC that vary depending on who has access and on the technology used: (a) digital central bank tokens that can be used by financial institutions (*e.g.* for interbank and securities settlements); (b) accounts at the central bank for the general public; and (c) digital "cash" that could be used by the general public in retail payments.[23]

Yet, notwithstanding such differences, all CBDCs' designs possess two key common and defining features that single them out from any other

[22] Norges Bank, Central Bank Digital Currencies, 1, 2021, 5; S. Allen, et al. Design choices for central bank digital currency: Policy and technical considerations, No. 27634, National Bureau of Economic Research, 2020, 11; R.P. Buckley, M. Trzecinski, Central Bank Digital Currencies and the global financial system: the dollar dethroned?, in Capital Markets Law Journal, Volume 18, Issue 2, April 2023, Pages 137–171, https://doi.org/10.1093/cmlj/kmad007

[23] A wholesale CBDC is not distributed to the public but only identified intermediaries to streamline their reciprocal settlement process. A retail CBDC could be assimilated to a traditional fiat currency in that it is distributed directly to all the participants of the market to be used in day-to-day transactions. A direct CBDC is one that is directly distributed by the Central Bank to its final users, whereas an indirect CBDC (which is the design embraced by the "digital euro", as further specified in the next paragraphs) an intermediate layer is introduced (while the issuance and the maintenance of the underlying network is still in the hands of the Central Bank, all user facing activities are performed by authorised intermediaries). For an overview of the characteristics of the three models, see, *e.g.*, N. Pocher, A. Veneris, Privacy and transparency in cbdcs: A regulation-by-design aml/cft scheme, in IEEE Transactions on Network and Service Management, 2021, 1; R. Auer, R. Böhme, Central bank digital currency: the quest for minimally invasive technology, in BIS Working Papers, No 948, 08 June 2021, 10; M. Klein, J. Gross, P. Sandner, The digital euro and the role of DLT for central bank digital currencies, 11; The White House, Technical evaluation for a U.S. Central Bank digital currency system, Washington, 2022; A. Kosse, I. Mattei, Making headway – Results on the 2022 BIS survey on central bank digital currencies and crypto, BIS Papers, No 136, July 2023.

type of digital asset: (i) they are issued by a central bank, as their liability,[24] and (ii) they serve as a legal tender within a defined jurisdiction.[25]

Despite the lively policy debate surrounding CBDCs and their potential uses, there is currently no specific reference to digital central bank money in the European AML regulatory framework.

The definition of "virtual currency"—quite obviously—is designed to capture different phenomena. Indeed, article 3 (1)(18) of AMLD4, as amended by AMLD5, refers to "a digital representation of value that is not issued or guaranteed by a central bank or a public authority, is not necessarily attached to a legally established currency and does not possess a legal status of currency or money, but is accepted by natural or legal persons as a means of exchange and which can be transferred, stored and traded electronically". The wording of art. 3 AMLD4 stresses out that "virtual currency" is a concept different from a digital asset (i) issued/guaranteed by a central bank and (ii) possessing a legal status of currency or money.

The same interpretation holds with reference to the upcoming AML regulatory framework and the legal category of "crypto-assets": indeed, the Proposal for the AMLR does not introduce its own definition of "crypto-asset", as previously noted, but it rather builds on the one enshrined in the MiCAR[26], which is formulated as widely as possible to capture all types of crypto-assets. Even though the MiCAR definition of "crypto-asset" is phrased much more broadly (vaguely, even) as compared to that of "virtual currency" of the AMLD4—for our purposes, *e.g.*, it lacks any explicit exclusion of digital assets issued by central banks from

[24] Bank for International Settlements, Central Bank Digital Currencies: system designs and interoperability, Basel, 2021, 4; Cheng-Yun Tsang, Ping-Kuei Chen, Policy responses to cross-border central bank digital currencies—assessing the transborder effects of digital yuan, in Capital Markets Law Journal, Volume 17, Issue 2, April 2022, Pages 237–261, https://doi.org/10.1093/cmlj/kmac004

[25] See the definition provided by the International Monetary Fund, "CBDC is a new form of money, issued digitally by the central bank and intended to serve as legal tender" in IMF Staff Discussion Note, Casting Light on Central Bank Digital Currencies, 2018; see also the definition provided by the US Federal Reserve, "CBDC is defined as a digital liability of the Federal Reserve that is widely available to the general public" in Federal Reserve, Money and Payments: The U.S. Dollar in the Age of Digital Transformation, 2022

[26] "A digital representation of a value or of a right that is able to be transferred and stored electronically using distributed ledger technology or similar technology" (see art. 3, par. 1, n. 5 of the MICA regulation).

its scope—it casts no doubt that CBDCs do not come within the notion of crypto-asset. This conclusion is corroborated by a recent amendment of the MiCAR, which, in the final version, introduced a reference to CBDCs in recital n. 13, where it states that "digital assets issued by central banks acting in their monetary authority capacity, including central bank money in digital form, or crypto-assets issued by other public authorities, including central, regional and local administrations, should not be subject to the Union framework for markets in crypto-assets. Nor should related services provided by such central banks when acting in their monetary authority capacity or other public authorities be subject to that Union framework". Therefore, this recital clarifies—should this ever be necessary!—that CBDCs do not come within the scope of MiCAR.

The fact that CBDCs are neither "virtual currencies" (today) nor "crypto assets" (tomorrow) for the purposes of the AML legislation, does not entail, in turn, that central bank digital currencies completely escape the AML regulatory framework.

Yet, the entry point of analysis should be the one emphasising the functional and substantial features as *currency* that characterise the digital assets issued by central banks. In other words, CBDCs are to be analysed keeping in mind their two key features as: (i) a claim towards the issuing central bank, and (ii) legal tender.

In this perspective, the FAFT, while confirming that a virtual asset "is a digital representation of value that can be digitally traded, or transferred, and can be used for payment or investment purposes. *Virtual assets do not include digital representations of fiat currencies*, securities and other financial assets that are already covered elsewhere in the FATF Recommendations" (emphasis added)[27]; it also pointed out (back in 2020) that the FATF's understanding of the ML/TF vulnerabilities of CBDCs is less clear than virtual assets, with their design at earlier stages and due to the fact that the money laundering risk associated with CBDCs will indeed differ depending on their actual design[28].

[27] FATF, *International Standards on Combating Money Laundering and the Financing of Terrorism & Proliferation*, Paris, February 2023.

[28] FATF, *FATF Report to the G20 Finance Ministers and Central Bank Governors on so-called Stablecoins*, June 2020, par. 90 and 91. In this perspective, "CBDCs could present greater ML/TF risks than cash. CBDCs could be made available to be used by the general public in retail payments or as accounts and, in theory, allow for anonymous peer-to-peer trans-actions. In this scenario, the CBDC would be acting as an instrument with the

The variable design of CBDCs calls for a proper application of the risk-based approach[29], and in fact jurisdictions are required to identify AML/CTF risks relating to new technologies and apply appropriate measures to mitigate those risks[30].

Despite the uncertainties surrounding the precise design of CBDCs, the FAFT fixes an important yardstick, in that it emphasises how "financial institutions, designated non-financial businesses and professions and VASPs that deal in the CBDC will have the same AML/CFT obligations *as they do with fiat currencies or cash*. A customer transacting using a CBDC will have the same customer due diligence obligations as if it were an electronic transaction using *fiat currency*"[31].

Thus, the AML regulatory treatment of CBDCs must be developed by emphasising that they amount to a new *form* (a technology-enabled digital form) of central bank money with legal tender which integrates the physical one already in use. Nonetheless, these two forms of currency (digital and physical) present differences in their *use* that justify (or may justify) a different AML approach.

In other words, what matters for AML purposes is *how* the CBDC allows financial users to make transactions. The way such token functions as a means of exchange. This means that the digital currency could be subject to different AML rules depending on the mechanics of their use

liquidity and anonymity of cash, but without the limitations on portability that come with physical cash. A point of comparison might be highly liquid bearer bonds, as these would be potentially high-value bearer instruments" (par. 91).

[29] S.L. Schwarcz, *Regulating Digital Currencies: Towards an Analytical Framework*, in *Boston University Law Review*, 2022, Vol. 102:1037, p. 1059. The Author argues that CBDCs could either present greater risk than cash (*e.g.*, CBDCs could be made available to be used by the general public in retail payments or as accounts and, in theory, allow for anonymous peer-to-peer transactions. In this scenario, the CBDC would be acting as an instrument with the liquidity and anonymity of cash, but without the limitations on portability that come with physical cash) or less risks than cash (for instance, a wholesale CBDC that can only be used among licensed financial institutions for interbank settlement may have lower risks than a retail instrument).

[30] See FATF Recommendation n. 1 and 15, FATF, *International Standards on Combating Money Laundering and the Financing of Terrorism & Proliferation*, Paris, February 2023.

[31] FATF, *FATF Report to the G20 Finance Ministers and Central Bank Governors on so-called Stablecoins*, June 2020, par. 94; see also U.S. Department of the Treasury, *Framework for International Engagement on Digital Assets, July 2022*: "FATF standards apply to CBDCs similar to any other form of fiat currency issued by a central bank".

(*e.g.*, as we will discuss in the next paragraph, the online digital euro transaction versus the offline digital euro transactions) and on whether or not, for instance, transactions between payer and payee are settled with the operational intervention by a third party (an intermediary).

4 The Proposal for a Regulation on the Establishment of the Digital Euro

4.1 Introductory Remarks

On 6 June 2023 the European Commission published the so-called Digital Euro Package, comprising a "Proposal for a regulation of the European Parliament and of the Council on the establishment of the digital euro" (COM(2023) 369 final) (DigEuro-Reg), a Proposal of the European Commission of 28 June 2023 for a Regulation of the European Parliament and of the Council on the legal tender of euro banknotes and coins, (COM(2023) 364 final) (Legal Tender-Reg) and a "Proposal for a Regulation on the provision of digital euro services by payment services providers incorporated in Member States whose currency is not the euro" (COM(2023) 368 final), which aim at setting out the legal framework for a possible digital euro as a complement to euro banknotes and coins. The Legal Tender-Reg is concerned with the definition of legal tender, in the perspective of ensuring legal certainty and consistency between its physical and digital forms, without prejudice to the differences between these two forms of the euro[32].

These three legislative measures integrate the set of policies that the EU policy-makers recently adopted in order to keep up with the new challenges associated with digitalisation, namely—among others—the "digital finance package" (the well-known "MiCAR", "DLT Pilot" and "DORA" package) and the "payment package" (the proposals for the Payment

[32] This Proposal is based and elaborates on the EU Court of Justice ruling from 2021: see judgment of 26 January 2021 in Joined Cases C-422/19 and C-423/19, *Hessischer Rundfunk*, EU:C:2021:63 point 46. See also European Commission, Remarks by Executive Vice-President Dombrovskis and Commissioners Gentiloni and McGuinness on the digital euro and the legal tender of euro banknotes and coins, Brussels, 28 June 2023.

Service Directive 3 ("PSD3") along with a brand-new Payment Services Regulation ("PSR")[33]).

In the context of the Digital Finance and Retail Payment Strategies, the European Commission in fact had stressed out how a retail CBDC (*i.e.*, the digital euro) could act as a "catalyst for innovation in payments, finance and commerce in the context of ongoing efforts to reduce the fragmentation of the Union retail payments market"[34].

In this perspective, the digital euro package addresses the design and functioning of a retail CBDC, laying down a legal framework for establishing a digital form of the euro with the status of legal tender[35]. Departing from a "silo-thinking" approach, the proposal embraces a perspective that emphasises the functioning of the digital euro vis-à-vis the other existing (public and private) means of payment, therefore considering the interaction between physical and digital forms of legal tender (cash and coins and digital euro, respectively), on the one hand, and central bank money and private digital means of payment, on the other. Indeed, in a world where a large variety of private digital means of payment are progressively taking over banknotes and coins—which represent the only current forms of central bank money with legal tender available to the general public—this could entail material risks connected to the sound functioning of the financial and monetary system[36]. The

[33] Proposal for a Directive on payment services and electronic money services in the internal market—COM/2023/366 final and proposal for a Regulation on payment services in the internal market—COM/2023/367 final, respectively.

[34] Communication from the Commission to the European Parliament, the Council and the Committee of the Regions on a Digital Finance Strategy for the EU (COM/2020/591 final). On the benefits of the digital euro, see also European Parliament's resolution of 16 February 2022 on the European Central Bank—annual report 20212021/2063(INI); Council of the European Union, Council conclusions on achieving the EU's economic and financial strategic autonomy in an open economy: one year after the Commission's Communication, Brussels, 29 March 2022, available at https://data.consilium.europa.eu/doc/document/ST-6301-2022-INIT/en/pdf; European Central Bank, Report on a digital euro, October 2020.

[35] "With a view to adapting the euro to technological changes and to ensuring its use as a single currency", this Proposal for a regulation of the European Parliament and of the Council on the establishment of the digital euro "establishes the digital euro and lays down rules concerning in particular its legal tender status, distribution, use, and essential technical features" (see art. 1).

[36] The recent ECB SPACE (*Study on the Payment Attitudes of Consumers in the Euro area*) showed that four Member States had reported a decline in cash acceptance of 5%

lack of a widely available and usable form of central bank money technologically adapted to the digital age could diminish trust towards commercial bank money, and ultimately towards the euro itself. Trust towards commercial bank money relies on the possibility of depositors to convert at par their deposits into central bank money with legal tender, which currently is only available in the form of cash. Lacking a form of a central bank money that can be used in the digital economy and is convertible at par with commercial bank deposits may undermine the monetary anchor role of central bank money, weakening financial stability and monetary sovereignty in the EU (see recitals nn. 3, 4 and 5 of the Proposal for the DigEuro-Reg).

The problem could be compounded should stablecoins gain traction and become a significant additional means to transfer value and transact among parties. Now that the MiCAR has been adopted, setting out, inter alia, harmonised rules for asset-referenced tokens (ARTs) and electronic money tokens (EMTs) issuance and offering to the public, those issues are in fact far from being merely speculative. The proposal for the DigEuro-Reg does not enter into the merits of the delicate interaction between digital euro and crypto-assets—at this stage—but it nonetheless accounts for their existence and the fact that they are an important component of the overall picture.

As anticipated, the proposal for the DigEuro-Reg aims at introducing the digital euro as a new form of central bank money (a digital form) that integrates the current physical form (euro banknotes and coins, the euro cash) in order to widen the options at disposal of financial users[37]. The digital euro thus is not supposed to replace the physical forms of the single currency, but it rather aims to complement euro banknotes and coins.

The digital euro poses therefore legal and regulatory issues on how a digital form of central bank money that possesses the legal tender status interacts with the wider payment ecosystem and finance at large.

(Belgium, Malta, Ireland, Estonia), and two reported a decline of 9% (Latvia and Finland). A Dutch National Bank study recently expressed concern about cash acceptance becoming too low in certain sectors, such as pharmacies (where 12% refuse cash).

[37] In fact, according to art. 128, par. 1 of the Treaty on the Functioning of the European Union and Article 10 and 11 of Council Regulation (EC) No 974/98 on the introduction of the euro, as of today, euro banknotes and coins are the only means of payment that have the status of legal tender.

This also entails that—for the coherent application of the provisions concerning payment services—the EU legislation on payment services and electronic money services needs to be adequately amended as to extend its application to the digital euro.

In this respect, art. 5, par. 3, provides that "in accordance with Article 4(25) of Directive (EU) 2015/2366 of the European Parliament and of the Council, of 25 November 2015, on payment services in the internal market, as replaced by Directive [Proposal for a Directive on payment services and electronic money services in the internal market—COM/2023/366 final] and [proposal for a Regulation on payment services in the internal market—COM/2023/367 final], the provisions of that Directive shall apply to digital euro payment transactions".

Indeed, the Proposal for a Directive on payment services and electronic money services in the internal market—COM/2023/366 final (the "PSD3") extends the definition of funds to central bank money issued for retail use, which includes central bank digital currencies[38]. While the current notion of funds (pursuant to art. 4, par. 1, n. 25 of the PSD2) refers to "banknotes and coins, scriptural money or electronic money as defined in point (2) of Article 2 of Directive 2009/110/EC", art. 2, par. 1, n. 23 of the PSD3 proposal provides that "funds" means "central bank money issued for retail use, scriptural money and electronic money".

Among other things, this change is instrumental to entitle payment service providers ("PSPs", *e.g.*, credit institutions, payment institutions and electronic money institutions) distribute the digital euro to financial users[39]. Not only will PSPs be executing account management functions

[38] Recital n. 15 of the Proposal for a regulation on a digital euro: "The definition of funds should cover all forms of central bank money issued for retail use, including banknotes and coins, and any possible future central bank digital currency, electronic money and commercial bank money. Central bank money issued for use between the central bank and commercial banks, *i.e.*, for wholesale use, should not be covered".

[39] In particular, art. 13 and 14 of the proposal for a regulation on a digital euro clarifies that PSPs may provide digital euro payment services, including additional digital euro payment services, in addition to basic digital euro payment services thanks to (and in accordance with) the authorisation they have been granted to provide payment services under PSD2, without the need to obtain an additional authorisation from their competent authorities to provide digital euro payment services. For the purpose of distributing the digital euro, payment service providers need to enter into a contractual relationship with digital euro users. The circumstance that PSPs, and not the Eurosystem directly, have a contractual account management relationship with financial users is without prejudice to the fact that the digital euro would remain a direct claim towards the Eurosystem.

and operations (for instance opening and closing digital euro accounts[40], providing front-end solutions, processing payment transactions), but they also will be involved—as further examined in the next paragraph—in carrying out the AML obligations.

4.2 *Digital Euro and AML Requirements*

The revolutionary nature of the Proposal for the DigEuro-Reg and its potential effects on the entire financial ecosystem raise plenty of questions regarding its consistency with existing regimes in the policy areas surrounding and intersecting this proposal. Within the vast and articulated set of such relevant regulatory frameworks affected by its entry into force, the coordination with AML legislation amounts most certainly to a high a priority in the policy agenda[41].

Art 5, par. 5 of the Proposal for the DigEuro-Reg is in fact concerned with the application of AML legislation. In this regard, it explicitly states that "without prejudice to Article 37 of this Regulation, Directive (EU) 2015/849 of the European Parliament and of the Council, of 20 May 2015, on the prevention of the use of the financial system for the purposes of money laundering or terrorist financing and Regulation (EU) 2015/847 of the European Parliament and of the Council of 20 May 2015 on information accompanying transfers of funds shall apply to digital euro payment transactions".

Setting aside the special regime designed by art. 37 (which will be analysed later), it seems—at least from a strictly literal interpretation—that *any* digital euro payment transaction—which, according to art. 2, par. 1,

[40] According to art. 2, par. 1, n. 5, digital euro payment account "means an account held by one or more digital euro users with a payment service provider to access digital euro recorded in the digital euro settlement infrastructure or in an offline digital euro device and to initiate or receive digital euro payment transactions, whether offline or online, and irrespective of technology and data structure".

[41] This is demonstrated, for example, by the great attention paid to AML implications in the Commission Staff Working Document, Impact Assessment Report accompanying the documents "Proposal for a Regulation of the European Parliament and of the Council on the establishment of the digital euro" and "Proposal for a Regulation of the European Parliament and of the Council on the provision of digital euro services by payment services providers incorporated in Member States whose currency is not the euro and amending Regulation (EU) 2021/1230 of the European Parliament and the Council" and "Proposal for a Regulation of the European Parliament and of the Council on the legal tender of euro banknotes and coins", Brussels, SWD(2023) 233 final.

n. 3 means "an act, initiated by a payer or on his or her behalf, or by the payee, of placing, transferring or withdrawing digital euro, irrespective of any underlying obligations between the payer and the payee"—is subject, as a general principle, to the AMLD4 (Directive (EU) 2015/849) and the so-called travel rule (Regulation (EU) 2015/847). Nonetheless, such provision is worth being further examined.

Despite art. 5 generally referring to "digital euro payment transactions" as any transaction initiated by (i) the payer, (ii) the payment service provider (on behalf of the payer) or (iii) the payee in order to place, transfer or withdraw digital euro, it is necessary to explore further *what* triggers the application of the AML regulatory framework and *how* such framework applies to digital euro payment transactions.

The entry point of analysis should disentangle the two subsets of the general category the "digital euro payment transactions" is composed of, and namely (i) "online digital euro payment transaction"[42] and (ii) "offline digital euro payment transaction"[43].

Such distinction is indeed essential for the correct application of the AML framework, especially in the light of the risk-based approach and proportionality principle that underpin such regulatory area.

In fact, while the settlement of the online digital euro (*i.e.* validation and recording of the transaction) will be made under the control of the Eurosystem, the settlement of the offline digital euro would rely on local storage (secure hardware) where no third party would be involved, thus approximating the former to private electronic payments and the latter to cash transactions (along with their higher level of privacy).

The different nature (and the respective different AML risk) associated with one and the other is reflected in recitals 78, 79 and 80 of the proposal, where it is illustrated that "[...] to ensure an effective application of AML/CFT requirements to the digital euro, this Regulation should provide that *online* digital euro payment transactions are subject

[42] Online digital euro payment transaction "means a digital euro payment transaction where the settlement takes place in the digital euro settlement infrastructure", that is the settlement infrastructure of the digital euro adopted by the Eurosystem (see art. 2, par. 1, n. 14).

[43] Offline digital euro payment transaction "means a digital euro payment transaction, made in physical proximity, where authorisation and settlement take place in the local storage devices of both payer and payee" (see art. 2, par. 1, n. 15).

to AML/CFT requirements laid down in Directive (EU) 2015/849" (*emphasis added*, author) (recital n. 78).

The dividing line between "online" and "offline" euro payment transactions for the purposes of the AML provisions is then confirmed in recital 80, which emphasises how the online ones "could present *greater AML/ CFT risks than cash* as they would be acting as an instrument whose liquidity is similar to that of cash but without the limitations on portability that are implicit in cash. It should therefore be laid down that an *online* digital euro payment transaction is to be subject to Directive (EU) 2015/849 of the European Parliament and of the Council, and Regulation (EU) 2015/847 of the European Parliament and of the Council" (*emphasis added*, author).

Unlike art. 5, those recitals seem to take a stance that confines the application of the AML rules to online digital euro payment transactions only. The puzzle is then ultimately complicated by art. 37 of the Proposal (which is the one and only provision of Chapter IX dedicated to "Anti-Money Laundering"). This provision in fact addresses the "anti-money laundering rules applying to offline digital euro payment transactions", thus, already by its name, in stark contradiction with the presumed limitation that comes with the mentioned recitals n. 78 and 80.

In the context of such conundrum, it is worth bearing in mind that "online" and "offline" transactions refer but to two different *uses* of the digital euro. On the one hand, the offline use has more cash-like functionalities, since it allows transactions to take place without the need of an intermediary to validate the transaction; it amounts consequently to a bearer instrument (*i.e.* peer-to-peer validated), which could be made available only by means of specific user devices (*e.g.* smartphone or cards) and would work without internet connectivity. On the other hand, the online use, on the contrary, requires transactions be validated by third-party intermediaries.

Consequently, for both offline (bearer based) and an online use (account based), therefore, AML requirements apply. Yet, the application of AML rules reflects the peculiarities of one use or the other.

In separating online and offline uses of the digital euro, it is possible to conclude that:

(i) Online euro payment transactions

The analysis of all the Proposal's provisions concerning AML (art. 5, par. 5 and art. 37), read in conjunction with recitals 78, 79 and 80, and along with the features and characteristics of those type of transactions bring easily to affirm that the AML requirements and obligations extend to such use[44].

Since, in this type of setting, transactions between payer and payee are settled online and with the operational intervention by the payments services provider (PSP), such third party would be in the position (and under the obligation!) to conduct checks and carry out the obligations enshrined in the AML framework. This means that PSPs will act as "obliged entities" within the meaning of the AMLD4 and would be responsible for performing the appropriate level of customer due diligence ("CDD"), reporting suspicious transactions, storing and processing of personal data of users for AML purposes and the sharing of information by competent authorities according to the principles and provisions of the AMLD4[45].

Like private electronic payments, PSPs will therefore apply CDD measures and obligations regarding online digital euro transactions on a risk-sensitive basis, when establishing a business relationship, when carrying out an occasional transaction or when there is suspicion of money laundering as set out in art. 11, 12 and 13 AMLD4[46].

[44] When used online, the digital euro, which can be transferred without payer and payee meeting in person, carries higher AML risks than cash (which is more difficult to carry in large quantity), and should therefore be subject to the same level of monitoring like other private electronic means of payment, while including the possibility for harmonised simplified due diligence for onboarding and online low value transactions. This differentiated approach would also be effective in supporting state-of-the-art payment solutions, by allowing the sharing of user's data for online transactions in compliance with GDPR and PSD2 requirements.

[45] On the pivotal role that supervised intermediaries—which are the natural candidates for distributing a digital euro—could play to manage the onboarding process, see ECB Report on the digital euro, October 2020, available at https://www.ecb.europa.eu/pub/pdf/other/Report_on_a_digital_euro~4d7268b458.en.pdf.

[46] Irrespective of the use of the digital euro (either "online" or "offline"), it is also important to recall when the AML requirements are triggered. For the customer due diligence, according to art. 11 AMLD4 obliged entities apply this obligation (a) when establishing a business relationship; (b) when carrying out an occasional transaction that: (i) amounts to EUR 15,000 or more, whether that transaction is carried out in a single operation or in several operations which appear to be linked; or (ii) constitutes a transfer of funds, as defined in point (9) of Article 3 of Regulation (EU) 2015/847 of the European Parliament and of the Council (30), exceeding EUR 1000; (c) in the case of persons trading in goods, when carrying out occasional transactions in cash amounting to EUR 10,000 or more, whether the transaction is carried out in a single operation or

In line with the general principles underpinning AML legislation (the risk-based approach underpinning the AML framework), obliged entities will be required to perform a risk assessment and adapt the AML obligations to the level of AML risks they will be exposed to, with the consequence that the extent of the monitoring of transaction data collected on clients would have to be adjusted on a case-by-case basis[47].

(ii) Offline euro payment transactions
As highlighted, offline digital euro payments pertain to transactions that are settled offline between payer and payee in physical proximity. Offline functionality would provide users with private transactions and holdings,

in several operations which appear to be linked; (d) for providers of gambling services, upon the collection of winnings, the wagering of a stake, or both, when carrying out transactions amounting to EUR 2,000 or more, whether the transaction is carried out in a single operation or in several operations which appear to be linked; (e) when there is a suspicion of money laundering or terrorist financing, regardless of any derogation, exemption or threshold; (f) when there are doubts about the veracity or adequacy of previously obtained customer identification data is triggered (i)(ii)(iii), the reporting of suspicious transaction is rather based on a different premises. Against this backdrop, the most relevant cases for the application of the CDD seem the circumstance business relationship is established between the financial user and the PSP (by means of the contractual account management relationship that empowers and mandates the intermediary to carry out digital euro payment transaction on behalf of the client/end user) and the possible occasional transaction (in this case, keeping in mind the proposed amendment of the notion of "funds" in order to incorporate also the "digital euro", as we discussed above). Regarding the reporting of suspicious transaction, according to art. 33 Member States shall require obliged entities to promptly inform the FIU when they know, suspect or have reasonable grounds to suspect that funds, regardless of the amount involved, are the proceeds of criminal activity or are related to terrorist financing.

[47] This may include the possibility to apply simplified due diligence, reducing the information accompanying certain digital euro transactions below a threshold, where justified by a risk assessment as laid down in the AML package adopted in July 2021. In this perspective, it is quite interesting that recital 79 states that "to facilitate the widespread uptake of the digital euro, it is essential that prospective digital euro users can easily access digital euro payment services provided by payment services providers in a harmonised manner across the euro area. It is therefore appropriate, without any prejudice to the risk approach underpinning the AML-package, for the anti-money laundering authority of the Union ('AMLA') to address the opening of digital euro payment accounts in its Regulatory Technical Standards on customer due diligence. For low-risk transactions or business relationships, AMLA should identify relevant simplified due diligence measures that payment services providers should apply. AMLA should prioritize the development of these Regulatory Technical Standards".

as transactions would be person-to-person and would not require an intermediary[48]. Consequently—unlike what recitals n. 78, 79 and 80 could make the reader believe—the offline use of CBDC remains subject to the AML regime, but with the necessary regulatory adjustments that the offline use requires.

In this perspective, art. 37 of the Proposal (which is the one and only provision of the Chapter IX dedicated to "Anti-Money Laundering") provides in fact for a risk-adjusted regulatory framework for offline digital euro payment transactions. After having clarified in par. 2 that, in case of offline digital euro payment transactions, the European Central Bank, the national central banks and PSPs will not retain transaction data, par. 2 states that PSPs will only be accessing "funding" and "defunding" data[49]—in accordance with the record-retention and data protection principles enshrined in art. 40 of the AMLD4—which should be transmitted, upon request, to Financial Intelligence Units and other competent authorities when users are suspected of money laundering or terrorist financing (see art. 37, par. 3).

[48] Offline digital euro transaction present cash-like features (offline functionality, peer-to-peer validation of transactions and high level of privacy), which seem quite appreciated by the potential digital euro users. Citizens in fact expressed clear preference for high level of privacy in both the ECB's and Commission's consultations. Indeed, the targeted consultation has shown that EU citizens are in favour of all features that enhance user privacy—with the ability to hide the identity of a payer and payee proving to be the most popular feature: see the survey conducted by the ECB and available in the Impact Assessment attached to the "digital euro package". According to ECB public consultation, "when confronted with a specific choice between an offline digital euro focused on privacy, an online one with innovative features and additional services, and a combination of the two, citizen respondents generally opt for an offline solution focused on privacy, while professional respondents consider a hybrid approach more appealing".

[49] Pursuant to art. 2, par. 1, n. 11 and 12 respectively funding means "the process whereby a digital euro user acquires digital euros, in exchange for either cash or other funds, creating a direct liability of the European Central Bank or a national central bank towards that digital euro user", and defunding means "the process whereby a digital euro user exchanges digital euro with cash or other funds". For offline digital euro payments, Payment service providers will only access funding and defunding data related inter alia to the identity of the user and the amount funded and defunded, similar to personal data processed by PSPs when users deposit or withdraw cash. More precisely, for the purposes of art. 37, par 3, the funding and defunding data means the following: (a) the amount funded or defunded; (b) the identifier of the local storage device for offline digital euro payment; (c) the date and hour of the funding and defunding transaction; (d) the accounts numbers used for funding and defunding.

Due to the peculiar way by which the digital euro is used, in case of offline transactions, AML requirements are thus to be adapted (by means of this special provision of art. 37) and applied with no operational intervention of PSPs.

Indeed, unlike obligations like customer due diligence and reporting of suspicious transactions that are known as so-called active cooperation activities (in the light of the efforts that are required to obliged entities, as private parties, as to pursue the public policies objectives underpinning AML legislation), in this case PSPs have—if any!—a very limited contribution to the potential detection of money laundering phenomena. In fact, not only does art. 37 limit the data to be collected and retained to the "funding and "defunding", but it also requires PSPs to share such data only in case the competent authorities and Financial Intelligence Unit so require.

In the light of the above, and considering that this provision, most likely, should be regarded as an exception to the general AML principles, it can be said that art. 37 amounts to the "gateway" for the ad hoc regulatory treatment of offline digital euro transactions.

Considering the characteristics and specific AML risks associated with offline digital euro payment transactions, art. 37, par. 5 empowers the European Commission to adopt implementing acts setting offline digital euro payment transaction limits and holding limits. In setting such limits, the Commission should keep in mind the trade-off between preventing money laundering and terrorist financing and allowing individuals to freely use any means of payment.[50].

The possibility of introducing transaction limits raises some questions, in particular in connection with the limits that Member States have introduced (or that the EU is introducing by virtue of the AML package of

[50] Pursuant to art. 37, par. 6 "the Commission, when drawing up the implementing acts referred to in paragraph 5, shall take into account in particular the following: (a) an assessment of the money laundering and terrorist financing threats, vulnerabilities and risks of the digital euro when funding and defunding their payment instrument; (b) relevant recommendations and reports drawn up by international organisations and standard setters with competence in the field of preventing money laundering and combating terrorist financing; (c) the objective of ensuring the usability and acceptance of the digital euro as a legal tender instrument. For the purposes of point (a), the Commission may request AMLA to adopt an opinion assessing the level of money laundering and terrorist financing threats associated with the offline digital euro and its vulnerabilities. The Commission may consult the European Data Protection Board".

20 July 2021, COM (2021) 420 final) to cash payments. Such questions will be formulated and dealt with in the next paragraph.

5 The Legal Characterisation of "Cash" for AML Purposes and Potential Consequences for the Digital Euro

The EU AML regulatory approach towards "cash" has been changing over time. In fact, from one directive to the following one, the EU legislator demonstrated a different understanding of the risks attached to this means of payment.

In this perspective, AMLD1, in setting the first brick of the European AML architecture did not make any reference to "cash".

The first time "cash" has been referred to is within the new subjective scope designed by art. 2 of the AMLD2. The second directive in fact provided that "all EU Member States ensure that the obligations laid down in this Directive are imposed on dealers in high-value goods [...] whenever payment is made in cash, and in an amount of EUR 15,000 or more".

Even though this Directive did not technically introduce anything specific about cash, it widened the regulatory net to capture certain phenomena involving cash as a means of payment. Indeed, dealers in high value goods are not per se subject to AML obligations. They might become subject to AML requirements and obligations insofar as they accept cash as a means of payment. In other words, cash becomes the triggering element for the application of the AML obligations upon certain obliged entities. Further, the AML obligations were to apply only if the cash payment is above the threshold of EUR 15,000.

The regulatory treatment of cash finds a turning point in the AMLD3[51].

[51] In this respect, see the explanatory memorandum to the proposal to the Directive where the European Commission states that "the new proposal seeks to complete certain gaps in coverage and to follow the revised FATF Forty Recommendations. It makes specific reference to trust and company service providers and also includes life insurance intermediaries" (see 'Proposal for a Directive of the European Parliament and of the Council on the prevention of the use of the financial system for the purpose of money laundering, including terrorist financing' COM (2004) 448 final).

The new approach could be inferred in Recital n. 18 which opens by overtly stating that "the use of large cash payments has repeatedly proven to be very vulnerable to money laundering and terrorist financing". For this reason, the same recital goes on by asking "those Member States that allow cash payments above an established threshold, all natural or legal persons trading in goods by way of business should be covered by the AML Directive when accepting such cash payments. Dealers in high-value goods, such as precious stones or metals, or works of art, and auctioneers are in any event covered by the AML Directive to the extent that payments to them are made in cash in an amount of EUR 15,000 or more". To ensure effective monitoring of compliance with this Directive by that potentially wide group of institutions and persons, Member States focus their monitoring activities in particular on those natural and legal persons trading in goods that are exposed to a relatively high risk of money laundering or terrorist financing, in accordance with the so-called principle of "risk-based" supervision. In view of the different situations in the various Member States, Member States may decide to adopt stricter provisions, in order to properly address the risk involved with large cash payments".

Consistently with the acknowledgement of the risks associated with cash, the Directive makes a substantial step forward in further expanding the subjective scope. In fact, unlike the AMLD2's approach—which was confined to those dealing in high value goods (*e.g.* metals, works of art, precious stones, etc.)—art. 2(1)(e) of the AMLD2 targets "natural or legal persons trading in *goods*, only to the extent that payments are made in cash in an amount of EUR 15,000 or more". This clearly demonstrates the intention to expose any kind of dealer, irrespective of the nature and even of the value of the good ***insofar the cash payments amount altogether to at least*** *15,000 euro*. In this respect, in fact, the same art. 2(1)(e) precises that AML obligations apply irrespective of "whether the transaction is executed in a single operation or in several operations which appear to be linked".

Furthermore, as mentioned above, recital 18 allows Member States to devise AML precautions to adequately manage the risks associated with large cash payments. Despite the literature stating that such last period of Recital 18 is vaguely formulated—not explicitly referring to cash limits—the reference to the possibility for Member States to "decide to adopt stricter provisions" seems rather straightforward in enabling them to devise additional safeguards to the money laundering risks that could most certainly amount to cash limitations[52].

The understanding of such stricter cash requirements should be read in conjunction with the developments of the law-making process behind the adoption of the third AML Directive and the intention of the European Parliament to account for the "particular risk of money laundering involved in cash transactions"[53].

The content of recital 18 translates into a new paradigm where cash calls for *(i)* stricter measures (*i.e.*, art. 2(3) and *(ii)* it can even call for specific precautions and safeguards, in the ambit of AML obligations, such as the introduction of limitations to the use of cash.

In the same direction, the AMLD4 does not contain any rules requiring Member States to restrict cash transfers between private individuals nor does it prohibit cash payments exceeding a fixed threshold. Despite this, the first period of Recital 6 recognises that "the use of large cash payments is highly vulnerable to money laundering and terrorist financing". For this reason, in order to increase vigilance and mitigate the risks posed by cash payments, any persons trading in goods should be subject to AML obligations provided for by the Directive "to the extent that they make or receive cash payments of EUR 10,000 or more". Furthermore, quite meaningfully, the last period of the mentioned Recital states that "Member States should be able to adopt lower thresholds, additional general limitations to the use of cash and further stricter provisions".

The relevance of Recital 6 AMLD4 is twofold.

First, from a general perspective, it shows an increased awareness of the risks associated with cash. In fact, it condenses in fewer lines the

[52] See, *e.g.*, F. Robert, *Euro As Legal Tender (and Banknotes)*, in Fabian Amtenbrink, Christoph Herrmann, and René Repasi (eds), The EU Law of Economic and Monetary Union (New York, 2020; online edn, Oxford Academic), p. 30.

[53] In fact, the Commission in triggering the law-making process and formulating the proposal for the 3 Directive did not mention any particular risk attached to the use of cash (see "Proposal for a Directive of the European Parliament and of the Council on the prevention of the use of the financial system for the purpose of money laundering, including terrorist financing" COM (2004) 448 final). For the rationale behind the introduction of recital 18 see also Committee on Civil Liberties, Justice and Home Affairs, *Report on the proposal for a directive of the European Parliament and of the Council on the prevention of the use of the financial system for the purpose of money laundering, including terrorist financing*, (A6-0137/2005, 3 May 2005) 11.

concept outlined by the long recital 18 and, at the same time, it is able to explain much more accurately the rationale (*i.e.* "to increase vigilance and mitigate risks") behind the extension of AML obligations to the persons trading in goods insofar the payments are made or received in cash.

Secondly, from a substantial point of view, Recital 6 details what Member States can do when adopting "stricter provisions", thus giving shape and substantiating to the possibility already envisaged by the AMLD3. Among the three options described by this last period of Recital 6, the one concerning "additional general limitations to the use of cash" is most certainly a measure that can go far beyond what the directive provides for by including the trader in goods within the scope of the obliged entities (the repeated art. 2(1)e), namely erecting a ban to the use of cash which can potentially affect every citizen and society at large. This raises some critical questions concerning the boundaries between what the EU legislator decided to regulate itself and what the same legislator had delegated to the discretion of national jurisdictions.

In this respect, it is critical to read Recital 6 in conjunction with art. 5 of the 4 Directive, which legitimates Member States, "to adopt or retain in force stricter provisions" with the aim to prevent money laundering and terrorist financing "in the field covered by this Directive" and "within the limits of Union law". Besides opening for additional national measures against money laundering, this provision is, most importantly, setting the boundaries on how Member States should use their discretion in pursuing a more effective national AML setting.

This raises pressing questions pertaining to what type of "general limitations" Members States can introduce *vis-à-vis* European Union law[54].

[54] This entails, for example, that it is necessary to ascertain the conditions that a limitation on payments in euro banknotes and coins should fulfil in order to comply with the legal tender status of euro banknotes and coins when general limitations to the obligation to accept cash payments are introduced (see paragraph 2.1 of ECB Opinion CON/2017/18; paragraph 3.1 of ECB Opinion CON/2017/20; paragraph 2.3 of ECB Opinion CON/2017/27, paragraph 2.2 of Opinion CON/2017/40, paragraph 2.2 of Opinion CON/2019/4 and paragraph 2.1 of ECB Opinion CON/2019/46). In this respect, Recital 19 of Council Regulation (EC) No 974/9811 states that "limitations on payments in notes and coins, established by Member States for public reasons, are not incompatible with the status of legal tender of euro banknotes and coins, provided that other lawful means for the settlement of monetary debts are available". Other lawful means for the settlement of monetary debts, ensuring similar benefits to those of cash, are generally available in Belgium for the transactions that are subject to the limits on cash

The Court of Justice of the European Union has recently considered the concept of "legal tender" and stated that the Union's exclusive competence for monetary policy in the Eurozone under art. 3(1)(c) TFEU does not prevent a Member State from adopting a measure that introduces, on public interest grounds, a derogation from the obligation in principle to accept banknotes and coins denominated in euro for payment purposes, subject to compliance with certain conditions[55]. The conditions established by the Court for restrictions on the legal tender status of euro banknotes in particular require (a) that the legislation does not have the object or effect of establishing legal rules governing the status of legal tender of euro banknotes; (b) that it does not lead, in law or in fact, to the abolition of those banknotes, in particular by calling into question the possibility, as a general rule, of discharging a payment obligation in cash; (c) that it has been adopted for reasons of public interest; (d) that the limitation on payments in cash which the legislation entails is appropriate for attaining the public interest objective pursued; and (e) that it does not go beyond what is necessary in order to achieve that objective[56].

Building on such ruling, recently the European Central Bank issued an opinion (ECB Opinion of 15 March 2022 on limitations to cash payments (CON/2022/9)) where it confirms that "when limiting the possibility, recognised by Union law, of generally discharging a payment obligation in banknotes and coins denominated in euro, Member States must ensure that any measures taken comply with the principle of proportionality, which, in particular, requires them to be appropriate for achieving the

postal payments under the draft law. According to par. 2.1.4 of ECB Opinion CON/2020/17 "measure taken to prevent money laundering and terrorist financing which may, in general, constitute a 'public reason' that justifies the establishment of limitations on cash payments".

[55] See judgement of the Court of Justice of 26 January 2021, *Hessischer Rundfunk*, joint cases C-422/19 and C-423/19, ECLI:EU:C:2021:63, paragraphs 55 and 56. On the compatibility of national laws restricting cash payments for AML purposes with EU law, see also Joined Cases C-422/19 and C-423/19, Johannes Dietrich and Norbert Ha¨ring v. Hessischer Rundfunk and Case C-544/19, Ecotex Bulgaria EOOD v. Teritorialna direktsia na Natsionalna agentsia za prihodite (Sofia).

[56] Court of Justice of 26 January 2021, *Hessischer Rundfunk*, joint cases C-422/19 and C-423/19, ECLI:EU:C:2021:63, paragraph 56.

legitimate objective(s) pursued by the legislation at issue and not to go beyond what is necessary in order to achieve those objectives"[57].

Against this backdrop, the Proposal for the AMLR proposes a Union-wide cash payment limit of EUR 10,000.

Indeed, art. 59 of the proposal provides that "Persons trading in goods or providing services may accept or make a payment in cash only up to an amount of EUR 10,000 or equivalent amount in national or foreign currency, whether the transaction is carried out in a single operation or in several operations which appear to be linked"[58].

In this way, not only does the proposal introduce an EU-wide limit to cash transactions, but it also provides a "figure" to a threshold that is to be considered compliant with EU law and with the proportionality principle.

Indeed, in this respect, the ECB noted that "the threshold for the intended prohibition of consumer-to-business and business-to-business transactions is to be set sufficiently high to avoid a factual impact leading to the abolition of euro banknotes. The de facto abolition of euro banknotes may occur, inter alia, if thresholds were set so low as to threaten the economic viability of cash as a general and widely accepted means of payment and endanger the functioning of the cash cycle, ultimately also affecting transactions below the threshold"[59].

[57] Paragraph 2.8 ECB Opinion CON/2022/9. The European Central Bank has also pointed out in other previous opinions that "the broader and more general a limitation is, the stricter should be the interpretation of the requirement for the limitation to be proportionate to the objective pursued" (See paragraph 2.7 of ECB Opinion CON/2017/8 and paragraph 2.11 of ECB Opinion CON/2021/18). In addition, when considering whether a limitation is proportionate, the adverse impact of the limitation in question and whether alternative measures could be adopted that would fulfil the relevant objective with a less adverse impact should always be considered (again, paragraph 2.7 of ECB Opinion CON/2017/8).

[58] The regulation allows Member States to adopt lower limits (see art. 59, par. 2). When limits already exist at national level which are below 10.000 EUR, they shall continue to apply (see par. 3). The limit however does not apply to (a) payments between natural persons who are not acting in a professional function and (b) payments or deposits made at the premises of credit institutions. On the rationale for the introduction of such threshold, see also Recital n. 14, 94 and 95 of the proposal and Impact Assessment accompanying the AML package of 20 July 2021, COM(2021) 420 final.

[59] See paragraph 4.6 of ECB Opinion CON/2022/5 and paragraph 3.4 of ECB Opinion CON/2022/9.

In order to apply such limitation, the Proposal encompasses a definition of cash, which "means currency, bearer-negotiable instruments, commodities used as highly-liquid stores of value and prepaid cards, as defined in Article 2(1), points (c) to (f) of Regulation (EU) 2018/1672 of the European Parliament and of the Council" (see art. 2, par. 1, n. 30).

In the light of the reference to Regulation (EU) 2018/1672, currency means "banknotes and coins that are in circulation as a medium of exchange or that have been in circulation as a medium of exchange and can still be exchanged through financial institutions or central banks for banknotes and coins that are in circulation as a medium of exchange" and bearer-negotiable instruments means "instruments other than currency which entitle their holders to claim a financial amount upon presentation of the instruments without having to prove their identity or entitlement to that amount. Those instruments are (i) traveller's cheques; and (ii) cheques, promissory notes or money orders that are either in bearer form, signed but with the payee's name omitted, endorsed without restriction, made out to a fictitious payee, or otherwise in such form that title thereto passes upon delivery".

Against this context, therefore, the digital euro might seem not to come within the notion of "cash"[60], and more specifically the category of "currency" which is—today!—confined to banknotes and coins.

[60] This appears to be the policy intention of the European Commission: "Cash is subject to limits that vary from one Member States to another on AML grounds. While the AML package of July 2021 provides for an upper ceiling of 10,000 EUR for transactions in cash, the AML package follows a minimum harmonisation approach and stricter rules are likely to stay after the adoption of the AML package. This means that the digital euro would be subject to diverging rules in terms of payment limits which would undermine its pan European use. Limiting all digital euro payments to *e.g.*, 10,000 EUR as proposed for cash transactions under the AML package would not provide an efficient means of payment, as certain use cases (*e.g.*, B2B transactions using a conditional euro) do not lend themselves to such limits. Finally, intermediaries would bear cost related to both the onboarding of customers and transactions, however these costs will be minimal in absence of transaction checks for AML/CFT and other purposes, like fraud detection. Based on previous onboarding and due diligence processes, most customers of PSPs would automatically qualify for holding digital euro. Hence, intermediaries are not expected to bear any significant additional cost related to this option. For these reasons, this option cannot be considered coherent with the applicable rules on payment transactions" (those are the words used in the Impact Assessment Report accompanying the documents "Proposal for a Regulation of the European Parliament and of the Council on the establishment of the digital euro").

Nonetheless, once again, online digital euro transactions and offline digital euro transactions should be maintained separate, because, as we illustrated above, they present quite different features, and the offline use of the digital euro could be assimilated to a cash-like transaction.

In fact, not only does this difference justify the special regime enshrined in art. 37 of the proposal for a regulation on the digital euro but it also entitles the European Commission to adopt implementing acts setting offline digital euro payment transaction limits and holding limits (see par 5, art. 37).

This power sounds pretty much like the possibility for Member States—*mutatis mutandis*—to set limits to cash transactions.

Therefore, as much as the digital euro could escape the cash limits enshrined in the AML legislation, this art. 37 seems to be acting, again, as a special rule that subjects the offline digital euro transactions to quasi-cash limitations.

Such possibility synthetises the delicate trade-off (and potential clash) between "privacy" and "other EU policy objectives", namely, in this case, the prevention of money laundering[61].

This also entails that all the vast amount on indications that the ECJ and the European Commission have over time distilled on the delicate balance between legal tender status and limitations to use cash will be applicable also to the digital euro.

Indeed, under this light it should be read the par. 6 of the same art. 37 that requires the implementing acts—setting the limits to take into account in particular:

(a). an assessment of the money laundering and terrorist financing threats, vulnerabilities and risks of the digital euro when funding and defunding their payment instrument;

[61] See, *e.g.*, C. Zellweger-Gutknecht, B. Geva, S.N. Grünewald, Digital Euro, Monetary Objects, and Price Stability: A Legal Analysis, in Journal of Financial Regulation, 2021, Volume 7, Issue 2, p. 285, https://doi.org/10.1093/jfr/fjab009; F. Panetta, *A digital euro that serves the needs of* the public: striking the right balance, Introductory statement at the Committee on Economic and Monetary Affairs of the European Parliament, Brussels, 30 March 2022, available at https://www.ecb.europa.eu/press/key/date/2022/html/ecb.sp220330_1~f9fa9a6137.en.html; Kantar study, *Study on New Digital Payment Methods*, March 2022 (commissioned by the European Central Bank and available at https://www.ecb.europa.eu/paym/digital_euro/investigation/profuse/shared/files/dedocs/ecb.dedocs220330_report.en.pdf.

(b). relevant recommendations and reports drawn up by international organisations and standard setters with competence in the field of preventing money laundering and combating terrorist financing;
(c). the objective of ensuring the usability and acceptance of the digital euro as a legal tender instrument.

6 Concluding Remarks

CBDCs are posing many pressing questions on the material consequences that such digital currency with legal tender nature could have on the entire financial ecosystem. This holds particularly true in the European Union, where the introduction of a CBDC indeed raises many issues concerning its compliance with fundamental principles of EU law as well as its coordination with existing financial regulatory frameworks.

Despite the European AML legislation has recently undergone several updates to take into account the new enabled-technology means of payment to transfer funds or value (*e.g.*, crypto-assets), it lacks any specific reference to CBDCs. At the international level, policy-makers gave some guidance pointing at the similarities between "CBDC" and "cash" but also acknowledging that the AML risk will depend on the actual design of the CBDC. For this reason, the AML regulatory engagement with CBDCs should be informed by the risk-based approach which requires to adequately account for the different "uses" of the digital currency and the specific AML risks those uses could be exposed to.

The Proposal for the DigEuro-Reg seems in line with this view and in fact provides for a diversified AML treatment of offline (bearer based) and an online use (account based) digital euro. While for the "online use" the AML requirements and obligations are like those for private electronic means of payment (and they will be discharged by PSPs), a bespoke regime—derogating the general rules—will be established for offline digital euro transactions in the light of their characteristics and of the foreseeable AML risks.

Yet, the coordination between the Proposal for the AMLR and the Proposal for the DigEuro-Reg is still surrounded by doubts (for instance with regard to potential the extension of "cash limits" to the digital euro) that can only partially be solved today and that most likely require an additional explicit intervention by the EU legislators.

References

Allen, Sarah, Srđjan Čapkun, Ittay Eyal, Giulia Fanti, Bryan A. Ford, James Grimmelmann, Ari Juels et al. "Design choices for central bank digital currency: Policy and technical considerations." Working Paper no. 27634, National Bureau of Economic Research, 2020. https://www.nber.org/system/files/working_papers/w27634/w27634.pdf.

Annunziata, Filippo. "Speak, if you can: What are you? An alternative approach to the qualification of tokens and initial coin offerings." *European Company and Financial Law Review* 17, no. 2 (2020): 129–154.

Arner, Douglas W., Janos Barberis, and Ross P. Buckley. "The evolution of Fintech: A new Post-Crisis Paradigm?." Research Paper no. 047, University of Hong Kong Faculty of Law, 2015. https://papers.ssrn.com/sol3/papers.cfm?abstract_id=2676553.

Auer, Raphael, and Rainer Böhme. "Central bank digital currency: The quest for minimally invasive technology." Working paper no. 948, Bank for International Settlements, 2021. https://www.bis.org/publ/work948.pdf.

Awrey, Dan. "Complexity, innovation, and the regulation of modern financial markets." *Harvard Business Law Review* 2 (2012).

Axelrod, Robert Michael. "Criminality and suspicious activity reports." *Journal of Financial Crime* 24, no. 3 (2017): 461–471.

Bank for International Settlements. *Central bank digital currencies: System designs and interoperability*. Report no. 2 in a series of collaborations from a group of central banks, 2021. https://www.bis.org/publ/othp42_system_design.pdf.

Bank of Italy. *Indagine* fintech *nel sistema finanziario italiano*. Bank of Italy, 2021. https://www.bancaditalia.it/pubblicazioni/indagine-fintech/2021/2021-FINTECH-INDAGINE.pdf.

Basel Institute of Governance. *Basel AML Index 2022: Ranking money laundering and terrorist financing risks around the world*. 11th Public Edition Report, 2022. https://index.baselgovernance.org/api/uploads/221004_Basel_AML_Index_2022_72cc668efb.pdf.

Basha, Leigh-Alexandra. "Overview on recent developments for the legislation, regulatory and anti-money laundering US update." *Trusts & Trustees* 25, no. 1 (2019): 138–148. https://doi.org/10.1093/tandt/tty173.

Buckley, Ross P., and Mia Trzecinski. "Central Bank Digital Currencies and the global financial system: The dollar dethroned?." *Capital Markets Law Journal* 18, no. 2 (2023): 137–171. https://doi.org/10.1093/cmlj/kmad007.

Chimienti, Maria Teresa, Urszula Kochanska, and Andrea Pinna. "Understanding the crypto-asset phenomenon, its risks and measurement issues." ECB Economic Bulletin no. 5, European Central Bank, 2019. https://www.ecb.europa.eu/pub/economic-bulletin/articles/2019/html/ecb.ebart201905_03~c83aeaa44c.en.html.

Chirulli, Paola. "FinTech, RegTech and SupTech: Institutional challenges to the supervisory architecture of the financial markets." In *Routledge Handbook of Financial Technology and Law*, pp. 447–464. New York: Routledge, 2021.

Chiu, Iris HY. *Regulating the crypto economy: Business transformations and financialisation*. New York: Bloomsbury Publishing, 2021.

Chiu, Iris HY. "The disruptive implications of fintech-policy themes for financial regulators." *Journal of Technology Law & Policy* 21, no. 1 (2017).

Costanzo, Paolo. "The risk-based approach to anti-money laundering and counter-terrorist financing in international and EU standards: What it is, what it entails." In *Research handbook on money laundering*, edited by Brigitte Unger and Daan van der Linde, pp. 349–367. Cheltenham: Edward Elgar Publishing, 2013.

Council of the European Union. "Council Regulation (EC) No 974/98 of 3 May 1998 on the introduction of the euro." *Official Journal L 139, 11/05/1998 P. 0001–000*. Council of the EU, 1998. https://eur-lex.europa.eu/legal-content/EN/TXT/?uri=CELEX%3A31998R0974.

Council of the European Union. *Council conclusions on achieving the EU's economic and financial strategic autonomy in an open economy: One year after the Commission's Communication*. Conclusion, March 29, 2022. https://data.consilium.europa.eu/doc/document/ST-6301-2022-INIT/en/pdf.

Court of Justice of the EU. *Judgment in Case C-544/19: Ecotex Bulgaria EOOD v. Teritorialna direktsia na Natsionalna agentsia za prihodite—Sofia*. CJEU: October 6, 2021. https://eur-lex.europa.eu/legal-content/EN/TXT/PDF/?uri=ecli:ECLI%3AEU%3AC%3A2021%3A803.

Court of Justice of the EU. *Judgment in Joined Cases C-422/19 and C-423/19: Johannes Dietrich and Norbert Häring v Hessischer Rundfunk*. CJEU: January 26, 2021. https://eur-lex.europa.eu/legal-content/EN/TXT/PDF/?uri=ecli:ECLI%3AEU%3AC%3A2021%3A63.

Dalla Pellegrina, Lucia, and Donato Masciandaro. "The risk-based approach in the new European anti-money laundering legislation: A law and economics view." *Review of law & economics* 5, no. 2 (2009): 931–952.

Dalla Pellegrina, Lucia, Giorgio Di Maio, Donato Masciandaro, and Margherita Saraceno. "Organized crime, suspicious transaction reporting and anti-money laundering regulation." *Regional Studies* 54, no. 12 (2020): 1761–1775.

European Banking Authority. *EBA Opinion on "virtual currencies"*. Opinion no. EBA/Op/2014/08, 2014. https://extranet.eba.europa.eu/sites/default/documents/files/documents/10180/657547/81409b94-4222-45d7-ba3b-7deb5863ab57/EBA-Op-2014-08%20Opinion%20on%20Virtual%20Currencies.pdf?retry=1.

European Banking Authority. *Joint opinion on the use of innovative solutions by credit and financial institutions the customer due diligence process*. Opinion no. JC 2017 81, January 23. EBA, 2018. https://www.eba.europa.eu/publications-and-media/press-releases/esas-publish-opinion-use-innovative-solutions-customer-due.

European Banking Authority. *Guidelines on customer due diligence and the factors credit and financial institutions should consider when assessing the money laundering and terrorist financing risk associated with individual business relationships and occasional transactions ('The ML/TF Risk Factors Guidelines') under Articles 17 and 18(4) of Directive (EU) 2015/849*. Final Report EBA/GL/2021/02, 2021. https://www.eba.europa.eu/sites/default/files/document_library/Publications/Guidelines/2021/963637/Final%20Report%20on%20Guidelines%20on%20revised%20ML%20TF%20Risk%20Factors.pdf.

European Banking Authority. *Opinion of the European Banking Authority on the risks of money laundering and terrorist financing affecting the European Union's financial sector*. Opinion no. EBA/Op/2021/04, 2021. https://www.eba.europa.eu/sites/default/files/document_library/Publications/Opinions/2021/963685/Opinion%20on%20MLTF%20risks.pdf.

European Banking Authority. *Report on the use of digital platforms in the EU Banking and Payments Sector.* Report no. EBA/REP/2021/26, 2021. https://www.eba.europa.eu/sites/default/files/document_library/Publications/Reports/2021/1019865/EBA%20Digital%20platforms%20report%20-%20210921.pdf.

European Central Bank. *Opinion of the European Central Bank of 21 March 2017 on limiting the obligation to receive cash payments*. Opinion CON/2017/8, 2017. https://eur-lex.europa.eu/legal-content/EN/TXT/?uri=CELEX%3A52017AB0008.

European Central Bank. *Opinion of the European Central Bank of 22 May 2017 on limitations to cash payments*. Opinion CON/2017/18, 2017. https://eur-lex.europa.eu/legal-content/EN/TXT/?uri=CELEX:52017AB0018.

European Central Bank. *Opinion of the European Central Bank of 30 May 2017 on the limitation of cash payments*. Opinion CON/2017/20, 2017. https://eur-lex.europa.eu/legal-content/EN/TXT/?uri=CELEX%3A52017AB0020.

European Central Bank. *Opinion of the European Central Bank of 11 July 2017 on the limitation of cash payments*. Opinion CON/2017/27, 2017. https://eur-lex.europa.eu/legal-content/EN/TXT/PDF/?uri=CELEX:52017AB0027&from=EN.

European Central Bank. *Opinion of the European Central Bank of 6 October 2017 on limitations to cash payments*. Opinion CON/2017/40, 2017. https://eur-lex.europa.eu/legal-content/EN/TXT/?uri=CELEX%3A52017AB0040.

European Central Bank. *Crypto-Assets: Implications for financial stability, monetary policy, and payments and market infrastructures*. Occasional Paper Series no. 223, 2019. https://www.ecb.europa.eu/pub/pdf/scpops/ecb.op223~3ce14e986c.en.pdf.

European Central Bank. *Opinion of the European Central Bank of 1 February 2019 on limitations to cash payments.* Opinion CON/2019/4, 2019. https://eur-lex.europa.eu/legal-content/EN/TXT/?uri=CELEX%3A52019AB0004.

European Central Bank. *Opinion of the European Central Bank of 30 December 2019 on limitations to cash payments.* Opinion CON/2019/46, 2019. https://eur-lex.europa.eu/legal-content/EN/TXT/?uri=CELEX%3A52019AB0046.

European Central Bank. *Opinion of the European Central Bank of 25 May 2020 on limitations to cash* payments. Opinion CON/2020/17, 2020. https://op.europa.eu/en/publication-detail/-/publication/e2a5e1ae-a4b1-11ea-bb7a-01aa75ed71a1/language-en.

European Central Bank. *Report on a digital euro.* ECB, 2020. https://www.ecb.europa.eu/pub/pdf/other/Report_on_a_digital_euro~4d7268b458.en.pdf.

European Central Bank. *Opinion of the European Central Bank of 14 May 2021 on the obligation to accept cash payments.* Opinion CON/2021/18, 2021. https://eur-lex.europa.eu/legal-content/EN/TXT/?uri=CELEX:52021AB0018.

European Central Bank. *Eurosystem report on the public consultation on a digital euro.* ECB: April, 2021. https://www.ecb.europa.eu/pub/pdf/other/Eurosystem_report_on_the_public_consultation_on_a_digital_euro~539fa8cd8d.en.pdf.

European Central Bank. *Opinion of the European Central Bank of 16 February 2022 on a proposal for a directive and a regulation on the prevention of the use of the financial system for the purposes of money laundering or terrorist financing.* Opinion CON/2022/5, 2022. https://eur-lex.europa.eu/legal-content/EN/TXT/?home=ecb&uri=CELEX%3A52022AB0005.

European Central Bank. *Opinion of the European Central Bank of 15 March 2022 on limitations to cash payments.* Opinion CON/2022/9, 2022. https://eur-lex.europa.eu/legal-content/EN/TXT/?home=ecb&uri=CELEX:52022AB0009.

European Central Bank. *Study on New Digital Payment Methods.* Kantar study: March 2022 https://www.ecb.europa.eu/paym/digital_euro/investigation/profuse/shared/files/dedocs/ecb.dedocs220330_report.en.pdf.

European Central Bank. *Study on the Payment Attitudes of Consumers in the Euro Area (SPACE).* ECB: December, 2022. https://www.ecb.europa.eu/stats/ecb_surveys/space/html/ecb.spacereport202212~783ffdf46e.en.html.

European Commission. *Proposal for a Directive of the European Parliament and of the Council on the prevention of the use of the financial system for the purpose of money laundering, including terrorist financing.* Proposal COM(2004) 448 final—2004/0137 (COD), 2004. https://eur-lex.europa.eu/legal-content/EN/TXT/?uri=celex%3A52004PC0448.

European Commission. *Communication from the Commission to the European Parliament, the Council and the Committee of the Regions on a Digital Finance Strategy for the EU*. Communication COM(2020) 591 final, 2020. https://eur-lex.europa.eu/legal-content/EN/TXT/?uri=CELEX%3A52020DC0591.

European Commission. "Beating financial crime: Commission reviews rules against money laundering and terrorist financing." Press Release, July 20, 2021, https://ec.europa.eu/commission/presscorner/detail/it/ip_21_3690.

European Commission. *Proposal for a Regulation of the European Parliament and of the Council on the establishment of the digital euro*. Proposal COM(2023) 369 final - 2023/0212(COD), 2021. https://eur-lex.europa.eu/legal-content/EN/TXT/?uri=CELEX%3A52023PC0369.

European Commission. *Proposal for a Regulation of the European Parliament and the Council on the prevention of the use of the financial system for the purposes of money laundering or terrorist financing*. Proposal COM(2021) 420 final, 2021/0239(COD), 2021. https://eur-lex.europa.eu/legal-content/EN/TXT/?uri=CELEX%3A52021PC0420.

European Commission. *Proposal for a Directive on payment services and electronic money services in the internal market amending Directive 98/26/EC and repealing Directives 2015/2366/EU and 2009/110/EC*. Proposal COM(2023) 366 final—2023/0209(COD), 2023. https://eur-lex.europa.eu/legal-content/EN/TXT/?uri=CELEX%3A52023PC0366.

European Commission. *Proposal for a Regulation of the European Parliament and of the Council on the legal tender of euro banknotes and coins*. Proposal COM(2023) 364 final - 2023/0208(COD), 2023. https://eur-lex.europa.eu/legal-content/EN/TXT/?uri=CELEX%3A52023PC0364.

European Commission. *Impact Assessment Report accompanying the documents "Proposal for a Regulation of the European Parliament and of the Council on the establishment of the digital euro" and "Proposal for a Regulation of the European Parliament and of the Council on the provision of digital euro services by payment services providers incorporated in Member States whose currency is not the euro and amending Regulation (EU) 2021/1230 of the European Parliament and the Council" and "Proposal for a Regulation of the European Parliament and of the Council on the legal tender of euro banknotes and coins" {COM(2023) 364 final}—{COM(2023) 368 final}—{COM(2023) 369 final}—{SEC(2023) 257 final}—SWD(2023) 234 final}*, Commission Staff Working Document SWD(2023) 233 final. https://eur-lex.europa.eu/legal-content/EN/TXT/PDF/?uri=CELEX:52023SC0233.

European Commission. *Proposal for a Regulation on payment services in the internal market and amending Regulation (EU) No 1093/2010*. Proposal COM(2023) 367 final—2023/0210(COD), 2023. https://eur-lex.europa.eu/legal-content/EN/TXT/?uri=CELEX%3A52023PC0367.

European Commission. "Remarks by executive Vice-President Dombrovskis and commissioners Gentiloni and McGuinness on the digital euro and the legal tender of euro banknotes and coins." June 28, 2023. https://ec.europa.eu/commission/presscorner/detail/en/speech_23_3576.

European Parliament. *European Parliament resolution of 16 February 2022 on the European Central Bank annual report 2021 (2021/2063 (INI))*. European Parliament, 2022. https://www.europarl.europa.eu/doceo/document/TA-9-2022-0029_EN.html.

European Parliament. *Report on the proposal for a regulation of the European Parliament and of the Council on markets in crypto-assets and amending Directive (EU) 2019/1937 (COM(2020)0593—C9–0306/2020—2020/0265(COD))*. Report, March 17, 2022. https://www.europarl.europa.eu/doceo/document/A-9-2022-0052_EN.html.

European Parliament and Council of the European Union. "Regulation (EU) 2023/1114 of the European Parliament and the Council of 31 May 2023 on markets in crypto-assets, and amending Regulations (EU) No 1093/2010 and (EU) No 1095/2010 and Directives 2013/36/EU and (EU) 2019/1937 (MICA regulation)." *Official Journal of the EU L 150/40* (2023). https://eur-lex.europa.eu/legal-content/EN/TXT/PDF/?uri=CELEX:32023R1114.

European Banking Authority. *ESMA, EBA and EIOPA warn consumers on the risks of virtual currencies*. EBA, 2018. https://www.eba.europa.eu/publications-and-media/press-releases/esas-warn-consumers-risks-buying-virtual-currencies.

European Securities and Markets Authority. *The distributed ledger technology applied to securities markets*. Report no. 50–1121423017–285, 2017. https://www.esma.europa.eu/sites/default/files/library/dlt_report_-_esma50-1121423017-285.pdf.

European Securities and Markets Authority. *Initial coin offerings and Crypto-Assets*. Advice no. 50–157–1391, 2019. https://www.esma.europa.eu/sites/default/files/library/esma50-157-1391_crypto_advice.pdf.

Federal Reserve System. *Money and Payments: The U.S. Dollar in the age of digital transformation*. Board of Governors of the Federal Reserve System, 2022. https://www.federalreserve.gov/publications/files/money-and-payments-20220120.pdf.

Financial Action Task Force. *Virtual currencies: Key definitions and potential AML/CFT Risks*. Report, 2014. https://www.fatf-gafi.org/content/dam/fatf-gafi/reports/Virtual-currency-key-definitions-and-potential-aml-cft-risks.pdf.coredownload.pdf.

Financial Action Task Force. *Guidance for a Risk-Based approach: Virtual currencies*. Report, 2015. https://www.fatf-gafi.org/content/dam/fatf-gafi/guidance/Guidance-RBA-Virtual-Currencies.pdf.coredownload.pdf.

Financial Action Task Force. *FATF report to the G20 finance ministers and central bank governors on so-called Stablecoins*. FATF, 2020. https://www.fatf-gafi.org/en/publications/Virtualassets/Report-g20-so-called-stablecoins-june-2020.html.

Financial Action Task Force. *International standards on combating money laundering and the financing of terrorism & proliferation*. FATF Recommendations, 2023. https://www.fatf-gafi.org/en/publications/Fatfrecommendations/Fatf-recommendations.html.

Freitag, Robert. "Euro As Legal Tender (and Banknotes)." In *The EU law of economic and monetary union*, edited by Fabian Amtenbrink and Christoph Herrmann, 12–36. New York: Oxford University Press, 2020. https://doi.org/10.1093/oso/9780198793748.003.0026.

Frame, W. Scott, and Lawrence J. White. *Technological change, financial innovation, and diffusion in banking*. Prepared for The Oxford Handbook of Banking, 2nd edition, ed. Allen Berger, Philip Molyneux, and John Wilson. SSRN, 2014. https://papers.ssrn.com/sol3/papers.cfm?abstract_id=2380060.

Halaburda, Hanna, and Miklos Sarvary. *Beyond bitcoin: The economics of digital currencies.* New York: Palgrave Macmillan, 2016.

Kelly, Brian. *The bitcoin big bang: How alternative currencies are about to change the world*. New Jersey: John Wiley & Sons, 2014.

Klein, Manuel, Jonas Gross, and Philipp Sandner. "The digital euro and the role of DLT for central bank digital currencies." FSBC Working Paper, Frankfurt School Blockchain Center, 2020. http://explore-ip.com/2020_The-Digital-Euro-and-the-Role-of-DLT-for-Central-Bank-Digital-Currencies.pdf.

Kosse, Anneke and Ilaria Mattei. "Making headway—Results on the 2022 BIS survey on central bank digital currencies and crypto." BIS Papers no. 136, Bank for International Settlements, 2023. https://www.bis.org/publ/bppdf/bispap136.pdf.

Lin, Tom CW. "Infinite financial intermediation." *Wake Forest L. Rev.* 50 (2015): 643.

Lowe, Richard John. "Anti-money laundering–the need for intelligence." *Journal of Financial Crime* 24, no. 3 (2017): 472-479.

Norges Bank. "Central bank digital currencies: Third report of working group." Paper no. 1, Norges Bank, 2021. https://www.norges-bank.no/contentassets/554ee1f1ac53417d99d43708f5abbe14/norges-bank-papers-1-2021.pdf?v=19052021132229.

Mancini, Novella. "Bitcoin: rischi e difficoltà normative." *Banca impresa società* 35, no. 1 (2016): 111–140.

Mancini-Griffoli, Tommaso, Maria Soledad Martinez Peria, Itai Agur, Anil Ari, John Kiff, Adina Popescu, and Celine Rochon. "Casting light on central bank digital currency." *IMF staff discussion note* 8, no. 18 (2018): 1–39.

Minto, Andrea, Moritz Voelkerling, and Melanie Wulff. "Separating apples from oranges: Identifying threats to financial stability originating from FinTech." *Capital markets law journal* 12, no. 4 (2017): 428–465.

Minto, Andrea, Stephanie Prinz, and Melanie Wulff. "A risk characterization of regulatory arbitrage in financial markets." *European Business Organization Law Review* 22 (2021): 719–752.

Panetta, Fabio. "A digital euro that serves the needs of the public: Striking the right balance." *Introductory statement at the Committee on Economic and Monetary Affairs of the European Parliament*. European Central Bank, 2022. https://www.ecb.europa.eu/press/key/date/2022/html/ecb.sp220330_1~f9fa9a6137.en.html.

Pellegrini, Mirella. "Anti-Money laundering legislation in the light of the proposal of the third EC Directive." *European Business Law Review* 16 (2005).

Pocher, Nadia, and Andreas Veneris. "Privacy and transparency in CBDCs: A regulation-by-design AML/CFT scheme." *IEEE Transactions on Network and Service Management* 19, no. 2 (2021): 1776-1788.

Schmidt, Alicia. "Virtual assets: Compelling a new anti-money laundering and counter-terrorism financing regulatory model." *International Journal of Law and Information Technology* 29, no. 4 (2021): 332–363. https://doi.org/10.1093/ijlit/eaac001.

Schwarcz, Steven L. "Regulating digital currencies: Towards an analytical framework." *Boston University Law Review* 102 (2022): 1037.

Siclari, Domenico. *The new anti-money laundering law: First perspectives on the 4th European Union Directive*. London: Palgrave Macmillan, 2016.

The White House. "Technical evaluation for a U.S. Central Bank digital currency system." September 2022. https://www.whitehouse.gov/wp-content/uploads/2022/09/09-2022-Technical-Evaluation-US-CBDC-System.pdf.

Thomson Reuters. *Cryptos on the rise 2022: A complex regulatory future emerges*. Special Report, 2022. https://www.thomsonreuters.com/en-us/posts/wp-content/uploads/sites/20/2022/04/Cryptos-on-the-Rise-2022.pdf.

Treaty on the Functioning of the European Union. Available at: https://eur-lex.europa.eu/EN/legal-content/summary/treaty-on-the-functioning-of-the-european-union.html.

Tsang, Cheng-Yun, and Ping-Kuei Chen. "Policy responses to cross-border central bank digital currencies—assessing the transborder effects of digital yuan." *Capital Markets Law Journal* 17, no. 2 (2022): 237–261. https://doi.org/10.1093/cmlj/kmac004.

U.S. Department of the Treasury. *Fact sheet: Framework for international engagement on digital assets*. Press release: July, 2022. https://home.treasury.gov/news/press-releases/jy0854

Walker, George. "Financial technology law–a new beginning and a new future." *The International Lawyer* 50, no. 1 (2017): 137–216.

Zellweger-Gutknecht, Corinne, Benjamin Geva, and Seraina Neva Grünewald. "Digital Euro, Monetary objects, and Price stability: A legal analysis." *Journal of Financial Regulation* 7, no. 2 (2021): 284–318. https://doi.org/10.1093/jfr/fjab009.

Zetzsche, Dirk A., Filippo Annunziata, Douglas W. Arner, and Ross P. Buckley. "The markets in Crypto-Assets regulation (MICA) and the EU digital finance strategy." Working Paper Series no. 77, European Banking Institute, 2020. https://papers.ssrn.com/sol3/papers.cfm?abstract_id=3725395.

Index

A

AML (Anti-Money Laundering), 19, 39, 57, 88, 92, 94, 224, 235, 240, 245, 287, 289, 290, 292, 295, 297, 299–301, 306–310, 312–316, 320, 321

B

Banking sector, 19, 30, 262, 264, 267, 275, 281

Blockchain, 24, 52

C

Cash, 4, 9, 11, 13–17, 20, 29–31, 34, 35, 37–39, 48, 52, 56, 72, 73, 76, 77, 81, 86–88, 91, 93, 94, 108, 118, 122, 129, 130, 132, 133, 135, 139, 143, 144, 148, 151–153, 170, 175, 197, 209, 225, 235, 238, 245, 258, 260, 261, 273, 274, 276, 277, 290, 291, 298, 301, 303, 304, 307, 308, 313–321

Cash payments, 5, 14, 84, 88, 90, 108, 109, 132, 141, 147, 148, 291, 313–315, 317

Central Bank Digital Currency (CBDC), 3, 4, 11, 15, 18, 19, 24–30, 32–34, 36–45, 47–49, 51, 52, 54–57, 72–77, 79, 80, 84, 89, 90, 93, 95, 106, 110, 124, 129, 138, 141, 150, 153, 162, 163, 167, 172, 174, 175, 183, 186–190, 192–195, 197, 198, 212–214, 218–220, 222, 227, 228, 232–235, 237, 238, 240–243, 245, 246, 258, 259, 275, 281, 290, 297, 298, 300, 301, 303, 311, 321

Central bank funding, 264–266, 269, 270, 272, 281

Commission, 15, 18, 20, 49, 53, 84, 216, 231, 303, 312, 315

© The Editor(s) (if applicable) and The Author(s), under exclusive license to Springer Nature Switzerland AG 2025

F. Annunziata et al. (eds.), *Central Bank Digital Currency*, EBI Studies in Banking and Capital Markets Law,
https://doi.org/10.1007/978-3-031-80957-6

Compliance, 55, 199, 203, 214, 221, 224, 226, 231, 240, 242, 244, 289, 295, 296, 309, 314, 317, 321
Consumer protection, 46
Cross-border payments, 38, 40, 41
Cryptocurrency, 293–295

D
Data protection, 17, 31, 46, 92, 200, 214, 218, 231, 235, 238, 241–246, 311
Digital currency, 41, 47, 72, 76, 77, 79, 89, 90, 94, 96, 112, 124, 144, 146–148, 150, 154, 155, 162, 165, 171, 187–189, 191, 192, 194, 196, 200, 202, 212, 213, 221–223, 229, 232, 234, 236, 240, 242, 244, 245, 301, 321
Digital Euro scheme, 10, 57, 75, 77, 83, 90, 91, 95, 118, 119, 122–124, 187, 188, 218, 220, 223, 225–229, 231, 233, 234, 236, 237, 241–246
Digitalization, 30, 33, 174, 218
Distributed ledger technology (DLT), 24, 192, 211, 295
DORA, 50, 53, 54, 114, 302

E
European Central Bank (ECB), 4–10, 12, 15, 17, 18, 20, 26, 32, 35–39, 41, 42, 44, 45, 47, 49, 51, 52, 54, 55, 57, 72, 73, 75–85, 88, 91, 92, 95, 107–109, 112, 117, 118, 120, 121, 130, 132, 135, 137, 138, 144, 151, 153, 154, 163–166, 170, 175, 187, 195, 198, 199, 201–216, 218–225, 229–233, 235–238, 242–244, 246, 261, 276, 278, 280, 303, 309, 311, 317, 318
Eurozone, 4–6, 8, 11, 21, 40, 138, 317

F
Financial inclusion, vii, 9, 17–19, 35, 38, 40, 49, 52, 90, 93, 141, 143, 150–154, 162, 164, 166–168, 170, 175, 218, 243
Financial innovation, 190, 290, 291
Financial integrity, vi, 218, 243, 293
Financial intermediaries, 25, 26, 44, 47, 49, 52, 53, 55, 90, 186, 194, 200, 209, 210, 220, 231, 243, 245, 289
Financial literacy, 141, 143, 152–154, 173
Financial markets, v, 57, 73, 186, 227, 267, 291
Financial stability, 15, 17, 51, 75, 118, 147, 155, 188, 193, 199, 231, 237, 240, 247, 259, 260, 264, 279, 280, 282, 304
Financial system, 27, 30–32, 35, 44, 76, 141, 175, 188–190, 192, 200, 202, 228, 233, 265, 275, 288, 298, 306, 315
FinTech, 6, 35, 43, 184, 194, 212, 222
Fraud detection, 9, 231

G
Governance, vii, 19, 110, 186–188, 193, 194, 197, 198, 203, 211–213, 227, 232, 233, 241, 242, 244–246

I
Infrastructure, 16, 17, 20, 24, 25, 29, 33, 40, 41, 45, 46, 52, 53, 56,

57, 79, 83, 91, 166, 192, 195, 196, 240, 247, 257
Interoperability, 25, 35, 36, 40, 56, 140, 190, 222, 232, 235, 245

K
KYC (Know Your Customer), 24, 26, 39, 41

L
Legal tender, 10, 12–14, 35, 75, 77–82, 84–87, 89, 90, 94, 95, 113, 165, 166, 189, 200, 210, 217, 290, 294, 299–304, 312, 316, 317, 320, 321

M
Market funding, 264, 265, 268, 269, 271
MiCAR, 50, 54–56, 114, 238, 245, 292, 295, 296, 299, 302, 304
Monetary policy, 17, 27, 32, 33, 37, 46, 51, 75, 77–80, 83–85, 90, 91, 93, 108, 137, 138, 154, 184, 188, 192, 199, 206, 209, 215, 219, 222, 240, 246, 260, 272, 277, 280, 317

P
Payment instruments, 52, 53, 112, 121, 122, 130, 154, 200, 216
Payments Directive (PSD2), 43, 53, 54, 57, 113, 114, 119, 121–123, 236, 305, 309
Payment system, vi, 8, 14, 18, 20, 25, 31, 34, 36–38, 46, 51–53, 57, 76, 78, 79, 107, 108, 110–113, 117, 119, 121, 122, 124, 129, 137, 139, 146, 164, 186, 190, 192, 195, 196, 198–201, 215, 218, 224, 228, 235, 237, 238, 245
Privacy, 5–7, 9, 16, 17, 20, 41, 42, 57, 58, 76, 91, 92, 117, 118, 133, 141, 143, 144, 147, 148, 154, 155, 224, 260, 307, 311, 320
Private money, 26–28, 30, 53–55, 118, 137, 233, 258, 260, 268, 279
Public consultation, 4, 5, 7, 8, 17, 114, 143, 185, 230, 311
Public money, 26, 28, 30, 34, 41, 46, 54, 72, 80, 85, 94, 139, 188, 246, 257, 258, 268, 274

R
Retail payments, 49, 72, 109, 110, 114, 129, 135, 137–141, 143, 144, 216, 227, 229, 259, 298, 300, 301, 303

S
Safeguard, v, 5, 18, 92, 93, 187–189, 199, 205, 210, 218, 224, 230–232, 234, 243, 246, 268, 275, 277, 280, 281, 315
Stablecoins, 15, 27, 31, 50, 54, 107, 110, 112, 122, 234, 235, 238, 304
Stakeholders, 5, 17, 91, 94, 186, 194, 208, 218, 220, 226, 228, 230, 231, 243

T
Token, 25, 27, 33, 34, 36, 40, 42, 54–56, 79, 146, 148, 152, 190, 211, 217, 233–235, 239, 245, 292, 298, 301
Treaty, 18, 38, 75–77, 81, 89, 200, 219, 225

The manufacturer's authorised representative in the EU is Springer Nature Customer Service Centre GmbH, Europaplatz 3, 69115 Heidelberg, Germany. If you have any concerns regarding our products, please contact ProductSafety@springernature.com

Printed and bound by CPI Group (UK) Ltd, Croydon, CR0 4YY

30/09/2026

02225565-0014